KING OF THE NORTH

King speaks to a crowd at the Robert Taylor Homes in Chicago.

KING OF THE NORTH

MARTIN LUTHER KING'S LIFE OF
STRUGGLE OUTSIDE THE SOUTH

Jeanne Theoharis

NEW YORK
LONDON

Requests for permission to reproduce selections from this book should be made
through our website: *https://thenewpress.com/contact*.

All photographs are by John Tweedle, photographer, from the collection of Hermene
Hartman.

An excerpt of Darius Simpson's poem "Mutulu Shakur Passed and No Streets
Trembled from Vigils" is reprinted with permission.

Published in the United States by The New Press, New York, 2025
Distributed by Two Rivers Distribution

ISBN 978-1-62097-931-0 (hc)
ISBN 978-1-62097-941-9 (ebook)
CIP data is available

The New Press publishes books that promote and enrich public discussion and
understanding of the issues vital to our democracy and to a more equitable world.
These books are made possible by the enthusiasm of our readers; the support of a
committed group of donors, large and small; the collaboration of our many partners in
the independent media and the not-for-profit sector; booksellers, who often hand-sell
New Press books; librarians; and above all by our authors.

www.thenewpress.com

Composition by Dix Digital Prepress and Design
This book was set in Palatino Linotype

Printed in the United States of America

10 9 8 7 6 5 4 3 2 1

Contents

King of the North:
Revising the Civil Rights Timeline, 1945-1968

June 1962: MLK highlights police brutality in LA; CSK goes to Geneva with WSP

1959: MLK supports 1199 strikes

September 20, 1958: King is stabbed

September 19, 1958: King speaks out on police brutality in Harlem

Fall 1951: MLK encounters housing discrimination in Boston

Sept. 3, 1958: MLK is victim of police brutality; photos go national

June 1950: MLK refused service at NJ bar. Discrimination suit goes nowhere

Fall 1953: Kings begin married life in segregated Boston

June 1950: CSK forbidden from student teaching at Antioch. Classmates refuse to join her protest

1956: MLK travels widely, makes connections with Northern activists and unions

Jan. 1956: Kings' house is bombed. CSK refuses to leave

Fall 1949: MLK confronts racism and segregation at predominantly white seminary in PA

Fall 1945: CSK starts Antioch

1951-54

1945-50

1955-62

Fall 1951: MLK starts Ph.D. at Boston Univ.

Fall 1945: MLK starts Morehouse

June 1953: MLK and CSK marry

Dec. 1955–Dec. 1956: Montgomery Bus Boycott

Fall 1949: MLK starts Crozer Seminary

Jan. 1957: SCLC forms

Fall 1954: Kings move to Montgomery; MLK begins pastorship

1961–62: SCLC Albany Campaign

1965–1968: CSK's anti-Vietnam War leadership and activism widens

Oct. 1965: Federal government withholds $32 million for Chicago's segregated schools. Johnson reverses

March 27, 1968: MLK meets with Baraka to build national Black political strategy

1963: CSK's global peace work expands

Oct. 1963: MLK supports Chicago school boycott. RFK approves FBI wiretap of MLK

July 1965: SCLC begins Chicago campaign

March 14, 1968: Historic PPC gathering.

Dec. 1967: MLK announces the Poor People's Campaign

Aug. 1963: MLK marches against LA school segregation

April 1965: MLK marches against Boston school segregation

Sept. 19, 1966: 1966 Civil Rights Act is killed by Senate

June 23, 1963: Detroit Great Walk to Freedom

Nov. 3, 1964: CA's Prop 14 legalizes housing discrimination

July 1966: Chicago open housing marches draw massive white violence. Johnson administration blames the marches

May 1963: MLK calls LA as segregated as Birmingham, condemns police brutality in massive rally

July 1964: Wagner invites MLK after NYC uprising; rejects all proposals

May 25, 1966: Jerome Huey lynched

April 1963: MLK supports NYC construction protests

Feb.–Nov. 1964: MLK campaigns against CA's Prop 14

Feb. 1966: Gang work and tenant organizing; baby Andre Adams killed by rats

March 1963: MLK calls Chicago as segregated as Birmingham

Feb. 1964: MLK supports school boycotts in NYC, Boston, Chicago

Jan. 1966: Kings move to Chicago

1964-65

1963

July 2, 1964: LBJ signs Civil Rights Act

1966-68

April 12, 1963: MLK arrested in Birmingham

March 1965: Selma to Montgomery March

Summer 1966: Chicago open housing marches

June 11, 1963: JFK introduces Civil Rights Bill

Aug. 6, 1965: LBJ signs Voting Rights Act

July 1967: Detroit Uprising

Aug. 28, 1963: March on Washington

Aug. 11–16, 1965: Watts uprising

April 4, 1968: MLK is assassinated

KING OF THE NORTH

Preface

Only the Language Was Polite

King of the North

An unarmed Black man had recently been killed by police when Martin Luther King Jr. arrived in the city in June 1962. At a packed church rally, he condemned police brutality, stressing there could be "no compromise on this issue."[1] The violent police chief needed to be replaced, and to have any hope of winning his ouster, King insisted, the city's Black community needed to increase its collective political power.

Over the next three years, King returned to the city many times to support the city's growing movement against school segregation, the drastic overcrowding and underfunding of Black schools, discrimination against Black teachers, and racist curricula. "We are tired of gradualism, tokenism, look-how-far-you've-comism,"[2] King proclaimed in May 1963. The local Black newspaper referred to him as a "militant cleric." Just weeks before the March on Washington, King returned to join with leaders of the other major civil rights organizations—James Farmer of the Congress of Racial Equality (CORE), Roy Wilkins of the National Association for the Advancement of Colored People (NAACP), and James Forman of the Student Nonviolent Coordinating Committee (SNCC)—in an even bigger demonstration against the city's rampant school segregation.

The city refused. Rather than desegregate, its leaders allocated more money toward addressing "juvenile delinquency" and what they saw as the real problem of Black "cultural deprivation." Even more ominously, whites across the state secured a referendum protecting the right of citizens to sell or rent their property to whomever they wished. The city's largest newspaper repeatedly editorialized in favor of the segregationist ballot measure, while white citizens, businesses, neighborhood associations, and real estate interests mobilized furiously to pass it. King called it a "vote for ghettos" and returned to the city over and over throughout 1964 to campaign against it. In November 1964, the measure passed overwhelmingly, with three out of four whites supporting it—doubling down on segregation.

This was not Birmingham or Selma, Jackson or Little Rock—but Los Angeles, California. Indeed, King would come to LA more than fifteen times before the 1965 Watts uprising to join local movements attacking the city's rampant segregation. Yet when Watts erupted in August 1965, California's Democratic governor, Edmund "Pat" Brown, had the audacity to call it "a state without racial discrimination."

White Angelenos, the national media, and many Americans were "shocked" by Watts. *What is the problem? Why are Black people so angry?* King knew why they were angry; he was angry too. That's why he, alongside so many others, had challenged LA's rampant segregation in schools, housing, and jobs as well as police brutality for years before the uprising happened, pointing out the dangers of continuing to ignore Black cries for change. Disgusted by the willful surprise after Watts, he took to the pages of the *Saturday Review*:

> In my travels in the North, I have become increasingly disillusioned with the power structures there. . . . Many of them sat on platforms with all their imposing regalia of office to welcome me to their cities and showered praise on the heroism of Southern Negroes. Yet when the issues were joined concerning local conditions, only the language was polite; the rejection was firm and unequivocal.[3]

This is a story of a King who challenged white Northerners to walk the walk and address the segregation and inequality rife in their own cities. It is a story of a King who well understood the gaslighting and tokenism, as well as the demonizing of local activists, as key white liberal resistance tactics. It is a story of a King who saw police brutality as a systemic problem, challenged legalized housing and school segregation, and highlighted the profit made from segregation and immiseration. It is a story of how King came of age in graduate school in the segregated North and fought alongside a phalanx of Northern Black activists from the late 1950s onward to highlight this structural racism with little systemic change or federal intervention resulting. It is, in short, a story of a King who saw—from the outset of his activism— the necessity of the Black freedom struggle in every corner of the United States.

But this is not the story of Martin Luther King Jr. that dominates the mountain of books, documentaries, and public commemorations of the civil rights leader today. A wealth of award-winning biographies and detailed studies have examined King's life, politics, particular campaigns, preaching, seminary experiences, intellectual thought, theology, and political evolution. But these works largely glance over King's long-standing attention to Northern racism, portraying a King who moved North only after the Watts uprising.[4] Even scholars who compellingly identify King's racial-capitalist analysis or detail the Southern Christian Leadership Conference's (SCLC) Chicago campaign or the Poor People's Campaign miss this early Northern focus.[5] King's lifelong challenge to Northern inequality remains largely hidden in plain sight—understudied and not understood.

The dominant story, then and now, focuses on the Jim Crow South—Montgomery, Atlanta, Albany, Birmingham, Selma, St. Augustine, Jackson—where a courageous movement of Black people led by King and many others changed the nation. This Southernification of King is—and was—a more comfortable tale. A courageous Southern movement with its eloquent minister leader alongside a phalanx of courageous local Black organizers gained the support of decent Northern whites, an upstanding national media, and finally a courageous president and succeeded in changing the country through the passage of the 1964 Civil Rights Act and the 1965 Voting Rights Act. Then, just five days after President Lyndon Johnson signed the Voting Rights Act came the Watts uprising. Shocked and dismayed, King journeyed to Watts and, as the story goes, realized the immense issues Northern Black people faced hadn't been addressed by this national legislation. Accordingly, this led him and SCLC to "go north" and base a campaign in Chicago the next year. But SCLC stumbled, not having the clear targets they had in the South nor widespread support from Black Chicagoans, particularly Black ghetto youth.

In this story, King is largely beloved by Northern liberal leaders, the national media, and President Johnson, until he turns against the Vietnam War. But Northern racism was harder to challenge, Northern Black people rejected nonviolent direct action, and rising Black Power in Northern cities alienated Northern liberals, who'd previously been friends of racial change. As King changed directions, challenging the war on Vietnam and building a multiracial Poor People's Campaign (PPC), he became more dangerous to the government and was assassinated before these efforts came to fruition.

Seductive as that narrative is, it is distorted. This book seeks to upend it by detailing how King understood and challenged the scourge of Northern racism in school and housing segregation, job discrimination, and police brutality across his adult life. Grounded in the racism both he and Coretta Scott experienced going to school in the North and the ways supposed allies left them in the lurch, King highlighted the limits of Northern liberalism from the beginning of his leadership in Montgomery. Racism was not simply a Southern malady, King underlined, but a national cancer, spread within the foundations of the country and the structures of society, North, South, East, and West. Black Northerners courageously and steadfastly organized a myriad of nonviolent direct-action movements alongside their Southern counterparts and faced unrelenting white opposition.

"The North was not the promised land," Coretta Scott King, his political partner, underlined. Crisscrossing the country, Martin Luther King joined with movements for years in Chicago, Los Angeles, Detroit, Boston, and New York, long before the Watts uprising, to challenge police brutality, housing and school segregation, job exclusion, and union discrimination rife in Northern cities. The courage and steadfastness Northern Black organizers showed rivaled the likes of Southern freedom fighters. But at the very same time that many Northern liberals came to support King's efforts in the South, they ignored or disparaged attacks on their own segregation. They branded Northern activists "troublemakers" and "Communists," just like their Southern white counterparts did. White Americans who stood in the way of change were not just bomb-throwing Southern racists but polite Northern ones. And Northern racism came in many forms, from bureaucratic priorities to school funding to violence against Black people who dared desegregate "white" neighborhoods.

Across the country in the early 1960s, one of King's favorite riffs was: "[T]his social revolution taking place can be summarized in three little words. They are the words 'all,' 'here,' and 'now.' We want *all* of our rights, we want them *here*, and we want them *now*." [6] *All* were the various manifestations of racial inequality in housing, jobs, policing, schools, public accommodations, municipal services, the courts, unions, and political power. [7] *Here* encompassed the whole United States. And *now* was now, not after some study or gradual process or electoral victory. From the 1950s onward, he called out segregation as a national problem and described LA and Chicago in 1963 as being as segregated as Birmingham, while engaged in the Birmingham movement. And he was hated and ignored for that work at the beginning of the 1960s as well as in 1967 and 1968. Northern politicians and journalists praised and welcomed him "as long as I was safe from [them] down in the South." In the midst of the Cold War, the United States was invested in framing racism as a regional anachronism, not a national condition.[8]

By the beginning of 1965, frustrated by Northern intransigence, the Kings and the SCLC doubled down on work he'd supported for years when they decided to expand an already robust freedom movement in Chicago. On the heels of the Selma-to-Montgomery March in 1965, he announced the SCLC's Northern campaign and kicked it off in Chicago in July (a month before the Watts uprising). In January 1966, the Kings moved to the city to further escalate that campaign. It was broad and audacious, with grassroots Black support including many gang members and numerous targets to challenge the myriad forces that maintained Chicago's Black slums. They encountered calls to go back down south and relentless criticisms of their disruptive tactics. Faced with Mayor Richard J. Daley's extraordinarily powerful political machine and massive white violence (worse than they had encountered in the South), the nation proved unwilling to address Northern injustice, no matter how systematic, inhumane, or violent it was. But King learned lessons from Chicago. Indeed, throughout his shortened life, King was listening and learning. To truly change the country's endemic inequality, they would have to transform the nation. This required bottom-up organizing and top-down pressure—local, national, and international—at the same time.

The origins of this book began more than fifteen years ago when I secured a yearlong fellowship at California State University, Los Angeles—partly to research LA's civil rights movement. As I delved into the archives and read earlier editions of the city's two Black newspapers to document the story of Black organizing in the decade before Watts, I was surprised to find Dr. King there. He had been in the city many times in the early 1960s, highlighting the city's segregation and police brutality and joining local marches and mobilizations. I'd bought into the idea that it had taken the Watts uprising to jolt King to turn his attention to Northern struggles and spurred the decision to build a campaign in Chicago. But it simply wasn't the case.

And then everywhere I looked I found him—Boston, New York, Detroit, Cleveland, Milwaukee, Chicago, Tempe. King traveled the country from the late 1950s onward, speaking over 2,500 times and charting

six million miles from 1957 to 1968, as he was asked to join local struggles from the West Coast to the Northeast, while he built support for
the SCLC and their work in the South.[9] From the very beginnings of
his public leadership in the 1950s, he called on Northern liberals to
challenge segregation at home along with the South's. In many ways,
this work was hidden in plain sight. His critiques of Northern racism
and the limits of Northern liberalism were clear and evident—and
simultaneously ignored or roundly criticized by journalists, many
Northern white politicians, and citizens *at the time*.

Looking at King outside the South changes the story of America
during the King years. It is at once more sobering and more beautiful.
We see Dr. King, the deep listener, his dedication to young people including gang members and his deep compassion for people's suffering.
We see his intellectual partner, Coretta, and their shared anticolonial
analysis both at home and abroad and long-standing fight against the
evils of war, poverty, and racism that commenced as their relationship
began in 1952. But we also see how much the national media (many
of whom liked him in the South) dismissed or demonized his Northern challenge and how hard white Northerners fought to preserve and
protect segregation and police abuse at home.

King used the term *North/Northern*—as did most Black activists of
the time—to encompass everything outside the South. They did so in
part to take on the prevalent conception that the race problem was a
Southern problem. Key to King's critique was how, despite their differences, white congressmen, city leaders, and local citizens from the
Northeast to the Midwest to the West took pride in being *not the South*.
"The North" derived its meaning not simply as a regional designa-
tion but as a vague though powerful evocation of the North's racial
liberalism (from the Civil War on) and the opportunities that Southern Black migration to Northern and Western cities had supposedly
opened. If Angelenos and Bostonians and Milwaukeeans proudly cast
themselves as open and good and tolerant—and so very different from
Southerners—King and many activists were going to use the blanket
term *North* to describe their shared position. And so I use *the North*
in this book, as they did, in its ideological and symbolic sense to refer
to all the places in the nation invested in seeing themselves as *not
the South*.

Years ago, historian Vincent Harding challenged Americans to listen
to King. "Beautiful voice, we said. But did we hear what he was saying?"[10] Picking up that call, I listened and read a mountain of Martin

and Coretta Scott King's speeches, interviews, and writings anew, bringing new questions and different frames. I saw the Kings come of age as activists and thinkers in the North, the partnership they found in each other, and the ways they bucked certain social and gender conventions of the time to find a path to take on the country's racial inequality, economic injustice, and war making. I pored over Dr. King's regular columns in the *Amsterdam News* and *Chicago Defender* from 1962 to 1966 to understand the story he wanted to tell during these years.[11]

Many scholars and activists today, myself included, have highlighted how the radical King is lost in the ways the country now memorializes him.[12] But the uncomfortable parts of his message were already being ignored and disfigured while he was alive. Many politicians and other civic leaders tried to use him to prove their own goodness while ignoring his message while he was alive. Across the 1960s, King was invited to speak to many colleges and civic and religious organizations and would even be honored by many Northern mayors and other politicians. Many Northerners wanted him to regale them with the horrors of the South. Comfortable in their own liberalism, they largely did not listen to—let alone act on—the issues of segregation and discrimination he highlighted in their own cities and often rejected the local movements he supported. And King spent years objecting and growing more exhausted by this blindness.

Not all Northern whites professed racial tolerance. Many organized and used violence, harassment, economic retaliation, and racial epithets to block Black advancement or foreclose any sign of desegregation, deriding white liberals for their stances and "naivete" about the threat Black people posed. The violent face of racism wasn't only Southern. So King faced death threats, violence, harassment, and picketing across the North as well as the South.

King did not simply turn radical at the end of his life; a structural analysis of racism and the myriad institutions that supported it animated his and Coretta Scott King's adult life. From her time in college supporting the Progressive Party's third-party challenge for president, Coretta also recognized the triple evils of racism, economic injustice, and war. Their personal experiences of Northern segregation and the limits of Northern liberalism laid a foundation for how they would understand American racism. That didn't mean their ideas were static. One of their greatest gifts was the ways they learned, expanded, and deepened their understandings of American racism, poverty, and global injustice and what it would take to address them. But the North was there from the beginning.

People across the country describe King as a deep listener. Changed by his experiences across the country, he refined his understanding of structural racism in the United States relentlessly over his adult life. Northern racism was not a pale version nor a vestige of the South's, nor was it the same as the South's. But it was based in a distinct set of laws, policies, social and business practices, and justifications. King was not saying white Americans were fundamentally compromised; he had deep experience with white people who saw and attacked racism wherever they were. But over and over, most white liberals didn't want change at home, so he took on the racism at the heart of American liberalism. He understood the varieties of white resistance that kept segregation and deep inequality intact—from violence to school policies to housing loans to state funding to culture-of-poverty arguments.

This book takes on the comfortable fable of a King who changes the South and the nation with a cast of Northern good guys—Northern white politicians, journalists, liberal citizens, social scientists. Many of these same good guys were actively denying challenges at home by Northern Black activists and King in *those very same years*. Indeed, one of the greatest fables ever told about the civil rights era was that Northern Black people were too angry and alienated to build organized nonviolent campaigns. Actually, Black people and their allies built a myriad of creative and long-standing nonviolent direct-action movements from LA to Detroit, Chicago to New York to Boston, and King traveled to support many of them from the late 1950s onward. But they were ignored, dismissed, or demonized by most white Northerners and the federal government. Thus rising Black militancy in many cities cannot be separated from the years of white obstructionism and intransigence that preceded it.

So why has a Southernized King persisted, amid the scores of books, articles, and films on him?

Part of why we see the movement in Birmingham as so different from those in New York, Chicago, or LA is that the mainstream media at the time told us so. The fact that a number of journalists and media organizations came to admire King in the South and do substantive reporting on key parts of the Southern struggle, yet at the same time dismiss and demonize King of the North, has largely eluded contemporary understandings of King. As Coretta explained to James

Baldwin, "The media never understood Martin."[13] Longtime friend Harry Belafonte talked about his anger at the reporters who clamored sorrowfully around King's grave, telling off a *New York Times* reporter at the funeral, "This grievous moment was in part the result of a climate of hate and distortion that the *New York Times* and other papers had helped create. . . . Just coming to grieve the loss was no cleansing of guilt."[14]

King himself wrote in 1963, "Few people realize that even our authentic channels of information—the press, the platform, and in many instances the pulpit—do not give us objective and un-biased truth. Few have the toughness of mind to judge critically and to discern the true from the false, the fact from the fiction. Our minds are constantly being invaded by legions of half-truths, prejudices and false facts."[15] Journalists praised and rigorously investigated conditions, King himself noted, "as long as I was safe from [them] down in the South," and refused to grasp, let alone expose, problems in their own cities that he and many others called out over and over. Reporters who proved heroic on the South often fell down on the North.[16]

There was not a single Black reporter on staff at the *Los Angeles Times* before the 1965 Watts uprising—a problem replicated in newsrooms across the country. Ninety-nine percent of the 1,750 daily newspapers across the US employed no Black reporters in 1963.[17] What white reporters framed as King's shock after Watts was often their shock. Black reporter Ted Poston tried to tell his *Washington Post* colleagues they had not met "their responsibilities to those of their readers who are hemmed in, hopeless, and sometimes helpless in their own backyards."[18]

Thus, to see the King of the North required unpacking the popular and media narratives of King and the civil rights movement from the time—narratives that have been compounded in the half century since his assassination by many writers and historians. Scholars of Malcolm X have long understood the need to read the media as a hostile source; the great movement historian Charles Payne warned thirty years ago about the ways media framings had wormed their ways into movement histories.[19] But few have expanded that media analysis to Martin Luther King.

Indeed, during King's lifetime, Northern officials and the mainstream media helped to prop up four myths that flattered Northern white sensibilities: first, that Southern segregation was state-supported and Northern segregation was not; second, that it was Black militancy that brought on Northern white backlash rather than the fact that Northern whites opposed desegregation and racial change at home from the outset; third, that King didn't understand the North and largely didn't connect with Northern Black communities, particularly Black youth; and finally, that nonviolence didn't appeal to Northern Black people and thus King failed when he moved North.

King himself critiqued a number of these media framings while he was alive.

> A simple explanation holds that Negroes rioted in Watts, the voice of Black Power was heard through the land; the white backlash was born; the public became infuriated and sympathy evaporated. . . . This pat explanation founders, however, on the hard fact that the change in mood had preceded Watts and the Black Power slogan. Moreover, the white backlash had always existed underneath and sometimes on the surface of American life.[20]

The mistaken belief that King only appealed to Southern Black people became a key media obsession during his lifetime. Paining him deeply, it was refuted continually by his experiences all over the country.[21] But the mainstream media loved Black division. "Healthy internal difference of opinion," as he put it, among Black organizers was distorted and weaponized: "there has to be an antagonist and a protagonist," King observed, "and if the antagonist is not there, the press will find and build one."[22] King repeatedly challenged narratives of "crime" and "cultural dysfunction" that many journalists, like many white Northerners, favored to explain Northern inequities—it was like "cutting off a man's legs and then blaming him for being a cripple." He longed in the last years of his life for a journalist to actually detail Black life and struggle more fulsomely and accurately.

These misapprehensions have continued in many King biographies. An avalanche of scholars and writers has expanded our understandings of the civil rights leader over the past half century—condemning the "Santa Clausification" of King—to foreground a "revolutionary Christian" who spoke out against the giant triplets of racism, capitalism, and war and whose politics drew closer to Malcolm X's.[23] Documentaries and miniseries have brought King's work and particular organizing campaigns to life.[24] While evidence can be found on the margins of many King books and films, most have not connected the dots. Despite the ways so many writers have documented how

Dr. King has been narrowed and sanitized, the civil rights leader remains trapped in the South—that is, until Watts exploded and he went North but then "failed" with the Chicago campaign.[25] A Southern preacher in a suit, he remains a bit distant and unapproachable to today's urban realities and Northern Black youth in particular.

This framing becomes a self-fulfilling prophecy—the questions asked lead to the answers found. Seemingly exhaustive works neglect crucial moments and fundamental aspects of his character. By *not* reading oral histories of movement activists in Los Angeles, Detroit, New York, and beyond or examining the Black press in those cities, it has been easier to overlook the variety of movements in these cities and King's work outside the South before Watts.[26] Without examining King's regular columns in the Black press, it has been easier to miss the ways he theorized Northern racism and the important struggles Black people were building across the country. Without listening to how he talked with young people, particularly gang members, it has been easier to frame King as a respectability-politics-upholding minister somewhat estranged from Northern Black people and Black youth in particular.[27] Without reading the Black press or listening to Black Chicagoans or SCLC's Chicago field staff, the Chicago campaign appears disorganized, unfocused, and unpopular with many Black Chicagoans. And because long biographies tell the story in a certain way, others follow their frameworks, assuming their length means that they are definitive. So key parts of King's work get lost over and over, perhaps because they don't fit the dominant story arc, which builds triumphantly in the first half of the 1960s with declension and tragedy in the second half.

King understood young people's anger because he was angry too, and not so old himself. His leadership spanned from age twenty-six until his assassination at age thirty-nine. His connections to Northern activists began during the boycott and escalated with the SCLC's beginning in 1957. He saw the ways young people's courage brought adults along with them from Birmingham to Chicago, and he worked to cultivate the leadership of young people, particularly gang members.[28] He believed in the power of the individual to push forward the struggle for racial and social justice and was clear that bootstraps and personal responsibility were not the antidote to Black freedom. King's nonviolence was fierce, "a warrior without a gun," Blackstone Ranger leader Jeff Fort called him. As King himself starkly put it toward the end of his life, "I have more in common with these young people than with anybody else in the movement. I feel their rage. I feel their pain. . . . It's the system that's the problem and it's choking the breath out of our lives."[29]

Neither incarcerating people nor retaliation, for King, got at the root of violence or inequality.[30] But when King called for a "love ethic," he didn't mean having a racist over for a beer; he meant love that "disturbs the contentment" to transform the situation and, potentially, the people themselves.[31] Inequality had to be exposed even if it made people uncomfortable, and he married a belief in disruptive nonviolent direct action with negotiation from the Montgomery bus boycott onward. Numerous Black moderates as well as whites decried his confrontational tactics over these dozen years. One of the twentieth century's most important practitioners of nonviolence, he nonetheless possessed a profound understanding about why oppressed people held down too long would turn to violence.

Doing this research, I have encountered the Kings anew. As I delved into the sources, I was stunned by how much there was to find about Dr. King's work in the North. I'd begun my career researching Boston's civil rights movement but hadn't thought deeply about the fact that Martin King and Coretta Scott went to school and met in Boston and thus how well acquainted they were from their young adult years with the venality of Northern liberal racism. I had written about the media's dismissive treatment of Northern struggles but had largely bought into the myth that it wasn't until the last years of the Vietnam War and the Poor People's Campaign (PPC) that King lost the national media. I had analyzed the contemporary misuses of King but hadn't seen how the tendency for public officials to take photos with him and try to use him to appear committed to civil rights (while ignoring his actual words) began while he was alive—and how he struggled mightily against it. Again and again, I was struck by how King's long challenge to Northern structural racism was hidden in plain sight.

Even though I had written about Coretta's lifelong activism, I had still let the mound of books on Martin cloud my vision of her as well. Books constantly quote King's many advisors, missing that perhaps his most important one was Coretta Scott King. She provides a key lens onto this work. As she explained, "I keep seeing these books and I say, 'It didn't happen that way.' . . . And that becomes history if you don't correct it."[32] It was a political and intellectual partnership from the beginning. Martin Luther King married a feminist intellectual freedom fighter with unflinching determination, and he could not have been the leader he was without her. She was the family leader on issues of peace, war, and the economy. Their relationship challenged certain dominant social and gender conventions of the time, even as it hewed to others.

At a 1986 conference with many leading King scholars, Coretta Scott King underlined that "[t]he next time we have a conference on him I want to see more women scholars. He allowed me to be myself and that meant that I always expressed my views . . . he was superior to a whole lot of people in his development."[33] Having spent the past decades being pushed aside by many men who jockeyed for power in SCLC and claimed Martin's story, she knew that fundamental aspects were missing from current understandings of her husband's life and their deep political commitments. Twenty years after her call, SNCC's Zoharah Simmons published a piece revisiting King as a Black feminist. In it, Simmons reconsidered her earlier criticisms of him as "hierarchical, sexist . . . out of step." She had "encased him in Albany Selma, and Birmingham" and missed key aspects—now seeing him as a "visionary" and "cherish[ing] him for the external and internal struggles he waged daily . . . his dogged determination to keep going in the face of harsh criticisms from friends and enemies alike."[34] In many ways, I have picked up their charge to return to him anew and have foregrounded the women freedom fighters around him.[35]

These Kings were so contemporary. Insisting on the necessity of disruption (school boycotts, rent strikes, blocking traffic), Martin Luther King understood uprisings as the results of years of unheard protests and delineated the difference between harm to property and harm to people. He recognized the leadership potential of urban Black youth, saw the profit made from racial inequality and Black immiseration, and foregrounded the need for collective Black political power. Working with local activists across the country, he understood that Northern segregation and "slumism" were built through policy and practice—and thus he had wide-ranging policy solution ideas for how to remedy it. Coretta Scott King understood that there could be no justice without peace. She saw the essential imperative of global solidarity and the interlocking systems of segregation and colonialism. She understood the ways that racist and sexist stereotypes of Black people underpinned state mistreatment and that poverty, hunger, and lack of health care were all state violence. The Kings' freedom dreams, to use historian Robin Kelley's brilliant formation, were wide, grounded, and pointed, as they took on the racism endemic to the nation.[36] Thus the ways in which Martin and Coretta Scott King have been stripped, sanitized, and taken from this generation is even more galling because their work provides much for recognizing and challenging the injustices persisting in this country today.

Understanding King also means seeing him in his body and the ways it was vulnerable. He had numerous experiences of police abuse, and the terror he felt in police custody was palpable. Arrested twenty-nine times over his shortened life, he had to fight his own fear of the police and what they would do. Over the years, police took him for joy rides, half-nelsoned and slammed him down on a counter, choked him, kicked him in the back, picked him up by his pants, and shackled and chained him to a police car floor for hours. Long before the Harlem and Watts uprisings and even more so after, he made common cause with Black people across the country around police brutality. He called for brutal cops to be fired, the creation of civilian complaint review boards to oversee police departments, and power for the Department of Justice to bring injunctive suits against departments that deprived people's civil rights. Perhaps most importantly, King didn't see the problem of police as a few bad apples but a structural one in Northern Black ghettos where police and the courts act as "enforcers."

Seeing both Martin and Coretta in their bodies means understanding the fortitude it required to keep speaking truth to power amid death threats, house bombings, violence, and red-baiting to their family, her as well as him. It means seeing the kind of pressure they fought from family and other Black leaders to be more pragmatic or nuclear family–oriented and the enormous commitments both felt called to assume. It means recognizing the toll this work took mentally and physically, the bouts of unceasing hiccups that began after his 1958 stabbing, the waves of depression and insomnia Martin lived with, the sacrifices to their family life. These Kings were much more human—the decisions harder, the toll greater—and yet more relevant and courageous than we have fully realized.

Over and over, then, I have continued to be struck by how much this King speaks to where we are today in this country. *How is it, then, that we didn't know this?*

Reckoning with the King of the North changes many of the ways we have come to think of King and the civil rights movement more broadly. First it expands how we understand his leadership. Because King is understood as a Leader (capital *L*) the fact that he lent support, showed solidarity for other organizations' campaigns, made appearances at marches and meetings organized by other people across the 1960s, and listened and learned is often missed. He wanted to be of service and was changed by the people he met and the movements they built. Thus, this is not just a story about a great man but about the many, many great people he met, worked with, was inspired by, and learned from.

King was, first and foremost, a religious leader who saw certain responsibilities flowing from that. In good faith, he could not stand in front of Northern white liberals, particularly those who considered themselves friends, without calling on them to examine the "plank in their eye," as the scripture demanded, before calling out the "splinter" in others. He thus demanded "a liberalism in the North that is truly liberal, that firmly believes in integration in its own community as well as in the deep South." To miss his religious responsibility to call in and call out his allies "mean[s] that the inquirers have not really known me, my commitment or my calling." [37] His and Coretta's Christianity was rooted in changing society and endowing Black people with a sense of possibility in their rightful justice on earth. It was not some sort of pull-up-your-pants, respectability politics, as his Christianity has often been caricatured. To be a person of God, for Dr. King, was not just to be concerned with saving souls but to be concerned with the structural conditions that harmed their souls. [38]

Second, following the King of the North changes the timeline of the struggle, disrupting the egregious myth that Northern Black people largely didn't organize nonviolent direct actions alongside their Southern brothers and sisters. 1963 wasn't an important year just in Birmingham, Alabama, but for movements in Los Angeles, Boston, New York, Detroit, and Chicago as well. So the movement didn't move north after 1965—it was already there. And the 1964 Harlem, 1965 Watts, and 1967 Detroit uprisings look far different after seeing the long history of Black struggle in those cities that preceded them.

Third means looking differently at the tactics. King called himself "militantly nonviolent." [39] Nonviolent direct action sought to bring inequality to the surface to challenge structural racism, not just individual prejudice. It wasn't just lunch-counter sit-ins and bus boycotts but rent strikes, school boycotts, and impeding city life to disrupt the normalizing of injustice. Thus King criticized "so-called friends" who celebrated the Southern struggle but attacked disruptive direct-action tactics when applied in New York or Chicago. Just like in the South, there was a long tradition of Black self-defense among Black Northerners, but that did not mean that many Black Northerners didn't take part in sustained nonviolent direct-action movements.

Understanding this means recognizing the considerable overlap between King and Malcolm X's politics. Both took on police abuse in New York and Los Angeles, joined militant union organizing of Black and Puerto Rican workers with New York's Local 1199, praised confrontational protests against white construction companies, supported the New York City school boycott, and had global, anticolonial perspectives from the 1950s on. Both men traveled the urban North making common cause with struggles happening across the country and connected with anticolonial activists across the world from the late 1950s on. And while they used different kinds of language, both were persistent critics of the limits of Northern liberalism and deeply criticized for it.[40]

Fourth, following King's challenge to Northern racism means meeting new heroes and reckoning with new villains. Mae Mallory, Milton Galamison, Marnesba Tackett, Rosie Simpson, Al Raby, James Orange, Ruth Batson, and Gilberto Gerena Valentin all grace these pages. They were steadfast in fighting the structures of racism, poverty, and Northern segregation yet are much less known than John Lewis, Fannie Lou Hamer, Septima Clark, Julian Bond, and Diane Nash, who were equally steadfast against Southern segregation.

History has rightfully condemned the racist politics of Birmingham's commissioner of public safety Bull Connor, Alabama governor George Wallace, Senators Strom Thurmond and James Eastland, and many other Southern legislators. It has excoriated the mobs outside Central High School in Little Rock and the many whites in Birmingham, Montgomery, and Jackson who joined White Citizens' Councils to prevent desegregation. But Northern leaders, journalists, and local citizens have largely escaped such blanket indictment—their racial politics are treated as more complicated, flaws certainly but not determinative of their legacy. Just as there was a Southern segregationist playbook, there was a Northern one too. Over and over, Northern officials said "we're not racist" but hired few Black people in municipal jobs and teaching positions, refused to zone Black students to open seats in white schools, moved Black schools to double-session days, and protected white residents' "right" to private property.

White mothers who opposed school desegregation in New York or attacked open-housing marchers in Chicago were also the mothers of massive resistance.[41] Mayor Richard J. Daley ran a violently segregated city and disabled a movement that dared to expose it; LA police chief William Parker's tactics toward Black Angelenos rivaled Bull Connor's. And President Lyndon Johnson refused to enforce the Civil Rights Act against Northern school districts, demonized King's Chicago campaign, and stayed silent when thousands of white Chicagoans brutally attacked nonviolent marchers in Chicago. In other words, reckoning with King in the North means seeing that many who maintained racial inequality and undermined the civil rights movement have eluded censure.

Finally, looking at this aspect of King's politics requires jettisoning a dangerous form of American exceptionalism that dominates how the civil rights movement is often understood: that injustice exposed in a democracy like the United States is injustice addressed. Dr. King and Rosa Parks have become the poster children for this idea—that in the United States, if you use the right plaintiff and go about change in respectable nonviolent methods, if you press long and hard and use the King's English and dress in nice suits and possess nearly unparalleled oratorical gifts, your protest will be heard, inequality will be recognized, and change will ultimately occur. While King helped inspire Northern advocacy for change in the South in the early 1960s, many of those same Northern supporters refused to recognize the segregation plaguing their own cities, even though he and many others challenged those inequalities at the very same time with similar language and tactics.

Moreover, even as he believed to his core in Black agency, King fundamentally understood that personal uplift was *not* a public philosophy.[42] Personal responsibility could not solve social problems—nor was it the driving cause of them. When whites asked why Blacks didn't clean up their own ghetto neighborhoods, he made clear "that was the job of sanitation." Taking issue with public obsessions with Black crime, King held that it was white criminality and the malfeasance of the state that bore investigating. He viewed the obsessive focus on Black "culture" and "crime" as another deflection to avoid confronting structural racism.

Today people regularly misuse King's quote "the arc of the universe is long but it bends towards justice." King explicitly challenged the myth of time and American progress that liberals preferred. To be sure, God stood on the side of justice, which provided ballast against the nihilism that white supremacy produced. But King was adamant that time did not produce change, nor did God—only "the tireless efforts and the persistent work of dedicated individuals" did. The "appalling silence and indifference of the good people" had long made time neutral, if not regressive.[43]

Reckoning with this aspect of his politics means coming face-to-face with King speaking directly to the racism of our time. A King who saw segregation as a national problem and called Northern segregation "a new form of slavery covered up with certain niceties." A King who highlighted the scourge of police brutality and described the police as the "enforcers" of "a system of internal colonialism" who "often demonstrate particular contempt for poor Negroes . . . in order that they might be controlled and 'kept in line.' "[44] A King who deconstructed the structural roots of racism, which required taking on slumlords, school officials, local mayors, police unions, welfare officials, and the federal government. A King who insisted that direct action from school boycotts to rent strikes to blocking traffic was necessary to expose the "thin veneer of Northern racial self satisfaction." A King who eviscerated the discourses of Black criminality and "cultural deprivation" used to justify inequity and highlighted white illegality and state malfeasance instead. A King who repeatedly called on allies to walk the walk with their own practices and not only point to the South. This is a King who addresses us today.

Listening to this King provides an urgent antidote to the ways he has been misused against contemporary movements like Black Lives Matter. King himself recognized the "deliberate manipulation of history" necessary to maintain inequality.[45] "Be more like Dr. King," commentators tell young protesters, framing King as a kind of respectability-politics-upholding Southern minister "of love and unity"—distant from, even critical of, urban Black youth.[46] "King would never take a freeway," then–Atlanta mayor Kasim Reed scolded BLM protesters in 2016. Except that Dr. King did take many a highway. The disruption of city life and commerce was a key tool from Montgomery to the PPC and King faced relentless criticisms for it from Black as well as white leaders across his life. Moreover, King saw young people as the vanguard who would bring their parents along and sought to cultivate the leadership of urban Black youth. These contemporary resonances may account for why this aspect of King's politics is considerably less recognized—as well as the urgency to excavate it.

———

This book is not a personal biography. It does not detail King's relationships with various friends and advisors, chart the internal workings of the SCLC, unpack his favorite biblical texts, or capture his rich sense of humor. A political biography, it moves largely chronologically through the two decades of Martin Luther King's adult life to tell a new story of the Kings and the nation. Nor is it a full biography of Coretta Scott King, though she is a key source throughout. By charting the evolution of their understandings of Northern racism and Northern liberalism from graduate school onward, his engagement with Northern movements, and their global vision, we see them both anew. It is not meant to suggest that King's work beyond the South and his growing critiques of American liberalism are the only strand of his thinking. Rather it seeks to explore how it constituted a *fundamental* aspect of his and Coretta's politics, work, and moral outlook *throughout* their adult lives—and analyze *why* it is still one of the least recognized. And by beginning with this new set of glasses, it brings a broader, more fulsome sense of King's politics, character, and solidarities and more accurate US history into view.

This book inserts New York, Los Angeles, Detroit, Boston, and Chicago into the hallowed pantheon of American civil rights sites like Montgomery, Birmingham, and Selma. And it adds Northern white liberals—politicians, journalists, and residents—as some of the most difficult opposition King faced. Changing the lens, we see King the listener who learned from the people he met around the country and continued to analyze the methods and discourses of structural racism, King the religious leader moved by injustice to get close to people's suffering and challenge Northern hypocrisy, and King the freedom fighter who bucked pressure to make common cause with activists leading disruptive struggles across the country.

Adopting a bird's-eye view, this book attempts to show the depths of Northern racism and the ways a host of Northern activists and King persistently challenged it. It is meant to be panoramic—and does not detail every movement in these cities nor explore all the internal movement dynamics. Since this is the first book focused on King's Northern work, its goal is to chart how King understood Northern segregation and structural racism across many cities, how many Northern movements challenged it, and how a phalanx of Northern whites from local citizens to the federal government resisted in violent, political, and bureaucratic ways. I hope it is just the beginning.

This book is possible only through access to an array of sources and by analyzing the blinders in some of those sources differently than many other writers.[47] Many writers on King have trusted the mainstream (white) press and largely overlooked the story of King told in the Black press.[48] The digitalization of both the white and Black press has allowed for much deeper investigation of what King was doing in trips around the country in the late 1950s and 1960s, the media narratives that emerged about it, and his regular Black press columns from 1962 to 1966 where he sought to define their work apart from the mainstream (white) media's distortions.

The national media, like most politicians and pundits of the time, also could not conceive of Coretta Scott King as Martin's political partner. Rendered a behind-the-scenes helpmate, even her name was lost in scores of mentions of "Mrs. Martin Luther King." She lamented how she was "made to sound like an attachment to a vacuum cleaner, the wife of Martin, then the widow of Martin, all of which I was proud to be. But I was never just a wife, nor a widow. I was always more than a label."[49] This helpmate framing was even sewn into her autobiography, *My Life with Martin*. Published a year after his assassination, the book was based on interviews done with her by white editor Charlotte Mayerson, ghostwritten by Alden Hatch, and rushed into print by Holt, Rinehart & Winston in 1969. Mayerson explicitly instructed white male ghostwriter Hatch (who did none of the interviews) that "the focus of the book be on Martin, not on Coretta" and that they wanted a "very female, personal, and sentimental story" in the "tone of Readers Digest."[50] Despite Coretta and her sister Edythe's objections to the book's tone and lack of attention to their family's work, Mayerson's and Hatch's racial and gendered blinders shaped the book and thus the ways generations of writers and readers understood how Coretta Scott King framed her own as well as her husband's work.[51] Some of the transcripts and recordings of those interviews survived, and they reveal a different story.

Many places that Martin Luther King visited in the Northeast, Midwest, and West have more recently sought to preserve the history of those visits, and so full texts of speeches, digitized recordings, and reconstructed itineraries have arisen in curious places.[52] Everyone now wants to document that King came to them. And what these sources show is King calling out Northern white leaders and residents on their homegrown injustices for years before Watts, alongside his descriptions of Southern issues, as well as the tendency for liberal Northerners, then and now, to be proud of the visit and ignore the call to change.[53] Finally, this book amply utilizes oral histories done over the past fifty years with local Black activists across the country along with my own interviews to document the rich life of the King of the North that has eluded many other writers.[54]

This book also stands on the shoulders of a vastly expanded field of Black freedom studies that has changed the ways we see the Black freedom struggle outside the South and the leadership and intellectual contributions of Black women. Over the past two decades, a bevy of scholars have richly detailed the systemic inequalities in housing, schools, jobs, and policing in the Jim Crow North and the rich and various movements across the Northeast, Midwest, and West that took them on.[55] A concerted focus on the work and ideas of women has reshaped how we see the Black freedom struggle and documented many of its unsung leaders and organizers. "Women have been the backbone of the whole civil rights movement," Coretta Scott King stressed in a 1966 interview.[56] So this book is indebted to that research.

Finally, this book owes a great debt to Black Lives Matter and the activists of this moment challenging the criminal legal system, climate change, gun violence, immigration policy, settler colonialism, and genocide. The kinds of framings around structural racism they have put before the nation, the interconnections they make between issues from the local to the global, and the ways they underline the necessity of learning a fuller, more accurate history of this country make it more possible and more urgent to detail this history. As King's historian friend Vincent Harding challenged, "Do we dare fantasize about what we would do now, if [King] came to our black-administered city to challenge our leaders; if he tried to question our values and our bank accounts, and our political machine?"[57]

The stakes of missing this Northern story are high. By not recognizing how much and how long King critiqued the practices and discourses of American racism, we make him unavailable for where we need him today.[58] Martin Luther King's twenty-year journey with his political partner Coretta Scott King has much to teach us about the nature of injustices we face and the creative methods people found to fight back. But that is only if the nation is more willing to listen and act than people were when he was alive.

A note: As Martin Luther King's public leadership enlarged, many people would help write his speeches and articles. It is impossible to document all the help. Wyatt Tee Walker, Bayard Rustin, Stanley Levison, Clarence Jones,

Dorothy Cotton, Vincent Harding, L. D. Reddick, Andrew Young, Coretta Scott King, and many others made an indelible impact on his thinking, on the framings he used, and in the writing itself. Certainly, many of the lines I quote in this book were not written by King himself and were likely influenced by the thinking of other people. Part of why I quote so many articles, speeches, and columns is to demonstrate how insistent and prevalent this theme was across his life—that even if some of these lines were not written by King, the sentiment was unequivocally his. I refer to him as Martin, like Coretta did (though many friends and family called him ML), and call her Coretta, as well as Scott King and Coretta Scott King, to restore her name and identity.[59] *And finally, the beautiful photos that grace these pages were taken by Chicago Black photographer John Tweedle. They provide a striking visual landscape of King in community and his challenge to US racism.*

Act I

1947–1960

Coretta Scott King and Martin Luther King Jr. in Chicago

1

Our First Protest

Martin Luther King and Coretta Scott
Come of Age in the North

Born on January 15, 1929, Martin Luther King Jr. grew up in Atlanta—
the middle child between older sister Christine and younger brother
A. D. of prominent Baptist minister Martin Luther King Sr. and Alberta
Williams King, the church choir director. Alberta's father and mother
had led Ebenezer Baptist Church before her husband took it over. "I
have to chuckle as I realize there are people who actually believe ML
just appeared," King's sister Christine observed. "They think he simply happened, that he appeared fully formed, without context, ready to
change the world. We are the products of a long line of activists and ministers."[1] Both of his parents joined the NAACP in the 1930s and his mom
also joined the Women's International League for Peace and Freedom.[2]
King's mother from the outset saw how hungry her middle son was for
education. She enrolled him in grade school early because Christine was
going, and he wanted to go too. And she supported his decision to take
the test to attend Morehouse College early.

   At fifteen, after his junior year of high school, King matriculated as
an early-admission student at Morehouse College. Both his father and
grandfather had attended Morehouse; his mother had gone to Morehouse's sister school, Spelman College. King had chafed against his
father's version of Baptist ministry—finding it too emotional, materialistic, and distant from the world and its suffering. He wanted to be a
lawyer. But his mentor Benjamin Mays introduced him to the possibilities of a religious calling grounded in social change and intellectual
thought. Mays exposed him to Gandhism and to the long tradition of
the Black social gospel—a ministry rooted in and committed to dealing with the great social problems besetting the country.[3] In 1945, the

young King accompanied his father to Detroit for the National Baptist Convention; his father delivered a sermon at Second Baptist Church during that visit. The Detroit they visited was deeply segregated in housing, schools, and leisure; Black people were not allowed to sit in the stands to watch the Detroit Tigers. Most bars, restaurants, and hotels didn't serve Black customers.[4] Detroit was not so different than Atlanta.

At Morehouse, he began to see the shoulders of the intellectual-activist Black ministers from abolition onward who had sought to transform the nation, upon which he could stand. He heard a call to the ministry that strove not just to change souls but to address the oppressive conditions that harmed Black people and stood as an affront to God as well. But to do that, he sought a graduate education to provide the intellectual and religious foundation he craved for his own ministry. That would take him far beyond Atlanta, providing experiences that would transform his understandings of Christian witness and American racism in the process.

In the fall of 1948, nineteen-year-old King left Georgia to attend Crozer Theological Seminary in Chester, Pennsylvania. He would spend six formative years, from age nineteen to twenty-five, getting a divinity degree at Crozer and then pursuing his doctorate at Boston University. He came into his own as a pastor, intellectual, and political thinker outside the South while confronting the depths and flavors of Northern racial inequality and the limits of Northern liberalism.

In 1945, eighteen-year-old Coretta Scott moved to Ohio to attend liberal Antioch College. Her family had endured tremendous racial violence in Marion, Alabama, because of her father Obadiah Scott's proud economic independence. Her mother Bernice McMurry Scott had been deeply committed to her children's education and ensured they got an education beyond the narrow one provided to Black children in rural Alabama. At Antioch, Coretta Scott became an activist, was introduced to the Progressive Party, and began to see the interlocking issues of racism, poverty, and war. In 1951, eager to continue her music education, she moved to Boston to attend the New England Conservatory of Music and met Martin.

So, as teenagers in the 1940s, both Martin Luther King and Coretta Scott joined over a million and a half Black people leaving the South for the North. Their experiences coming of age in the North would indelibly shape how they understood American racism and Black struggle.

———

As a teenager, King had spent two summers working on a tobacco farm in Connecticut, a job many Morehouse students had come to hold. Beginning in 1916, tobacco growers recruited Morehouse students to serve as summer labor, in part because Black college students from the South were less likely to demand better working conditions. They also recruited white high school women from the South for similar reasons. The work was hard labor, and the students also lived in dorms controlled by the growers.[5] The Black students' mobility in particular was constrained, in part because neighboring whites didn't want young Black men wandering about town.[6] Moreover, according to historian Lerone Martin, dotting the Connecticut landscape near the Simsbury dorm where King stayed were a number of sundown towns, places where Black people could work but not live and thus were unsafe to be seen there after sundown. Still, King's first summer in Connecticut, right before he began at Morehouse, opened his eyes to different possibilities from what he'd experienced in Georgia.

The fifteen-year-old wrote his mother, "I never though[t] that a person of my race could eat [in any location] but we ate in one of the finest restaurants in Hartford."[7] It also gave him space and perspective to find his own religious calling, feeling a different kind of freedom both being out of the South and being away from his family, particularly his father. He spent hours every day in conversation with the other Morehouse students working alongside him at the tobacco farm, talking about American society and how they might change it. "I was at the point where I was deeply interested in political matters and social ills."[8]

He saw how Black and white workers were exploited together—and racism was used to prevent solidarity. King returned to Connecticut for a second summer in 1947 after his junior year at Morehouse, according to biographer Taylor Branch, because "pressures at home were so severe" that he needed to be away.[9] King had his first experience with law enforcement that second summer in Connecticut, when police detained him after he had been drinking and horsing around with friends. Little is known about what ensued.[10] Still, King felt a new freedom in those summers away from Georgia and felt stifled on his return. "I felt as though that curtain had dropped on my selfhood."[11]

Graduating from Morehouse in 1948, King now saw a religious calling steeped in possibilities of liberation in this world and applied to seminary. He chose the predominantly white Crozer Seminary in Chester, Pennsylvania, which had a liberal theological foundation centered on the engaged ministry he wanted. With the guidance of Rev. J. Pius Barbour, the young King forged forward. King had met Rev. Barbour through his father as well as Professor Mays. A Morehouse graduate and the first Black person to graduate from Crozer, Barbour pastored at Calvary Baptist Church near the seminary in Chester and would be a big influence not just on King's decision to attend the seminary but in his years there as well.

Part of the decision to attend Crozer likely stemmed from the freedom he felt away from home in the North to pursue both his intellectual and political passions. His father, an overbearing figure, would have preferred his son just start co-pastoring Ebenezer Baptist Church with him in Atlanta. Neither of King's parents had ever lived outside the South, and a divinity degree was not necessary to join his father as co-pastor at Ebenezer. But King Junior set out to carve his own political, intellectual, and religious path.

The nineteen-year-old arrived at this predominantly white seminary as one of six Black students in his class and one of only eleven Black students in a student body of about fifty men and one woman.[12] There were other foreign students of color and women in certificate programs as well. But the faculty was entirely white.[13] Crozer offered much to nurture King's intellectual growth, but his experiences in Pennsylvania and at Crozer led to confrontations with the various faces of Northern racism and a growing realization of the significant gap between the profession of openness and the practice of many Northern whites. It was no promised land.

While the seminary's student body was somewhat integrated, the surrounding communities and Crozer's faculty were not. Chester was segregated, as were nearby Camden and Philadelphia. Black students like King felt a tremendous pressure to perform, since many faculty didn't see them as the intellectual equals of their white peers. Some of Crozer's faculty, as historian Patrick Parr demonstrates, tended to stereotype Black students, shortchanging their potential and finding their preaching styles overly "emotional."[14] This weighed on King, who was anxious to disrupt white stereotypes of Black people. "If I were a minute late to class, I was almost morbidly conscious of it and sure everyone noticed it," he recalled. He was fastidious about his personal presentation. "Rather than be thought of as always laughing, I'm afraid I was grimly serious for a time. I had a tendency to overdress, to keep my room spotless, my shoes perfectly shined and my clothes pressed."[15] While many historians have detailed King's Crozer and Boston University experiences in forming his broader intellectual-political foundation, the Northern context of his graduate studies was just as crucial.[16] Being a twenty-year-old Black religious intellectual with a growing political consciousness in a predominantly white institution in the Jim Crow North meant grappling with old and new manifestations of racism.[17]

Crozer had a pool table, a Ping-Pong table, and a shuffleboard court underneath the chapel—and Martin began regularly playing pool, scandalizing his father when he came to visit. With his Black classmates, the small group able to access this sort of education, it also meant figuring their way forward amid the racism around them. One of those friends was Walter McCall, whom King had met at Morehouse. An army veteran five years older than King, McCall had grown up in South Carolina and served during World War II. Having friends like McCall meant King would have experiences beyond the campus and a friend to discuss everything with. "We used to sit up oh way into the morning discussing the social issues of the day," McCall recalled.[18] The two young men liked to have fun—drinking, playing pool, dating, and exploring the leisure possibilities off campus. That meant getting to leave Crozer for more welcoming Black spaces—but also grappling with the racism they encountered.

In his second term at Crozer, King and a white student, Dupree Jordan, went into Philadelphia and tried to get lunch at Stouffer's. Minutes ticked by and no one served them. Finally, according to Jordan, "we demanded service and we got service. . . . Unfortunately in one or more of the vegetables that he was served, he [King] got sand on his plate."[19] King did not want to make a scene, and they left quietly. Another time, James Beshai, an Egyptian student, and King were denied service at a restaurant in Philadelphia. Beshai had eaten there before but with King was told they couldn't dine without a reservation. Beshai said King took it in stride.

To relax in Black spaces, King and McCall periodically stayed in Camden with McCall's relatives Benjamin and Ella Hunt. But this too led to discriminatory encounters. In 1945, New Jersey passed a law prohibiting discrimination in all places of public accommodation. But that didn't mean it was enforced. King and McCall were thrown out of Federal Street Bowl when the two young Black men tried to take a stand against discrimination at the all-white bowling alley.[20]

A year later, a much more significant encounter happened as historian Patrick Duff has worked to document. School had ended. King had gone home to Atlanta to preach but returned to New Jersey to visit McCall, staying with him at the Hunts' while auditing a class at the University of Pennsylvania. On June 12, 1950, a twenty-one-year-old King, McCall, and two women, Pearl Smith (who was a police officer) and Doris Wilson, stopped for a drink at Mary's Café in Maple Shade, New Jersey, across the Pennsylvania border from Crozer.[21] They asked for a beer but bar owner Ernest Nichols refused them service, citing the fact that it was Sunday. They were shocked. So they asked for a soda. Again, Nichols refused. He told them to leave. When they protested, Nichols went and retrieved his .45-caliber handgun. He fired his gun in the air, yelling, "I'll kill for less."[22] King and McCall cited New Jersey's antidiscrimination law to no avail. The four young people were summarily kicked out at gunpoint.

Angry, they decided to file a police report. McCall explained, "It was the first time that we had ever been in any kind of civil rights struggle."[23] They came back with the police to talk to witnesses, and the police confiscated Nichols's weapon.[24] Still furious, King went to visit his mentor Rev. Barbour. He often went to Barbour's to discuss issues, writing his mother that Barbour had "one of the best minds of anybody I ever met."[25] The minister's daughter, Almanina, was attending the University of Pennsylvania Law School and was similarly outraged when King recounted what had happened to them. She advised them to sue. Almanina recruited three white classmates to go to the bar and see if they would be served. They were indeed served.[26] With the help of the local Camden NAACP and New Jersey NAACP leader Ulysses Wiggins, McCall and King decided to file a racial discrimination complaint.

King testified the next week on the gun charge against Nichols. To do so, he had to convince his brother A. D. to put off his wedding so he could stay in New Jersey to testify. A. D. was "mad as the devil" but ultimately agreed.[27] Nichols's lawyer claimed in a statement that firing the gun "was not intended as a threat to his colored patrons. . . . [Nichols] has been held up before and he wanted to alert his watchdog who was somewhere outside on the tavern grounds."[28] But the solicitor found King to be an effective witness—"direct and positive with his answers."[29] The judge found Nichols guilty on the firearms charge.

But the three white University of Pennsylvania students whom Almanina had recruited backed out, refusing to testify to the grand jury about the disparate service because "they felt testifying would hurt their careers."[30] Their parents, McCall recalled, "brought pressure

against them and they couldn't appear." This meant they had no witnesses to attest to the discriminatory service that would have violated
New Jersey's antidiscrimination law. "We couldn't be our plaintiff and
defendant at the same time," McCall explained. "I'm sure that Ernie,
who ran this place, was very happy."[31] After the witnesses pulled out,
the racial discrimination case against Nichols was dropped.

This encounter was a pivotal experience for King, revealing to him
that laws could exist but not be enforced and allies disappear under
pressure. It didn't matter that New Jersey had an antidiscrimination
law—it hadn't protected them. Violence often lurked behind the surface.
And the white students initially willing to testify to the differential service backed down because it might affect their careers. This experience
likely affected how King came to see Northern antidiscrimination laws
as more symbolic than substantive practice, a theme he would return to
again and again, helping to lay the groundwork for his persistent critiques of the limits of Northern liberalism across his life. People in the
SCLC would later say he would recount the incident often as pivotal to
his development to fight for civil rights.[32] Eleven years later, in an interview with the *Philadelphia Tribune*, King highlighted the importance of
the event in Maple Shade: "They refused to serve us. It was a painful
experience because we decided to sit-in."[33]

There are some hints that King and McCall might actually have intended to confront segregation that night. Howard University students
in 1943 led by Pauli Murray had sat in at white stores in Washington, DC, that refused to serve Black people; the next year Black New
Yorkers boycotted the buses to get Black bus drivers hired, and similar actions had taken place in restaurants in Philadelphia. In 1946, the
NAACP's *Crisis* magazine published "how to" instructions for challenging Jim Crow in restaurants, including, if refused service, to ask
for something in sight and go to the police and tell the officers you
want to file a complaint around the civil rights law.[34] King and McCall
likely had heard of some of these actions.

According to the Hunts' daughter Thelma interviewed sixty years
later, "Daddy told him, don't go to Maple Shade. He told him many
times, they're racist and they won't serve you." She continued, "And
Martin said, well, it's a free country, you know. They shouldn't be
segregated, you know. And they went, and they got locked up." But
King and McCall didn't actually get arrested—they went to the police to press charges.[35] At the station, King listed the Hunts' Camden
address as his own, suggesting he may have strategized that a New

Jersey address might help his case.[36] Or he might have decided in the moment not to involve Crozer or his parents in a possible case, since he initially tried to buy alcohol on a Sunday night.

Planned or spontaneous, King's experience as a twenty-one-year-old—their "first time" in a civil rights protest, as McCall put it, a "sit-in" King would later call it—was a potent one. Staying put when asked to leave, deciding to press charges, discussing the potential case with friends and mentors, preparing to go before a grand jury, having witnesses leave you in the lurch—all that work was educational for the young King in the pragmatics of fighting for very basic rights. As a young adult figuring out his own ideas, this experience would indelibly shape his understandings of American racism and Black struggle.[37]

When he was fifteen, returning to Atlanta from a public speaking contest in Dublin, Georgia, King had been made to give up his seat on the bus and stand for hours. It was a traumatic event—"the angriest I have ever been in my life"; nearly all of his biographers cite this as pivotal to his leadership in the Montgomery bus boycott.[38] The "painful" Maple Shade event had similar impact. That he made his first civil rights protest in the North and that his supposed allies ultimately refused to testify to discrimination (ostensibly illegal under the law) was a formative experience for King in understanding the North as a site of racial discrimination, struggle, and hypocrisy.

Five months after the Maple Shade incident, in November 1950, King went to hear Howard University president Mordecai Johnson deliver a lecture on Gandhism at Philadelphia's Fellowship House.[39] Johnson had returned from a trip to India, where he had learned from Mahatma Gandhi himself the techniques of satyagraha (or truth force) and the power of nonviolent resistance. The lecture made an electrifying impression on the twenty-one-year-old King, who bought several books on Gandhi after that.[40]

King absorbed Gandhi's teachings in a deeply segregated context. As Fellowship House founder Marjorie Penney, who sponsored Johnson's talk, described, "Philadelphia as a Jim Crow city had not a movie in town where a black could be sure of getting a seat. . . . Your child better not want a soda fountain because the chances are that you would not be served there." [41] The only restaurant open to their interracial gatherings was a Chinese restaurant. All these experiences—the tremendous learning Crozer exposed him to, his professors' varying treatment, the confrontation in Maple Shade, Johnson's lecture in segregated Philadelphia—served as a crucible for King's developing understandings of US racism and nonviolent resistance.

At this same time, King had begun a romantic relationship with a young white woman, Betty Moitz, the daughter of the cook at Crozer.[42] They had met in the kitchen where her mom worked during King's first year. Becoming friends, King liked talking to Moitz. Their friendship blossomed into romance in King's second year at Crozer. King's friends tried to discourage him, but the couple grew serious. While the climate at Crozer was not friendly to an interracial couple, as Martin began his third year at Crozer, he had fallen in love with Betty and began to think of marriage. He refused his friends' concerns, seeing this as an opportunity to break down this artificial racial barrier. But then Barbour sat him down and gave him "a long fatherly talk" cautioning against the relationship. Subsequently the couple split up. King would later talk about the pain of this decision and the prejudice that existed in the North along with the South.[43] King was "a man with a broken heart. He never recovered," according to Barbour.[44]

King and his friends often went to Rev. Barbour for counsel on issues they faced as Black students at a predominantly white graduate school. According to Barbour, King "was in and out of my house just like one of my sons."[45] King sought Barbour out when his white professors seemed to denigrate Black preaching styles and Black students' intellectual substance. Several of King's professors lacked any urgency regarding American racism, and he wrestled with how those supposedly bound by religious commitments could harbor such complacency against oppression. According to Coretta, Martin grew more active around civil rights at Crozer because of the need for "these kinds of committees at white institutions."[46] Going to Rev. Barbour's was a way to try to figure this all out.

Barbour was devoted to the intellectual freedom the North allowed for Black ministers—and urged King not to go back to the South to pastor. But he also had a critique of Northern liberals and their lack of urgency toward racial justice and Black class divisions that likely affected King. As Barbour wrote, "The white liberals must stop sipping tea with well-to-do Negroes and drawing the conclusion that the Masses are doing all right. THE MASSES ARE NOT DOING ALL RIGHT. They are . . . cheated at the grocery store, double-crossed by prejudiced law leaders."[47]

While King had enrolled at Crozer because it was theologically liberal, he began to reject some aspects of liberal theology. He described "liberalism's superficial optimism"—how it failed to see that "reason by itself is little more than an instrument to justify man's defensive ways of thinking" or "realize that many of our present ills result from the sins of men."[48] Historian Clayborne Carson attributes this shift partly to King's experiences with Northern racism and "events in his personal life that contradicted Crozer's ethos of interracial harmony."[49] King had experienced the sins of some of his Crozer professors and classmates and their unwillingness to interrogate their own practices. The gap between their professed ministry as open and tolerant and their actions that often upheld racist practices affected his emerging theology.

In his last year at Crozer and subsequently at Boston University, King came to embrace the writings of ethicist-theologian Reinhold Niebuhr. At first King had been drawn to the writings of social gospeler Walter Rauschenbusch, who recognized that the church had a social responsibility in a world plagued by inequality and war. Rauschenbusch saw the urgency and role for a fearless Christian leadership—which resonated with the young minister. But increasingly, King gravitated to Niebuhr's critique of Rauschenbusch as overly romantic, overlooking power relations, economic imbalance, and the "persistence of man's self concern."[50] King increasingly saw Rauschenbusch as a "victim of the nineteenth-century cult of inevitable progress."[51] Niebuhr didn't think Christian suasion was enough to move people beyond their own self-interests. White Americans wouldn't embrace equality for Black people unless forced to do so. Already, King was rejecting the myth of time and evolving progress, which didn't account for individual benefit in systems of power. In Niebuhr, he found a "necessary corrective of a kind of liberalism that too easily capitulated to modern culture."[52] Justice on earth was a Christian imperative but required sacrifice and pressure to disrupt systems of power.

Not a Cradle of Liberty

After finishing his divinity degree at Crozer, King decided he wanted to pursue a doctorate. Accepted in various graduate schools, including Yale Divinity School and the University of Edinburgh, he chose Systematic Theology at Boston University, seeing it as the best place to deepen the prophetic intellectual work he had begun at Crozer. Black theologian Howard Thurman would become a key mentor, picking up from Mays's example and surrounding King with the theological and intellectual foundations of the Black social gospel.

The Boston that Martin Luther King called home from 1951 to 1954 was a tremendously segregated, unequal city that also fabulously denied its racism. Most housing was off-limits to Black renters or buyers. The city's African American population had grown considerably in the 1940s and 1950s, while school segregation expanded and job discrimination worsened in the post–World War II era.[53] Many restaurants, hotels, and clubs didn't serve Black people and the schools were continually segregated. Black sociologist Adelaide Cromwell, who joined BU's faculty the year that King arrived, talked about the "dark side of the city":

> Boston was a funny place, a paradoxical place . . . the image that this was freedom's birthplace . . . first of all, people were not particularly well-off . . . not many professional people. And what's more there were places you could not go and did not go. Restaurants did not welcome you. . . . The local people conspired to keep the silence. . . . Everybody maintained this fiction that this place was a free place. It wasn't a free place.[54]

Arriving in Boston in 1951, driving a green Chevy his father gave him, King first found an apartment in a rooming house at 170 St. Botolph Street, where he lived briefly. Then he moved to 397 Massachusetts Avenue, close to the bustling Black community of Lower Roxbury, with a Morehouse classmate, Philip Lenud. King would later talk about the housing discrimination he encountered when he moved to Boston. "I remember very well trying to find a place to live. I went into place after place where there were signs that rooms were for rent. They were for rent until they found out I was a Negro, and suddenly they had just been rented."[55] He got to know firsthand the housing discrimination he would challenge in Northern cities for the rest of his life.

King and Lenud's apartment sat right across from the Savoy Cafe. But given Boston's racism, they never attended the almost-nightly dances there for fear of trouble.[56] Between 1952 and 1953, King and Lenud's apartment became a meeting place for a group of Black male students.[57] The Dialectical Society, as they called it, met on the weekend to discuss philosophers from Plato to Aristotle and grapple with the issues of the day "to solve the problems of the world."[58] Their discussions "often focused on discrimination and segregation," according to classmate David Briddell, unavoidable topics as they navigated the city's racism.[59]

The combination of these discussions, his studies, particularly with Thurman, and his own experiences of Boston's racism deepened King's political analysis. His father worried about him shifting "too far to the left." [60] Daddy King grew concerned that his son's political ideas were "drifting away from the bases of capitalism and Western democracy that I felt very strongly about. There were some sharp exchanges; I may even have raised my voice a few times." [61]

Some of the city's most ardent civil rights activists whom Martin would later join forces with got their start in the years that he lived in Boston. In 1949, Ruth Batson, a Boston native and now mother of three, began attending the interracial Parents Federation meetings, which were documenting racial disparities in Boston's schools. Batson had learned from a white friend in the Parents Federation that her son had science in school but Batson's own daughter did not. This marked difference in the quality of education galled her and so she called the local NAACP. At first they said they didn't have a committee to deal with school issues, but the next day they called her back and asked her to chair a new subcommittee. After this call, Batson's life "changed profoundly. . . . Some black citizens scolded me for raising the issue of segregation and discrimination in Boston, the seat of culture and the home of abolitionists. . . . Some white citizens— usually officials and press representatives—argued my declarations to be without foundation." [62]

From the outset in 1950, the NAACP Public School subcommittee focused on segregation, educational inequity, and the differential allocation of school resources within Boston's public school system. And from the outset, it faced opposition over whether segregation even existed in the Cradle of Liberty. In 1951, the year King moved to the city, Batson decided to run for School Committee, the first Black person to do so in the twentieth century. She did not win. Mel King (no relation to Martin Luther King) had also grown up in Boston, attending college in South Carolina, but returned home in 1952. "There was a sense of arrogance that this was Boston but at the same time, the denial of access was much greater here." [63] Batson and Mel King would help build a nonviolent direct-action movement against school segregation in the years to come, against unbending white resistance.

This is the Boston where Martin Luther King spent his early twenties—a deeply segregated city that nonetheless trumpeted its openness and where Black activists were beginning to collectively raise their voices. Given the schizophrenic nature of Boston's racial politics, King and Lenud's group must have had a lot to discuss.

Most of King's personal life thus took place within Boston's segregated Black community. Biographer Lewis Baldwin describes how King "discovered in Boston a Black community that afforded so much of what he needed for his material well-being and spiritual sustenance."[64] But Coretta Scott King observed how this wasn't fully by choice: "Blacks were isolated. . . . The neighborhood we had lived in before, and still were part of, was almost completely black."[65] King's friends were Black; while there were white students at BU, "there was very little socializing. . . . Negro students were very clannish for self protection."[66]

King became very involved in Black Boston, mainly through his work at Twelfth Baptist Church in Roxbury.[67] Serving as their student minister, King became the "adopted son" of the church—worshipping, teaching religious classes, delivering some Sunday sermons, and playing basketball and shooting pool with young people across the street at the social services center.[68] Both Rev. Michael E. Haynes, Twelfth Baptist's pastor, and the church itself (which had been founded by abolitionists in the 1840s) had a long history of social justice engagement. Haynes underscored the impact coming to Boston had on King's thinking: "He wanted to get a different perspective on world issues and race issues than he would be getting if we were directly in the south." Alongside Twelfth Baptist, Professor Howard Thurman's mentorship helped King lay the foundation for a revolutionary Christian nonviolent movement to challenge US social injustice.[69] So what he was learning alongside his experiences in Boston widened King's political outlook.

Meeting the Formidable Coretta Scott

Part of why King had gone to Boston was to deepen his intellectual foundation in the social gospel and praxis for social change. He would find part of that grounding in a formidable New England Conservatory of Music student named Coretta Scott. Politically engaged, religiously driven, and more of an activist than Martin when they met, Coretta would help expand the various strands of his political and religious convictions.

Coretta Scott had grown up in a proud, independent farming

family near Marion, Alabama. Nearly all the Black people in their Alabama community owned their own land, angering neighboring whites. Their family was harassed and threatened repeatedly. When her father started transporting lumber, a business reserved for whites, whites torched their house to the ground. And when her father refused to sell his business to a white man, they burned the business too.[70] "Our father was the subject of almost constant threats," her older sister Edythe explained.[71] Those experiences and the pride her parents instilled in her helped prepare Coretta for what she would encounter as an adult.

Coretta Scott was a "tomboy" growing up: "I was tough . . . I would fight; real fight, real hard. And I used to fight my sister and my brother when they did anything that I didn't like, so they used to call me mean. . . . [A]s I got to become a teenager, I began to be much more ladylike, and I stopped fighting."[72] Her mother had been keenly determined that her children get a good education (beyond what was available to Black children locally) so she enrolled Edythe and Coretta at Lincoln Normal School in Marion. To attend, Coretta lived for the first years with other Black families, until her mother learned to drive a bus to transport them so her daughter could live at home the last two years. At Lincoln, Coretta was introduced to Bayard Rustin, who came to the school to speak about nonviolence.[73] She and her classmates were awed when he said he refused to sit in the Jim Crow sections of trains and buses and showed his scars to prove it.[74]

Following her older sister Edythe (who was the first African American to attend Antioch College in Ohio in decades), Coretta Scott received a scholarship to Antioch, where she majored in music and elementary education. Her mother's tenacity, plus her own feelings "that something must be done about discrimination against the Negro," meant she arrived at Antioch already determined.[75] Like Martin, she left the South for new opportunities, and Antioch opened many. But like Martin, it was daunting being one of only a few Black students on the campus. "I was so inhibited. . . . My previous study habits would not suffice. . . . I found myself baffled when asked to make comments in ordinary conversations."[76] Self-doubt accompanied much of her time at Antioch, though a school counselor helped her to scale back the self-recrimination and find her own pace.[77]

Attending the nearly all-white college also provided a key launching pad for Coretta's own politics, as she became active in the NAACP, the Race Relations Committee, and the Civil Liberties Committee on campus. She met Rustin again at a campus talk. "It was at Antioch that I first became aware of the relationship between peace and justice and came to see without justice there can be no peace."[78] But she also confronted being the "token" Black and the limits of her classmates' and the school's progressivism. Her classmates would periodically ask offensive questions like "why are Negroes loud and immoral," then qualify them by saying how she was "different." She felt compelled to try to challenge their assumptions and explain how "conditions make them that way."[79]

Being an education major qualified Coretta Scott to student-teach, but Antioch sided with the local school board's decision not to allow her or any other Black person to student-teach in the city's schools. She was dumbfounded and very, very hurt. "Well, it happened here. The same thing I left Alabama to get away from."[80] Antioch wanted her to student-teach at a segregated Black school in Xenia, Ohio. But she refused, writing the school a powerful indictment of US Cold War liberalism: "My precious time and money have been spent for a commodity which I never received only because my skin color happened to be darker. . . . Do you then wonder why America as a leader among the nations in the world cannot command more respect among the common people who make up the majority of the world?"[81]

She also attempted to get her white classmates to protest the college's decision with her, but they refused, worried that their opportunities might be taken away too.[82] "Most of the students would not even discuss the subject with me." So even her classmates, who prided themselves on their progressivism (and many were active in various causes), grew wobbly when addressing racism in their midst, fearing it would impinge on their own standing.[83] She took her case directly to Antioch's president, but he refused to do anything. Coretta was "shattered," according to her sister. She had become "the victim of racism at one of the most liberal white colleges in the country."[84] She felt abandoned; she talked with a fellow student from Kenya but had "no body of support around me." Her counselors whom she loved, including the one Black faculty member at Antioch, were supportive but said they couldn't do anything.[85] Later, she said that Antioch's failure to live up to its values helped her develop "a sense of fortitude" and "made me determined to become more involved in addressing issues of social and political injustice."[86]

Coretta dated a handful of men, including a Jewish student, at Antioch for two years but, like Martin, she grew wary of life in the US in

an interracial relationship, and they split up.[87] Even though her classmates were unwilling to confront the college's racism, many Antioch
students were deeply critical of Cold War militarism. Because of this,
some young men filed as conscientious objectors to the Korean War.
She and other students organized to support them, and Coretta's own
global peace politics grew as a result. Introduced to the Progressive
Party by some of her professors, Coretta Scott supported Henry Wallace's third-party campaign for president in 1948. Wallace was challenging incumbent Democrat Harry Truman and Republican Thomas
Dewey from the left for the US presidency around issues of segregation, economic justice, and Cold War militarism. But the Progressive
Party's interracial antiracism and global vision were treated by many
Americans as Communist sympathy.

Nonetheless, Scott attended the Progressive Party convention in
Philadelphia in July 1948, one of only 150 Black people of more than
three thousand delegates. At the convention as a student delegate, she
heard political activist-author Shirley Graham (who married W. E. B.
Du Bois three years later) deliver a powerful keynote speech denouncing war; linking militarism to decreased social spending for education, health care, and housing; and demanding an end to Jim Crow in
America.[88] Pete Seeger performed.

Many FBI agents were on hand to surveil the proceedings. Wallace,
Franklin Roosevelt's former vice president, supported voting rights
and a national health care system while opposing segregation and the
United States' hawkish Cold War policy. Many leftists and civil rights
activists welcomed Wallace's campaign, as Wallace's run would force
Democratic presidential incumbent Truman to become more forthright on civil rights. Both Harry Belafonte and Paul Robeson were
key Progressive Party supporters, speaking at rallies throughout
the country. For that work, both would be blacklisted and Robeson's
passport revoked.

Coretta Scott had heard Robeson sing at Antioch and speak in
Philadelphia—and admired him incredibly for the ways he combined
singing with social issues. At a state meeting of the Progressive Party
in Columbus, Ohio, she met and sang for him. He encouraged her
to continue with it.[89] The Progressive Party, according to her sister
Edythe, "exposed her to the national debate regarding racial equality,
economic justice, and international peace—issues she would spend the
rest of her life promoting."[90] These were courageous politics, putting
Coretta Scott on the left when it was being massively red-baited. She

didn't talk about it publicly much. "I didn't want it to become a noose around Martin's neck," she later explained.[91]

Determined to pursue a singing career, Coretta Scott received a scholarship to attend the prestigious New England Conservatory of Music. It didn't cover her living expenses in Boston; worried about how she would survive, her father didn't want her to go. But she forged ahead. Her mother had told her to "get an education. Be somebody. And you won't have to depend on anyone. Not even a man." Music was a way forward.[92] She wanted to be a female Paul Robeson.

In the first weeks after arriving in Boston in fall 1951, Coretta ran out of money. Terrified and proud, she didn't want to ask for help, but she did, calling on a network of Antioch alums, who stepped in to find her a job, albeit in a racially gendered position. She began doing live-in domestic work for an Antioch alum in the fashionable neighborhood of Beacon Hill. Along with three Irish women who served as maids and a cook, she scrubbed floors, cleaned the bathrooms, and did washing and a variety of household tasks to be able to live and eat.[93] She was "the only black living in the Beacon Hill section and I did not feel comfortable going to the churches in that area."[94] (Housing for conservatory students, had she been able to afford it, was also segregated.) Still, she worried, "I have to prove I am worthy of this."[95] Some classmates found her aloof, both because she was a reserved young woman and likely in part because she was busy balancing her work off-campus with her conservatory study.

Initially, when her friend Mary Powell, who knew Martin King from Atlanta, brought up meeting the young minister, Coretta Scott said she wasn't interested in a "whooping Black preacher." In her experience, people who wanted to be ministers were often "very narrow" and "overly pious"—"trying to look the part but . . . not intelligent, committed persons." She wanted someone with a political and religious vision closer to hers. She too was a deep Christian, but it was rooted in what you did in your life, not in the suits and sanctimony of many of the preachers she had experienced. Like Martin, her Christianity pushed her to pursue social change in this world, which hadn't been the case in most of the churches she knew.[96]

But King pursued her. Martin dated a variety of women in Boston and was also still dating Juanita Sellers, his longtime sort-of girlfriend from Spelman whose family was prominent in Atlanta's Black community like King's.[97] But he was looking for more. He wasn't bothered, she later learned, when Mary had told him Coretta didn't go to church.

"That's alright," he told Mary. He did not want someone who was "a fundamentalist."[98]

They had their first lunch date in January 1952. To her surprise, she found "a thinker," and he found an intellectual as well.[99] Coretta Scott's influence on Martin King began on their very first date. Their first discussion was about racism, war, and peace.[100] He had never met a woman like her. "He wanted to test me to see whether or not I was a thinker," Coretta recalled, "because he always placed a great value on thinking . . . not having someone who was, who looked well, but shallow, you know. So anyway, the conversation . . . had something to do with communism versus capitalism—and I made an intelligent comment. And he said, 'Oh, I see you know something other than music.' And I thought to myself, 'of course I do. I've been to Antioch College.' But anyway, I didn't say that to him."[101] Martin was trying to see how she thought and got more than he bargained for. He was awed and, frankly, seduced by the ways she raised the bar on what he had imagined in a woman.

At the end of their first date, he told her that she had "all the qualities he wanted in a wife—beauty, personality, character and intelligence." Incredulous, she responded, "you don't even know me." On the phone before their date, he had been charming, trying out some of his best lines—he was Napoleon and she was his Waterloo—"intellectual jive," she thought.[102] She didn't let him get away with some of the easy charm or general statements he was used to proffering. Martin was going to have to bring out his substance to win her over.[103] But she agreed to another date.

In many ways, meeting Coretta Scott opened new worlds for Martin Luther King. Indeed, when their courtship began, she was more committed, according to SCLC colleague Andrew Young, "to get into the struggle to do something about race than either Martin or I."[104] From the beginning, according to his sister Christine, Martin liked how self-assured and unapologetically Black Coretta was.[105] She liked how "relaxed and free" Martin seemed, so "secure with himself."[106] And funny; he could keep her in stitches for hours.

As they continued dating, they talked about her disillusionment with the church and its narrowness. Martin "didn't criticize me." He didn't judge. In many ways, Coretta was living the radical Christianity that Martin had also sought. "I had realized," she said, "that carrying all the forms out did not make you religious. What you did in your life . . . really mattered."[107] Her faith didn't need a building; it was rooted in the kinds of justice and life choices that they as Christians pursued on earth. While men like Benjamin Mays and Howard Thurman have been credited for providing Martin Luther King with the foundations for a liberatory Christianity, Coretta Scott also played a crucial role. If Martin had left Atlanta to acquire a more grounded Christian praxis, he found that in her.

Coretta became increasingly impressed with his vision and determination to be a minister who challenged the American racial system. "He sounded so much like he went to Antioch." She thought, "[H]ow can you talk this way? . . . [T]his is so wonderful, you know, that he really is very serious about working to change society. And he seemed so sure that he was going be able to do it." In their conversations, she saw her views were "more global and pacifist, while his were more focused on direct action to change the oppressive structures of black America."[108] She sent him a copy of Edward Bellamy's utopian socialist novel *Looking Backward*. Perhaps to try to impress his activist girlfriend, Martin wrote back laying out his own philosophy. He was "much more socialistic in my economic theory than capitalistic," he wrote, and the gospel he wanted to preach to the world would be for "a warless world, a better distribution of wealth, and a brotherhood that transcends race or color."[109]

Martin liked that he had to work to impress her. With her politics and Progressive Party experience, Martin "stepped into her space," Harry Belafonte explained.[110] Martin told Coretta that he didn't like how capitalism was practiced in the US, "taking all you can get and not being concerned about other people." He shared with her that his father "loved money" and cared about his own family more than the broader needs of the community, which was not what Martin wanted to do.[111]

Independent and "ferociously informal," according to James Baldwin, Coretta still worried about how "circumscribed" her life would become if she married the young minister.[112] "I didn't want a man that would lead me, I was thinking in terms of where I would go myself."[113] She hadn't planned on marrying till after her career was established, but he was "so persistent and determined."[114] Key to their emerging love was this shared political-intellectual companionship they found in each other, a vision of a partnership that defied certain social norms of the day. Martin wanted a wife he could communicate with and was as dedicated as he was to pursuing change.[115] She agreed. "I didn't learn my commitment from Martin, we just converged at a certain time."[116]

"It wasn't love . . . at first sight," she explained. "But he was such an extraordinary human being, and our values were so similar and our outlook were so much alike, we made a good couple. . . . [I]t took a lot of praying to discover that this was probably what God had called me to do to marry him."[117] A cerebral person, according to her sister Edythe, Coretta thought through their relationship for months—what her life and career would become, if he would be serious in challenging racism, what her own contribution would be, if they could have a big and different life.[118] Fifteen years later, as she was interviewing Coretta Scott King, editor Charlotte Mayerson was incredulous at this story of their romance: "Wasn't it unusual to think all of this out so thoroughly?" No, it wasn't, Scott King said firmly. Thinking through things was always her way. "I tried to face them. I didn't try to run away from them." That thinking, the ability to face things and move forward, lay at the core of her inner strength and the partnership they found in each other.[119] Indeed, Coretta was perhaps the more analytical and Martin the more emotional of the two.[120]

Her friends worried about her career and whether Martin would amount to much. But she decided that despite the sacrifices, she loved his spirit, commitment, and vision and how well it dovetailed with hers. He reminded her of her father.[121] By the end of her first year, Coretta moved from Beacon Hill to Martin's neighborhood, renting a room from the League of Women for Community Service in the South End.[122]

King was still dating Juanita Sellers, whom his parents, particularly his father, wanted him to marry; they had an easy companionship, and she came from the right kind of family. But Juanita didn't fully share his political vision and willingness to go where they were needed.[123] After Martin's prodding, Coretta visited him in Atlanta in June on her way to Alabama. King's father wasn't wholly welcoming, talking to Coretta about what other young women like Juanita had to offer his son. Coretta bristled, sternly telling him, "I have something to offer too." She felt a "bit provoked by this. . . . He didn't know me." Coretta wasn't afraid to take on King's father.

When Edythe met him, he also grilled her. Edythe bristled: "I assured the Kings that Coretta was one of the strongest people I knew and that she had an iron will and inexhaustible physical stamina. . . . In my opinion, Coretta had no need to bargain for a husband."[124] Then, when the Kings came up to visit them in Boston that fall, Daddy King told Coretta not to take his son too seriously because he had another woman more suited to marry. Martin just sat there not saying a word, "grinning . . . like a little child. . . . He was always so respectful of his father." It made her angry. Why wasn't he saying something? Instead Martin got up and left her with his dad; he was going, she later learned, to tell his mother that he was going to marry Coretta. Martin was not good at confronting his father directly, Coretta explained. "He made his decisions and whenever he didn't want to tell his father something he would just go out and make it. And his father would hear about it." [125] Later, according to his father, Martin made clear: "She's the most important person to come into my life." [126]

They got married June 18, 1953, on her parents' lawn in Alabama. But their wedding too bucked the conventions of the time. She told her imposing father-in-law to take the word *obey* out of their vows. She and Martin didn't want to promise to obey—"it made me feel too much like an indentured servant." [127] Against traditional forms of marriage, she decided, "I'm not going to wear a white dress." Instead she wore a light blue, waltz-length (not floor-length) dress—testament to the early feminist she was and that Martin had fallen in love with. Not interested in materialistic things, she refused to select a china pattern. [128] She would be Coretta Scott King for the rest of her life—keeping her maiden name as part of her name, unlike most women of her generation, but perhaps inspired by the example of Shirley Graham Du Bois, who had impressed her years earlier.

That is not to say Martin was the kind of feminist Coretta was. He surely was not. In some ways he wanted a "shared relationship," but in other ways he wanted to work and provide for her and, in time, the kids they would have. He had wished his mother questioned his father more—and so he sought and had found this quality in a life partner. Yet he was also used to spaces where men led and women followed—not to mention all-male spaces of leadership and discussion. He did not always listen to women in the ways he listened to men. Coretta said "it was an adjustment to make" from her time at Antioch, where women were encouraged to "assert themselves." [129] Many of the people who gravitated to the Progressive Party and the kinds of race-class politics that Coretta Scott possessed were also thinking critically about gender roles, historian Dayo Gore shows. [130] And so she was far ahead of him in her thinking about gender. This independence would provide a foundation for the ways she would enable their civil rights activism and his leadership in the years ahead.

But one of the gifts Martin embodied that she most appreciated was that he "let me be myself and that meant I always expressed my views."[131] He was a listener and didn't make her feel weird for how she was. He wanted her to be a thinker and not always agree with him. Admiring the activist-intellectual she already was, he moved toward her politics and activism, and she gravitated toward his vision and determination.

Toni Morrison's *Beloved* captures the gift of love that is having "a friend of my mind."[132] This, in slightly different ways, is what Martin Luther King and Coretta Scott brought each other—to love each other's minds, their spirit and personhood, their deepest aspirations for change and the self they wanted to be in the world. Martin had chosen Coretta for a wife *because of* who she was, because of her willingness to challenge things (including him), because she imagined that the ways of their parents and American society did not have to be the way they would be, and because she lived her Christianity and was determined to have a different life that challenged racism, war, poverty, and social convention. He would not have become the leader he became without her.[133]

Martin and Coretta's married life began in the segregated Cradle of Liberty, where white Bostonians liked to boast of their openness and Black people were relegated to certain parts of town with poor schools and inferior municipal services. Coretta referred to Boston as "up South."[134] But this segregated reality has been left out in most accounts of their early life together.

They first lived at 3396 Northampton, a dilapidated six-story former hotel in Boston's South End that would get torn down in the 1960s.[135] They were both busy, him writing his dissertation and her studying, teaching music, and preparing for final recitals. They went food shopping together. In that first year, he did "all the cleaning . . . and the washing." And on Thursday nights, when her class ran late, he would cook dinner—smothered cabbage, corn bread, and fried pork chops were some of his specialties.[136] Martin was "sure in his manhood," she noted, not self-conscious about sharing the housework.[137]

While they didn't meet, in the winter of 1954 Malcolm X lived five minutes away—and the Cradle of Liberty's racism and performative liberalism had a decisive impact on all of them.[138] When an interviewer in 1968 asked about their experience as newlyweds in "integrated" Boston, Coretta Scott King scoffed. She and Martin had talked a lot about how "the integration in the North was not real yet . . . there was not law that you couldn't mix but it was just that the negroes were still isolated . . . the whole thing was superficial really . . . that was the reason that even now in the north really you have so much segregation." While she made some white friends, she noted how little contact Martin had with white Bostonians.[139]

In September 1954, Martin accepted a call to the pulpit at Dexter Avenue Baptist Church in Montgomery, Alabama. He had told Coretta when they were courting that he imagined moving back south "to where I was needed."[140] Describing a "moral obligation to return," King wrote three years later that "we had the feeling that something remarkable was happening in the South."[141] But moving back to the South was a difficult decision, and he and Coretta talked through what it would mean to return to the strictures of Southern-style racism and the kind of education their children would receive.[142] According to Edythe, Coretta wanted to stay in the North; she knew Alabama "too well" and was sure a singing career would be easier in the North.[143] Moving to the South to be a preacher's wife meant giving up the career she had been training for, and Coretta worried about their marriage narrowing her. But Martin was determined.

Upon moving to Montgomery, he finished his dissertation, writing BU in 1955 that he could not afford to come back for graduation. "King . . . never forgot what he had learned in and about Boston," Rev. Haynes observed. The civil rights leader that King became over the next years was indelibly shaped by spending his formative young adult years in the North. Both he and Coretta had come of age amid the segregation and disappointing limits of Northern liberalism. If Martin had gone north for opportunities, perhaps the greatest opportunity he found was a life partner who understood the trifecta of racism, poverty, and war and was hell-bent to challenge them.

Three crucial facets that would set the course of their lives—their understanding of the breadth of American racism, the importance of a Christianity rooted in social justice, and a partnership that attempted to challenge conventions of the time—had been set in motion. Scott King would tell the *Pittsburgh Courier* just a few years later, "Our romance prepared us for our ordeal. It would have been a most difficult period if the strong bond between us didn't exist."[144] And so it is no surprise that as an unexpected opportunity emerged in Montgomery to put their convictions into practice, they heard the call.

2

There Lived a Great People

King's Leadership Emerges,
as Does His Critique of the North

Sometimes who you are is enough.

—Omar, *The Wire*

Their first year in Montgomery kept the Kings busy. They adjusted to life at Dexter Avenue Baptist Church, Martin finished his dissertation, and Coretta got pregnant. Martin was "particularly attentive" during her pregnancy.[1] From the beginning, Coretta helped Martin with his sermons. She was his sounding board. He would tell her the subject and then say, " 'I'm going to have three points. Now what would be my first point?' And of course I would come up with something. . . . I felt very much involved in what he was doing."[2] An intellectual partnership, they talked through many ideas together.[3]

Dexter had a largely middle-class congregation, with many college-educated parishioners. The church had let go of its previous minister, Vernon Johns, for being an agitator. Johns preached sermons like "It's Safe to Murder Negroes in Montgomery" and sold watermelons out of the church basement. Little did the congregation realize just how bold the new minister and his wife would prove to be.

Finding the class and political divisions of Black Montgomery dispiriting, King worried about the middle-class snobbery that Dexter was known for and attempted to begin to change it.[4] His father had begun arranging guest sermons for him, and so he returned to Second Baptist in Detroit in 1954, this time to give his own sermon. "There is something wrong with our world, something fundamentally and basically wrong," he preached.[5]

He also started working with the local NAACP. The first time

Rosa Parks, the forty-one-year-old chapter secretary, encountered the twenty-five-year-old King was at an NAACP meeting where he addressed the thirty or so people on the US Supreme Court's recent *Brown v. Board of Education* decision. Parks and her fellow activists Johnnie Carr and E. D. Nixon had spent the past decade working to transform Montgomery's NAACP into a more activist chapter—pushing for Black voter registration and desegregation, seeking justice for Black women who had been raped, and challenging the wrongful convictions of Black men. Parks's and Carr's jaws dropped when King started speaking that day. They were "amazed that one so young could speak with so much eloquence and to the point."[6] King considered running for NAACP branch president but decided not to, since Coretta was due with their first child. But he did join the executive committee and Parks sent him a letter welcoming him.[7] On November 17, 1955, Coretta and Martin's daughter Yolanda was born.

Shortly after, events came together leading King to step forward into a new leadership role. From the beginning, the movement made King. At the same time, he and Coretta made hard choice after hard choice— the substance of their religious and political commitments becoming real and visible. They were young and felt insufficient but stepped forward anyway. And in those choices and learning, many people found their own courage.

Catching a Vision

On December 1, 1955, coming home from work at the segregated Montgomery Fair Department Store, longtime activist Rosa Parks refused to give up her seat on the bus when bus driver James Blake ordered her to and was arrested: "I felt like if I got up, I approved of that treatment and I didn't approve." Late that night, she decided to pursue a legal case against bus segregation and called her friend Fred Gray, a young Black lawyer, to represent her.[8] Even later that night, hearing from Gray of Parks's decision, the Women's Political Council sprang into action, calling for a boycott of the city's buses on Monday, when Parks would be arraigned in court.

The Women's Political Council was a Black women's political organization, made up largely of women who attended Dexter Avenue Baptist Church, who had been challenging bus segregation for years. Following the *Brown* decision the year before, WPC head Jo Ann Robinson had sent the bus company a letter saying that if changes were

not made, they would boycott the buses. In the middle of the night
after Parks's arrest, Robinson headed to Alabama State College, where
she was a professor. With the help of two students and a colleague,
they ran off thirty-five thousand leaflets announcing: "another woman
has been arrested on the bus . . . stay off the buses Monday."[9]

Around 3 a.m., Robinson called E. D. Nixon, one of Montgomery's
most stalwart organizers, to apprise him of their plan. But she did not
call Parks. Perhaps because of the class divides in Montgomery's Black
community (Parks was working-class, did not attend Dexter, and lived
in the Cleveland Court projects), Robinson did not feel she had to in-
form her.[10] Early that morning, Nixon began to mobilize Montgomery's
handful of political ministers to support the Monday boycott. His first
call was to Rev. Ralph Abernathy. The twenty-nine-year-old Abernathy was one of the few politically active ministers in town and a
member of the NAACP. Then, at around 6 a.m., Nixon phoned King
to tell him about the boycott. Nixon wanted to use King's church, cen-
trally located downtown, for a meeting that evening to coalesce support for the protest.

The twenty-six-year-old King hesitated. Yolanda was only two
weeks old, and he wasn't sure he could commit, given his new family
responsibilities. "Let me think about it a while and call me back," he
told Nixon.[11] A few hours later, when Nixon called back, King agreed
they could meet at his church. Nixon, Abernathy, and King worked
through the morning to find other ministers and community leaders to attend that evening. Then Nixon called Parks to tell her about
the meeting that evening. Surprised, she asked what it was for. "You
know—about your being arrested," he replied. Parks said she would
be there.[12]

Looking back on that Friday morning, it is important to recognize
there was nothing destined about King's leadership, no lightning bolt
that showed him what to do. Similar to Rosa Parks, part of King's gift
was the ability to act on convictions despite fear and uncertainty. This
decision would have significant consequences for their families—and
by the end of the boycott, King had gained national notice. But there
was nothing easy about the roles he and Coretta would come to play
or the many choices ahead. Coretta and Martin had already decided
they would not be bound by the limits society imposed. This would
give them both the will and the vision to make decisions most people
would have either missed or regarded as impossible.

Nearly fifty ministers and other local leaders, including physicians, teachers, and union leaders, gathered that evening at Dexter. Parks was nervous as she approached the church, wondering if the community would support her. "I didn't know whether my getting arrested was going to set well or ill with the . . . leaders of the black community." At first the answer seemed to be no.

The meeting began poorly. Nixon, who had to be out of town for work as a Pullman porter, had put Rev. Roy Bennett in charge, who lectured for thirty minutes without even mentioning Parks or the Monday boycott. People started to leave. King joked with a friend that he wanted to leave too but couldn't because this was his church. Finally, Parks addressed the group, explaining that she had reached her breaking point with segregation. Robinson also took the floor and spoke about the urgent need to take action. Besides, the WPC had already set the plan in motion, distributing thousands of leaflets calling for the Monday boycott. Ultimately the meeting ended with those gathered deciding to promote the one-day protest. The small cadre of Montgomery's Black activists—including Parks—were nervous that weekend. Most Black Montgomerians had been unwilling to engage in mass action in the past in fear of repercussions. King had taken note of the "appalling lack of unity" among them.[13] Would people actually stay off the buses?

On Monday, the Kings were up and dressed by 5:30 a.m. to see if the boycott had worked. Martin felt that if even 60 percent of Black people stayed off it would be a success. A bus rolled by nearly empty of Black passengers; another bus passed empty. They were elated. Martin drove around for an hour to see the rest of the city. Nearly every Black person in Montgomery had stayed off the bus. "I was jubilant," King wrote later. "A miracle had taken place."[14]

On Monday afternoon, after Rosa Parks's appearance in court, a group of Montgomery's Black leaders, including Parks's lawyer Fred Gray, met to discuss the success of the protest. Neither Parks nor Jo Ann Robinson was invited; in fact, Parks was back answering Gray's phones. Despite the multiple roles women would play as organizers, fundraisers, and boycotters, the formal leadership would remain overwhelmingly male. Awed by the day's protest, many of the men still feared being publicly associated with the boycott and didn't want to speak at the mass meeting planned for that evening. Finally, Nixon exploded in anger at their hesitation: "Where are the men? We need to turn history around and stop hiding behind these women who do all the work for us."[15] Nixon threatened to take the microphone and tell their congregations these clergy were "too cowardly to stand on their feet and be counted." [16] King, who had entered late, said he wasn't a coward and agreed to speak that night at the mass meeting.

Then Rufus Lewis, a member of King's congregation, nominated King to lead this effort. A number of people, including Lewis, didn't want Nixon to lead the new group, finding him too low-class, unsophisticated, and, likely, too bold. And so they put the relatively unknown King forward as the leader of the Montgomery Improvement Association (MIA), as they called it. Because he was new in town, the twenty-six-year-old King hadn't made enemies in Montgomery's Black community. The only woman elected was Erma Dungee, as financial secretary.

That evening, a huge crowd packed into Holt Street Baptist Church. It was so crowded that thousands of people had to congregate outside, and the church turned on its outdoor loudspeakers for people to hear. Parks struggled to even get inside. Upon seeing the crowd, several ministers changed their mind and decided to make speeches, as did E. D. Nixon. Despite a minutes-long standing ovation, Rosa Parks did not get to speak.

King was terrified. He had only a few minutes to prepare his thoughts. Coretta couldn't go with him to the meeting because her doctor had ordered her to stay home that first month after Yolanda was born. But once King mounted the pulpit, he became comfortable, offering prophetic words about the historical significance of their actions: "Right here in Montgomery, when the history books are written in the future, somebody will have to say, 'There lived a great people—a Black people—who injected new meaning and dignity into the veins of civilization.' " Stunned by the power of King's speech, the crowd was silent for a moment after he finished. Then they rose to their feet, cheering and clapping. Outside, the crowd erupted into thunderous applause. That night, the people decided to extend that one-day protest into an indefinite boycott. It would last for 382 days.

The power and unity of Montgomery's Black community kept the boycott going, and weekly mass meetings helped buoy people's spirits. As Coretta Scott King explained, "coming together in solidarity" each week helped the people boycotting the buses "go back out the next day to face whatever insults that they were going to have to face." [17] While the popular image of the Montgomery bus boycott has focused on walking, what made the boycott succeed was a massive Black organizing effort and the cross-class solidarity. The Montgomery Improvement

Association built an intricate car-pool system to maintain the boycott—establishing forty pickup stations across the city so people could get a ride to work or school or the doctor and stay off the buses. At its peak, they were giving out fifteen thousand rides a day.

Many middle-class Black people offered their cars in the car pool (which surprised and delighted longtime organizers like Parks and Nixon, who hadn't seen this kind of cross-class unity). The backbone of the effort was working-class Black people, particularly women, who stayed off the buses and fundraised to maintain the car-pool system. Many women worked as domestics and constantly had to bite their tongue as their employers disparaged the protest, but then regularly showed up at the mass meetings at night. Many of these women were so proud of this brave young minister who had emerged as a leader that, as their employers then moved to try to discredit him, a number risked their jobs to defend him.[18] The power of this activism, and these women's resolve, deepened King's conviction in the power of working-class people to challenge their oppression collectively.

The police harassed the car pool intensely, giving out hundreds of tickets. When the city began negotiations, they treated the MIA and the White Citizens' Council as two different interest groups to be reconciled. When King criticized the inclusion of the openly segregationist WCC, city leaders treated King as unreasonable and intolerant for suggesting this.

To maintain the car-pool system, the MIA needed funds far beyond what Montgomery Black people could provide. So King and Parks (who had lost her job five weeks into the boycott) spent much of that year on the road—Detroit, New York, Pittsburgh, San Francisco, Detroit, and on—raising attention and money for the movement at home. In the first months of the boycott, besides the largely negative coverage in the *Montgomery Advertiser* and *Alabama Tribune*, it was just the Black press paying attention. But these trips helped turn this local movement into a national struggle. As King began the travel that would escalate for the rest of his life, he brought the urgency of Montgomery, his experiences living in segregated Chester, Boston, and Atlanta, and the lived religious commitments he and Coretta had forged together.

The boycott inspired Black people across the country and the world, including some of New York's most seasoned organizers—Ella Baker, Stanley Levison, and Bayard Rustin—to lend their assistance. Baker, Rustin, and Levison were part of a vanguard of activists who saw the need to challenge racism and economic injustice in tandem.[19] Baker had grown up in Norfolk, Virginia, and attended Shaw University but after graduation in 1927 moved to Harlem, where she worked in a variety of community organizations. In 1940 she began working with the NAACP, serving as director of branches from 1943 to 1946. She left the position because she saw the organization as too hierarchical but remained active challenging the city's injustices, heading the Harlem NAACP beginning in 1952.

Rustin was a longtime pacifist-socialist who had resisted the draft during World War II and worked with labor leader A. Philip Randolph around the first March on Washington movement to protest segregation in the defense industries and armed forces. With a global vision of peace and belief in Gandhian nonviolence, Rustin had worked for the Fellowship of Reconciliation. Rustin was gay and had been forced out of the Fellowship in 1953 when he was arrested on a morals charge and now worked for the War Resisters League. Levison, a Jewish attorney who had grown up in New York, had spent decades working on racial justice and left-wing movements involving the Communist Party, including the defense of Julius and Ethel Rosenberg.

Baker, Levison, and Rustin recognized the power of what was happening in Montgomery and formed In Friendship to provide a range of support from fundraising to tactical guidance for the boycott and King himself. These three would play an indelible role in the coming years in shaping King's thinking and connecting him to movements across the country. From the boycott on, King's work reached beyond Montgomery. The boycott inspired bus boycotts from Johannesburg, South Africa, to Tallahassee, Florida—and activists across the country began reaching out to him.

It also inspired a tremendous amount of hate mail and calls. By January, King was receiving thirty to forty hate letters a day and their home was bombarded by obscene calls and death threats, sometimes as many as twenty-five a day.[20] Montgomery authorities and many whites across the country had fingered Communist influence on the boycott and King. So it wasn't just Southerners who called but Northerners as well. For Coretta, at times, it reminded her of childhood when her dad had received repeated death threats. But her steeliness emerged as well.

Sometimes when people would call in the middle of the night asking for "that N– who's running the bus boycott," Coretta would reply, "My husband is asleep. He told me to write the names and number of anyone who called to threaten his life so that he could return the call and receive the threat in the morning when he wakes up and is fresh."[21] Occasionally, it would get so bad that she would take their phone off the hook. When one hate caller noted this, she shot back, "It's my phone and I'll do what I like with it."[22] Their home had become an MIA office. "The phone rang from five in the morning until midnight; and all day long, groups of people were meeting there." People would stop by, all sorts of meetings took place, and Coretta was routinely expected to have enough dinner to accommodate whatever guests showed up. They stopped having any real privacy.

A lot has been written about King's eloquence and charisma. But key to his leadership was the ways he expanded people's sense of their own power. People found their own courage in his courage.[23] His and Coretta's example encouraged others to act. We are the people to do it, they embodied, and we *must* do it. Not everyone appreciated this empowerment. King and the MIA were also criticized for the boycott's impact on the bus company and putting people "out of business."[24] But that was the point—to upset the material comforts of the status quo and make segregation bad business. It wasn't just white Montgomerians who disapproved. The national NAACP, while supporting the legal challenge, had not supported the boycott.[25]

Police continued to harass the car-pool system mercilessly. Within a few months, Jo Ann Robinson got seventeen tickets. On January 26, after King gave some people a ride, police pulled him over, supposedly for going 30 in a 25 mph zone. Asking for his license, one officer was overheard saying, "It's that damn King fellow."[26] Instead of giving him a ticket, the police made him get in their car and drove him around the city. He was terrified that they intended to kill him. Finally, they took him to jail and put him in a cell with other Black men. Recognizing King, the men began telling him their stories and asking for his help getting out. "Fellows, before I can assist in getting any of you out, I've got to get my own self out," King said. Everyone laughed. The fear of the day began to dissipate. A crowd of Black people gathered outside to demand his release.[27] That night, he shared with Coretta how frightening the ride had been; to comfort him, she didn't let on how terrified she'd been when she heard the police "got Martin."[28]

King grew increasingly anxious about this police harassment and the potential for white violence. One night, deep in the throes of this fear, he felt God speak to him in a way he had never felt before. A sense of calmness—of the presence of God—transformed his "despair into the buoyance of hope." "I can stand up without fear," he reflected.[29]

With his commitment to a more confrontational nonviolent activism and engaged ministry, Martin was cutting a different path from his father. Daddy King was a proud man who challenged racism but also urged his congregation to be patient, prized material success, and was exacting with his children. He beat Martin as a child and teenager, but Martin refused to let his father see him cry. When his father wanted him to spank his siblings, Martin preferred to take the punishment himself.[30] At times, King's father did not appreciate this "sensitive" son he had.[31] Martin's intellectual ideas were well to the left of his father's, as was his calling to a more politically active ministry. He had gone to Crozer, BU, and Dexter because he had seen the possibility of a ministry grounded in justice in this world. And now he heard God directly.

Four days after his speeding arrest, the Kings' home was bombed. Both Coretta and baby Yolanda were there. She heard a thump and moved fast to the back of the house. Thankfully, she and Yolanda got out unscathed. She wanted to report it but thought, "I'm not going to call the police."[32] Yet the mayor and police chief were suspiciously some of the first to arrive on the scene. Martin was quickly summoned home. A crowd of Black people gathered. Frightened and angry, he came out and quieted the crowd: "Brothers and sisters, . . . don't get panicky. . . . Don't get your weapons. . . . I want it to be known the length and breadth of this land that if I am stopped, this movement will not stop."[33]

Furious and terrified by the news, both Martin's and Coretta's fathers came to Montgomery to encourage them to leave immediately—or, at the very least, to get Coretta and Yolanda out of there. "It's better to be a live dog than a dead lion," King's father pronounced.[34] Coretta's father, who had braved this sort of violence for years, wanted his daughter to come home with him. The pressure was intense. How could Martin put his family in danger like this? His father preached at them all through the night. Exhausted by the next morning, Martin and Coretta wouldn't budge. "I knew I wasn't going anywhere," Coretta explained. Her experiences growing up had prepared her for this moment.[35]

This was a moment of truth for both her and Martin, Coretta later explained.[36] "When everyone seemed frightened, I realized how important it was for me to stand with Martin. And the next morning at breakfast he said, 'Coretta, you have been a real soldier. You were the only one who stood with me.' "[37] In that pressure, where it would have been more than understandable to leave with the baby or to insist Martin put their family's protection first, she cut a different path. Had she flinched in this moment, the trajectory of the bus boycott and Martin's emerging leadership would have been very different.

Coretta Scott King's sense of purpose was immense: "I just prayed for strength that whatever came that I would be able to endure it." From that night on, they lived with the understanding that if they continued in the struggle, she too might be killed. While most King biographers focus on dangers to his life and how they lived with it, the first violence the Kings faced was not to Martin personally but to their home and family space, to Coretta and their baby. He had to reckon with the possibility of her death, just as she had to reckon with his. And that danger would not lessen as his work expanded.[38] But she would remind him when he grew frightened that the movement was bigger than them. In key ways, Martin and Coretta were forging a way of family life and leadership different from many of their generation and their parents, by rejecting the "promise of protection" that good men were supposed to provide and prioritizing a life of freedom fighting instead.

After the bombing, and when the Montgomery police wouldn't protect the Kings, the Black community stepped in to protect their home with around-the-clock armed guards.[39] But in time, they stopped this as well. "Ultimately one's sense of manhood must come from within," Martin decided.[40] He didn't want to live in a fortress. She didn't either. For a number of days, they talked it over. Guns weren't the solution, so they got rid of the one weapon they owned.[41]

Like Martin, out of the fear, Coretta felt her prayer produced a new strength. Shortly after the bombing, she too had a religious experience. "For the first time in my life, my religion became real."[42] It put her worries about their marriage and whether she was curtailing her ambitions to rest. "I felt that there was a larger force working with me and that I was not alone. . . . participating in this Movement was the right thing for me. . . . I was making a contribution."[43]

Coretta had realized years earlier how much Martin departed from many Black preachers who relished the stability and measure of independence being a pastor provided and did not want to rock the boat for fear of reprisals. Now Martin's unusual approach of pastor-activist-leader was becoming publicly clear as well.[44] In the early months of the boycott, veteran Black journalist Ethel Payne pronounced, "A NEW TYPE OF LEADER is emerging in the South." Not an NAACP leader or

CIO labor union organizer, Payne wrote in surprise, "this new, vocal, fearless, and forthright Moses who is leading the people out of the wilderness into the Promised Land is the Negro preacher."[45]

Along with Coretta, Bayard Rustin helped nourish Martin's political-religious approach. The forty-three-year-old Rustin came down to Montgomery in February to offer his service. Having met Rustin years earlier, Coretta welcomed him into their home. Coretta and Martin saw Rustin's gifts; he pulled together approaches that meshed with their own politics and would become a key mentor-advisor. As Rustin biographer John D'Emilio explains, "Rustin had melded Quaker, Gandhian, and Marxist persuasions in ways that were unusual if not unique. . . . Putting these influences together made Rustin a radical strategist able to combine vision, values, and program."[46]

Rustin became an important sounding board for the Kings on nonviolence, political strategy, and civil disobedience. Martin came to see nonviolence as the "way of the strong man."[47] Violence was "cowardice because people who commit violence usually run away," Coretta explained. With nonviolence, people stay "to take the consequences."[48] "You fight the injustice, not the person," SCLC organizer Dorothy Tillman elaborated.[49] By exposing oppressive systems and forcing people to reckon with their racism in the process, nonviolent action brought the tension of injustice to the surface, refusing to let your oppressors define the world you want or the terms of engagement: "The end we seek was preexistent in the means we use."[50]

The Point of No Return

When the police harassment and bombings didn't stop the boycott, the city dredged up an old anti-syndicalism law and on February 20 indicted 101 "boycott leaders," including King. Activists like Rosa Parks and E. D. Nixon, rather than wait for arrest, went to the police station to present themselves. Many Black Montgomerians stood watch with guns outside.

The Kings were away when the news broke. The indictments made Martin's parents sick with worry. His father, crying, tried to enlist the support of King's mentor Benjamin Mays to insist his son stay in Atlanta; he had done enough. During this heated discussion, Coretta took baby Yolanda upstairs. "You ran out on me," Martin accused her later. "No, I didn't," she said. "[T]here comes a time in your life when— in every person's life I suppose—when there are decisions that you have to make and only you can make them." Coretta was committed to press on, "not only because of Martin . . . I was doing it for myself too." [51] But he had to face his father and the decision himself.

Distressed by his parents' panic, King stood firm. "I must go back to Montgomery. My friends and associates are being arrested. It would be the height of cowardice for me to stay away. I would rather be in jail ten years than desert my people now. . . . I have reached the point of no return." [52] She agreed. The *Pittsburgh Courier* the next year would underline Coretta Scott King's importance as "one of the strong weapons that have made the boycott a successful venture." [53] There is no way to understand the leader Martin was becoming without her.

The family pressure against King's growing activism was intense. King's father came back to Montgomery with Martin and Coretta and tried again to intercede by calling a prayer session with his son, Coretta, and Bayard Rustin. He prayed aloud that his son had done his duty and now had to take care of his family. Martin began crying. "Daddy, you ought not to do this to me. . . . You know, I will have to pray this through myself." Biographer Stephen Oates writes that "humiliating though it was, the prayer session proved a liberating moment in King's life, Rustin said. After that, he was firmer with his father than Rustin had seen him before." [54] Coretta remained resolved as well.

These indictments proved to be a tremendous miscalculation for the city. Instead of scaring people, they redoubled the Black community's resolve and led to the first significant national media attention to the boycott. The *Washington Post* and *New York Times* sent reporters to Montgomery; the *Post* termed the indictments a "monumental display of folly" and the boycott "impeccably lawful, orderly, dignified and effective." [55] Reporters swarmed to Montgomery. The nation was now watching. In Montgomery, reporters found a story they felt comfortable casting in clear, moral terms and a young, educated, tremendously eloquent minister-leader they were captivated by. As SNCC organizer Julian Bond later explained, given how segregated the country was, most white Americans, including most white journalists, hadn't ever heard a Black person give a speech, let alone the oratorical power of a Black Baptist preacher-scholar like King. [56]

After King's trial, the judge found him guilty, ordering either a year of hard labor or a five hundred-dollar fine. His attorneys appealed the decision. On the steps of the courthouse that day, Coretta affirmed her support: "whatever happens to him, happens to me." [57] Alongside the city's attempts to break the boycott, in February, lawyer Fred Gray decided to pursue a federal case on behalf of four women: Aurelia Browder, Susie McDonald, and two teenagers, Claudette Colvin and Mary Louise Smith. Gray, Parks, and Nixon knew from earlier cases against bus segregation that the state might tie up Parks's appeal, so Gray decided to file a proactive case, *Browder v. Gayle*, into federal court to start another legal front in challenging bus segregation. He wanted a minister on the case, but none came forward.

The boycott endured, still in need of money to sustain the intricate car-pool system, and Parks and King continued to travel to raise funds. Black churches like Detroit's Second Baptist, where King had preached before this all began, did fundraisers and sent thousands of dollars.[58] This hectic travel schedule established the practice of Martin being away a lot and his honoraria going to the movement. "If I hadn't been so sure of his loving and so on, I guess I would have gotten upset," Coretta observed. "But if you're going to serve humanity, you're going to neglect your family to some extent."[59] King's grueling travel across the United States gave him an opportunity to meet, strategize with, and learn from people around the country, making connections with Black reporters, Northern Black churches, and interracial trade unions in Los Angeles, New York, Chicago, and beyond that would shape the rest of his life. Coretta would underline how Martin "evolved" from these experiences.[60]

King decided to call singer-actor Harry Belafonte to solicit his help. This began a lifelong friendship. Belafonte's first impression of the young minister was that Martin Luther King was a listener. To Belafonte, who wasn't particularly religious, King's faith and fortitude would also prove astonishing: "Martin had virtually no possessions. . . . His kindness, his sense of justice, above all his humility—these were astounding to me."[61]

King's connections to the more radical side of the labor movement began during the boycott as well. In February he traveled to Chicago to address the United Packinghouse Workers of America (UPWA) and make common cause between the boycott and union activists. King, according to UPWA union leader Rev. Addie Wyatt, "clearly recognized that the most effective means for working people to achieve economic, political and social justice was thru the labor movement."[62] The radical National Negro Labor Council reached out to support the boycott, as did New York's Drug Health and Hospital Workers Union 1199, beginning King's lifelong association with the union. Indeed, many of the unions willing to support the boycott were being red-baited for their civil rights activities. So King's willingness to associate with activists being cast as "Communist sympathizers," including Rustin and Levison, started in the mid 1950s amidst the white heat of the Cold War.

On June 5, a US district court in Alabama, in a surprising 2–1 decision, sided with the Black community's case in *Browder v. Gayle*. The city appealed. On November 12, the US Supreme Court affirmed the district court's decision declaring laws segregating the buses unconstitutional. And on December 21, 1956, 382 days after the boycott had begun, Montgomery's buses were desegregated. It was a jubilant day. King was photographed all day getting on and off the buses. Coretta Scott King described the "great sense of fulfillment" she experienced, reaffirming her decision that in marrying Martin, they would have "a different kind of life." [63]

But the pressure and the violence continued. Two days later, the Kings' door was destroyed by a shotgun blast. People were attacked at bus stops. Other leaders' homes were bombed. The family had "learned to live under the constant threat of death," Coretta explained. [64] "Should the bombs stop either of us," she told the *Courier* in March 1957, "it would not mean the end of the fight." [65] In his annual report to the church that year, King made note of his "unbelievable schedule" and how it had impacted his health, mental equilibrium, and work life. "Almost every week—having to make so many speeches, attend so many meetings, meet so many people, write so many articles, counsel with so many groups—I face the frustration of feeling that in the midst of so many things to do I am not doing anything well." [66] Pulled in many directions, King's life had changed, and his work now extended far beyond his Montgomery church. This self-questioning would follow him for the rest of his life. He struggled with living up to people's expectations of him and his own expectations for himself, a kind of imposter syndrome.

Perhaps King's greatest talent was his ability to refuse easy answers, to take in new information on what more needed to be accomplished and then summon the will to do so. But it was also an area of tremendous personal anxiety. As Coretta observed, "He constantly reevaluated his position himself in light of each new circumstance. He was quick to say, if he felt he had erred, 'I was wrong that time.' . . . [H]e criticized himself more severely than anyone else ever did." [67] Over the next dozen years, this tendency meant that both victories and setbacks led him to reassess, reconsider, and then double down on his efforts to push further for change.

SCLC

On January 15, 1957, Martin Luther King turned twenty-eight. Rustin, Levison, and Baker had been strategizing over the past year about the possibilities the boycott opened to develop a more permanent organization as "a counterbalance" to the NAACP, according to Baker.[68] With their encouragement, Martin Luther King, Ralph Abernathy, and a group of other political Black ministers based in the South, including T. J. Jemison of Baton Rouge (who had helped lead a bus boycott there), K. C. Steele (who had helped organize the Tallahassee bus boycott), and Fred Shuttlesworth in Birmingham, decided to take the Montgomery example to a bigger scale. They formed the Southern Christian Leadership Conference "to redeem the soul of the nation." The SCLC, according to Scott King, was "a militant organization which believed the most powerful weapon available is nonviolence."[69]

Their direct action was insistent and impatient. "The Negro says in no uncertain terms that he doesn't like the way he's being treated," King underlined. Repeatedly, interviewers over the next decade would try to shame King for insisting on this uncompromising pace. And over and over, he would say that "with this aggressive attitude . . . we will bring the gains of our civil rights into being much sooner than . . . waiting for these things to be given voluntarily."[70] This also meant challenging Black people who objected to their approach. Some, according to King, had "adjusted" to segregation; some thought that a more gradual, legal approach was superior; many were "not willing to confront the sacrifices involved"; and some "profit from segregation."[71]

Departing from many of their fellow Black ministers, the SCLC framed the church as a foundation for challenging racial inequality and highlighted the need for an organized mass movement to supplement the NAACP's legal approaches and bring God's work to this world.[72] SCLC was concentrating its efforts in the South, but from the beginning of SCLC, King made clear that racism was a national cancer, not a Southern malady. Moreover, he believed the venality of Northern racism and the ever-present threat of violence (economic, social, and physical) often hid under the cloak of liberalism and of the church.

Rustin helped draw up the papers and pushed King to see the broader fight against racial inequality.[73] Ella Baker would become the first acting executive director, moving to Atlanta and spending the next three years helping get the fledgling organization off the ground. These young ministers had little experience with political organizing, and Baker brought with her decades of political experience and organizational skill. But the "patriarchal ethos" of the Black church often dominated the organization, and her expertise was not always recognized by the men of SCLC.[74]

Two months later, in March 1957, the Kings joined United Nations mediator Ralph Bunche (the first African American Nobel Peace Prize winner), Congressman Adam Clayton Powell Jr., A. Philip Randolph, actress Etta Moten Barnett, and other antiracist activists from around the world, including Pan-Africanist George Padmore and Trinidadian Marxist writer C. L. R. James, to attend Ghana's independence ceremony and Kwame Nkrumah's inauguration as president. The MIA and the Dexter Avenue Baptist Church paid their expenses—and the congregation thrilled in following the Kings' travel to Africa.

Delighted to see the crowd of tens of thousands in Accra and the Ghanaian people gaining control of their own government, Coretta described the surge of Black pride she experienced: "We had never seen this happen before."[75] Martin described weeping for joy (one of the few times he describes himself crying). "I knew about all of the struggles, and all of the pain, and all of the agony that these people had gone through for this moment."[76] Both took key lessons from Ghana and Nigeria (which they visited afterward): first, "freedom only comes through persistent revolt, through persistent agitation,"[77] and second, as Coretta observed, "both segregation in America and colonialism in Africa were based on the same thing—white supremacy."[78] The trip to the land of "my father's father" stuck with them and became one of the most important experiences of Martin's life.[79] Black people had thrown off the shackles of white colonial rule—and the Kings, in their late twenties, had gotten to see what had previously seemed unimaginable become real.

Stopping in London on their way home, they had a five-hour lunch and far-ranging conversation with C. L. R. and his wife, Selma James, and Barbadian novelist George Lamming. The Jameses were eager to hear about the organization of the boycott. "The story of his work was told by Coretta, not him," Selma James recalled. "He just listened for long periods. . . . You could see that he could be angry [militant and fierce], but he kept it in check."[80] James also underlined how Martin acknowledged the education he got from women.[81] The Kings were thus part of a new generation of Black radicals across the diaspora throwing off the chains of old. This global perspective would infuse their thinking going forward. As King would later observe in Los Angeles, "Wherever you turn, whether it's Accra, Nairobi, Johannesburg, New York, Los Angeles, Montgomery, Alabama to Little Rock, Arkansas, the cry is for freedom."[82]

Four months after SCLC's founding, the first major civil rights march took place in Washington, DC. Launched at a meeting of seventy-seven civic, church, fraternal, and labor organizations, the Prayer Pilgrimage marked the third anniversary of the Supreme Court's *Brown* decision and the urgent work ahead. King, A. Philip Randolph, and Roy Wilkins of the NAACP co-chaired the event. People journeyed to DC from all over.[83] King's speech, arguably his first national address, is remembered as "Give Us the Ballot." He highlighted how Southern states were rising up in "open defiance" of *Brown*. But he also spoke directly to Northern liberals and challenged the superficiality of their commitments:

> There is a dire need today for a liberalism which is truly liberal. What we are witnessing today in so many northern communities is a sort of quasi-liberalism which is so based on the principle of looking sympathetically at all sides that it fails to become committed to either side. . . . We call for a liberalism from the North which will be thoroughly committed to the ideal of racial justice and will not be deterred by the propaganda and subtle words of those who say: "Slow up for a while; you're pushing too fast."[84]

What would become his searing critique of the white moderate in "Letter from a Birmingham Jail" began six years earlier at the Lincoln Memorial, with King calling out the both-sides-ism of many white liberal Northerners and how they denigrated the urgency of Northern injustice. US racism was a many-headed hydra, its tentacles north, south, east, and west, he made clear. Indeed, there was no moment in King's public leadership when he was not challenging Northern liberals to move beyond "lip service" to substantive action both in the South and at home.[85]

In September 1957, King journeyed to Highlander Folk School, an interracial organizer training school founded in 1932 in Tennessee, to

build grassroots leadership for social change. Highlander was celebrating its twenty-fifth anniversary, and King zeroed in that day on
the ways the activists who gathered from across the country had been
made to feel crazy for refusing to accept the status quo. He exhorted
them to push forward and continue to be maladjusted:

> I never intend to adjust myself to the evils of segregation and the
> crippling effects of discrimination . . . to adjust myself to the tragic
> inequalities of an economic system which takes necessities from
> the masses to give luxuries to the classes . . . to the madness of
> militarism and the self-defeating method of physical violence. . . .
> [T]he salvation of the world lies in the hands of the maladjusted.[86]

Over the next decade, King would return to this theme of
maladjustment—refusing the normalizing of injustice, he would ex-
hort fellow activists to take pride in *not* accommodating themselves
to inequitable systems and people's suffering. Speaking at Highlander
would escalate the red-baiting of King. A photo taken there with Rosa
Parks, Highlander co-founder Myles Horton, and others would be
blasted across white supremacist pamphlets and billboards throughout the South for a decade, proclaiming that King had gone to a "Communist training school."

Numerous publishers had contacted King to write a chronicle of the
Montgomery bus boycott. In October, with Levison's help, he signed a
book contract with Harper & Brothers and, with help from many colleagues, began work on *Stride Toward Freedom: The Montgomery Story*.
There he laid out the work and lessons of the yearlong boycott for attacking US racism. Amid commencing the work on the book, on October 23, the Kings had their second child. They named him Martin
Luther King III, though Coretta worried about the burden of the name.

In *Stride Toward Freedom*, published the following year, King underlined how the "racial issue we confront in America is not a sectional
one but a national problem. Injustice anywhere is a threat to justice
everywhere." And he laid out his critique of Northern liberals:

> There is a pressing need for a liberalism in the North that is truly
> liberal, that believes in integration in his own community as well
> as in the deep South. . . . Today in too many Northern communi-
> ties a quasi-liberalism prevails, so bent on seeing all sides that it
> fails to become dedicated to any side. . . . A true liberal will not be

deterred by the propaganda and subtle words of those who say: "Slow up for a while; you're pushing things too fast." [87]

Stressing the lessons of Montgomery to the nation, King was already highlighting a Northern unwillingness to confront segregation discrimination, at home. Segregation was a national issue, as he and Coretta knew from experience. From the late 1950s onward, King challenged a Cold War liberalism that framed racism as a regional anachronism and held up the Southern struggle as proof of the power of American democracy to reform its own troublespots. [88] The difficulty of seeing the Northern movement and King's challenge to Northern racism was a "structured blindness" of the time, to use philosopher Charles Mills's concept, that supported Northern liberal allies and American global interests. [89] Many Americans were invested in *not* seeing what King and many others were saying about Northern racial inequality and the limits of American democracy and liberalism.

In *Stride Toward Freedom*, King also highlighted the psychic toll that segregation took on Black people who "lost faith in themselves." The bus boycott "demonstrate[ed] to the Negro, North and South, that many of the stereotypes he has held about himself and other Negroes are not valid." [90] Part of what the boycott had done, Coretta Scott King observed, was renew people's faith in their own power and the necessity of their own actions. "The nonviolent revolution that we launched in Montgomery spread like a prairie fire," not only in cities across the South but Chicago, Cleveland, and other cities in the North. [91]

Showing Up

In 1958, Detroit NAACP head Arthur Johnson wrote King to ask him to come to support their local campaign. "A helping hand from you is ten, twenty-five, one hundred times more productive than that of countless other friends." [92] From the late 1950s to the end of King's life, Johnson's sentiment was echoed by scores across the country who asked him to join rallies, fundraisers, marches, and pickets they were planning to challenge racial inequality across the country. Showing up for struggles across the country was precious to local organizers, and King was moved by the role he could play. Joining people's rallies and mass meetings buoyed people's determination for change and sometimes galvanized city and media attention. He understood he was a symbol—because "others helped me to stand there." [93] Thus a hallmark of King's leadership from 1957 onward was lending his voice against a range of Northern injustices.

But because King has been seen as a capital-*L* Leader, this crucial aspect of his leadership has not been fully recognized. This travel and learning changed him as well. SCLC's Dorothy Cotton underscored what a "listener" King was and so he learned from meeting scores of local activists.[94] The movement made Martin not just in Montgomery and Birmingham but in Detroit, Los Angeles, Cleveland, and Chicago as well. Yet, many King scholars have reduced this travel to SCLC fundraising—missing the key role he played in supporting local movements, how crucial he saw this facet of his leadership, and the ways it deepened his thinking on American racism and economic inequality.[95] While King's work as the president of SCLC was essential, King was not just concerned about the success of his own organization. He was, first and foremost, a minister who felt called to go where needed and to do what he could wherever he could to support the broader mission of Black freedom.

Important criticisms that fellow organizers Ella Baker and Septima Clark of Highlander Folk School made of King's charismatic leadership style have also contributed to the historical blinders around King's movement support. Baker and Clark's philosophy of grassroots leadership differed from many SCLC ministers, but their calls for change in the organization largely fell on deaf ears.[96] Septima Clark, a long-time teacher turned Highlander organizer, wrote King asking him "not to lead all the marches himself but to develop leaders who could lead their own marches. Dr. King read that letter before the SCLC staff. It just tickled them." [97] King had been raised toward and embraced a charismatic leadership position in the church among other men. Used to this sort of leadership, the SCLC ministers were not very welcoming of Baker's and Clark's philosophies or criticism.

But King was also listening and learning, at times perhaps more than he let on. He had a life partner in Coretta Scott King, who was also pushing him. For the rest of his life, he not only led from the front but showed up to support struggles in other cities and marched in marches he did not lead. He didn't have to be in charge to join people's protests. And show up he did. He also bore the religious responsibility to tell people what they needed to hear. Just as he challenged his Montgomery congregation on the gap between their professions and actions, so too he did with Northern white liberals who professed racial tolerance. King zeroed in on the tendency to point elsewhere and avoid one's own sins, a practice condemned in Matthew 7: "How can you say to your brother, 'Let me take the speck out of your eye,' when all the time there is a plank in your own eye? You hypocrite, first take the plank out of your own eye, and then you will see clearly to remove the speck from your brother's eye."

King's staggering amount of travel meant encountering segregation in its many forms throughout the Jim Crow North as well as the South. Like many cities from the Northeast to the West, Detroit's downtown hotels didn't serve Black people. Nor did many of its finest eating establishments; the acclaimed Joe Muir's Seafood served Black customers in the back, wrapping their fish dinners in newspaper. As Detroit activist Dorothy Aldridge explained, "You didn't need a sign to know to stay in your place."[98] In fact, the *Negro Motorists' Green Book* was initially created by Harlem postal worker Victor Hugo Green in 1936 because many of New York's clubs, hotels, and restaurants were racially segregated. As the guide grew, it helped Black people safely navigate travel throughout the Northeast, Midwest, and West as well as the South.

King routinely stayed in people's homes to avoid these problems. Staying over with local people throughout the country brought him much closer to the issues and the struggles in these cities, but it also was more exhausting, since he often had to be on with his hosts. King also frequented Black-owned hotels, like Detroit's Black-owned Gotham Hotel, which he loved. The owner put copies of *Stride Toward Freedom* in each room and sent copies to the Detroit Police Department to educate them.[99] In Detroit in 1958, Black congressman Charles Diggs toured King through the Black neighborhoods of Paradise Valley being destroyed to build Detroit's highways, showing him the devastation of urban renewal on the city's Black community. Nearly three hundred Black businesses and about 100,000 Black people lost their homes due to the demolition of Detroit's Black Bottom neighborhood. Such visits deepened King's understandings of the different forms racial oppression took throughout the country.

From early on, King took issue with Northern desire to finger just the South's racism and ignore it locally. In an address to interracial religious leaders in 1959, he emphasized the employment discrimination "shamefully widespread in the North, particularly in great urban communities which often pride themselves as liberal and progressive centers in government and economics."[100] Zeroing in on the self-satisfaction of many religious leaders, he highlighted how many people professing to be racially progressive countenanced inequality at home.

While he used the term *de facto segregation*, King saw Northern segregation as state-supported and systematic. While Southern states had laws mandating white and Black schools, white and Black public accommodations, white and Black drinking fountains, and other explicitly separate institutions, there were other kinds of laws and policies from the Northeast to the West Coast that maintained segregation. School zoning lines, state hiring practices, the distribution of municipal services, and Federal Housing Administration (FHA) redlining maps all were state policies that furthered school and housing segregation, as he would point out. Many white Southerners in the 1950s and 1960s reacted angrily to Northern liberals who criticized the South without being willing to examine, much less change, their own racial systems. During the bus boycott, Montgomery's main newspaper, the *Montgomery Advertiser*, had run a series spotlighting segregated Northern locales. It was easy to dismiss these Southerners as hypocrites themselves, but King saw this double standard too.

King and the SCLC relied on Northern white attention to shine a light on organizing across the South and push for national action. Part of the power of nonviolent direct action came from the national attention it received and the moral outrage it engendered against these Southern injustices. And the nation grew increasingly invested in highlighting these Southern trouble spots and the movements challenging them as proof of the power of American democracy.[101] And yet, King's bedrock understanding of American apartheid meant he recognized that many people he was relying on for outrage regarding the South were enabling oppression at home. He could have chosen the easier path. But they were "co-workers with God," and so he couldn't stay silent about the consistent unwillingness from Northern whites to address racism at home.[102] Part of how he reconciled this, at least in the early 1960s, was by this dual message: a moral appeal to the conscience of white Northern liberals and laborites about Southern racism and at the same time a challenge for them to address segregation and inequality endemic around them. For years, many Americans ignored this second part of his message, leading many historians to miss King's double approach as well.

King needed more time to build SCLC and travel to support other movements. And so in November 1959, he made the difficult decision to move back to Atlanta to permanently co-pastor Ebenezer Baptist Church with his father. (Atlanta also had many more airlines, which would make the travel easier.) It was hard to leave their Montgomery community. The farewell was "so deeply touching; we felt exalted yet unworthy of their admiration," Coretta explained.[103] This put him back in his father's church, which was challenging. He also worried about measuring up to the fame he now had. "I find myself struggling to catch up with my image." They also thought intensely about how to raise confident Black children. Five-year-old Yolanda seemed to feel that "only white people can be beautiful," so Coretta took to cutting out photos of beautiful Black girls and women to show her.[104]

As he continued to travel beyond the South, King zeroed in on the federal government's role in segregation. In late 1960, when the *Nation* magazine asked for his recommendations to the incoming Kennedy administration, King described the federal government as the "nation's highest investor in segregation" in housing, jobs, health, and urban renewal in the North and South. "Negroes are almost totally excluded from skilled, clerical and supervisory jobs in the federal government."[105] In other words, King saw racism as a constitutive element of postwar American democracy, not just Southern malfeasance.

King was not willing to let Northern audiences simply feel the catharsis of focusing on Southern horrors. Across the 1960s, King was invited to speak at scores of colleges—from Whitewater State College in Wisconsin to Cornell College in Iowa to Arizona State in Tempe. At all of them, he both extolled the Southern struggle and challenged students and faculty to look at jobs, housing, and schools in their own cities. "We must come to see that this problem in the United States is not a sectional problem, but a national problem. . . . In other words, genuine liberalism will see that the problem can exist even in one's front and back yard."[106]

From the outset of his public leadership, King also challenged the "myth of time" that framed US democracy as naturally, inexorably improving. Visiting Seattle, he lamented the illusion of "giving it time" that many Northerners proffered—making clear that only concerted action ever produced change. King challenged the concept of patience and prayer as the Christian ways to push for change: "don't get me wrong. Prayer has been one of the great resources in my own life . . .

but I am saying: That God never intended for prayer to be a substitute for work and intelligence." [107]

In September 1960, he addressed an interracial audience celebrating the National Urban League's fiftieth anniversary in New York City. Once again, he identified "a pressing need for a liberalism in the North that is truly liberal, that firmly believes in integration in its own community as well as in the deep South . . . who not only rises up with righteous indignation when a Negro is lynched in Mississippi, but will be equally incensed when a Negro is denied the right to live in his neighborhood . . . or secure a top position in his business." [108] Four years before the passage of the Civil Rights Act, Dr. King insisted that those gathered that day in New York not simply call out Southern travesties but attend to the segregation and discrimination endemic around them.

Act II

1958–1965

King addresses the largest civil rights rally ever held in Chicago, at Soldier Field on July 10, 1966.

3

The Thin Veneer of the North's Racial Self-Righteousness

King and the Black Freedom Struggle in New York

> Down home, our bigots come in white sheets.
> Up here, they come in Brooks Brothers suits.
>
> —Paul Zuber

On September 18, 1958, as Black people across the country reeled from news images of him being abused by police, Martin Luther King traveled to New York City. For Black people in 1958, this was a Rodney King moment, a George Floyd moment. One of the first times that images of police brutality against Black people were published in the mainstream news media, the photo of King being assaulted by the police struck a chord with Black people far beyond the South.

The week before, the Kings had attempted to attend a Montgomery court hearing for their good friend Ralph Abernathy, when the police accosted them. Refusing to let Martin into the courtroom, they manhandled him in the hallway and threatened Coretta from intervening. The police then charged King with loitering and marched him down the street to the police station, twisting his arm behind his back and pinning him down on the station counter. A passing photographer snapped picture after picture as the brutality unfolded. Further angered by the photographer, they choked and kicked King in his cell, out of sight of the camera.[1] "They tried to break my arm," King later explained, and "grabbed my collar and choked me, and when they got me to the cell, they kicked me."[2]

King was shortly released, but pictures of him dressed in a suit and hat, wincing in pain as an officer pinned him on the counter and twisted his arm behind his back, spread over the news wires.

Prisoner-activist Martin Sostre described the impact of these photographs: "You'll notice in the photos the pain reflected on King's face. . . . Having personally experienced this identical type of brutality I know exactly what King felt in having his arm viciously twisted behind his back and lifted towards his head while being bodily pushed forward."[3] For Black people across the country, the identification, the shared sorrow and outrage at this police abuse captured for the nation to see, was palpable.

That spirit of deep identification came out the evening of September 18, when King spoke to an overflowing crowd at Williams CME Church, rallying Harlemites to refuse second-class citizenship.[4] Then, the next night, in front of Harlem's Hotel Theresa on 125th Street, he addressed an even larger outdoor evening rally of seven thousand people. The rally had been organized by Bayard Rustin to prepare for the Youth March for Integrated Schools to protest school segregation, police brutality, and mob violence in the North and South.[5] That night in Harlem, King shared his own experience of being manhandled by police.

A year earlier, Nation of Islam member Johnson X Hinton had been brutally beaten blocks away from where King was speaking. Hinton had tried to intervene when he saw police beating up another Black man outside his Mosque #7, where Malcolm X was in charge. "You're not in Alabama," Hinton told the officers. "This is New York."[6] Enraged, the police beat Hinton savagely and arrested him. A huge crowd gathered outside the Harlem police station on 123rd Street where he had been taken. Malcolm X arrived on the scene and insisted that the masses would stay until Hinton received medical care. When they were finally assured that Hinton would be transferred to Harlem Hospital to be treated for his extensive injuries, Malcolm X dismissed the crowd.

Now, a year later, a short walk from where Hinton had been brutalized and Malcolm X's speaker's corner, Martin Luther King addressed an outdoor night rally and highlighted the problems of police brutality and school segregation—two pressing issues for Harlemites. King's account of police brutality likely resonated deeply with the crowd that night, but little detail has survived because of what happened the next day.

The next afternoon, September 20, King came to Blumstein's Department Store in Harlem to sign copies of *Stride Toward Freedom*. Izola Curry, a forty-two-year-old Black woman suffering from paranoid delusions, approached the table where he was signing. Georgia-born

Curry had moved to New York when she was twenty-one and struggled to maintain steady work. The media's red-baiting of King had taken its toll on Curry. She had come to believe that King was a Communist threat conspiring to prevent her from being employed. She asked if he was Martin Luther King. When he said yes, she pulled out a letter opener and plunged it into his chest.

Curry meant business. She had a gun tucked in her bra and had attended the rally the night before, but with so many people, she couldn't get close to King. She believed she was acting in self-defense because "he was going to kill me."[7] King was rushed to Harlem Hospital with the letter opener still in his chest. While he was lying on the gurney, waiting for the surgeon to assemble the necessary equipment and staff, the police brought Curry in for him to identify her. But instead she immediately identified him. "Yes, that's him. I'm going to report him to my lawyers," Curry declared. "Martin said it struck him as being so funny," Coretta later recounted. "He smiled in spite of the terrible pain."[8]

That night, two surgeons, Aubrey Maynard and Emil Naclerio, and a team of other medical personnel took two and a half hours to carefully remove parts of King's two ribs and sternum to take out the letter opener lodged in his sternum between his lung and heart.[9] Born in Guyana, Maynard had been the first Black intern hired at Harlem Hospital in 1930. An authority on chest and abdominal wounds, Maynard was the hospital's chief of surgery in 1958. "For [King] to be brought to Harlem Hospital for a dangerous thing like that, it was a challenge," Maynard explained. "It was a city hospital, and it was looked down upon. It was up to me to show the world that it could be done there."[10] The stabbing had grazed King's aorta. If the letter opener had punctured his aorta or if they had removed it at the store like some onlookers wanted to, it would have killed him.[11]

Coretta flew up to New York, the nurses telling her Martin had been calling for her through the night.[12] When she got to the city, she ended up consoling Levison and Rustin, who'd come to meet her, her calm strength in crisis outstripping the men around her.[13] When she visited Martin, one of the first things he asked was about Curry's situation. "He felt as I did—that the woman was sick and needed treatment, not punishment," she told the *Pittsburgh Courier*.[14] While this is usually reduced to King's commitment to nonviolence, King's reaction was as much an awareness that the remedy lay in treatment, not punishment.

His desires revealed an abolitionist impulse—his point was *not* to ignore violence but to treat the cause of it.

King came out of the stabbing with a lifelong disability, according
to Rev. William Barber. It left him with a breathing problem he would
have to manage during his public appearances for the rest of his life.[15]
One of King's parishioners in Montgomery, Claressa Chambliss, described the toll of the constant threats on King's life and then the 1958
stabbing. "One time he got the hiccups. It would not cease. Reverend
King had it for about a week. All we could do is pray."[16] Other scholars describe King's "extended fits of hiccups" that would last for hours
linked to depression, anxiety, and insomnia.[17] One of the causes of
prolonged hiccups, alongside stress, is impact to the phrenic nerve,
which goes through the heart and lung area where King was stabbed
and sends signals to the diaphragm to expand and contract. It is possible that the stabbing impacted King both physically and psychically.
Barber, who also managed his own leadership role as co-chair of the
new PPC with a disability, stressed what it took for King to persevere
as a public figure, given this breathing difficulty.[18]

The stabbing didn't just impact King's own sense of mortality. It also
brought home the larger responsibilities of his new leadership role and
the possibilities that someone would be killed in the process. Martin
was a "guilt-ridden" man, Coretta recalled, and used his weeks in a
Harlem hospital to "rethink his personal philosophies" and reckon
with his "awesome responsibilities."[19] In many ways, King was coming to terms with his new calling.

> If anybody had told me a couple of years ago, when I accepted the
> presidency of the MIA, that I would be in this position, I would
> have avoided it with all my strength. This is not the life I expected
> to lead. But gradually you take some responsibility, then a little
> more, until finally you are not in control anymore. You have to
> give yourself entirely. Then once you make up your mind that
> you are giving yourself, then you are prepared to do anything
> that serves the cause and advances the Movement. I have reached
> that point.[20]

Part of Coretta and Martin's bond stemmed from the profound ways
both felt called to the role they would play in the Black struggle—
local, national, and global. But it was also a burden far greater than
they could have imagined. They spent those weeks of his recovery

discussing the awesome responsibility and pressure he felt. "I can't afford to make a mistake," he worried.[21] The next month, Coretta Scott King went to DC to give the speech at the Youth March he was supposed to give—starting the practice of her periodically filling in for him.

At the end of 1958, in his annual review for the church, King said the year had been "rather difficult" personally, citing "the brutality of police officers, an unwarranted arrest and a near fatal stab wound." But he was tremendously grateful for the congregation's care and the support that had flowed from across the country because of the book and stabbing. King understood that he was also a symbol and embodiment of many people's deep hopes for freedom: "this affection was not for me alone. It was really for you," he wrote his congregation.[22]

"My Favorite Union"

New York City would be an important base for King intellectually, politically, and religiously for the rest of his life. Home to a wide range of direct-action moments challenging the city's school and housing segregation, job discrimination, and police brutality, King called the city "the center of the Negro struggle for equality," and he would join the work challenging the city's racism.[23] To do so, he wanted to define the issues for Black people unmediated by the mainstream white press and commenced a biweekly column in the *Amsterdam News*, one of the nation's most important Black newspapers, from 1962 to 1966.

King understood the power of unions for Black workers. One barrier Black people faced in securing stable, well-paying jobs in cities like New York was union discrimination. King would spend much of the 1960s pushing unions to see their role in Black economic exclusion, as well as supporting strikes across the country. But some unions demonstrated the role organized labor could play in uplifting and protecting Black workers. The Drug and Hospital Employees' Union Local 1199 in New York City would become King's "favorite" union, demonstrating the power of multiracial, militant unionism that asserted workers' rights and challenged racism head-on.[24]

Founded in 1932 by Jewish pharmacists and interracial from its earliest years, 1199 launched a campaign in Harlem in 1937 to get Black people hired as pharmacists and Black porters promoted to soda men. The union would become an example of what organized labor could do on behalf of some of the poorest workers of color; in 1956, 1199 had sent money to support the Montgomery boycott.[25] For this radical interracial work, 1199 was red-baited and brought before the House Un-American Activities Committee (HUAC).

In 1957, 1199 committed itself to organizing the city's lowest-paid hospital workers, largely made up of Black and Puerto Rican women often forced to work split shifts from 8 to 11 a.m. and then again 4 p.m. to 11 p.m., six days a week.[26] The 1935 Wagner Act gave many Americans the right to join and organize a union, but whole categories of workers—many of whom were women and people of color—were excluded from that protection. These private hospital workers were among those excluded. Given the difficulty of organizing workers without protection, most unions stayed away; many then blamed the workers themselves for being "unorganizable."

To force the hospital to negotiate, 1199 understood that the women would have to strike. In 1959, through Stanley Levison, King met with 1199 to learn about their hospital worker organizing plans. King was on board: "Count me in . . . whatever I can do, call on me," he told them.[27] He was not scared off by the union's "Communist" reputation. As King would later highlight, "if all of labor would emulate what you have been doing over the years, our nation would be closer to victory in the fight to eliminate poverty and injustice."[28] In May 1959, hospital workers with 1199 struck six hospitals across New York. King described the struggles of these Black and Puerto Rican workers as "more than a fight for union rights . . . it is a fight for human rights and human dignity."[29] He issued a statement that "the hospital struggle was against degradation, poverty and misery; that it was against all the evils that afflict poor black people in society."[30]

King's die-hard support over the years, according to 1199 public relations director Moe Foner, made a difference in getting other New York civil rights leaders to support 1199 and recognize this urgent civil rights issue. King lambasted the ways that hospital workers were "working fulltime jobs at parttime wages."[31] As 1199 head Leon Davis, who had helped found the union twenty-five years earlier, observed, "We talk so much about the conditions in the South . . . we forget about the conditions in our own backyard."[32]

The work 1199 did on behalf of some of the city's lowest-paid workers gave King "renewed courage and vigor to carry on."[33] In 1961, King attended a hospital workers' mass meeting to help boost their hospital organizing. He visited the headquarters regularly when he was in town, attending rallies and sending messages every year.[34] In 1962 he supported the 1199 strikes for recognition at Beth El and Manhattan Eye and Ear. Rustin, along with A. Philip Randolph and Puerto Rican labor leader Joseph Monserrat, helped head the Committee for Justice for Hospital Workers in 1962; that committee included Gilberto Gerena Valentin, a Puerto Rican community leader and union activist. This 1199 work led King and Rustin to see more clearly the interconnections between the Black and Puerto Rican struggle and the power of multiracial organization. The next year, they reached out to Gilberto Gerena Valentin to organize Puerto Rican turnout to the March on Washington.

During the 1962 strikes, 1199 head Leon Davis defied an antistrike injunction and was jailed for thirty days. Both King and Malcolm X admired that decision, and it inspired Malcolm to make his only union address in July 1962 to 1199. Deep in a campaign in Albany, Georgia, King sent a taped message of support, underlining how the victory "will have a profound effect upon millions of unorganized workers throughout the nation."[35] Under pressure from these strikes, Governor Nelson Rockefeller pledged legislation to grant hospital workers coverage under the state's collective bargaining rights. But the New York State legislature balked. King called Rockefeller to push him to support statewide legislation, but in 1963 the law passed covering only voluntary hospitals in New York City.

Calling himself "a fellow 1199-er," King referred to 1199 as the "authentic conscience of the labor movement"—in part because many unions excluded or marginalized Black workers.[36] Many white union members saw Black workers as an economic threat who, if organized, would downgrade their own position. Thus 1199 was both an exception and a model of what was possible in a union.

In May 1960, King joined Randolph in Detroit for the founding convention of the Negro American Labor Council, proclaiming, "Negroes are disheartened and weary of discrimination and segregation in the labor movement . . . that thin veneer of acceptance masquerading as democracy." About 1,500 Black delegates from New York to Los Angeles attended and testified to the "hypocrisy" of Jim Crow locals across the North, the ways in which training programs excluded Black workers, and other methods used to keep union jobs in the hands of white workers.[37] A follow-up workshop was held in DC in 1961 attended by eight hundred people, with many highlighting various types of job discrimination—from lack of access to apprentice programs to discrimination by unions and the federal government. There King also charged the federal government as the "nation's highest investor in segregation and discrimination."[38]

In December 1961, King addressed the national AFL-CIO convention. Underscoring how labor has "no firmer friend than the 20 million Negroes," he also stressed the problem: "Labor has not adequately used its great power, its vision, and its resources to advance Negro rights." He expected more from the labor movement than other institutions in society, "just as a member of a family expects more from a relative than he does from a neighbor." King highlighted the pervasive discrimination Blacks faced in the labor movement across the country. "Negroes have been barred from membership in certain unions and denied apprenticeship training and vocational education," he declared. "In every section of the country, one can find local unions existing as a serious and vicious obstacle when the Negro seeks jobs or upgrade in employment."[39] Defending Randolph's criticism of the labor movement's racism, King's fortitude in challenging white union members showed.[40] Many of King's remarks, according to historian Michael Honey, "elicited grim silence from his audience." They were *not* pleased with his message calling them out.[41] He would never address the national AFL-CIO convention again.

Black Pushback Against King's Politics of Confrontation

As he did at the Urban League anniversary and AFL-CIO convention, King repeatedly called on Northern liberals to challenge segregation in New York, not just Alabama. His emerging national leadership and more confrontational approach also put him at odds with some national Black leaders like the NAACP's Roy Wilkins and Congressman Adam Clayton Powell Jr.[42] Powell had spearheaded "Don't buy where you can't work" protests in the 1930s and became the first Black congressman elected from New York or any other Northeastern state in 1944. A complex persona, Powell confronted segregation from businesses in Harlem to the congressional dining hall. But he also guarded his power zealously, increasingly criticized mass action, and was known for his lavish spending. In 1960, Randolph, Rustin, and King prepared to launch the March on the Conventions Movement to put both the Democratic and Republican parties on notice around issues of racial justice. They highlighted the double disfranchisement Black people, North and South, faced "because they are barred from the polls, and secondly, because they are denied political representation through the existing parties." They decried the tepidness of so-called liberal politicians. "At present, no candidate for the presidency has measured up to the courage of the Southern students [leading sit-ins]."[43] King, like Ella Baker and many fellow activists, had been inspired by the courage and resolve of young people across the South who had started sitting in at lunch counters and other public establishments in the spring of 1960. He agreed when Ella Baker wanted to use $800 of SCLC's money for a conference to bring these young people together Easter weekend of 1960. Baker was determined to ensure the young people build their organization (which became the Student Nonviolent Coordinating Committee) and not get subsumed by SCLC or the NAACP.

Powell and Wilkins were livid at such confrontational tactics, particularly, for Powell, that the protests were also aimed at the Democratic Party. Wilkins would become such a persistent critic of King that, according to Rustin, Martin "simply couldn't stay in a room where he had to contend with Wilkins."[44] To try to shut down the March on the Conventions Movement, Powell first red-baited King, saying he was "the captive of socialist interests" and dangerous.[45] When those criticisms didn't slow the momentum of the proposed marches, Powell became concerned about Rustin's "undue influence" on King and privately threatened to say that Rustin and King were having a sexual affair.[46] King was terrified—even though, as Rustin observed, "Martin knew goddamn well [Powell] couldn't have that kind of information. You can't sleep with a guy without knowing it."[47] Randolph urged King not to cave to Powell's threat. According to Rustin, "Martin had one very major defect. He did not like contention with people who were supposed to be friends. He sort of folded on in-fighting."[48]

Rustin and King had come to represent a type of masculinity threatening to many Black male politicians and clergy. Black sociologist E. Franklin Frazier had published *The Negro Family in the United States* in 1939, arguing that racism and slavery had damaged the Black family.[49] Determined to prove otherwise, many men of King's generation underlined the importance of a vigorous masculinity and nuclear, male-headed family. King was invested in upholding this family role but at the same time challenged certain norms of masculinity. The politics of confrontation King and Rustin pursued was not blustery debate or backroom deals like Powell's but rather nonviolent direct action, putting one's body and personal safety on the line in public and, for King, ahead of his family's safety, *even* when it might fail or compromise his own personal advantage. Leaders like Wilkins and Powell felt this was the wrong public presentation for a "race man."[50] Seventeen years King's senior, Rustin was proving to be an important mentor to King. Threatened, Powell would use homophobia to undermine Rustin.

Powell's attack impugning King's masculinity also frightened King, perhaps because, alongside his fear of being painted as gay, it fell close to his father's criticisms of his growing activism as not being properly masculine. Daddy King continued to argue with Martin about his family responsibilities, telling him "how bullheaded he was being," but Martin had refused to bend.[51] It was no coincidence that Powell first painted King as a socialist and then moved on to impugn his gender and sexuality. The climate of the Cold War zeroed in on proper gender presentation and heterosexuality as key sites of Americanism.[52] Those who deviated were dangerous and potentially traitors. And so when Rustin offered to resign, King did not object. This betrayal devastated Rustin, who had been pivotal to King's work since Montgomery. He would reemerge as a mentor and political sounding board to King after Randolph tapped him to organize the 1963 March on Washington, but their relationship would never be quite the same.

King's own fears and the pressure he felt led to this devastating fissure with Rustin. But in other significant ways, King's masculinity eschewed dominant ideas of masculinity of the time that foregrounded individualism and nuclear-family protection. He and Coretta forged a different path, embodying a kind of anti-respectability politics that foregrounded love, vulnerability, and broader community needs. While on a personal Christian level he embraced the importance of individual agency and responsibility (he wrote a series of advice columns for *Ebony*), he rejected personal responsibility as a public philosophy. The solution was to change the conditions that produce oppression or violence; he asked for treatment over punishment when Izola Curry stabbed him. Black people couldn't bootstrap their way to full citizenship. When a BBC interviewer noted how some of King's critics thought he wasn't fiery enough, hoping for King to react, King instead referred to himself as "soft and gentle."[53] King wasn't going to apologize for being sensitive, for eschewing violence, for not bullying, and for rejecting many markers of manly self-expression.

Martin Luther King's gender politics were complicated and, at times, contradictory. As much as he wanted an intellectual equal like Coretta for a partner, his own thinking on women's roles was not as forward-thinking. He didn't listen to women on his staff as seriously at times as men and favored men in leadership. While veteran organizer Ella Baker had played a pivotal role getting SCLC off the ground in its first two and a half years, they wanted a man to permanently lead the organization—and recruited Wyatt Tee Walker, one of SCLC's founders, to move to Atlanta and head the organization. This had caused a breach with Ella Baker that, as Coretta observed, "even [Martin] could not heal."[54]

On January 31, 1961, Coretta gave birth to their third child, Dexter, named for their Montgomery church. She chafed at the ways Martin saw her as having the primary responsibility for raising their family, explaining:

> Martin had, all through his life, an ambivalent attitude toward the role of women. On the one hand he believed that women were as intelligent and capable as men and they should hold positions of authority and influence. . . . But when it came to his own situation, he thought in terms of his wife being a homemaker and a mother for his children. He was very definite that he would expect whoever he married to be home waiting for him.[55]

Martin embodied such contradictions around women's roles in a society that had very firm ideas about where women belonged. But Coretta Scott King knew she had more to contribute to the movement.[56] She also understood she was expected to carry herself a certain way as a minister's wife, and now a wife of a national leader, and fastidiously kept up those personal appearances. She didn't want him criticized for her.

Martin looked for her opinion on matters political as well as personal. They discussed everything, according to friends.[57] She would often get recordings of his speeches so they could talk through them afterward. Ella Baker pushed Scott King to demand a seat at the table: "You need to be among the councils of the men. You have a lot to say."[58] Coretta felt she did too and periodically pressed for it—and was frustrated by Martin's reluctance. She wanted to get arrested like many women, but he said no; someone needed to be home for the children.

Dorothy Cotton, who would come to play a crucial role directing SCLC's Citizenship Education Project and as a confidante of Martin's, also noted this contradiction. "I did have a decision-making role," Cotton noted, but she saw how King "had to learn and a lot of growing to do" around issues of sexism and women's roles. "I really loved Dr. King but I know that that streak was in him also."[59] Cotton would become one of the few women in SCLC's inner leadership circle. From a very young age growing up in North Carolina (her mother died when she was three), unsettled by the racism, poverty, and cruelty around her, Dorothy Lee Foreman "felt like I was in the wrong place." Her high school teacher opened her world—getting her into Shaw University and finding her two jobs to enable her to go. When her employer became president of Virginia State, she transferred there, where she married George Cotton and began attending Wyatt Tee Walker's church. Walker was already active in numerous civil rights groups and recruited the spirited Cotton to organize young people. When Walker was tapped to run SCLC, he asked Cotton to go with him. She told her husband she would go for three months but "the movement became my life," and she stayed for twenty-three years.[60]

Through Highlander Folk School, Septima Clark and Esau Jenkins had developed the citizenship schools to empower and provide literacy training so working-poor Black people across the Deep South could register to vote and be empowered to push for the change their communities needed. Black people were denied the vote partly through literacy tests of state constitutions and other arcane knowledge, so Highlander set out to address the problem and build grassroots leadership through a web of citizenship schools. The state of Tennessee did not appreciate this organizing and had red-baited Highlander for years. Now they were threatening to shut the school down altogether on bogus charges. King and the SCLC were committed to ensuring the Citizenship Schools kept going. He tasked Cotton to go to Highlander to learn and confer.[61] Cotton saw the ways they transformed people's sense of possibility and refusal to be victims, and they moved the Citizenship Schools under SCLC's auspices—political education, empowerment, and literacy all wrapped up in one—with Cotton as the director alongside Andrew Young.

SCLC was a collection of different strong personalities, talented, strong-willed, some arrogant, and some wildly chauvinistic. But King was "a great listener . . . to his team of wild horses," Dorothy Cotton explained.[62] Buoyed by her ebullient spirit, King and Cotton became fast friends. She described King in meetings "as more silent until he needed to speak." Often the only woman at executive staff meetings, she stressed the ways "we were all growing and evolving into new definitions of ourselves and our roles." Still, she was always the one sent to fix the coffee until one day Jack O'Dell, one of the most progressive SCLC men, announced, "Dorothy needs to stay at the table." And then she stayed. Cotton herself knew "I had an important role to play and I knew I was smarter than some of those guys at the table."[63]

At home, Coretta and Martin differed on what her role should be, but that did not mean she wanted Martin to curtail his activism for the good of his family.[64] As SCLC administrator Edwina Smith Moss observed, "If Dr. King ever wanted to quit, she wouldn't have let him. . . . Coretta had steel."[65] King himself explained, "When I needed to talk things out, she was ready to listen or to offer suggestions. . . . She never allowed her fears to worry me or impede my work in the protest."[66] Historian Vicki Crawford has thus laid out an ambivalence in Martin's ideas about Coretta and their marriage: on the one hand, he held to certain traditional ideas about family roles (like Coretta having the primary role of raising the children), and, on the other hand, he saw Coretta as an intellectual equal and valued counsel. But, in recent decades, most writers who touch on King's gender politics often focus only on sexism. Neglecting the other ways the Kings subverted certain dominant social and gender norms, this has obscured Coretta Scott King's intellectual power and full personhood in the process.[67] As Martin himself would note, Coretta had "a calmness that kept me going . . . and a unique willingness to sacrifice for the [movement's] continuation."[68]

Calling Out Hypocrisy and New York's School Segregation

King increasingly found himself called to challenge liberals to recognize segregation at home. In 1963, he accepted the invitation to be the City College of New York's commencement speaker. "The Harvard of the Poor," founded in 1847, sat in the heart of Black Harlem, and tuition at City College was free—which meant that the people of New York were paying so that the children of the city could get an excellent public higher education. City College's president, Buell Gallagher, had a long history of civil rights commitments. A white ordained minister, he had previously been the president of Talladega College, a historically Black college in Alabama, and his research focused on racial inequality in American higher education. Hours before King was scheduled to speak, Mississippi NAACP leader Medgar Evers was shot in front of his home in Jackson. Evers's assassination sent shock waves through the country and reverberated for the King family, who received regular death threats like Evers had. But Martin summoned the fortitude to go on to New York anyway.

Gallagher beamed in pride at his decision to invite King. But, as historian Tahir Butt documents, King addressed a staggeringly white audience of 15,000 people in Harlem on June 12, 1963. Fewer than thirty-six of the 2,800 students graduating that day were Black. In the heart of Harlem, arguably the Black capital of the United States, the city's flagship free public college was overwhelmingly serving only white students. Black and Puerto Rican New Yorkers paid for a public good that their children could not access. New York's school segregation, just like Mississippi's, went from kindergarten to college, a problem that civil rights advocates, including City College's own professor Kenneth Clark (whose research had been crucial to the Supreme Court's *Brown* decision), had been calling out for years. King looked out on that sea of white and made clear that racial injustice was "not a sectional problem. . . . De facto segregation of the North is as injurious as the legal segregation of the South." That day, King questioned the self-satisfaction of many Northerners, like Gallagher, who zeroed in on the travesties of Southern racism but didn't look as critically at how their own systems perpetuated racial inequality.[69]

A *New York Times* article covering the graduation mentioned neither how white the graduates were nor the portion of King's speech that referenced Northern segregation.[70] Instead, five days later, the *Times* published a long piece on a study done by a nonacademic who claimed the problem Black New Yorkers faced was *not* racial discrimination but poverty. The thirty-two-paragraph article falsely claimed Black New Yorkers weren't "terribly concerned" about school desegregation and neglected to mention a decade-long movement in the city challenging school segregation. This class-over-race approach was one of the many tactics of Northern white deflection. The *Times* did not interview anyone in the Harlem or Brooklyn NAACP or CORE, or scholars like Clark who had been challenging New York's school segregation for years.[71] This kind of skewed coverage typified the paper's treatment of the city's endemic school segregation and the city's movement against it.

The movement against the city's segregated and unequal schools had accelerated after the Supreme Court's 1954 decision in *Brown v. Board*. Kenneth and Mamie Clark and Ella Baker, who headed Harlem's NAACP in the 1950s before moving to Atlanta in 1958, challenged the city's school segregation. While the city claimed the schools weren't segregated (just "separated," as New York superintendent, William Jansen, instructed administrators to say), Black community leaders highlighted the ways zoning was being used to segregate the city's schools. They also exposed that the resources for schools serving Black and Puerto Rican children were far fewer than those serving white students, and the education far more limited, which also contributed to the near exclusion of Black and Puerto Rican students from the city's free public colleges. On top of the treatment of students, the teacher-hiring process discriminated by including an in-person oral test that weeded out people with "foreign" or "Southern" accents, screening out most Black and Puerto Rican candidates.[72] The overall percentage of Black New York City schoolteachers in 1963 was 8.28 percent of the teaching force (and much lower at the high school level, 3.89 percent).[73]

Despite the overwhelming evidence of school segregation in cities like New York, the national NAACP still prioritized the South, with Wilkins claiming that in New York "some responsibility rests with parents and the community." According to historian Christopher Hayes, Wilkins instructed the city's local chapters to relax: "in the North we have time, freedom, power and allies to achieve our ends."[74] But New York's civil rights activists and Black parents vehemently disagreed. "[The national NAACP] were always talking about the poor people down South," lamented Ella Baker. "And so the question was, what to do about the poor children right here?"[75] Baker had long believed in empowering people to participate in the decisions over their lives.[76] In the face of New York City's stonewalling and the national NAACP's neglect, she traveled throughout the city urging parents to demand change and excellence for their children and helping to organize this moment against the city's segregated schools.

Black parents and organizers attended school meetings, took their kids out of school, protested at City Hall, built independent parent organizations, and picketed to call attention to the city's segregated and deeply unequal schools. At a 1957 public hearing on school integration, Black parent-activist Mae Mallory asserted that the Harlem public school her daughter attended was "just as 'Jim Crow' as the Hazel Street School that I attended in Macon, Georgia."[77]

Mallory was part of a growing parents' movement "trying to shame New York because they would always talk about the South and segregation, when their hands were dirty too." Mallory recounted how shocked she was by the stench of her children's school in Harlem: "There were only two bathrooms for sixteen hundred kids. They were very old fashioned, with one single wood sheet that went from one end of the place to the other with holes cut in it. You couldn't flush it.... And that made the school smell terrible."[78] Mallory found the conditions intolerable and took her case to the capitol in Albany, New York. "They were not prepared for this angry Black woman. Brand new toilets were put in immediately."[79] After her son Keefer, a fifth grader, came home with an assignment to count the pipes under the sink, Mallory confronted his teacher about the school's low expectations of its students. The teacher bristled: "Are you questioning my integrity as a teacher?" recounted Mallory. "So I told her you god damn right. Are you challenging my integrity as a parent? This child isn't a moron. What does he need to count pipes under the sink for? The teacher answered, 'How do you know he is not going to be a plumber.' " This incident propelled Mallory to get involved in challenging the school's curriculum and ultimately to file a suit against the New York City Board of Education.[80]

Mallory joined a group of nine mothers who kept their kids out of school in the fall of 1958 to protest their children's segregated schools. The mothers, who came to be known by the Black press as the Harlem Nine, had been told that their kids, not the segregated schools, were the problem and that was why they didn't learn. The women were determined to fight back, according to Mallory, for "our children to be educated the same way as everybody else's."[81] Having taken their grievances to school officials but getting nowhere, the mothers decided to stop schooling them entirely, as a protest gesture. "We will go to jail and rot there, if necessary, but our children will not go to junior high schools 136, 139, or 120," Viola Waddy explained.[82] The FBI heavily monitored Mallory's actions and the other Harlem Nine mothers, fearing communism lurked in demands to equalize education.[83] The city then charged the nine mothers for failure to comply with compulsory education requirements. Ultimately the charges were dropped, but the segregated schools remained.

Rev. Milton Galamison, pastor of Brooklyn's Siloam Presbyterian Church, helped spearhead the school organizing in the 1960s. One key obstacle they faced was "the astounded Northern White. Somehow it was easy to be liberal and generous toward the Negro when he was fighting to ride a bus in Montgomery, Alabama, or to sit at a lunch counter in Atlanta, Georgia . . . [they] now find themselves confronted with the need to remedy an inequity they pretended did not exist in the North."[84] Back in 1956, King had made clear "laws don't enforce themselves."[85] King well understood that many white New Yorkers, not just white Southerners, opposed desegregation and so Black people would have to organize to demand enforcement. He joined their struggle.

At the start of 1963, in his *Amsterdam News* column titled "New Year Hopes," King highlighted the "educational crisis" besetting the country—the "inadequate and inferior education" that many children were receiving and the "critical shortage of classroom space."[86] Increased Black migration to New York combined with the city's housing and school segregation had produced drastically overcrowded Black schools. Rather than alter zoning lines to bring Black students into less crowded, predominantly white schools, school officials proposed double session days in predominantly Black schools: one set of students would go to school for the first four hours of the day to accommodate a second group in the afternoon who also got a four-hour school day. Parents rose up in anger at this egregious school shortening. "Segregation is a national problem," King wrote two weeks later in the *Amsterdam News*. The problem "will not be solved until enough people North and South, come to see it is wrong and are willing to work passionately and unrelentingly to get rid of this cancerous disease."[87]

King was not the only one fed up with the city's segregation. In June 1963, James Baldwin convened a secret meeting with US attorney general Robert F. Kennedy at Kennedy's New York apartment. Baldwin invited Kenneth Clark, Harry Belafonte, Clarence Jones, Lena Horne, and Lorraine Hansberry to bring the issue of Northern segregation to the Kennedy administration and urge action, fearing that the lack of change could lead to unrest. Nothing came out of it. "We might as well have been talking different languages," Clark explained after.[88] Kennedy bristled at the ways they treated him that evening and complained that they had not properly credited what the administration was doing. But Belafonte told him, "You don't live with us, you don't even visit our pain."[89] Baldwin would later call Harlem "occupied territory" where the police are "hired enemies of the population" and "the Northern liberal thinks of himself as already saved."[90] Malcolm X too would echo this critique: "The North's liberals have been for so long pointing accusing fingers at the South and getting away with it that they have fits when they are exposed as the world's worst hypocrites."[91]

Clark interviewed King in the spring of 1963 and asked him about the Kennedy administration's approach to civil rights. King underlined a similar message to the Baldwin meeting: "time is running out, and the Negro is making it palpably clear that he wants all of his rights, that he wants them here, and that he wants them now." Clark was surprised and delighted by King's "extremist" position, writing that there was "little about his personal appearance that suggests the firm, courageous leader" that King actually was.[92] King's robust politics had been obscured, even to a Black intellectual like Clark.

All the News That's Comfortable to Print

One driver of the city's blinkered liberalism was the news media. The city's—arguably the nation's—flagship newspaper, the *New York Times*, was increasingly providing serious coverage of the Southern struggle. But any time civil rights activism got closer to home, the coverage became less rigorous. From 1962 to 1966, Martin Luther King wrote his biweekly column in the *Amsterdam News*.[93] While many columns focused on aspects of SCLC's Southern work, King repeatedly took on issues closer to New York City (like the housing segregation Jackie Robinson encountered in the city), but the *Times* ignored them.[94]

While the *Times* did occasionally cover civil rights protests at home, they did so largely in ways that refused to see a systemic problem in the city. They were a nearly all-white paper invested in not seeing itself that way. As *Times* reporter Gay Talese observed in 1969, any Black people allowed on the *Times'* editorial floor in the 1960s were most likely to be elevator operators.[95] Looking at their more fulsome, rigorous coverage on the South by the early 1960s provides a lens on what their coverage could have looked like in New York.[96] While they detailed horrific scenes of racism and poverty in the South, they provided significantly less serious coverage to the inequitable living conditions and decrepit schools Black people in New York, Chicago, and Los Angeles were forced into and less urgency to get federal intervention against Northern school or housing segregation than the South. Taking Black New Yorkers' protests less seriously and often actively disparaging them, they under-covered King's work outside the South and, if they did cover it, were often more dismissive, preferring stories of Black division.

On May 15, 1963, the *Times* ran an article titled "Newsman Beaten After Rally Here" highlighting violence at a Harlem rally against segregation; the piece pushed a Martin/Malcolm rivalry (even though both men were currently highlighting the city's segregated schools and housing) and ignored King's repeated trips and exhortations condemning the city's segregation. Two weeks later, the paper ran an article worrying again about Black violence in the North.[97] This focus on violence treated Black New Yorkers as a problem, not the city's segregation, discredited years of local protests, and disregarded King's admonitions about ignoring Black grievances. Repeatedly, the *Times* highlighted disagreements between civil rights leaders and groups. The year before, at the NAACP's Freedom Fund dinner, King decried the media tendency to cast the civil rights movement as "a seething admixture of organizations seething with disunity." King recognized that people could have different tactics or visions for Black freedom but still be understood as part of the Black struggle. But the *Times* ignored this criticism and "exploited [division]," King observed, "to disfigure our appearance" and avoid the substance of inequality.[98] By featuring and amplifying Black division, national outlets implicitly downgraded the urgency of the problem by making it seem like Black people couldn't even agree on the issue.

Another tactic the *Times* employed was brief mentions of the city's inequality in long articles on racial inequality overwhelmingly focused on the South. By devoting much more space to the urgent problem in the South, Northern inequality was downgraded.[99] Three days after the March on Washington, for instance, the *New York Times* published a long piece titled "Status of Integration: The Progress So Far Is Characterized as Mainly Tokenism."[100] While the piece touched on unemployment, police brutality, public accommodations, schools, and housing, the only direct mention of the North was a single one about housing. School segregation was discussed only in the South—despite a decade-long school desegregation movement in New York City itself (not to mention Los Angeles, Chicago, Boston, and elsewhere).

By the fall of 1963, King was emphasizing the extent of white resistance to housing and school desegregation in Northern cities. "Demonstrations in . . . New York and Chicago aroused the ire of many [white] persons in the North," King explained, revealing "more deep-seated prejudices than they had realized." King warned that "if the North isn't very careful, the South may very well outrun the North in human relations."[101] While the *New York Times* quoted him as saying this, it did not actually report on the vehemence of white resistance or document the level of housing and school segregation that King was referring to, as it might have done for a Southern-based issue. So the reader was left with a sense that King was making wild claims and fear-mongering.

On September 15, 1963, four members of the Ku Klux Klan bombed the Sixteenth Street Baptist Church in Birmingham, killing four girls and wounding more than a dozen other people. Absolutely devastated, King joined the call from New York artists and radicals for a nation-wide boycott of Christmas shopping to highlight the racial climate across the country that had given succor and cover for such acts to occur.[102] Galled by the idea that King saw the nation as responsible for the climate of violence precipitating the church bombing, the *Times* editorial board, in a piece titled "Strike Against Santa Claus," slammed the plan as "singularly inappropriate," "dangerous," and "self defeating." Such a boycott, the *Times* claimed, would turn Christmas into "a day of hate" and put "civil rights activists on the same level as those who did the church bombing."[103] The paper was quick to condemn King when he fingered the need for national accountability for the racial climate in the US. This was the frontlash that King would highlight time and again—Northerners reacted swiftly and negatively when their own segregated schools, homes, or pocketbooks were targeted.

The King family themselves decided to have a much more modest Christmas that year. Each child got one toy—so they could give the money to the families of the girls killed in the church bombing as well as Medgar Evers's family. Six years later, Holt editor Charlotte Mayerson was incredulous at this decision, speculating whether it had hurt the children. Coretta Scott King shot back, "I think it helps them to understand better their relationship toward other persons in society and the fact that they are all tied together in a common bond."[104]

A Movement Deepens in the Big Apple and King Sides with Disruption

For a decade, Black parents and local activists had pushed the city to follow the *Brown* decision and desegregate the city's schools. But the city continued to deny the very fact of segregation. After years of Board of Education intransigence, Black parents and New York's civil rights activists escalated their tactics. They decided to call for a citywide school boycott to highlight the fact that a decade after *Brown*, there was not even a comprehensive plan for desegregation by the city, let alone desegregation itself. King supported this escalation. Citing the many efforts Black community leaders and parents had made to draw attention to school inequality, King emphasized that more disruptive actions like school boycotts were essential—"the harvest of past apathy to tragic conditions that were allowed to exist without any serious concern."[105]

On February 3, 1964, the largest-ever civil rights demonstration in the country took place, organized by Black parents across the city, Rev. Milton Galamison, Annie Stein, Bayard Rustin, Gilberto Gerena Valentin, and many others. Almost double the numbers at the March on Washington the previous August, nearly half a million students and teachers stayed out of school to protest New York's lack of school desegregation. More than three-quarters of the students in the heavily Black and Puerto Rican schools of Harlem, Washington Heights, and the Lower East Side boycotted.[106] The Board of Education threatened to discipline the teachers who participated.

The *Times* lambasted the protest as a "violent, illegal approach of adult-encouraged truancy." It dismissed the demand for a comprehensive desegregation plan ten years after *Brown* as "unreasonable and unjustified," claiming that "few things could be more destructive to the welfare of all of the city's children" than the boycott; overcrowded classrooms, truncated school days, decrepit buildings, outdated and insufficient textbooks paled in comparison. The day after the boycott, acknowledging the significant numbers of students who stayed out, the *Times* still called the boycott "misguided."[107]

When King spoke to Rustin three days later in a call captured by the FBI, he began by praising the success of the boycott. King joked that it was "the greatest fizzle ever seen" (the BOE's president had tried to characterize the massive protest as a "fizzle").[108] King was clearly impressed by the boycott and dismayed by the ways white New Yorkers disingenuously deflected issues of segregation in their schools. Over and over, Northern liberals would say such tactics increased "tensions" and were counterproductive. But King would counter that tension was needed and inevitable. "We would not be integrated in Montgomery, Alabama, if we had taken this attitude."[109]

King devoted an entire *Amsterdam News* column in April to extoll "The School Boycott Concept," and castigated city leaders who refused to address the city's segregated schools. King underlined his support of school boycotts in New York, Chicago, and Boston, which "proved very effective in uncovering the injustice and indignity that school children in the Negro–Puerto Rican minority community face. . . . School boycotts have punctured the thin veneer of the North's racial self righteousness." Part of why school boycotts elicited such hysterical attacks, King saw, was precisely because they pierced the ways white Northerners saw themselves as good and righteous.

The next month, terrified the huge school boycott might weaken the Board of Education's resolve, about 15,000 white mothers marched over the Brooklyn Bridge. They asserted "their rights" to "their schools" as parents and taxpayers and protested even a modest school-pairing program being floated that would impact a small number of schools for desegregation. The media coverage they received was enormous. Print and TV reporters flocked to cover white mothers marching to protect their rights. Two days after the white mothers' protest, addressing the largely white United Federation of Teachers, King underscored the urgency of addressing New York's school segregation to the 2,500 teachers gathered. "Poor quality and segregated education will not be overcome without some cost to the white majority." He then contextualized the depth of the frustration of Northern black communities: "They are trying to loosen the manacles of the ghetto from the hands of their children."[110]

White New Yorkers demanded protection for "their" schools and their congressmen—then debating the 1964 Civil Rights Act—heard their call. John F. Kennedy and Burke Marshall had worried about enforcement against Northern schools the year before.[111] Working to pass the Civil Rights Act, which would tie federal funding to school desegregation, many Northern congressmen sought to protect their local schools from its mandates. Facilitated by Brooklyn congressman Emanuel Celler, Northern sponsors of the bill included a loophole in Title IV, Section 401b, reading: " 'Desegregation' means the assignment of students to public schools and within such schools without regard to their race, color, religion, or national origin, but 'desegregation' shall not mean the assignment of students to public schools in order to overcome racial imbalance." (*Racial imbalance* was the preferred Northern term for their own school segregation.) Southerners like Mississippi senator James Eastland highlighted the hypocrisies of the act's sponsors who sought to exempt their own schools. Referring to New York's senators as "pretty good segregationists at heart," he did "not blame the two distinguished Senators from New York for their desire to protect New York City as well as Chicago, Detroit, and similar areas. But why should they attempt to penalize our part of the country?"[112]

And so, the year after the Civil Rights Act's passage, to mark *Brown's* eleventh anniversary, King blasted the persistence of school segregation in the South and North. The decision "has meant very little to the millions of school children crippled in segregated schools in the South and . . . North." He called school boycotts "one of the most moral acts a parent may support. The cost paid daily by our youth is far greater than the cost to the school systems." While many whites slammed Black boycotts for "depriving their kids of education," King cast school boycotts as essential moral acts. He wrote about the educational deficiencies of his own segregated schooling, which meant he arrived at college years behind. "I could have remained out of school in protest for a year and if the protest remedied the injustice and inadequacy in my education, I would have still been years ahead of where I was when I graduated." Providing Black people inferior schooling, King reminded his readers, "continu[ed] the availability of cheap labor as the basis of economic expansion. This is but a sophistication of slavery." Understanding the economic as well as educational ramifications, King cast New York's segregated school system as "the most difficult school situation in America."[113]

So-Called Friends

Alongside his robust support of school boycotts, King endorsed disruptive protests at construction sites that erupted across the city in 1963. Even though African Americans and Puerto Ricans comprised a quarter of the city's population in 1960, they held under 8 percent of construction jobs. Racism within the building trades unions meant 92 percent of the twenty-one building trades unions were white, shutting out Black workers from these well-paying union jobs.[114] To highlight the problem, Black New Yorkers staged sit-ins at construction sites in Brooklyn and Queens, City Hall, and Governor Rockefeller's office to hold the government accountable for doing business with racially discriminatory construction companies.

In Brooklyn, a movement exploded as the state-funded Downstate Medical Center prepared to build a new 350-bed hospital addition and expand the State University of New York medical school housed there. The state had allocated $20 million to these upgrades, but the jobs were poised overwhelmingly to go to white workers. So a number of Brooklyn ministers, Brooklyn CORE, and many other Black Brooklynites mobilized to stop it, until they hired more Black workers. In July 1963, activists staged pickets intended to disrupt—and ideally halt—the construction work, sometimes lying down in front of construction vehicles. (Malcolm X came, though he didn't lie down or get arrested.)

On the day King endorsed these actions, 116 people had been arrested, 211 the day before. Arriving in New York for a March on Washington organizing meeting, King extolled the demonstrations, stressing that "Negroes here feel that not enough has been done by political leaders" and that the demonstrations would end "when the Negro feels he is getting a fair deal in housing and job opportunities." [115] King understood that part of the importance of these protests was to get in the way so the injustice could not proceed. Similar to Birmingham, the police roughed up many Downstate protesters; given these NYPD abuses, King called on the federal government, according to the *Chicago Tribune*, to create "a special civil rights police force to prevent what he called police brutality on the local and state levels in the integration drive." [116]

King repeatedly stood with disruptive protests that angered many white liberals. In the winter of 1964, despite calls from moderate white and Black leaders, King refused to condemn Brooklyn CORE's proposed stall-in. For years, Brooklyn CORE had challenged the city's housing segregation, school segregation, disparate municipal services, and job discrimination. Its members protested discriminatory realtors and Brooklyn's segregated schools, dumped trash on Brooklyn's Borough Hall to highlight differential sanitation services, and picketed racial exclusionary hiring at Brooklyn's Ebinger Bakery and the Downstate construction. Despite this creative, sustained organizing, as historian Brian Purnell shows, CORE had garnered little substantive change. [117]

Frustrated by city intransigence, the group sought to expose New York's rampant inequality—and force people to confront it. Their plan was to stall cars on highways leading to the opening of the World's Fair at Flushing Meadows, Queens, in April, an event that would draw international attention to the city. CORE understood that even the location of the World's Fair underlined the city's segregation. City planner Robert Moses had blocked plans to extend the subway to Flushing Meadows, which would have made it possible for more Black and Puerto Rican New Yorkers to attend the fair. The protest's demands were listed on flyers Brooklyn CORE handed out through the city: "We want jobs now, integrated quality education [and an] end [to] slum housing." [118]

City leaders were outraged. Mayor Robert F. Wagner called it "a gun at the heart of the city," while Moses enlisted the state commissioner not just to fine the protesters but to take their driver's licenses.[119] Many Black and white moderates furiously attacked the idea of the stall-in and called on King to do the same. But King refused, highlighting the "grinding poverty, and humiliating denial of access to public accommodation, voting, housing education and jobs" in New York. He noted the ways Congress was using a similar "stall-in" tactic to delay passing meaningful legislation. "We do not need allies who are more devoted to *order* than to *justice*," King explained. "I hear a lot of talk these days about our direct action talk alienating former friends. I would rather feel they are bringing to the surface latent prejudices that were always there. If our direct action programs alienate so-called friends . . . they never were really our friends."[120]

King took this position despite disagreement by close advisors like Clarence Jones. Jones privately decried the proposed stall-in as "counter revolutionary" and "a distortion of non-violent, mass direct action and politically seeks to substitute individual guerrilla-type confrontations with the power structure for direct mass action."[121] King wasn't sure how effective the protest would be, but tellingly he did not bow to the pressure to speak out against the stall-in. He certainly wasn't going to castigate fellow activists trying to get New Yorkers to confront long-ignored injustice.

The stall-in did not materialize. In his *Amsterdam News* column, King noted that it might have been for the best, because the "general public was not aware early enough of the issues at stake." But again, he refused to condemn it. He criticized the "silent good people" who spent so much time decrying this idea of stall-in and wished for them "to work up as much fervor for the full emancipation of the Negro as they did against the Stall-in." He then drew a parallel to Congress's filibuster around the civil rights bill: "What is worse, a 'Stall-in' at the World's Fair or a 'Stall-in' in the US Senate? The former merely ties up traffic of a single city while the latter seeks to tie up the traffic of history and endanger the psychological lives of 20 million people."[122]

We've Known Our Good Fridays

As he had done in Harlem in 1958 and around the Downstate protests, King continued to highlight the urgency of police brutality in the South *and* the North. King's repeated experiences of police abuse would connect him to Black people across the country. Back in October 1960, King was again arrested, this time for taking part in an Atlanta sit-in organized by SNCC students. Authorities released the other sit-inners but held King on an old traffic violation. In the middle of the night, police picked him up and drove him two hundred miles, handcuffing him, shackling his feet, and chaining him to the floor for the four-hour ride. When King complained about the handcuffs being too tight, they tightened them.[123] Terrified, he didn't know where they were taking him. He later told Andrew Young, "That kind of mental anguish is worse than dying, riding mile after mile, bound and helpless, waiting and not knowing what you're waiting for."[124] They deposited him at a maximum-security prison in Reidsville, Georgia.

Coretta didn't know what had happened to him. In a DeKalb County court a week later, the judge sentenced King to six months of hard labor. Coretta, terrified, exhausted, and six months pregnant, unprecedentedly broke down crying. Martin was deeply shaken: "Corrie, I've never seen you like this, you have to stand up for me."[125] In many ways, he relied on her to be a rock, and Coretta rarely cried, and never in public. But they both understood what the police and jailers could do. Every police encounter scared him, and he had to conquer that fear over and over as he was arrested nearly thirty times over his life. In his Easter sermon at Ebenezer Baptist Church in 1962, he likened Jesus's persecution to Black experiences of police brutality: "We've known our Good Fridays in the fact that we've seen with our own eyes police brutality."[126]

In July 1963, King returned to speak at Salem Methodist Church in Harlem. Over five hundred people lined the streets around the church. A few young men outside threw eggs at King's car.[127] The *New York Times'* front-page headline blared "Dr. King Is Target of Eggs in Harlem."[128] About six eggs were actually thrown, but journalists became obsessed with this incident. The eggs grew and grew in the media over the years. In the *Los Angeles Times* a year later, it expanded to "Harlem greeted Dr. King with rotten eggs."[129] Indeed, it's a story now featured in nearly all King biographies, though most don't mention the many other times King had spoken in New York, the love many Black New Yorkers felt for him, the fact that it was only a handful of eggs by a few people, and most importantly the ways King zeroed in on the devastating segregation and police brutality that Black New Yorkers faced.

Writer Robert Penn Warren the next year tried to push King on this egg incident. King contextualized the incident: "they've heard all of these things about my being soft, . . . they began to fear that I'm saying love this person that they have such a bitter attitude toward." Warren clearly wanted more of a condemnation of these young men; he pressed again on the egg incident's "emotional" impact on King. But King responded,

> I was able very quickly to get my mind off of myself and feeling sorry for myself. . . . I started including them into the orbit of my thinking that it's not enough to condemn them for doing this . . . but what about the society and what about the conditions that are still alive which made people act like this? . . . I'm concerned about the fact that maybe all of us have contributed to this by not working harder to get rid of the conditions, the poverty, the social isolation, and all of the conditions that cause individuals to respond like this.[130]

King would return to the point repeatedly, as he tried to move white Northerners to get beyond their own feelings to address the oppressive conditions that produced Black people's actions. In a piece for the *Nation* in 1964, he observed, "For many white Americans in the North there is little comprehension of the grossness of police behavior and its widespread practice." [131]

4

A New Form of Slavery Covered Up with Certain Niceties

Rethinking 1963 and King's Growing Frustration with Northern Intransigence

By 1963, King's pace was relentless. Knowing he was a "symbol," he had "constant moments" of feeling inadequate to the responsibilities of this leadership.[1] In 1961 and 1962, SCLC had set out alongside SNCC in Albany, Georgia, joining local people in a campaign to desegregate public facilities. But it had been a mixed success—it had built a robust local movement but widened disagreements with SNCC over strategy. Police chief Laurie Pritchett outfoxed them by arresting scores of Black Georgians but keeping his police nonviolent in public while abusing people's rights and bodies in private. This kept the national media from coming down on Albany's leadership.

In December 1961, the SCLC and Albany Movement reached an agreement for a biracial committee for integration as long as King left town, but it proved unenforceable. In January the city then about-faced and denied any concessions, so the movement redoubled its efforts. After a difficult spring and SNCC urging a strategy of jail-no-bail, in July King was arrested and decided to stay in jail. But Pritchett secretly got a group of white businessmen to bail out the civil rights leader so he wouldn't gain public sympathy—and then lied for years saying a Black man had done it to make King and the movement seem untrustworthy. Then the movement was served with a federal injunction against protesting; while uncharacteristically yelling at Robert Kennedy about how problematic it was, King still hesitated to break it. Arrested again while trying to visit an activist in jail, King was beaten by the sheriff with a heavy cane. In August, King and Abernathy were tried and given sixty-day suspended sentences, so long as they didn't continue to protest.[2] Unlike SNCC, SCLC had not committed to organizing in Albany for the long term and so in September 1962 SCLC sat together at a retreat to learn lessons from the campaign for their work ahead.

One of the "most frustrating aspects" of his life, King would tell interviewers, was trying to be a father in the midst of this relentless schedule. It was "just impossible."[3] He was out of town for multiple days nearly every week. The kids regularly asked why and wanted him home. Sometimes they would see ads for Atlanta's Fun Town, a segregated amusement park. Yolanda (whom they called Yoki) asked over and over to go. For a while, he and Coretta dodged it. But then they told her the truth and how they were fighting to change it. "His absences became more meaningful" after that. When their father was arrested in Albany and Coretta told the kids, six-and-a-half-year-old Yoki piped up: "well that's fine. Tell him to stay in jail till we get to go to Funtown." When the park was finally desegregated in 1963, Martin and Coretta took Yoki and Marty and had a "glorious" time. They went on all the rides, Coretta recalled, and "Martin was boyishly happy." She loved how "the children had been able to see that what their daddy was doing had got some results."[4]

Fielding many comments from classmates and others about their "troublemaking" father, the kids would periodically ask, "why don't people like my daddy?" She would try to explain that "God uses people to do his work . . . and he's using your daddy."[5] They seemed to understand, but it wasn't easy. Marty, who was now six, would talk about his father's huge workload: Daddy "has a lot of work to do in this country, but he's fighting, trying to get freedom for everybody and when he finishes with this country he has to go to some foreign countries and do the same thing . . . as a matter of fact, he has to fix up the whole world, he and uncle Ralph." Martin wasn't around a lot, but when he was, it was "something special."[6] On extremely rare occasions when she left Martin home with the kids, they would "dismantle" the house. And sometimes when she returned, all three kids would be sitting on him—a pile of Kings.[7]

A few months later, at the invitation of SCLC co-founder Fred Shuttlesworth, who had been fighting the fight in Birmingham for years, King and SCLC prepared to join the campaign in Birmingham, hoping to have learned lessons to take with them. The city was one of the most segregated in the country and so infamous for its violence, Black people called it "Bombingham." In early March 1963, King flew to New

York to get Harry Belafonte's help in raising bail money, lots of it, to be able to mount the campaign, a massive movement of disruption.

Coretta was very pregnant at the time. "We were waiting for the baby to come so Martin could go to jail." On March 28, Bernice was born. Martin drove Coretta home from the hospital and then returned to Birmingham. This was difficult for both of them—she had been his rock in Montgomery. It was hard to be without her, and she struggled with being left behind.[8] With four children, Atlanta was harder, Coretta felt. "In Montgomery we had gone through the struggle together" and the community helped.[9] After Bernice was born, they began to get more regular help in the house. Ultimately, Belafonte would help pay for a caretaker for the kids; then the next year, they also hired a young Black ex-marine, Cody Perry, to be the kids' driver, guardian, and "playmate."[10]

The Birmingham campaign faced criticism from white and Black people in the city, since moderate Albert Boutwell had just defeated the segregationist commissioner of public safety, Theophilus Eugene "Bull" Connor, for Birmingham mayor. Many said this was a new day and wasn't the time for such protests; Black people needed to give the new administration a chance. Then the city won a state injunction against the protests. But, having learned lessons from Albany, on April 12, King and Abernathy made the difficult decision to disobey it, which meant spending the Easter weekend in jail. There, locked up in solitary confinement, King wrote a letter on scraps of paper and toilet paper responding to white clergy who had called him an extremist and criticized the movement as "unwise and untimely." He observed how the white moderate who "preferred order to justice" might pose a greater danger than the KKK. Then he extolled, "the question is not whether we will be extremist but what kind of extremists we will be.... Will we be extremists for the preservation of injustice, or will we be extremists for the cause of justice?"[11]

Those arrests didn't move Birmingham leadership or the Kennedy administration. With not enough adults willing to get arrested and the media coming down on the movement, SCLC made the controversial decision to let young people who field secretary James Bevel had been working with for months pick up the charge. Day after day, the young people—over one thousand high school and middle school students—marched and were arrested. In the face of mounting criticism from many Black people, King proclaimed on May 5, "don't worry about your children. Don't hold them back if they want to go to jail." King recognized how these young people were stepping up, like Jesus had, "carving a tunnel of hope through great mountains of despair."[12] He saw these young students' determination and how they might bring their parents and teachers past the fear to see the necessity for action.

On May 2, hundreds of young people marched. The next day, hundreds more marched. Police commissioner Bull Connor sicced police dogs and fire hoses on the young people, arresting them in droves. The water lifted some kids off the ground and tore through their clothes. Black parents, teachers, and some of the more moderate Black leaders, including millionaire A. G. Gaston (who had wanted King to leave town), were outraged at what was being done to these young people, and mobilized.[13] Media coverage blasted images of these attacks across the nation.

National outlets provided intricate, emotional descriptions of the movement and the police violence against it, which prompted national outrage.[14] Belafonte held a clandestine fundraiser at his New York apartment that raised $472,000 to bail out hundreds more young people carrying forward the Birmingham movement. The relentless marches combined with this national media outrage finally forced the city's political and business leadership to the table.[15] Part of what also pushed them to negotiate, according to Coretta Scott King, was that alongside the public demonstrations there had been a months-long Black boycott of downtown businesses, eroding these businesses' bottom line.[16]

On May 10, the Birmingham Agreement was announced; it included the removal of "colored" and "white" signs, plans to desegregate lunch counters, a program to upgrade Black employment, and a biracial committee to monitor. Fred Shuttlesworth, who was in the hospital injured from the protests, disagreed; they shouldn't call off the demonstrations, he believed, as the agreement lacked an enforcement mechanism or concrete job commitments. The night after the agreement, white supremacists bombed the Gaston Motel, where King was staying, along with his brother A. D.'s Birmingham home. (A. D. had also been a key leader in the Birmingham Campaign.) Black Birmingham exploded in anger, with fires and some looting. The next day, seeing that Black people were at an understandable breaking point, President Kennedy endorsed the agreement. A month later, on June 11, Kennedy addressed the nation saying the US had been "founded on the principle that all men are created equal." Kennedy stressed, "Those who do nothing are inviting shame as well as violence," and announced he would be sending civil rights legislation to Congress, addressing segregation in public accommodations and schools.[17] The Birmingham movement had yielded federal action.

The story of 1963 has become the story of Birmingham—of difficult struggle, long-awaited success, and finally a national move to address civil rights. But King also spent much of 1963 crisscrossing the nation supporting struggles against school and housing segregation and police brutality from LA to Boston, Chicago to New York. These equally long-standing, creative movements garnered little change. In a television interview, King explained that while in the South "you can see pockets of progress," the North was different: "often the Negro can only see retrogress."[18]

The Great Marches

Two weeks after President Kennedy's national address, King journeyed to Motown to join Black Detroiters in the Great Walk for Freedom. Detroit's civil rights activists had grown tired of the runaround by city officials. They had protested the city's pervasive housing and school segregation, job discrimination, and police brutality—variously holding meetings, rallies, and housing marches, organizing the Black political party, Freedom Now Party, and challenging urban renewal as "Negro removal." But mostly they had been brushed aside by city leaders and white Detroiters.

Frustrated with the lack of change, civil rights leaders Rev. Albert Cleage and Rev. C. L. Franklin called for a citywide march—a Great Walk to Freedom—as an "unprecedented show of strength" of Detroit's Black community.[19] As Franklin told the *Detroit News*, the march would serve as a "warning to the city that what has transpired in the past is no longer acceptable to the Negro community."[20] Splits in the coalition led Franklin, against Cleage's entreaties, to let Detroit's mayor, Jerome Cavanagh, who had long stonewalled the movement, march in the front.[21]

On June 23, 1963, King, Cleage, Franklin, and Rosa Parks (who had been forced to leave Montgomery for Detroit in 1957) led what King called "the largest and greatest demonstration for freedom ever held in the United States."[22] Between 125,000 and 200,000 people marched that day, 90 percent of them Black.[23] Dressed in their Sunday best, "a mighty sea of black faces" spilled down the city's mighty Jefferson Avenue, filling block after block after block.[24] "We didn't have to walk but were pushed up Jefferson," recalled Detroit labor activist General Baker.[25] Indeed, the crowd's enthusiasm pushing forward lifted King's feet off the ground that day.

At the end of the march, at Cobo Arena, many people spoke. Mayor Cavanagh paid tribute to King but did not signal any subsequent change in action by his administration, while both Cleage and King spoke candidly of the city's racism. When King was introduced, the *Michigan Chronicle* reported, "the roar of the crowd sounded like a sudden burst of thunder shaking the rafters of the vast arena."[26] King praised this "magnificent new militancy"—and described Detroit's segregation as "a cancer in the body politic" and "a new form of slavery covered up with the niceties of complexity." Then he reiterated a message that he would underline in Northern cities across the country: "if you want to help us in Alabama and Mississippi and over the South, do all that you can to get rid of the problem here." Underscoring the severity of Detroit's segregation, "We must come to see that *de facto* segregation in the North is just as injurious." Then he returned to the refrain that suffused his speeches in the early 1960s: "All-Here-Now." "[T]his social revolution taking place can be summarized in three little words," he said. "They are the words 'all,' 'here,' and 'now.' We want *all* of our rights, we want them *here*, and we want them *now*."[27]

Parks thought his speech the best she'd ever heard him give, "reminding everybody that segregation and discrimination were rampant in Michigan as well as Alabama."[28] Motown Records produced its first spoken-word recording of that speech; founder Berry Gordy Jr. pronounced it "required listening for every American child, white or Black."[29] Yet, as historian Suzanne Smith observed, that speech has been largely lost to the general public because it "acknowledge[d] that the fight against segregation and injustice did not stop once one crossed the Mason-Dixon Line."[30]

The *New York Times* did two stories on the Detroit March but made no mention of King's critique of Northern segregation, Detroit's segregated schools, job discrimination, and police brutality that the march focused on, or Cavanagh's inaction. One article focused on the white participants in the march, even though more than 90 percent of the participants had been Black.[31] Quoting King saying that such marches were necessary "until there's freedom from Boston to Birmingham . . . Michigan to Mississippi," the *Times* provided little sense of specific conditions in Detroit, where Black people were not free.[32] The *Washington Post* didn't cover the march at all.

King's speech at the Great Walk was a preview of the one he would give two months later at the March on Washington. Organized by A. Philip Randolph, Bayard Rustin, and Anna Arnold Hedgeman to mark the hundredth anniversary of the Emancipation Proclamation, the March on Washington for Jobs and Freedom would see a much more sizable contingent of white supporters. Hedgeman, the only Black woman on the march committee, had a long career of race work, serving as the executive director of the Fair Employment Practices Committee (FEPC), the first Black woman to serve on the New York City mayor's cabinet, and now the newly formed Commission on Race and Religion for the National Council of Churches. Hedgeman helped turn out large numbers of white Christians, historian Jennifer Scanlon documents, and so the March on Washington would be the first mass civil rights event with a large percentage of whites (estimated at nearly 25 percent of the marchers). Hedgeman also facilitated many of the day's logistics, including Operation Sandwich, in which she commanded a massive volunteer effort to produce eighty thousand box lunches for marchers.[33]

Getting Puerto Ricans to the march was also a priority. Having served on the 1199 strike support committee in 1962 with Gilberto Gerena Valentin, Randolph and Rustin had reached out to Valentin about organizing Puerto Ricans for the march.[34] A union organizer, Valentin was president of Congreso del Pueblo and New York's Puerto Rican Day Parade.[35] According to Valentin, King invited him and another Puerto Rican community organizer, Manny Diaz, to Atlanta and asked them to "organize the Latinos of New York, New Jersey, Pennsylvania, Connecticut, and Massachusetts, and so I did."[36]

Valentin and Diaz spent six months systematically organizing for the march.[37] Active in his local union at Adams Laboratory, Valentin used some of his work time to organize for the March; the labor movement helped "tremendously" with transportation and expenses for Puerto Ricans to attend the march.[38] On August 22, twenty-four Puerto Rican leaders from a variety of organizations met in New York to declare they would "join and support" the March on Washington the next week.[39] While a number of unions including the AFL-CIO didn't endorse the March, about a thousand 1199ers came to the nation's capital.[40]

Coretta and Martin traveled to DC the night before the march. Nervous and excited that night, Martin "ask[ed] me to give him synonyms for various words . . . he was trying get the right word for what he wanted to say," Coretta explained.[41] Much like the night before the Montgomery bus boycott began, they worried about how many people would show up.

Over a quarter of a million people made the journey to DC. Rendered invisible in the ways the march has been remembered, historian Evelyn Higginbotham has observed, "were the many delegations from the West Coast, the East Coast and the Midwest . . . with banners and placards that identified the civil rights issues of their locales: 'We March for Integrated Schools Now'; 'We Demand an End to Police Brutality Now'; 'We March for Higher Wages.' "[42] More than a thousand Bostonians marched; Rosie Simpson, Lawrence Landry, Timuel Black, Peggy Terry, and 2,500 others made the seven-hundred-mile journey from Chicago; twenty-four buses came from Harlem alone.[43] Malcolm X had been very critical of the march and the compromises organizers made with the Kennedy administration. Nonetheless, he was in DC that day—and had made it known that if they needed his help, he was there.

In Gilberto Gerena Valentin's account, over thirty thousand Puerto Ricans went to the March on Washington. Manny Diaz said that Rustin affectionately referred to Diaz as "the one percenter" because Diaz took one percent [two thousand] of the two hundred thousand people to Washington on the bus from New York.[44] Busloads of Puerto Ricans traveled to DC from across the East Coast to take part in the march. The large Puerto Rican contingent made front-page news in New York's largest Spanish-language newspaper, *El Diario*, but was overlooked in most of the rest of the media and subsequently by historians.[45]

When they reached the Lincoln Memorial, part of the Puerto Rican contingent waving the Puerto Rican flag spontaneously burst into "La Borinqueña," the Puerto Rican anthem. The crowd applauded.[46] Various speeches took place across the day that were not in the official program; King had asked Valentin to give one in Spanish. Extremely nervous, Valentin had memorized his speech. "I said that there was discrimination not only against blacks, but also against Puerto Ricans and Hispanics."[47]

The many women who had led, organized, and helped build the march itself were marginalized in the march's official program, despite Hedgeman and Dorothy Height's pivotal roles and protests.[48] Height, head of the 800,000-women-strong National Council of Negro Women, had been meeting with the other leaders and was a key fundraiser for the march. She was extremely dismayed at their exclusion that day. Martin's sister Christine was also deeply frustrated at Height's omission and the ways historians always marked the "Big Six" organizers of the march: "There is another name that should forever be enshrined . . . Dr. Height."[49] When Hedgeman, Height, and Pauli Murray protested of the lack of women on the program, Rustin and Randolph agreed on a "compromise" where Randolph would introduce a handful of key women to the crowd to be recognized.

The wives of the leaders were not allowed to march with their husbands. "Not pleased," Coretta had "pleaded" with Martin to march with him, but the leadership council thought wives would "sort of be in the way. I resented this. . . . I should have the privilege of sharing this experience" like the many hardships over the years they had shared. No woman got to address the crowd. Randolph gave a "Tribute to Women" and then introduced Daisy Bates, who delivered a brief women's pledge to the movement, written for her by the NAACP's John Morsell. Then Rosa Parks, Diane Nash, Myrlie Evers, Gloria Richardson, and Prince Lee were announced to the crowd.

Coretta insisted that at least she wanted to sit near Martin. Finally, a seat was made for her on the platform; "it was the biggest crowd I had ever seen." King was tremendously moved by the crowd; choked up, his voice was "husky" when he began, Coretta noticed.[50] Hedgeman was tremendously moved by the day but wished Martin had ended his speech with "We have a dream." The "I" detached him from the broader history, she felt, from all the men and women there. "Only because we didn't educate him," Hedgeman later regretted.[51] The ten-person delegation that met with President Kennedy afterward included no women either. Hedgeman was galled that Rosa Parks was not invited. Coretta wanted to go, but Martin told her she was "not invited." At the meeting, the men pushed Kennedy on Black economic needs that had been lost in the civil rights bill.[52]

When Martin finally made it back to the hotel that evening, he and Coretta stayed up and talked for hours, reliving and analyzing the events of the day.[53]

The FBI Escalates Its Campaign

King's eloquent power, on full display at the march, amplified the Kennedy administration's and FBI's fears. While the Bureau had monitored King since Montgomery, as his influence spread, the FBI grew more concerned. Extensive FBI surveillance led up to the march, and

150 FBI agents were on hand that day to monitor the crowd. The Kennedy administration had rigged the microphone so it could be turned off and a recording of Mahalia Jackson played instead.[54]

In the wake of the march, the FBI described King as "the most dangerous Negro . . . in this Nation" and pursued greater surveillance of him.[55] The justification was potential Communist influence over King; the Bureau particularly worried about Stanley Levison but Bayard Rustin and Jack O'Dell as well. Two months after the march, Attorney General Robert Kennedy signed off on wiretapping King's home and office phones. In early 1964, the FBI would extend that permission to bugging King's home, office, and hotel rooms and other friends' homes where he stayed. They monitored the Kings' bank account.[56] Both Robert and John Kennedy warned King directly to stop associating with Levison. While King put distance between them, at times going through intermediaries, according to Andrew Young, Martin "defied the FBI and the president of the United States for their friendship."[57]

When Lyndon Johnson became president after Kennedy's assassination in November, the White House began an even closer relationship to FBI director J. Edgar Hoover and the Bureau's campaign against King. Friendly with Hoover and neighbors for a time, Johnson had used the FBI to vet his Senate staff. From the beginning of Johnson's presidency to King's assassination in 1968, Hoover apprised Johnson directly almost weekly on the FBI's surveillance of King, and Johnson did not stop the FBI's campaign against King in all those years.

Rather, Johnson and Hoover set up a protocol for direct and private communication that went from late 1963 to King's death. Mildred Stegall, Johnson's personal aide since 1956, was crucial to that system.[58] She later became the primary liaison between the White House and the FBI. The memos typically sent from Hoover to Johnson's top aide (Walter Jenkins, then Bill Moyers for a time) were for the president's eyes only. After Johnson read the pages from Hoover (and he likely didn't read all of them), Stegall locked them in a vault that also contained Johnson's personal business papers, as well as the tapes Johnson made of his telephone conversations. In more than 250 memos in the four-and-a-half-year period, Hoover fed Johnson a steady diet of information on King's conversations with his top advisors, travel plans, personal life, extramarital affairs, and various events King was planning, treating King like a foreign adversary.[59] Gleaned from telephone wiretaps, bugs, and informants, this extensive political espionage was handy for a president who prized the power of information and used it to manage his relationship with King. Hoover reported that an administration official wanted King to participate in a memorial for John Kennedy, what King planned to say to the Republican platform committee, that Senator Hubert Humphrey planned to ask King to write an introduction to a civil rights pamphlet he was doing (this never happened), and on and on.[60]

In April 1964, King publicly criticized the FBI for its refusal to investigate violence against civil rights workers, calling it "completely ineffectual." Hoover was furious. At a press conference with women journalists, he called King "the most notorious liar." Hearing about this, according to Dorothy Cotton, was "the first time I saw [King] cry . . . it was just so painful for him."[61] Yet Hoover retained public support. A Harris poll in February 1965 found that "despite recent criticisms" he still had the backing of eight in ten Americans—a full 50 percent took Hoover's side and only 16 percent took King's.[62]

When an FBI wiretap picked up Coretta and Martin discussing how the White House hadn't called to congratulate Martin on the Nobel Prize, Hoover reported it to Johnson. (A week later, Johnson telegrammed his congratulations.)[63] Like a high school tattletale, numerous memos described private comments that King made about Johnson. Hoover justified this political espionage by constantly reminding Johnson of the suspected Communist ties of the civil rights leader's advisors, in particular Levison and Rustin, though the FBI found nothing to suggest that King or anyone in his circle had ongoing interest in or ties to the Soviet Union. This surveillance got so bad that Atlanta's police chief, Herbert Jenkins, came to warn King's father. "They even know when he goes to the bathroom."[64]

While the FBI's surveillance did not succeed in finding any Communist control of King, it did find evidence of his extramarital affairs. The Johnson administration wanted to use that titillating information to undermine King, even though it had nothing to do with national security. Johnson's special assistant Walter Jenkins told FBI deputy director Cartha "Deke" DeLoach "that the FBI could perform a good service to the country if this matter could somehow be confidentially given to members of the press." Soon after DeLoach's memo, journalists at many of the nation's biggest news outlets—including the *New York Times, Los Angeles Times, Chicago Daily News, Newsweek,* and *Atlanta Constitution*—were handed salacious files about King's extramarital affairs and presented with lists of questions the FBI wanted reporters to ask King.[65] These reporters have been praised for not publishing the prurient details of the FBI's surveillance.[66] But at the same time, *none* of them chose to report that the FBI was conducting a massive surveillance campaign against the civil rights leader.

Hoover was beside himself when the news broke that King was to be awarded the Nobel Prize. An FBI agent was dispatched to Florida to send King a letter written to appear to be from a Black person along with a tape made from recordings of King's hotel room assignations. The letter told King to kill himself before he was exposed as a fraud. Since Montgomery, Coretta had started archiving papers, letters, and newspaper clippings, organizing their files, and answering some of Martin's correspondence.[67] When Coretta discovered the package, according to Edythe, she intuitively understood that the FBI had sent it "to disrupt the Movement's work."[68] This didn't stop them, but the constant harassment took its toll.

Make no mistake, the FBI's campaign against King could have been stopped. While Hoover is often portrayed as possessing more power than even US presidents, Lyndon Johnson wielded significant authority over him. On January 1, 1965, Hoover turned seventy and would have been forced to retire, given the then-mandatory US government service retirement age. Instead, on May 8, 1964, Johnson signed an executive order waiving the mandatory order for Hoover for "an indefinite period of time."[69] Johnson had left himself an out—and could have rescinded the order at any time (or threatened Hoover with the possibility). But he never did.

Ignored

King had been highlighting the costs of ignoring Black protests against police brutality and segregation for years. On July 16, 1964, an off-duty New York City police lieutenant, Thomas Gilligan, killed fifteen-year-old James Powell outside the teenager's Manhattan summer school. Students often loitered after school, which annoyed some of the white building superintendents. That day, one superintendent turned his hose on some of the young men, calling them "niggers." The boys responded by throwing stuff. Gilligan pursued the boys, shooting Powell twice and killing him.

Powell's murder sparked a six-day uprising in Harlem. There were organized protests by many of Powell's classmates and other New York activists as well as bricks, bottles, and Molotov cocktails thrown. The police crackdown was brutal. *Time* magazine ran a photo of an armed white cop chasing a group of skinny Black boys with his baton poised to smash their heads.[70] Many white New Yorkers and politicians blamed Communists for the uprising and for exaggerating charges of police brutality.[71]

Mayor Robert Wagner decided to invite King to come to New York, hoping to help ease tensions between Black residents and city leaders. Local activists worried that King was being used by Wagner to quiet them. Ruby Dee, Ossie Davis, and Kenneth and Mamie Clark warned King privately that he might be used to "muffle the cries of an outraged community."[72] Turf wars that had played out for years erupted when Congressman Adam Clayton Powell Jr. declared he'd been organizing since King was "still in diapers."[73] "No leader outside Harlem," Powell told his congregation, "should come into this town and tell us what to do."[74] But King didn't have the stomach to spar with other Black leaders.[75] So again, King didn't take on Powell directly.

In his July 18 *Amsterdam News* column, King laid out "A Plan for New York" to address the city's long-standing housing and school segregation and job discrimination to avoid further unrest. King called for a "massive public works project to employ the unemployed and give hope to those who have lost it as a result of . . . their disadvantaged position" and underscored the role the federal government needed to play.[76] Over and again, when uprisings happened, King would point out the changes needed that had long been ignored and how white intransigence laid the ground for these uprisings. While praising the start made with the Civil Rights Act, he stated that the law was "not nearly strong enough to deal with the magnitude of the problem" of structural discrimination in employment and housing.[77]

Then, on July 27, 1964, after the violent police arrest of a twenty-year-old Black man led to an uprising in Rochester, New York, King spoke out from Atlanta about the conditions that had produced these two uprisings. Criticizing the "shallow rhetoric condemning lawlessness," he called for

an honest soul-searching analysis and evaluation of the environmental causes which have spawned the riots. . . . If law and order are to be maintained in New York City, Rochester or Mississippi, it can be done when there is an ever-increasing measure of justice and dignity accorded all persons. The president of the United States, the mayors of New York City and Rochester and the governors and mayors of every city and state throughout our country

have a responsibility to see that millions of black Americans acquire an ever-increasing amount of justice.[78]

King slipped Mississippi into his speech here to underline the
parallels—the "white power structure" was responsible in New York
as well as the South.[79]

Then he headed to New York City. King felt obliged to come but refused to play by the mayor's script. In a call with Rustin recorded by the
FBI, King worried about the role he could play. Committed to supporting the demands of local leaders, King had informed Wagner that the
mayor had to meet with local Black leaders and then refused Wagner's
request for an off-the-record meeting so he was free to publicly criticize the mayor. Rustin and King seemed to be on the same page about
the approach: violence could be prevented only if Wagner took action
to address the city's inequalities in housing, schools, and jobs.[80] Rustin
accompanied King through two days of meetings, helping him maintain a strong stand with Wagner.[81] King's first stop was Harlem to meet
with local leaders, including Livingston Wingate of Harlem Youth Opportunities Unlimited, a key community group in Harlem. King had
made it clear to Wagner, the *Amsterdam News* reported, that "under no
circumstances would he meet with the mayor without first meeting
with local people."[82] But bizarrely, the *New York Times* chose to report
that King had no plans to go to Harlem that day, quoting Wingate as
upset about King's (alleged) decision. The *Times* was eager to play up—
and indeed distort—divisions between Black leaders.[83]

Over the next three days, King had a series of meetings with the
mayor. While he politely described them as "frank, fruitful, and ami-
cable," the four meetings led to *no* concessions from Wagner. King was
clear: "profound and basic changes" around jobs, housing, schools, and
police would have to happen to avoid further uprisings, including "a
master plan to put all youth, Negro and white back to work in New York
City."[84] He slammed New York's police commissioner, Michael Murphy,
as being "utterly unresponsive to [Black] demands" and "intransigent"
and called for Officer Gilligan's suspension.[85] Wagner refused it all, instead increasing police presence on the subway. Indeed, King was nearly
run out of town when he dared to suggest the city would benefit from
a Civilian Complaint Review Board to oversee the police department.[86]

King's press release laid out clearly what he had told Wagner was
necessary to address the city's endemic inequality and avoid further
uprisings. The mayor needed to implement the demands of the Unity

Council of Harlem Organizations, including a civilian complaint review board. "I told the mayor that 'law and order' cannot exist in a
vacuum—that law and order are byproducts of justice and of sincere
and genuine efforts to relieve injustice." King highlighted the "biased
behaviors" of the police; "unless the police treat Negroes with courtesy, dignity and respect, we cannot . . . get on to solving basic economic problems that beset us not only in New York but nationally."
King stressed how Wagner and Governor Rockefeller needed to "appeal to President Johnson to institute an adequately funded program
to deal with the problems of unemployment." [87]

Despite how many of the city's civil rights activists as well as
Dr. King had clearly articulated the ways New York's segregation and
police abuse *could* be addressed, the *New York Times* instead maintained the "baffling question of what could be done to relieve the basic
problem—the need for better housing, better education, and more and
better jobs." Making it seem mysterious if not impossible to do anything, they assiduously refused to use the word *segregation*.[88] Faced
with Wagner's intransigence, King left the city more pessimistic about
change in the North than in the South, but many King biographers
miss this New York work altogether.[89]

Because they condemned police misconduct, King and other civil
rights leaders faced a $1.5 million lawsuit from Officer Gilligan, for libel
and "printing and distributing handbills bearing Gilligan's picture and
the words 'wanted for murder.' " The suit accused King of using the
word *murder* in public statements, claiming Gilligan had been "held up
to ridicule and contempt by his friends and standing as a man and a
police officer have been irreparably injured."[90] This nuisance suit was
partly an attempt by Gilligan to launder his reputation in public, and
many newspapers obliged, citing his awards for good police work.[91]

Meanwhile, civil rights leaders had grown increasingly nervous
about rising Northern white resistance and how it might help Republican Barry Goldwater in the upcoming presidential election. What
would later be termed Nixon's "Southern strategy" of appealing to
moderate anti–civil rights whites was actually happening in the North,
where whites gravitated to anti–civil rights candidates like Goldwater
and then Nixon.[92] That fall, a *New York Times* poll found that 57 percent of New Yorkers believed the civil rights movement had gone too
far—"a large number of those questioned . . . spoke of Negroes' receiving 'everything on a silver platter' and 'reverse discrimination' against
whites." Fifty-four percent felt the movement was going "too fast."[93]

Nearly half said demonstrations hurt the Negro cause, and 80 percent opposed school pairings to promote school desegregation in New York City public schools. King took note of the poll in a conversation with Dorothy Cotton (that the FBI was monitoring) and worried about Northern white support for Goldwater.[94]

The Limits of the Civil Rights Act

On July 2, 1964, Johnson signed the Civil Rights Act, with Martin Luther King flanking him. The next month, in his August 15 column, King focused on the riots in Harlem and Rochester and laid out, in a powerful riff similar to "Letter from a Birmingham Jail," the urgency and impact of Harlem's segregation on Black people:

> As long as thousands of Negroes in Harlem and all the little Harlems of our nation are hovered up in odorous, rat-infested ghettos; as long as the Negro finds himself smothering in an air-tight cage of poverty in the midst of an affluent society; as long as the Negro finds himself as an exile in his own land . . . as long as he has to attend woefully substandard schools and use grossly inadequate facilities; . . . as long as the Negro finds his flight to freedom constantly delayed by strong headwinds of tokenism and small handouts from the white power structure, there will be an ever-present threat of violence and rioting.[95]

But this "why we can't wait" passage detailing Northern racism is much less known than the similarly poetic rendering in the Birmingham letter the year before. Amid his work pressing for the Civil Rights Act in 1964 and his joy at its passage, King was clear that the act was insufficient and inadequate in terms of housing segregation, unemployment, and job discrimination—some of the key areas of Northern racism.[96]

After Johnson's election in November, King observed how "federal, state and municipal governments toy with meager and inadequate solutions while the alarm and militancy of the Negro rises" and reiterated that local leaders like Wagner needed to "look critically into their own law enforcement agencies."[97] He highlighted how the Civil Rights Act "just barely begins to deal with the problems of racial injustice in the South. It does not touch the de facto segregation and injustice of the North."[98]

Then, in the *Saturday Evening Post* just days after the November presidential election, King reiterated that the responsibility for uprisings such as Harlem's lay at the feet of government leaders. "The white leadership—the power structure—must face up to the fact that its sins of omission and commission have challenged our policy of nonviolence." He called the tendency of Northern liberals to attack Black militancy and say Black people were being aggressive or going too fast "cruel and dangerous." He zeroed in on the role of law enforcement: "The mayors of troubled cities . . . would do to look critically into their own law enforcement agencies."[99]

Late in 1964, King sat down for a long interview with Alex Haley in which he reiterated that Harlem's uprising resulted from the lack of change in segregation and inequality in New York: "Violence grows to the degree that injustice prevails," King told Haley. "If you will notice, there have been fewer riots in the South. The reason for this is that the Negro in the South can see some visible, concrete victories in civil rights . . . the fellow in Harlem, to name one Northern ghetto, can't see any victories."[100]

Haley, a Black Republican and friend of the FBI, was invested in pitting Malcolm and Martin against each other. He had hyped that division in a May 1963 *Playboy* article on Malcolm.[101] When he published this interview with King in 1965, Haley put words in King's mouth that King never uttered. Haley quotes King saying "I feel that Malcolm has done himself and our people a great disservice. Fiery, demagogic oratory in the black ghettos, urging Negroes to arm themselves and prepare to engage in violence, as he has done, can reap nothing but grief." In the interview transcripts biographer Jonathan Eig found, King *never* said Malcolm did "our people a great disservice" or "can reap nothing but grief."[102] But Haley knew this feud made for good copy and the FBI wanted to ensure that Malcolm and the Nation of Islam "remained at war with King and the civil rights movement."[103] King, by this point, was so used to being misquoted that he couldn't possibly take on every reporter.

Despite some of their public words, King and Malcolm's political commitments—supporting 1199's hospital strikes, the New York City school boycott, the Downstate Medical Center construction protest—had converged numerous times. But they met only once, just briefly, earlier that year in DC. The year before, in July 1963, Malcolm had written King a letter suggesting that the racial inequality Northern urban Black people continued to face was a "powder keg" and proposing a "united front." [104] King too saw this and increasingly took up the "powder keg" framing and the need for such united-front organizing. Over and over, King highlighted how the Civil Rights Act hadn't taken on the structures of Northern racism; over and over, the public, the media, and political leaders didn't listen until Watts erupted.

International Attention

In September 1964, King had journeyed to Rome, where he met with Pope Paul VI. There he described the progress taking place in the South following the passage of the Civil Rights Act and zeroed in on Northern white resistance, particularly in large Northern cities around housing and school desegregation, jobs, and other matters. He asked the pope to intervene; "in these counties the Catholic Church is very strong and a reaffirmation of its position [on civil rights] would mean much." [105] In other words, when Dr. King met the pope for his first and only time, the problem he chose to focus on was not the South but the North—to ask for the pope's assistance in trying to address white Northern resistance and moving white Catholics toward desegregation and racial justice in their parishes and cities. The next year, in an *Ebony* column, he decried the "Un-Christian Christian," one version of whom marched in the South but returned home to congregations who "were disturbed that a Negro was about to move into their neighborhood." [106]

On October 14, Coretta called Martin in the hospital, where her worn-down husband had been admitted for exhaustion. She had just gotten a call that he had been awarded the Nobel Prize. Stunned, her "joy mixed with panic" at this great honor but also the responsibility they now bore. [107] This was a collective award: "I felt pride and joy and pain too, when I thought of the added responsibilities my husband must bear and it was my burden too." [108] They had a job to do, she felt, around Vietnam and global justice. She stressed to him "the role you must play in achieving world peace, and I will be so glad when the time comes when you can assume that role." [109] In many ways, part of what distinguished the Kings was that at their highest moments, like the Nobel Prize, they saw that these honors came with increased responsibilities.

In late November, King devoted a column to what the Nobel Prize meant to him. On a plane delay from Chicago's O'Hare International Airport to Los Angeles, King recounted, he had watched the ground crew repair the plane. He thought about how the pilots get the credit, but the ground crew made the plane's flight possible. This was true in the movement as well. The ground crew's "names will not go down in history nor splendor of the courage taught in classrooms. They are the unknown soldiers in the second great American Revolution." [110] Again, he understood he was a symbol of a far bigger, courageous group whose work had now gained international recognition.

On his way to Oslo, Norway, to accept the Nobel Prize, King joined an 1199 hospital picket line in Newark, New Jersey. He then stopped off in London, where he highlighted the "hardcore de facto segregation" in the US and the kinds of liberal arguments that "go on ad infinitum about 'crime' and 'culture' "—blaming Black communities for their situation to deflect addressing inequality. He then turned his attention to South African apartheid and the United States' and United Kingdom's "unique responsibility, for it is we, through our investments, through our governments' failure to act decisively, who are guilty of bolstering up the South African tyranny." King underlined the need to pursue what Black South Africans had called for—"a massive movement for economic sanctions." [111] He condemned Britain's own racism and racist immigration policies. Black British radical Diana Collins, who arranged the event, noted how King appeared "a deeply solitary person, a man who has wrestled with God. . . . [H]e came to London from a sick bed and was clearly exhausted. But the feeling of his inner strength remains with one; he moves through the crowds, through both execration and exclamation, his eyes fixed on a distant goal." [112]

Then he headed to Norway. The Kings took separate planes—even for the Nobel Peace Prize. These were their constant calculations; that way, if one plane failed or was targeted, the children would not lose both parents. Speaking to the media in Oslo, King highlighted the limits of the Civil Rights Act: "We are not finished. . . . It will not be a battle to integrate lunch counters but a problem of dealing with de facto segregation in schools, jobs, housing and other such areas." [113]

Coretta observed how Martin seemed melancholy in Norway. For both of them, this honor brought a combination of joy and sorrow, highlighting the immensity of the task at hand, the work that hadn't been done, the expectations it placed on them, and, particularly to Coretta, their responsibility to a broader world community. [114] But she encouraged him to see what he had accomplished. "God has allowed you to see the promised land"—to envision a different world was possible. [115] They had seen the unimaginable become possible—from Montgomery to Ghana to the Civil Rights Act's passage. We may not get to see real justice or equality, she underlined to him, but few people even get to see its possibility. On their way back from Oslo, they stopped in New York City. Happy to be back in the US, they were relaxing for a moment when their hotel phone rang with a vile death threat. Martin was suddenly drained—angry and unraveled. "Maybe this is a sick society," he said to Coretta.[116]

Doing a clever about-face, Mayor Wagner presented King with the city's Medallion of Honor, heaping praise upon him—a far cry from how he'd treated King just five months earlier.[117] This liberal tendency, so pronounced in Wagner, would frustrate King time and again. A certain stripe of liberal would embrace King and even honor him, only so far as King could be positioned as a mascot for change in the South. When King highlighted local problems, problems outside the South, that was a bridge too far, and they would shut him down. Mayor Wagner would see no contradiction in bestowing the medallion while rejecting King's urgent recommendations to address the city's inequality.

Later that day, the celebration continued with an official city reception at the Waldorf Astoria. Vice President Hubert Humphrey was photographed shaking the Kings' hands. Humphrey too would shirk King's demands. Many prominent liberals wanted to take pictures but couldn't be counted on for sustained commitment to enact justice across the country. For his part, King contrasted his visit to Scandinavia, where they "have no unemployment and no slums," with the "deep but unnecessary economic malady in our country"—and called for a broad alliance to address it.[118]

That night, King spoke to a massive crowd of more than ten thousand New Yorkers at Harlem's 369th Armory. Malcolm X was in the audience that night, but they didn't speak. King had made it clear in his Nobel speech in Norway that the award wasn't for him alone but also for the ground crew driving the movement forward. But that night in Harlem, he explained to the crowd what the award meant to him personally, living "almost every day under the threat of death. . . . This isn't the usual pattern of my life, to have people saying nice things about me. Oh this is a marvelous mountaintop. . . . I wish I could stay here tonight. But the valley calls me."[119]

Returning to Boston

Well acquainted with Boston's racism from his student days, King returned to the city multiple times in the early 1960s to join a burgeoning movement for school desegregation. The movement attacking Boston's segregated and unequal schools, led by Ruth Batson, Mel King, and parent organizer Ellen Jackson, had heated up. But Black organizers were constantly gaslighted and told that all was well in the Cradle of Liberty.

Under Batson, the NAACP did its own research, finding that the city spent $340 on white students but only $240 for Black students. Four elementary schools serving Black children had such health and safety violations that they'd been recommended to be shut down; eight others were below code.[120] Most schools had no Black teachers, as Black people made up less than .5 percent of the teaching force. Speaking at the Ford Hall Forum in Boston on March 24, 1963, King called out the Cradle of Liberty's racism.[121] Three months later, community organizers called for a "Stay Out for Freedom" school boycott—and three thousand students, nearly half of all Black high school students in Boston, stayed out of school.[122] King came to Boston to support it.[123] The city condemned it and threatened to discipline the parents of the students.

White Bostonians reacted angrily to charges of racism and segregation. And the nation joined them. When Black reporter Ted Poston tried to get his *New York Post* editor to send him to Boston in 1963 to cover the city's growing school desegregation movement, his editor refused, saying, "What have Negroes in Boston to complain about?"[124] The head of Boston's School Committee announced, "We don't have problem schools. We have problem students."[125] When Black community members en masse tried to bring up the issue of desegregation at a School Committee meeting (filling the meeting with hundreds outside), the committee shut it down. "They told us our kids were stupid and this was why they didn't learn," Batson recalled.[126] The vehemence of white antagonism and the personal attacks on their children stunned Black organizers.

A second school boycott was called for February 26, 1964, drawing nearly twenty thousand students and teachers.[127] King "heartily endorsed" the second school boycott, for exposing the myth of segregation as "inherently sectional problems."[128] The city flatly rejected Black demands for school desegregation, Black teacher hiring, and school equity. But white leaders framed their opposition around preserving "neighborhood schools" and opposing "busing"—though busing was amply being used in Boston, in part to keep students segregated. School Committee chair Louise Day Hicks grew increasingly popular among white Bostonians for her opposition to desegregation—and the national media lapped up the busing language, never questioning that white Bostonians actually had no problem with busing when it was used to maintain segregation.

In April 1965, King came to town for a series of events. Organizers sought a meeting for King with the Boston School Committee to build further pressure around the city's school segregation. In response, Hicks sought to limit the number of people at the meeting and who could speak.[129] In much of this support work across the country, King walked a tightrope, trying to use his presence to influence white power structures, even as those structures attempted to use him as an intermediary to the Black community. He "questioned his own motivations time and again," Coretta recalled.[130] In Boston, King insisted local leaders got to speak; he wouldn't allow limits on his ability to share his time with them. Organizers had hoped King's attendance would make the School Committee listen to their demands. But when King tried to highlight Boston's school inequality and urge desegregation, the School Committee shut the meeting down.[131]

During this visit, King addressed both houses of the Massachusetts legislature. King pointedly explained that "segregation, whether it is de jure segregation of certain sections of the South or de facto segregation of the North, is a new form of slavery covered up with certain niceties."[132] This "de facto" framing for Northern segregation that King regularly used had arisen after the *Brown* decision. It appealed to Northern sensibilities seeking to distinguish the segregation in their cities from the segregation many decried in the South. Black lawyer Paul Zuber, who litigated cases in New York, New Jersey, and Chicago, wrote:

> The word *de facto segregation* was never heard until the historic Supreme Court decision of 1954. . . . Now the law is clear, segregation by legislative act was illegal and in violation of the Constitution of the United States. Now the North needed a rationalization to continue its brand of racial segregation.[133]

The term helped cast their segregation as more innocent and thus requiring no action, historian Matthew Lassiter argues, even though there was ample evidence "of comprehensive State action in producing deeply entrenched patterns of residential and educational segregation."[134] While King used the term, he tried to make clear that

Northern "de facto" segregation wasn't accidental or naturally occurring but in fact systematic and venal, a prettified form of slavery.

"Now is the time to end segregation in the public schools," King told the Massachusetts State House gathering, urging the legislature to pass the Racial Imbalance Act to combat school segregation.[135] The law required racially imbalanced (more than 50 percent nonwhite) schools to desegregate or else risk losing their state funding and passed in August 1965.[136] Boston Public Schools appealed the law for years in court to stall and never lost their funding.

On April 23, King led a march of twenty-two thousand to the Boston Commons.[137] Massachusetts governor John Volpe had proclaimed the day Martin Luther King Day—but King made clear the day would be devoted to the urgent issues facing Boston: slum housing, municipal code enforcement, antipoverty programs, and segregated education.[138] There were false claims in the media (later picked up by biographers) that this was the *first* march King had led outside the South, which contributed to the misimpressions that King was largely divorced from the struggles of Blacks in the North, that this march wasn't a product of robust organizing in Boston but one King needed to head for it to happen, and that King marched only in marches that he led.[139]

The march began at the Carter Playground in Roxbury, where King had played pickup basketball as a grad student. "Little did I imagine that such a day was possible when I walked through this same Boston Common as a student 10 years ago." Speaking through a bullhorn, King declared: "Now in the North, the twin evils of housing and employment discrimination stand out as they do all over this country. These must be grappled with in a very significant and determined manner."[140] The sickness in the South, he underlined, was also in the North.[141] King visited Roxbury to see some of the city's deteriorated segregated schools and housing but was not allowed inside any school buildings. King seemed uneasy during the march, as white crowds of counterprotesters kept surging out from the sidelines toward him. The police received at least seven death threats on King's life that day; police and the National Guard formed a "flying wedge to keep the way clear."[142] King's life was in danger not just in the South but across the country as well.

The determined spirit and size of the march stunned Ruth Batson.[143] In her address on Boston Common, she extolled how "this cradle of liberty has lulled too many into a state of apathy—into a state of smug false security where we had really come to believe that all was well.

But all was not well and all is not well."[144] After the march, King and a twelve-member delegation of local civil rights leaders presented Mayor John F. Collins with a "bill of particulars" that called for ending racial discrimination in housing, welfare, and employment in Boston. That evening, King highlighted his own experiences of Boston's housing discrimination as a student before a crowd of a thousand people at Temple Israel.

King had become familiar with white Northerners welcoming him only to react furiously when attention turned to local inequality. He was criticized so much for helping to lead this march "in the home of abolitionism" (as the media referred to Boston) that the next week the *Chicago Defender* leapt to his defense. "Some of us are yet clinging to the erroneous view that racialism flourishes only below the Mason-Dixon line," the *Defender* wrote. "Negroes who dwell in the North know that it is not so. Dr. King has called for an end to racial restrictions on housing, to job descriptions and to segregation which exists in fact . . . in Boston public schools."[145]

King's repeated trips to the Cradle of Liberty reveal how robust Boston's school desegregation movement was in the mid-1960s, as well as the ways many white Bostonians were outraged for having their own segregation called out. "We're not racist," they said again and again, while massive white resistance swelled in Boston as it did across the country, North and South. It would take another decade and an NAACP federal lawsuit before federal judge W. Arthur Garrity Jr. would step in and order the comprehensive desegregation of Boston's public schools to begin in 1974. And still, the nation continued to view Boston's problem as "busing."

Indeed, the United States looks very different in the years 1963–1965 from the vantage of Northern movements and King's efforts to support them. King's supposed popularity and access to political officials in these years existed so long as he didn't use it to point out local problems or systemic national racism. If only Northern politicians and citizens had been willing to address their own segregation and inequality, if only federal enforcement of civil rights legislation had actually extended to the North, King would say repeatedly, then what happened on the streets of cities across America could have been avoided.

5

Voting for Ghettos

King and the Struggle in Los Angeles Before Watts

> White people are astounded by Birmingham. . . . They
> don't want to realize that there is not one step, morally or
> actually, between Birmingham and Los Angeles.
>
> —James Baldwin[1]

Two weeks after negotiating the Birmingham agreement, King headed to the West Coast. Describing King as a "militant cleric," LA's Black newspaper the *Los Angeles Sentinel* trumpeted excitedly, "Dr. King to Get a Hero's Welcome."[2] On May 26, 1963, an audience of fifty thousand people gathered at Wrigley Field in South Los Angeles to cheer for King as he underscored the urgency of challenging local racism as well.

"Birmingham or Los Angeles, the cry is always the same: We want to be free," King declared to massive applause from the crowd.[3] Thanking Angelenos for their support of the Birmingham campaign, he emphasized that what was even more important was fighting LA's system of racial injustice. "You asked me what Los Angeles can do to help us in Birmingham. The most important thing that you can do is to set Los Angeles free because you have segregation and discrimination here, and police brutality."[4] King stressed how behind the city's liberal façade, many Northern urban power structures were just as racially intractable as Birmingham's.[5]

King was familiar with LA's systemic racism and the multivarious movements against it. In the decade between the Montgomery bus boycott and the Watts uprising, King made at least fifteen trips to Southern California and stressed the city's "segregation and discrimination here, and police brutality."[6] Indeed, King would join more than fifty LA rallies, mobilizations, freedom meetings, and marches in the years before the Watts uprising, raising his voice to challenge the city's pervasive inequality.[7]

Segregation and Police Brutality in the City of Angels

Portrayed as a city of possibility and innovation, Los Angeles was a destination for more than half a million African American migrants in the post–World War II period. Yet segregation worsened alongside the migration. King came to understand the structured inequality Black Californians faced—from housing to jobs to schools to policing—and the city's various power structures, from the mayor to the police chief to organized white citizens to the media, that kept it in place. The city's segregation was both similar to and different from Birmingham's. Most public swimming pools, hotels, and other business establishments in LA barred Black patrons but didn't necessarily have signs. Redlining and restrictive covenants formed a legal wall around South Los Angeles that Black Angelenos largely could not scale.

Over the course of a series of trips between 1958 and 1961, King became familiar with the city's entrenched segregation. In February 1958, he held a three-day residency at Caltech in Los Angeles, giving three speeches during his stay, and helped raise money for the Youth March that Rustin was organizing in Washington, DC. The *Los Angeles Times* did not cover his appearances.[8] In March 1960, he spoke to crowds of thousands at churches across LA.[9] Three months later he returned to hold a Civil Rights Rally drawing five thousand to push the Democratic Party to include a civil rights platform at its national convention.[10] His multiple visits in 1961 drew tens of thousands of people—and helped familiarize King with LA's many inequalities.

These issues would crystallize in 1962 as the city faced a police-brutality crisis. On April 27, having witnessed two men getting clothes out of a car trunk and deciding they were selling stolen goods, Los Angeles Police Department officers assaulted members of LA's Nation of Islam outside their mosque. The NOI members bristled at the treatment and fought back, one man taking one of the cop's guns.[11] As dozens more cops arrived, they moved inside the mosque, lining up members inside. "We ought to shoot these n—s," one cop taunted. "We got them lined up and we ought to kill every one of them." The unarmed secretary of the mosque Ronald X Stokes had been attempting to help one of the men when Officer Donald Weese shot him. The autopsy found Stokes had been stomped, kicked, and bludgeoned while dying. Meanwhile, officers shot and paralyzed William X Rogers and seriously wounded five other members outside the mosque.[12] "There was an obscene obsession with Black men's genitals as they were prodded, kicked, and their pants torn off," according to writers Mike Davis and Jon Wiener. "Two of the wounded Muslims, moreover, had been shot in the groin."[13] A police officer was also shot.

Fourteen NOI members—and not a single officer—faced charges of resisting arrest and attempted murder stemming from this police-instigated melee. In response, a united-front movement of Black Angelenos from the NAACP to the NOI grew to challenge the pattern of police abuse in the city. For years, the local NAACP had brought tabulations of police brutality to city attention with "no results." On May 13, 1962, Malcolm X came to LA to demand justice for Ron Stokes and address a 1,200-person mass meeting billed as the "Citizens Protest Rally Committee." He was in the midst of helping build this movement when Elijah Muhammad recalled him from LA.

Less than a month later, King threw his support in as well. At a packed address at Zion Baptist Church, he spoke directly on police brutality. "There is no compromise on this issue," he stressed.[14] Many commentators hoped to pit King against Malcolm X and get him to denounce the NOI. Refusing to fall for the bait, he emphasized, "I am more concerned with getting rid of the conditions that brought this sort of organization into being than the organization itself."[15]

Part of the solution, King believed, was increased Black political power.[16] Given ongoing police violence, Black Angelenos sought the ouster of longtime police chief William Parker. After becoming chief in 1950, Parker had professionalized and militarized the LAPD while treating Black LA as a community to be contained. Police brutality and harassment was rampant; historian Gerald Horne described how officers "randomly and arbitrarily beat and tortured black men, even those who were not suspected of anything."[17] Yet Chief Parker claimed there was no segregation problem in LA; in fact, he proclaimed that the most "dislocated minority in America today is the police."[18] Black Angelenos' repeated calls for Parker's dismissal had been ignored. King now called for organized voting power "so that you can say to the political leaders of this city . . . this particular chief of police or this particular person will have to go."[19] King's speech at Zion also condemned "the three major social evils" of war, economic injustice, and racism.[20] Concerns about police brutality, housing discrimination, and war that have typically been associated with the last two years of King's life were on ample display in 1962.

These interlocking concerns had in large measure been underlined by Coretta Scott King for years. In fact, as Martin was speaking about these issues on the West Coast, she was preparing to go to Geneva, Switzerland, with a Women Strike for Peace (WSP) delegation to take part in a nineteen-nation disarmament conference. Present at the creation of the National Committee for a SANE Nuclear Policy in 1957, she had spoken out against war and nuclear weapons in Washington, DC, in 1961.[21] Having gotten interested in the Women's International League for Peace and Freedom (WILPF) in Montgomery because it made no distinction between peace and freedom, she attended some meetings and then joined the organization.

Scott King was one of three Black women who traveled to Geneva in the fifty-person WSP delegation. Martin had supported her decision to go. "You need to do that," he made clear, even though Dexter was only a year old.[22] The delegation sought "to express the hopes and fears of all women in their deep concern for the survival of mankind," their statement read, to pressure the United States and Soviet Union to sign a Nuclear Test-Ban Treaty.[23] Scott King told the press that "the rights that we had achieved were meaningless unless there was a world to exercise those rights."[24] The US representative was disdainful of this group of "hysterical females." The WSP delegation met with the Soviet delegation and, according to historian Amy Swerdlow, "was a visible and audible presence in Geneva."[25] Given this direct challenge to US Cold War prerogatives, WSP leaders would be hauled in front of HUAC six months later.

The punishing climate of the Cold War made peace advocacy exceedingly rare for Black or white Americans. But Scott King pushed forward, the Geneva trip deepening her global commitments.[26] In 1963, she addressed a WSP rally in New York and led a march to the UN carrying a sign saying "Let's Make Our Earth a Nuclear Free Zone" to mark the signing of the Nuclear Test-Ban Treaty and press for further disarmament.[27] They met with UN secretary-general U Thant. She left these New York events for Washington, DC, and another WSP action, telling the press she was proud to be identified with the peace movement.[28] She wasn't going to let red-baiting make her shrink. "I can never be free until every black man from Johannesburg, South Africa, to Jackson, Mississippi, is free."[29]

Growing even more outspoken as US involvement in Vietnam escalated in the early 1960s, Coretta Scott King became "the family spokes-
person on the peace issues."[30] Martin agreed, telling an interviewer he
left it to her to "take the stands and make the meetings on the peace
issue." The reporter pushed King on how he had found such a political
companion. Did he "research her before your marriage that she had
the potential? Or train her in this direction?" King laughed and said,
"It may have been the other way. When I met her, she was very concerned with all the things we are trying to do now. . . . I wish I could
say to satisfy my masculine ego that I led her down this path but I
must say we went down here together."[31]

In Los Angeles, King reiterated his "ALL-HERE-NOW" demand.
Because he used this ALL-HERE-NOW mantra in so many of his
speeches in the early 1960s across the country, the next year, television
talk show host David Susskind questioned King about it and whether
"in your lifetime you will see 'all, now, and here' in terms of equality
of opportunity, equality of education and housing and employment?"
King answered that "in between seven and ten years, we will be able
to see all over the South a desegregated society—that is, the legal barriers will be broken down," but he completely avoided answering the
question about when it would be achieved in the North.[32]

King gave ten speeches in that June trip, speaking to huge crowds
in Pasadena and San Diego. He returned repeatedly to LA in 1962 and
1963. Governor Brown and Mayor Sam Yorty welcomed him to the
city. It was a media opportunity. They wanted to celebrate the King
of the South while refusing to address what he was saying about the
segregation and police brutality endemic to California. Yorty had been
elected mayor in 1961 in part by promising Black voters he would
"school" police chief Parker but then refused to do so once in office.[33]
The mayor was a member of a segregated private club, did not support
school desegregation, helped expand highway construction that further segregated LA's metro area, and became a passionate supporter of
the police. He would favor token gestures like Freedom Days to try to
assuage Black LA without having to take substantive action.

The day before King spoke at the LA rally in May 1963, the jurors
in the Stokes trial went into deliberation. Many Black Angelenos were
galled that the NOI was being put on trial rather than the police. In the
year since Stokes's murder, police and city leadership had remained

intransigent in the face of growing Black outrage, blaming Black Angelenos for the problem. In a public forum with the mayor in September 1962, even national NAACP head Roy Wilkins called attention to the city's "long reputation" under Chief Parker for police brutality.[34]

Mayor Yorty lashed out at the city's NAACP branch for its "agitation," claiming that "they are bringing about the very condition they are complaining about."[35] He reiterated his 100 percent support for Chief Parker. LA's NAACP struck back, claiming the Muslims were "scapegoated" to cover up a pattern of police brutality in the city. A coalition of activists pressed the issue, leading the city to create a blue-ribbon committee to "study" the problem. But little change in police practice resulted. LA NAACP president Christopher Taylor blasted the committee's report: "They have ignored all complaints of the community and now they can keep on doing the same thing."[36] Taylor's influence helped King foreground the urgency of addressing police abuse in the North. Alongside police brutality, Black Angelenos objected to the extreme overpolicing of Black and Chicano neighborhoods and the relentless stop-and-frisking of Black and Chicano youth.[37]

With police abuse continuing despite steady organizing, the NOI tried to use the trial to expose police brutality in the city. Joining that effort, King highlighted LA's problem of police brutality at Wrigley Field. The May 26 Freedom Rally was part of a full day of action around the city's racism. Dorothy Dandridge, Rita Moreno, Paul Newman, Sammy Davis Jr., and Dick Gregory all took part. The *Los Angeles Times* described it as "the largest civil rights rally ever held here," but then tried to cast it as rally-fundraiser for the Southern movement; deep in the article they were forced to note that King had "charg[ed] that de facto segregation here is as bad as Birmingham's segregation."[38] *Segregated as Birmingham*, King stressed. Like in New York, King confronted LA's political leaders who denied any systemic problem and offered token solutions. "We are tired of gradualism, tokenism, look-how-far-you've-comism," King emphasized that May afternoon.[39]

Inspired by the Freedom Rally and King's visit, seventy-six community and political groups across the city formed the United Civil Rights Committee in June 1963 to create a new united-front direct-action movement.[40] They issued their own version of "Letter from a Birmingham Jail" attesting that "all deliberate speed has meant no speed at all."[41] The UCRC demanded total integration of schools through rezoning district lines, desegregation in housing and jobs, and a civilian complaint review board of the police. And they promised relentless direct action to follow if nothing changed. The *Los Angeles Times* described it as "an unprecedented ultimatum."[42]

Schools were a key concern. Similar to New York, LA's schools were deeply segregated and grew desperately overcrowded in the decade after *Brown*. As the city kept adjusting zoning lines to keep white schools white, schools serving Black students were moved to double-session days—despite many open seats in white schools. Textbooks often contained "happy slave tales" and other demeaning portrayals of Black people in history and literature.[43] The teaching staff was overwhelmingly white. LA's NAACP had done a survey, finding that less than 5 percent of the city's teachers were Black; some districts refused to hire Black teachers altogether.[44] Into the 1960s, some white teachers used corporal punishment on Black students and more extreme forms of school discipline like expulsion were introduced into the city's schools in the wake of *Brown*.[45] So LA's educational segregation did not derive simply from racialized housing patterns, as school officials liked to claim, but from the ways school officials drew and redrew zoning lines, restricted hiring, apportioned school resources unequally, and provided few college preparation classes while increasing school punishment in Black schools.

A leading activist in this fight was Marnesba Tackett. Born February 4, 1908, in St. Louis and active in the NAACP as a teenager, Tackett had lived in Georgia; in 1952 she moved to Los Angeles, where she found "very little better than what I found in the South."[46] Tackett and other community leaders saw how, as more Black people migrated to the city, the Board of Education redrew district lines to keep Black children in Black schools. Attacking the board's claim of color blindness, Tackett, who became the UCRC's education chair, compared Los Angeles schools to "those of Alabama and Mississippi."[47] She embarked on a project to examine textbooks for racist stereotypes and lack of exposure to African American history and culture and would sue the schools for these racist representations. Beginning in 1963, the FBI contacted Tackett every six weeks for the next four years—making it known agents were watching her.[48]

The UCRC drew up a list of demands: calling on the city to redraw district lines, transfer Black students out of overcrowded schools, diversify the curriculum, and change the teacher-hiring process to increase the number of nonwhite teachers and distribute them throughout the entire district. Tackett found it "unthinkable" that LA

continued to "concentrate Negro, Mexican-American and other minorities into overcrowded and segregated schools" when there were
numerous "under-enrolled schools in 'white areas.' "[49] But the board
did nothing, preferring to "study" the issue.

Refusing to even put a plan forth for desegregation, LA's Board of
Education made clear that its constituency was white families and cast
Black parents as putting inappropriate pressure. The city's schools were
not segregated; rather, nonwhite families and Black students themselves were blamed for "negative attitudes toward education," and "the
lack of hope and motivation among some of these families which leads
them into negative attitudes toward education."[50] The BOE proposed
increased funding to "culturally disadvantaged" schools, including
money for new programs aimed at addressing "juvenile delinquency."

Many neighborhoods, like South Gate, which bordered Black South
LA, were all-white enclaves that the city protected by repeatedly ad-
justing the school zoning lines.[51] Finally, in the last week of school in
June 1963, five Black students desegregated South Gate High School.
White Angelenos threw eggs and bricks, waved Confederate flags, and
spewed racial epithets at them.[52]

When Tackett asked King what Black Angelenos could do to assist
Birmingham, he answered, "Set Los Angeles free."[53] The UCRC began
holding weekly protest marches downtown throughout the summer
of 1963. King joined them in August for a mass march on the Board of
Education alongside CORE's James Farmer, the NAACP's Roy Wilkins,
and SNCC's James Forman, hoping to escalate the campaign against
LA's segregated schools.[54] The Los Angeles Times called it a "protest
against alleged de facto segregation" and downplayed the event.[55] That
these four major civil rights leaders joined together to march against
LA's school segregation attests to the urgency of the city's school inequality and the vigorous movement against it. This might have been
the only local struggle where the four marched together, yet this is
ignored in most King histories, as it was in the national press. While
Birmingham had been covered as a movement with national implica-
tions, Los Angeles was not.

Unlike in Birmingham, this multivarious nonviolent movement garnered little change or even acknowledgment. In Birmingham, Attorney
General Robert Kennedy sent Burke Marshall to negotiate. No such
thing happened in LA. In Birmingham, business leaders and the city
finally agreed in early May to desegregate public accommodations, a
program of upgrading Black employment, and a biracial committee

to monitor the progress. In LA, the city agreed to nothing—no deseg-regation of schools, no new hiring of Black and Chicano teachers. In fact, faced with this growing desegregation movement in the city, LA's Board of Education in September 1963 issued another report placing responsibilities for school problems again on the "negative attitudes towards education" and "lack of motivation" of Black and Latino stu-dents and families.[56] For King, such cultural arguments "go on end-lessly" about "standards" but simply "blamed [Black people] for their own victimization."[57]

Three weeks after LA's mass march for school desegregation came the March on Washington. "We can never be satisfied as long as the Negro is the victim of the unspeakable horrors of police brutality," King extolled in a less-remembered part of his speech. It's usually assumed that King was referring to Birmingham's police—but King knew police brutality wasn't just a Southern problem. In fact, one of the march's unfulfilled demands was to establish the US attorney general's authority to issue injunctive suits—including against police departments—when people's constitutional rights were violated.[58] Black communities needed a concrete way to take on the racism of po-lice departments like the LAPD.

Throughout the fall of 1963, Black parents, students, and community leaders continued holding sit-ins, sleep-ins, hunger strikes, and study-ins to protest LA's school inequality. Hundreds of student protest-ers marched. Young people lined the halls of the Board of Education building with a study-in and disrupted a meeting with a sing-in in the fall.[59] But the board remained intransigent, and most white Angelenos didn't see a problem.

California Moves to Legalize Segregation and King Steps Forward

Late in the year, Black community organizers were forced to shift focus to try to defeat a menacing proposition on the state ballot.

Housing in California was deeply segregated. The postwar hous-ing boom, aided by the GI Bill and federal highway construction, had transformed the state's landscape and put homeownership in reach of many white Californians. It had fueled massive housing development and deepened housing segregation in the state. Redlined Black and Latino neighborhoods grew impossibly overcrowded, as most Black and Latino Angelenos found much of the city's metro area off-limits to rent or buy. While the population density was 5,500 people per square mile in most of LA, in the Black neighborhoods of South LA it was 16,400.

Activists had fought for years and finally won a statewide fair housing act in September 1963, called the Rumford Fair Housing Act after its sponsor, Assemblyman William Rumford, the first Black person elected to the California legislature. The new law made discrimination in public housing, in publicly financed homes and properties, and in all residential properties with more than four units illegal (pressure by homeowners and real estate interests had exempted smaller units and single-family homes without government financing).

Almost immediately, developers, business leaders, real estate leaders, block associations, and white residents rose up to block it. Many white Californians saw any fair housing law, even if it didn't touch the sale of most single-family homes, as a dangerous opening to "losing their neighborhood." Similar to their Southern counterparts, *any* desegregation was too much desegregation. Referring to the Rumford Act as the "Forced Housing Act," they used contrasting images of happy suburban white families with deviant families of color.[60] They managed to secure an obliquely worded proposition to overturn the act on the state ballot—prohibiting the state from abridging Californians' right to discriminate in the sale and rental of properties.

A broad coalition of Black, Latino, and Asian American groups came together to try to defeat Proposition 14, and King crisscrossed the state multiple times in 1964 to join their fight. King made clear its passage would be "one of the most shameful developments in our nation's history."[61] Labeling King a "Communist" for this work, many white Angelenos picketed the SCLC's Western office, run by King's longtime friend Rev. Thomas Kilgore Jr. Carrying signs reading "King Has Hate, Does Travel" and "Thank God for [LAPD police] Chief Parker," they viewed advocating for fair housing as a destruction to the "sacred" right of private property.[62] Many white Californians saw Black nonviolent direct action around school and housing segregation as a problem—and un-American—and looked to Chief Parker and the LAPD to keep Black people in their place.

In February 1964, King came to LA blasting Proposition 14; if it passed, "the nation would be set back, civil rights would be set back, and the cause of Democracy would be set back." The *Los Angeles Times* covered his speech but provided no substance as to why King was so outraged about it.[63] A second article noted a "standing room only" crowd but provided nothing of what King said regarding LA's endemic housing segregation and the threat of overturning the Rumford Act.[64]

Instead, the *Times* supported the ballot initiative. On February 2, the *Times'* editorial board endorsed Proposition 14. In a classic move, the newspaper praised the *goal* of the Rumford Act and *general principle* of antidiscrimination. But it made clear that private property was a sacred right and attacked the Rumford Act as an "artificial law" that infringed on a man's right to private property: "The philosophical fallacy of the Rumford Act, unhappily, lies in seeking to correct a social evil while simultaneously destroying what we deem a basic right in a free society."[65] This framing of the issue was reflected in the paper's coverage over the next nine months. The *Times* covered Proposition 14 repeatedly, publishing at least an article a week. Largely replicating the ways proponents highlighted private property and personal freedoms, the paper assiduously covered real estate interests and other backers of the proposition.[66] In the coverage, the *Times* largely did not expose the rampant housing discrimination that the Rumford Act sought to address and how Proposition 14 would further legalize segregation. Rather than describing white people who wanted to repeal the fair housing law as "fair housing opponents" or "segregationists," like they did in the South, they preferred the awkward "housing law's foes."[67]

In April 1964, Yorty was reelected as LA's mayor in a landslide. No longer dependent on Black voters, "his inner racist was now given full scope."[68] Yorty refused federal guidelines that would have made millions of dollars available for youth jobs and in 1965 canceled a recreation program for twenty thousand LA teenagers. Yet Yorty would proclaim the city's race relations the best in the nation.

While Governor Brown had come out decisively against Proposition 14, he decried *any* kind of disruptive civil rights protest around housing, jobs, or schools as counterproductive. So he too cast Black activism as a problem, occasionally intimating that these activists were the cause of the white "backlash" behind Proposition 14.[69] He wanted civil rights organizers to stand down. The *Los Angeles Times*, like Brown, linked rising Black militancy to the white "backlash" against the Rumford Act, as they termed it, implying that Black militancy had forced white Angelenos to oppose fair housing.[70] Then, in May, when a California poll found confusion among voters about Proposition 14's "consequences" in terms of legalizing housing segregation, the paper expressed surprise— refusing to see its own responsibility in this confusion.[71]

By spring, Republicans were predicting that Proposition 14 would sail to victory. "The people are fed up with this type of ramrod legislation," Barry Goldwater's state finance director crowed. The next week, a state senate committee began investigating "the nature, extent, and causes of racial segregation in housing in California"—in effect leaving open the question of whether racial segregation in housing existed at all. The committee would take testimony from both pro– and anti–Rumford Act residents and business interests on questions such as "family and cultural influences," "apprehension of loss of property values," "apprehension on the part of builders of their ability to sell other houses," and "apprehension on the part of landlords of their ability to rent other apartments and the financial responsibility of proposed tenant."[72] In other words, the California Senate was convening a two-day public hearing that reduced housing segregation to fears and property values—the framings that Proposition 14 proponents favored. It did not ask property owners to outline the racial makeup of their buildings or Black and Latino Californians to testify to the discrimination they encountered in trying to rent or buy housing.

For nearly a week in late May and early June, King stumped across California, railing against Proposition 14. He traveled to San Francisco's Cow Palace for an interfaith rally to raise money for the Southern movement and campaign against Proposition 14. Repealing the Rumford Act, King again stressed, would be a major setback for California and American democracy. Next, at the Los Angeles Palladium, he extolled: "Every citizen must rise up and save [the fair housing law]." But his alarm was largely confined to the Black press.[73]

Alongside his anti–Proposition 14 work, King was simultaneously engaged in a campaign against public segregation in St. Augustine, Florida, and was arrested protesting a segregated restaurant. This campaign in St. Augustine garnered a tremendous amount of serious news coverage by national outlets like the *New York Times* and *Los Angeles Times*. While the campaign against Proposition 14 was just as serious a fight against segregation, it wasn't covered that way. In two different articles, the *New York Times* took note that King was in California on a "speaking tour" but made no mention of why.[74] While the *Los Angeles Times* did cover some of King's appearances, the paper continued to obscure the state's rampant housing segregation—largely casting Proposition 14 proponents as reasonable and civil rights activists as unreasonable.[75]

On June 1, King spoke before more than fifteen thousand people at

Los Angeles Memorial Coliseum. Saying Proposition 14 "would legal-ize segregation," he stressed the urgency to vote no, arguing that its passage would be "one of the great tragedies of the 20th Century for democracy."[76] Then, in an interview with the local CBS station in San Diego, he challenged the host, who spoke of a growing "backlash," given Alabama governor George Wallace's support in the presidential primary in many pockets of California. Many white Northerners "had never been committed" to civil rights, King emphasized.[77] The CBS in-terviewer tried to bait King by criticizing Brooklyn CORE's stall-in and the lack of "responsible Negro leadership" in Northern cities. King pushed back. "If there is not a strong move to do something about the injustices the Negroes face, if there isn't something dramatic done . . . I'm sure it will increase the discontent, the restlessness, the frustra-tion, and the despair of the Negro that it will be much more difficult to keep the struggle disciplined and non-violent."[78] Here and elsewhere across California—more than a year before the Watts uprising—King pointed out the costs of ignoring Black cries around the dramatic racial inequalities in the state and the potential for unrest if white intransigence continued.

Massive resistance was happening in California, but to call it such was anathema.[79] At the same time, a *Los Angeles Times* columnist de-fended Wallace supporters as "a genuine reaction of many Democrats who are not racists to the violent demonstrations that have rocked the nation."[80] This was another persistent deflection that King and North-ern activists encountered: White Northerners who sought to protect "their homes" and "their schools" were not racist. They were taxpay-ers and committed parents just reacting to excessive Black militancy.

On October 18, two weeks before the election, the *Los Angeles Times* doubled down on its support of Proposition 14. While stressing their "consistent support to the national and local struggle for basic civil rights," they again endorsed Prop 14 to provide "absolute discretion in the choice of buyer or renter," and decried how the Rumford Act "abridge[d] property rights."[81] Just like Southern newspapers that as-serted the right of business owners to decide whom to serve at their lunch counter or store, the city's paper of record supported the sacred right of Californians to decide whom to rent or sell to.

A week before the election, King returned to LA. He urged a "thun-derous no" on Proposition 14. Calling it "sinful," he emphasized how it would "write segregation in the California Constitution."[82] Despite King's forcefulness and repeated trips to the state, the *New York Times* continued to ignore his urgency on how California was poised to legalize segregation.

Despite the vigorous efforts of this broad, multiracial coalition, Proposition 14 passed by a staggering two-to-one margin—even as 60 percent of Californians voted to return Lyndon Johnson to the White House. (Orange County and San Diego County—the heart of the white homeowners' movement—voted for Goldwater.) With three out of four white California voters supporting it, Proposition 14 united a bipartisan coalition of white bedfellows—a harbinger of the rise of Ronald Reagan and the New Right, the power of real estate interests in the state, and the prerogatives of many white Democrats who didn't want desegregation coming to their neighborhoods either.

The message was stark: this was massive resistance, West Coast–style. Civil rights were all right, as long as they didn't come home to California.[83] King termed it a "vote for ghettos."[84] Nine months later, he would finger Proposition 14's passage as the kindling for the Watts uprising.

King returned to Los Angeles in February 1965, a few days after the assassination of Malcolm X.

Three weeks earlier, Malcolm X had come to Selma to join the voting rights movement that SNCC and SCLC were building in Alabama. Martin was in jail. Both Malcolm and Coretta addressed a mass meeting and talked afterward. Malcolm told her he had hoped to visit her husband in jail to tell him, "I didn't come to Selma to make his job more difficult but I thought that if the White people understood what the alternative was that they would be more inclined to listen to your husband." Malcolm saw a role he could play to help their movement.

Malcolm made a significant impression on Coretta Scott King, who noted how different he was from his portrayal in the media. He "had such a gentle manner."[85] According to Harry Belafonte, he and King talked about Malcolm "all the time . . . Martin loved Malcolm's power, his discipline, his self-education, his clarity."[86] Belafonte stressed the "most wanted goal" of King and Malcolm coming together and how many in the movement, like himself, were working on it.[87] Coretta described the work they could have done together; Malcolm "could have been a tremendous bridge, you know, in bringing Black Muslims and other Black people in the Civil Rights Movement together."[88]

The assassination of Malcolm X sixteen days later terrified and saddened both Kings. In his *Amsterdam News* column, King praised Malcolm X's "personal depth and integrity" and wrote how Malcolm was "growing at the time of his brutal and meaningless assassination." He underscored Coretta's recent meeting with Malcolm and his "interest in politics as a way of dealing with the problems of the Negro."[89] King also noted the trauma of white violence that ran through Malcolm's family history: "A man who lived under the torment of knowledge of the rape of his grandmother and the murder of his father under the conditions of the present social order does not readily accept that social order or seek to integrate into it."[90]

Scott King described the "feeling of depression" that descended on her after Malcolm X's assassination, "as if I had lost someone very dear to me."[91] Stressing the great respect both she and Martin had for Malcolm, she felt that if Malcolm had lived they would "have come closer together and would have been a very strong force in the total struggle for liberation and self-determination of Black people in our society."[92]

With fears heightened after Malcolm's assassination, King was heavily guarded in LA in February. He was supposed to attend a movie screening at the Cinerama Dome, but police found dynamite in the theater.[93] Fourteen hundred pounds of dynamite were reported stolen from a storage shed and an anonymous threat called in "to blow up that nigger." The *Los Angeles Sentinel* reported four white supremacists were arrested and the LAPD was still searching for the fifth man, "in whose apartment a large quantity of the explosives were found."[94] Alongside the policy and bureaucratic racism of cities like LA ran a core of violent racism, from the attacks on Black students desegregating South Gate High to this planned attack on King.

Addressing the World Affairs Lunch at the Palladium, King received a proclamation from Mayor Yorty, who declared it Freedom Day. "The welcome mat is always out for you," the mayor told King.[95] At Temple Israel of Hollywood, King highlighted the urgency of economic injustice and poverty in the United States and the "50 million of our brothers and sisters in this country who are poverty-stricken . . . perishing on a lonely island of poverty in the midst of a vast ocean of material prosperity. Certainly, if we are to be a great nation, we must solve this problem."[96]

Coretta Scott King came to LA in March for a concert and to address a Women Strike for Peace event. For years, she had been wanting to play a more central role in the movement. She and Martin had talked repeatedly and, at times, argued about it. Sometimes, after these arguments, he would send her to give a speech in his stead.[97] But they weren't making a seat at the SCLC table for her. With years of musical training that had lain fallow and receiving many speaking requests, she conceived of the idea of doing a set of freedom concert fundraisers. Patterning them after her hero Paul Robeson, she wrote an original program to tell the story of Black struggle through song. Beginning with the origins of the US and slavery and going through the ongoing civil rights movement, she interspersed commentary, explanation of Black musical traditions, and a dozen songs.[98] Calling it a "people's revolution," the program contextualized the Black struggle in its global anticolonial context. "While the Negro suffered in America, his brothers and sisters in Africa were being suppressed by the British, the Dutch, the Belgians, the Portuguese and the French."[99] The first one took place at New York City's Town Hall on November 15, 1964. In March 1965, she embarked on a five-city, nine-day West Coast Freedom Concert tour.[100] The money raised would help support the Selma-to-Montgomery March. Martin was supportive, though initially skeptical about how much money they would make. But they did. She sometimes raised $50,000 a concert.[101]

Interviewed by the *Los Angeles Times*, Scott King stressed the fear they continually lived with. But when asked if she wished her husband would "ease his determination to seek Negro rights in the South and elsewhere," she answered a definite no.[102] While underlining the dangers they faced, she stressed the importance of pressing forward. Full freedom was what would protect them in the long run—implicitly saying fellow Americans needed to step forward, rather than her husband step back.

While in LA, she addressed a Women Strike for Peace event in Beverly Hills and saw some of the women from the Geneva trip. There, to the overwhelmingly white gathering, she highlighted "the very brunt of the load" Black women were carrying in the fight against racial discrimination.[103] Even these peace activists had trouble attending to the urgent injustices in their own backyard.

Then, at an SCLC retreat in early 1965, she explained how the Vietnam War "drains resources from education, housing, health and other badly needed programs," making clear to those gathered, "Why do you think *we* got the Nobel Prize? . . . Peace and justice are indivisible."[104] Coretta understood *they* had gotten the award and thus the responsibilities and further actions demanded of them. She tried unsuccessfully to convince the SCLC to take a stand on Vietnam. To be a peace activist in 1965 was to be seen as un-American. Most civil rights activists, most people the Kings knew, didn't have the courage to stand out on this issue, but Coretta Scott King was "beyond steel," as fellow activists noted.[105]

Suspicious of her peace focus, the FBI and Justice Department had surveilled her for years—noting her singing with Paul Robeson in Columbus in 1948, letters she'd sent in college, her and Martin's 1957 trip to Ghana, her 1962 trip to Geneva and WSP work, her 1963 march to the UN.[106] In May, when she also addressed the fiftieth-anniversary celebration of Women Strike for Peace in Chicago, on "Peace, Jobs, and Freedom," they again took note, fearing the ways she might tie the peace movement with the civil rights struggle.[107]

A month after Coretta's visit to the city, Martin returned to LA. Speaking at UCLA on April 27, he charted a history of the United States since 1619, from slavery and segregation to a widening of possibilities and a change in Black consciousness. Then King paused. This would be a nice place to stop, he remarked, with this sense of progress and accomplishment. But then the audience would remain "victims of an illusion wrapped up in superficiality."[108] Black people were "covered up in ghettos" in cities like LA—trapped in "woefully inadequate" schools with outright job discrimination. There would be significant costs if the audience did not act, he warned: "When people are walking the streets hungry and they have no jobs, and they see life as a long and desolate corridor with no exit sign, they become bitter."[109] Increasingly, by the mid-1960s, King challenged the history of progress that liberal Americans favored and stressed the perils of ignoring Black cries for change in LA and elsewhere outside the South. Here in LA, four months before the Watts uprising, he did it again.

While the city's two Black newspapers provided a drumbeat of coverage of the myriad grassroots actions challenging the city's rampant racism, white newspapers attempted to dodge this reality. Instead the *Los Angeles Times* ran an op-ed from the NAACP's Roy Wilkins claiming that those attacking Northern segregation (he didn't name King specifically) overstated the problem.[110] In July, a month before the Watts rebellion, King returned again to LA, criticizing Mayor Yorty and other LA officials for excluding poor Black and Latino city residents from leading local War on Poverty programs. Twenty-three million dollars of War on Poverty funds were at stake and city leaders wanted to ensure their own control of the funds, proposing a county-wide board with little representation from poor Black or Latino

Angelenos. Arguing that poor people were intelligent and knew what they needed, King declared the programs would fail if "the victims of poverty" were excluded from policymaking.[111]

King himself had reached a turning point. For many Black Californians, and King himself, Proposition 14's passage had decisively shown white California's commitment to segregation and ghettoization despite a wide, multiracial movement that had tried to challenge it and King exhausting himself flying back and forth. As Coretta proclaimed in May, "The South is moving so much faster than the North."[112] The cost of the city's worsening segregation and deafness to Black grievances would soon become clear.

6

As Segregated as Birmingham

King in Chicago Before the Chicago Campaign

> We do not have segregation in Chicago.
>
> —Mayor Richard J. Daley, 1963

Like Los Angeles, Chicago was so deeply and institutionally segregated that in 1963, in the midst of the Birmingham campaign, King deemed the Windy City as segregated as Birmingham. Given the magnitude of segregation and inequality Black Chicagoans faced, King traveled to the city numerous times in the late 1950s and early 1960s for rallies, fundraisers, and demonstrations.[1] Chicago's movement challenging school segregation was so vibrant, vigorous, and relentless that King would later say that if it had been somewhere in the South, change would have ensued. Black Chicagoans' robust organizing would lay the groundwork for SCLC's decision to pursue a campaign in the city in 1965.

The second-largest city in the nation at the time, Chicago was home to over a million Black people, a third of its population. In the 1960s, Chicago's segregation was intentional, systematic, and relentless. Mayor Daley and Superintendent Benjamin Willis, like their other Northern counterparts, would persistently deny it and as persistently work to maintain it. They used a variety of strategies, including the building of massive, segregated housing projects, aggressive policing, school zoning, double-session schools, and urban renewal—all designed to cordon off Black Chicago. Half of Black Chicagoans lived in poverty. The city spent $366 per white student but only $266 per Black student. Tackling the city's segregation and entrenched inequality, King knew, was an urgent fight.

Like in other cities, FHA residential security maps created by the federal government to encourage banks to increase their lending put a premium on racial segregation. King would deem the creation of Chicago's slums a "historic conspiracy involving real estate codes, mortgage practices, federal, state and local housing authorities."[2] Blacks were hemmed into neighborhoods in Chicago on the near South Side. These neighborhoods grew desperately overcrowded, with a population density three times other parts of the city.[3] A swell of Black migration after World War II led to the creation of a second ghetto on the city's West Side.

Between 1950 and 1960, Black people went from being 15 percent to 90 percent in these West Side neighborhoods and the population of school-age children nearly doubled. Ghettoization led to decreased city services; the parks weren't kept up, sanitation happened much less regularly, few pools served Black Chicagoans, and yet Black people paid more in rent than their white counterparts. Only 1 percent of the city's residential listings were open to African Americans, so landlords could gouge Black renters as did businesses serving the city's southside and westside Black ghettos.[4] The city was ringed with white neighborhoods and suburbs; many were sundown towns, where it was dangerous for a Black person to be seen at night.

Schools serving Black students in Chicago grew decrepit and increasingly overcrowded, as the city refused to rezone. By 1958 the city moved nine of the fifteen Black secondary high schools to double-session days.[5] Twelve elementary schools in Chicago by 1962 were over the required capacity of 1,200, but the city refused to do anything. According to historian Elizabeth Todd Breland, per-pupil spending on Black students was two-thirds of what it was for Chicago's white students.[6] These tactics paralleled those of New York, Los Angeles, and many other Northern cities—a Northern segregation playbook. This under-resourcing of Black schools and neighborhoods was accompanied, as historian Simon Balto documents, by throwing money "hand over fist" to the Chicago Police Department.[7]

Mayor Daley maintained this regime of segregation through the most far-reaching political machine in the nation. He had a number of Black politicians in his pocket, which provided further cover for his actions. Daley had grown up in Chicago and been a member of a Bridgeport Irish gang—the Hamburg Athletic Club—that helped touch off Chicago's 1919 race riot, where white mobs killed thirty-eight African Americans.[8] The Hamburg Club also provided muscle to the city's neighborhood machine bosses. Daley became club president in 1924

and held that post for fifteen years, using that position and the lever-
age it provided to climb the ranks of Chicago's Democratic machine.[9]
Becoming head of the Cook County Democratic Party (and thus the
machine boss) in 1953, Daley was elected mayor in 1955 by playing on
white racial fears while still commandeering the Black vote. Daley's
campaign covertly spread the word among Chicago's white communities that he was opposed to racial integration (no matter the *Brown* decision). They printed smear leaflets, making up stories that his opponent
Robert Merriam was for open housing and had a mixed-race wife.

Daley wasn't simply looking to preserve the status quo—he would
modernize Chicago while hypersegregating it.[10] By Daley's orders, the
construction of the Dan Ryan Expressway swerved to miss the may-
or's neighborhood of Bridgeport, instead hitting a swath of Black businesses and effectively cordoning off Chicago's Black community. On
top of that, by 1963, urban renewal to "upgrade" the city largely meant
"Negro removal," and by 1963 more than fifty thousand families had
been displaced. The mayor purposefully built massive housing projects, according to journalist Mike Royko, to contain Black people.[11] On
the South Side, the segregated seventeen-story Stateway Gardens and
twenty-eight-story Robert Taylor Homes projects ran for thirty blocks;
nearly all the residents were Black. The Kings were stunned by this
version of the Berlin Wall, as they saw it. Martin called them "cement
reservations," Coretta "upright concentration camps."[12]

Daley wasn't simply a powerful local politician; he was pivotal to
the Democratic Party nationally. John F. Kennedy would credit Daley
for securing the presidency for him and Lyndon Johnson understood
the mayor's power and reach as well.[13] Biographers Adam Cohen and
Elizabeth Taylor minced no words in describing Daley. "He ruled over
his empire with pharaonic power, the kind of absolute power that few
American politicians have ever wielded."[14] While Daley professed
support for the Southern struggle, his power in the Democratic Party,
both locally and nationally, left Black Chicagoans out in the cold. King
would call it a "colonial situation"—Black people could vote, but their
vote was basically controlled. So even though Black voters were key to
electing a half dozen Black aldermen, those aldermen were selected
and beholden to Daley. When Daley asserted that "there are no ghettos
in Chicago," the aldermen publicly agreed, while repeatedly denouncing Black protests as unnecessary and unwise.[15]

Daley actively protected the whiteness of his own Bridgeport neighborhood, as did white gangs, from "Negro invasion."[16] In 1964, when

two Black students tried to move into an apartment in Bridgeport, Daley let his white neighbors run them out.[17] Then, when the growing movement against the city's school segregation marched into his neighborhood and his neighbors threw rocks, eggs, and firecrackers at the marchers, the mayor had the marchers, rather than his neighbors, arrested. When even moderate civil rights leaders spoke out against this, Daley described his rock-throwing neighbors as "fine people, hard-working people."[18]

As Segregated as Birmingham

Housing and school segregation plagued Black Chicagoans. In 1959, King applauded a new interracial housing development in Chicago's all-white suburb of Deerfield, where twelve of fifty-one single-family homes would go to Black families.[19] White resistance to this modest open-housing project demonstrated how "discrimination is not a sectional issue," King emphasized.[20] Many Deerfield whites took offense at King's stance and voted overwhelmingly to scuttle the project. In December 1960, King was listed as a sponsor of a committee organized to pursue a legal case against Deerfield's segregation.[21] In 1962, he headlined a fundraising dinner for groups trying to secure Freedom of Residence legislation during the next state legislative session and spoke out in Evanston, Illinois, another white suburb, about fair housing.[22]

Understanding the significant role the federal government played in Chicago's housing segregation and white homeownership across the country, King joined the National Committee on Discrimination in Housing in 1960. The FHA had facilitated $30 billion in home loans for white subdivisions since 1934.[23] White homeownership had shot up with the GI Bill: 43 percent of Americans owned a home in 1940 but 61 percent did in 1960. Federal loan guarantees enabled burgeoning white homeownership in segregated white neighborhoods that now ringed Chicago and other cities. Kennedy had campaigned in 1960 that, if elected president, he could eliminate housing segregation "with the stroke of a pen." But he hadn't used his pen to do anything related to housing segregation. In a TV interview with Mike Wallace in 1961, King underscored the urgency for Kennedy to act.[24] In 1962, in Illinois, he again criticized Kennedy's inaction, particularly around public housing.

Finally, in November 1962, Kennedy banned discrimination in any housing with financing from the federal government, including public housing as well as homes financed through the FHA—but the order did not cover mortgages by lending institutions supervised by the federal government or previously constructed public housing.[25] Thus Chicago's massive, segregated housing projects went untouched. In his *Amsterdam News* column, King noted his gratitude for Kennedy's action but criticized how the order didn't go far enough, particularly the "absence of a retroactive clause" to remedy the millions of dollars the federal government had already invested in segregated public housing and the fact that the order did not include savings-and-loan companies.[26] In January 1963, King again called for federal legislation to address the widespread discriminatory housing the government had already funded and to ensure that savings and loans didn't discriminate. King also stressed that the real test was going to be implementation of Kennedy's order.[27]

At an interfaith conference held in Chicago in January 1963, King called on the religious leaders gathered to buy houses in white neighborhoods and sell them to Black people and to use "selective buying" to pressure local stores that didn't hire Black people.[28] But few churches took him up on the idea. It was at this Religion and Race conference that King met Rabbi Abraham Joshua Heschel. A Polish-born Jewish theologian Heschel was a professor at the Jewish Theological Seminary in New York and, like King, saw the deep religious imperative to confronting racism across the country and the complicity that well-meaning white people shared. "Another way of dealing with a bad conscience is to keep the Negro out of sight," Heschel pronounced at the conference "Let a Negro move into our neighborhood and madness overtakes the residents." Heschel then laid out how one-sixth of the country's Black population now lived segregated and ghettoized in the nation's five biggest cities, including Chicago and New York City.[29] One of the most famous photos of King came two years later with him linking arms with Rabbi Heschel in the Selma-to-Montgomery March. But King had gravitated toward Heschel partly because he too saw the sin of Northern racism and ghettoization.

Segregation marred recreation as well. Chicago's Parks and Recreation Department had deliberately located most of the city's public swimming pools in white neighborhoods. While they were officially open to all residents, white Chicagoans greeted Black people who dared to try to swim with open hostility and violence. Most of the dozens of public beaches on the city's beautiful lakefront were also in practice off-limits to Black residents. In the summer of 1960, Black police officer Harold Carr and his family attempted to use Rainbow Beach on the city's South Side and were attacked by a gang of rock-throwing white youths. Following the attack, members of the South Side NAACP Youth Council decided to stage a wade-in at the beach. These wade-ins at Rainbow Beach continued in the summer of 1961.[30]

Many white Chicagoans were angered that King continued to highlight Chicago's housing segregation and support freedom-of-residence legislation. But he pressed forward. King's brother A. D., a pastor in Birmingham, also traveled to Illinois and Wisconsin multiple times in the 1960s to highlight their segregation. On the heels of the May 1963 LA rally, at a Freedom Fund rally/fundraiser in Chicago, sponsored by the singer Mahalia Jackson, King made clear that the city was just as segregated as Birmingham—one of the "most segregated" cities in the nation.[31] He urged Black Chicagoans to press President Kennedy for another executive order outlawing segregation in housing.[32]

As segregated as Birmingham. Just a month after his arrest in Birmingham, knee-deep in that campaign, King declared, "We are through with we've-done-more-for-your-people-than-anyone-elseism."[33] White Chicago was outraged by the comparison. Their city was not segregated, just "separated." Alderman Vito Marzullo told King "to go back to Alabama if he thinks this way about this city."[34] Labeling King "arrogant" and an "outsider," the *Chicago Tribune* fantastically claimed "in Chicago, there was little to no segregation," and when "Chicago Negro leaders speak, they are listened to respectfully."[35] The *Saturday Evening Post* asked, "Is Martin Luther King Harming the Negro?"

The *Tribune* made crystal clear that King was not welcome in the city anymore. "We don't need any agitators from the South."[36] Interestingly, five years earlier, when King's work seemed contained in the South, the *Tribune*'s editorial "Portrait of a Christian" praised him as "an influential champion of both egalitarian ends and nonviolent means."[37] King had not changed. He was still championing nonviolence and still calling for egalitarian ends. But the *Tribune* now found it unacceptable when Dr. King's call for change was trained on Chicago itself. The vitriol would only increase as King and the SCLC's work in the city expanded.

Building a Broad-Based Movement

In 1962, Chicago organizers under the leadership of the Urban League's Bill Berry and Rev. Arthur Brazier formed a new group—the

Coordinating Council of Community Organizations (CCCO)—to bring together a broad coalition of Black community organizations and a handful of white and Latino groups to challenge school and housing segregation in the city.[38] The council encompassed a range of groups employing different kinds of tactics, including the more militant, direct-action CORE, into one powerful but at times internally contentious front. Two years later, they selected Al Raby, a local Black teacher who'd been involved in the coalition from the start, to lead the group.

Raby had grown up in Chicago. His father died when he was a baby, and his mother struggled to raise him and his three siblings. Raby dropped out of school before finishing eighth grade and ended up joining the army. When he returned, he completed his high school diploma and a certificate in teaching from Chicago Teachers College and then taught seventh and eighth grade at the nearly all-Black Hess Upper Grade Center on Chicago's West Side.[39] So Raby was well familiar with segregated education in the city. In 1962, Raby and Meyer Weinberg, a professor at Wright Junior College, grew concerned that the teachers union hadn't taken an organized stand against Chicago's segregation and formed Teachers for Integrated Schools. As Weinberg explained, "It became clear, at least to me, that this whole distinction between de facto segregation and de jure segregation was a fake kind of distinction . . . and that segregation in the North was a conscious creation of the school system working along with city government." From their work in Teachers for Integrated Schools, both men became delegates to the CCCO.

On the side of the "radical impatient activists" of the CCCO, Raby became the CCCO's convener in 1964.[40] Other CCCO radicals were CORE leaders Lawrence Landry and Bob Lucas and parent organizer Rosie Simpson, a single mother and welfare recipient who would become one of the city's most determined school activists. This broad coalition formed part of CCCO's strength but also meant there was considerable internal struggle. The more moderate civil rights groups like the Urban League and NAACP at times were threatened by the CCCO and tried to box Raby out from meetings.[41] Like in New York, Black women formed the front line of activists challenging the city's entrenched school segregation. Through 1963, they picketed to expose how school zoning lines established segregation and constantly adjusted to maintain it. They pressed Superintendent Benjamin Willis and the Board of Education to redraw school district lines.

Appointed by Daley, Benjamin Willis had become the highest-paid school official in the country. Willis actively worked to keep the schools segregated, while claiming color blindness.[42] This was another Northern playbook strategy: school officials claimed, despite the segregation apparent to the eye, that they didn't keep track of race and that to do so would be racist (even though they well knew the demographics of their schools *and* kept readjusting zoning lines to preserve that segregation). Indeed, 90 percent of the city's schools were segregated with Black schools consistently overcrowded with fewer resources.[43] But school officials gaslighted Black activists highlighting the city's segregation that they were putting race into the equation when it wasn't there. In 1963 the CCCO filed suit against the city's school segregation, and a year later, two reports confirmed the rampant school segregation and recommended change. Like in New York, the Board of Education and Daley, with massive pressure from white parents, refused to implement any desegregation plan.[44]

White Chicago celebrated Superintendent Willis for improving school quality for their children, while Black class sizes skyrocketed, 25 percent larger than white schools.[45] While half of Chicago's students were Black, Black people held only about a quarter of all teaching and school administration jobs so the teaching staff at most Black schools was predominantly white. Like LA's officials, part of how Willis and other city leaders justified the differentials in education was through cultural arguments that cast Black children as educationally and culturally deficient. As the *Chicago Tribune* editorialized in 1963, "We doubt that any city has tried harder than Chicago to solve the immensely difficult problems caused by the migration to the north of hundreds of thousands of needy, poorly educated Southern Negroes."[46] The *Chicago Sun-Times*, while not as rabid, also largely stood against local desegregation efforts, even editorializing against the "intimidation" of the March on Washington.[47]

Chicago's premier Black newspaper, the *Chicago Defender*, dedicated an issue to exposing Willis's actions.[48] "Incredibly arrogant and contemptuous of citizens who differ with him," the *Defender* described Willis's ten-year tenure building "one of the most beautiful physical school plants in America and unquestionably one of the most segregated." Willis and other school officials had made a myriad of choices about zoning, school resource allocation, building renovation, and teacher placement.[49] By 1963, the *Defender* had taken to referring to Willis as "the Governor Wallace of Chicago."[50]

Refusing to rezone Black students to empty seats at white schools,

Superintendent Willis instead ordered the purchase of two hundred mobile trailer classrooms for Black schools to serve growing numbers of Black students.[51] The Board of Education approved his request and prevented Black students from transferring to other white schools. Black community leaders like Rosie Simpson named these 20-by-36-foot aluminum trailers "Willis wagons."[52] The trailers— which cost $2 million—were placed on school playgrounds and parking lots to add extra "classrooms" to Black schools.[53] Over the next years, Willis would order 625 of them.[54]

Schools serving Black students grew so overcrowded that even after using auditoriums, basements, cafeterias, and hallways as classrooms, Willis and the board moved schools to double-session days. While their Southern counterparts limited Black education by the crop schedule, Northern officials simply shortened the school day for Black schools to accommodate two sessions. More than thirty thousand of Chicago's Black students by the early 1960s went to school only four hours a day.[55] At the same time, research by Chicago's Urban League revealed "whole floors were vacant in white neighborhoods."[56]

Black community activists—including parents, young people, union members, and longtime organizers—employed a host of tactics to challenge these school policies. In 1961, a group of parents initiated "Operation Transfer," attempting to register their children in white schools with open seats; school officials refused to grant the transfers. School boycotts, sit-ins, and protests targeted individual schools in 1962 in an attempt to achieve change on the individual-school level but largely hadn't succeeded.[57]

In July 1963, the national NAACP convention met in Chicago and invited Daley to speak. When Daley had the audacity to proclaim that there were "no ghettos in Chicago," he was booed off the stage with people shouting "Down with ghettos" and "Daley must go!" The head of Illinois's NAACP was astonished by Daley's "foolishness. Everybody knows there are ghettos here and we've got more segregated schools than you've got in Alabama, Mississippi and Louisiana combined."[58] To protest Daley and Willis's segregationist policies, on July 4, thirty thousand people marched through downtown Chicago demanding educational equality.[59] Six days later, Chicago CORE started a weeklong sit-in at the Board of Education.[60]

The struggle against Chicago's school segregation expanded. Twenty Black parents filed a class-action suit against the Willis wagons and Chicago Public Schools (CPS) for forcing them to send their children to segregated, unequal schools.[61] The district judge denied their request for a temporary injunction against CPS in November 1963 because Willis "categorically den[ied] I and my office has ever been motivated to maintain or perpetuate racially segregated schools." So the judge decided nothing "intentional" or "irreparable" was going on.[62] Then the board agreed in an out-of-court settlement to commission another study that would recommend desegregation measures; while the study was approved in principle in 1964, it was never implemented.[63]

Community activists began calling for Willis's firing, circulating petitions advocating his dismissal. Activists with CORE began holding "lay downs" to prevent the Willis wagons from being installed at schools.[64] Rosie Simpson and parents on the South Side launched a protest of wagons being installed at Seventy-Third Street and Lowe Avenue.[65] Discovering where the trailer classrooms were going to be put, "we were not going to allow that to happen. . . . We laid down in front of the bulldozers and when the paddy wagons came to take us to jail, we chained ourselves to the paddy wagons and threw the keys away after we'd locked the locks."[66]

The Chicago police responded brutally to these protests, the *Defender* likening this police treatment to Mississippi.[67] When Daley claimed the protests were the work of a small group of "outside agitators," Simpson spearheaded a petition signed by 1,300 local parents and forced Daley to meet with her.[68] Birmingham leader Fred Shuttlesworth came to support Simpson's protests and gather support for the March on Washington, calling it a "tragedy and shame" that they had to be challenging school segregation eight years after *Brown*.[69] The next day, Simpson and hundreds of other Chicagoans headed to Washington, DC, for the March on Washington.

While he ignored Black community grievances, Willis protected white parent concerns to limit *any* desegregation. A new Illinois state policy allowed high school students in the top 5 percent of their class to transfer to schools with honors classes. When *three* Black students sought to use the policy to transfer, white parents protested. They did not want these highly successful Black students transferring to "their" schools. As a result, Willis took a number of white high schools off the list of possible transfer sites. Black parents went to court to force Willis to abide by the state's transfer policy and celebrated when the state agreed with their petition. But rather than follow the court order, Willis tendered his resignation.[70] Mayor Daley and the board were "distressed" by Willis's resignation and rebuffed it, deciding instead to extend his contract. White parents celebrated.[71]

The message was clear: the political establishment backed Willis's segregationist policies. He didn't have to proclaim segregation from the rafters, as Alabama governor George Wallace was doing, just ensure it time and again through policy and administrative decisions. And Mayor Daley, the Board of Education, and business leaders had his back. Willis was a hero for many white Chicagoans.[72] On top of that, Illinois governor Otto Kerner weighed in, celebrating the state's "great progress" in race relations and criticizing King's contention that the degree of segregation in Chicago's metropolitan area rivaled the South. Kerner blamed the ongoing school protests on "militants."[73]

Black community leaders and parents with King's backing had succeeded in making Chicago's school segregation a visible issue, but the city's political and business elite hunkered down to protect it. As the city backed Willis, activists escalated their tactics. Raby described how angry they were about Willis's continued reign but "even more determined to carry on the protest."[74] They made "Willis loves Wallace" buttons, picketed Daley's house, held sit-ins, and blocked construction of the Willis wagons. Comedian Dick Gregory was one of 250 people arrested in August at an anti-Willis march. In town for an event, King visited Gregory in jail to show his support for the protests.[75] A young Bernie Sanders, then a University of Chicago student, was also arrested protesting the Willis wagons.[76]

Angered by the various attempts to maintain Chicago's segregated schools, the CCCO decided to call for a district-wide "Freedom Day" school boycott for October 22, 1963.[77] King came to Chicago and met with them, encouraging them in their school boycott to highlight the urgency of the situation.[78] Part of the rationale behind the boycott was that the school system received money for each student's attendance, and so it would hurt the school system's finances and underline the gravity of the situation.

On October 22, an astonishing 225,000 students—50 percent of the city's total school enrollment—stayed out of school to protest the lack of school desegregation, an end to the Willis wagons, and a racial count to document what they already knew about Chicago's widespread school segregation.[79] "Black people had had enough," CORE's Lawrence Landry explained; "it was a stunning effect."[80] Now chair of the Chicago Area Council for Integrated Schools, Simpson was a key organizer of the boycott.[81] Keeping her six kids home, they took to the streets that day in protest. One hundred and seventy-six of Chicago's overcrowded Black schools sat largely empty while many students attended freedom schools in churches or community centers.[82] Ten thousand students and parents picketed City Hall and the Board of Education carrying signs reading "Willis Must Go" and "No More Little Black Sambo Read in Class."[83]

The school boycott cost the city nearly a half million dollars. While the *Chicago Defender* celebrated the boycott as a "thumping success," many white Chicagoans accused Black leaders of encouraging lawlessness.[84] Daley was furious. Shortly after the boycott, King again publicly criticized Willis's wagons and ongoing support for the city's segregated schools. King said he favored "busing students to less crowded schools."[85] The city remained intransigent. Thus 1963 ended in Chicago with two things clear: Black people had built a creative, multi-front nonviolent movement, and white Chicagoans had rejected it.

In January 1964, Chicago activists traveled to New York to join thirty organizers from other cities, including New York's Milton Galamison, to organize a nationwide school boycott in February. Having misjudged the first boycott, Daley attempted to mobilize his Black surrogates to try to thwart a second. Still, a second boycott occurred in Chicago on February 25, alongside massive school boycotts in New York, Boston, and dozens of other cities.[86] Despite Daley's efforts to discredit the boycott along with Black congressman William Dawson and Black aldermen William Campbell and Claude Holman, 175,000 Chicago students stayed out.[87] King was deeply supportive of these boycotts, terming them "one of the most creative nonviolent methods developed to dramatize the intolerable conditions" in city schools.[88] The CCCO marched on City Hall carrying signs declaring "If we don't get rid of Daley, we'll have boycotts daily" and bearing a mock coffin with the names of Dawson, Willis, and the six Black aldermen in Daley's pocket who supported his school policies.[89]

Many Chicagoans also stood against the Civil Rights Act being debated in Congress that spring; the *Chicago Tribune* editorialized against it as a "vast invasion and usurpation by the federal government." And the *Tribune* condemned the second school boycott, saying it was "a payoff to Martin Luther King who says laws not to his satisfaction are to be broken."[90] But King pressed on. In June 1964, he came to Chicago for a massive rally at Soldier Field to highlight the city's school segregation and the growing movement challenging it.[91] More than 75,000 people came out—young and old, about 90 percent Black, according to the *Defender.*[92]

King underscored the need to keep up demonstrations, school boy-cotts, rent strikes—the arsenal of Northern protest. "Now is the time . . . Now is the time!" he trumpeted. Just as the Civil Rights Act was being signed, King was clear and vocal highlighting the depth of inequality in Chicago and the need for massive, disruptive protest to change it.

The Decision to Join Forces with the Chicago Movement

Since 1963, King had been considering a Northern campaign for SCLC. He had joined with movements challenging school segregation, job discrimination, housing discrimination, and police brutality from the Northeast to the Midwest to the West Coast for years. And yet, while many Northern liberals increasingly supported action on the South, they protected their own local inequality and demonized those who challenged them. King's own Northern work felt piecemeal—showing up when called and when he could fit it into his increasingly impossible schedule. And despite all these robust nonviolent efforts, many white Northerners continued to deflect, supporting the "real" movement in the South as a shield to demonstrate their own goodness and not address local segregation.

This campaign would need to be different—a campaign that SCLC would spearhead alongside local activists, like they had done in Birmingham, but bigger than anything previously attempted. After returning from Chicago in June 1963, he explained, "I will have to face the decision soon on whether I should be limiting myself to the South. In the North, there are brothers and sisters suffering discrimination that is even more agonizing. . . . In the South, at least the Negro can see progress, whereas in the North all he sees is retrogression."[93] The NAACP was threatened by this, according to the *Saturday Evening Post*, because it would make SCLC "truly national."[94] Before the March on Washington, King was already thinking about SCLC taking on a Northern campaign.

By the beginning of 1965, King, like many SNCC activists, had reached a turning point with Northern liberals. Northern Black people were "constantly kept at a boiling point by the misery of rats, filth, unemployment, and *de facto* segregation."[95] The decisive passage of California's Proposition 14 alongside Johnson's victory had underscored for King how Northerners might support change in the South but "voted for ghettos" at home. New York's Mayor Wagner threw him a party but had refused his ideas for change after the Harlem uprising.

Alongside the voting rights campaign they were helping build in Alabama, King began meeting with organizers in Boston, Philadelphia, New York, Cleveland, Washington, DC, and Chicago in the spring of 1965. With an explicit invitation from Chicago organizers, King explained to *Ebony* magazine that he had received requests from several cities, including Washington and Los Angeles, "but I decided to come to Chicago mainly because of Al Raby. I had been watching Raby for some time . . . and I became enormously impressed with his work and the sincerity of his commitment." [96] Chicago had a broad-based nonviolent movement and not the factionalism or testy personalities like some other cities. The appeal of Chicago's CCCO—with its wide coalition of groups in the city, years-long direct-action movement, and seasoned leaders like Raby, Simpson, and CORE's Bob Lucas—was part of the draw. As Rev. C. T. Vivian explained, "We weren't coming North. They asked us." [97] This is not to say everyone in Chicago was on board with SCLC—a number of Black Chicagoans worried about whether King and the SCLC were committed to building on their organizing or just interested in high-profile events. But with the years-long movement facing setbacks, dwindling energy, and little change from Daley, many like Raby hoped that King and the SCLC would bring new energy, power, and militancy to their struggle. [98]

One of King's right-hand advisors, James Bevel, had recently moved to Chicago and urged King forward: "You've got to go for broke." [99] He pressed the importance of breaking the Chicago machine to improve Black life chances in the city. But many SCLC advisors weren't on board to base a campaign in a Northern ghetto. [100] Georgia native Hosea Williams initially worried, "We need to clean up at home . . . Chicago is not our turf." Andrew Young felt the best way they could transform the nation was by concentrating on voting rights in the South. [101] Worried that with the Daley machine "you'll come away with nothing meaningful for all your efforts," Bayard Rustin also lambasted the idea of SCLC joining a campaign in the Windy City. [102] Daley's Democratic machine and its phalanx of Black politicians were a liability. Plus, Rustin felt there was unfinished business in the South. So the decision was difficult.

On March 7, 1965, voting rights activists who had been sickened by the death of civil rights worker Jimmie Lee Jackson two weeks earlier were viciously attacked by Alabama state troopers as they marched over Selma's Edmund Pettus Bridge. King had not been on the bridge that day, but two days after the attack, he returned with two thousand marchers. Faced with a court injunction and pressure from the Johnson administration, he turned the march around when they reached the bridge. Many activists, particularly from SNCC, were furious at King's decision. That night, a white Episcopalian minister from Boston, James Reeb, who had heeded the call to join them in Selma, was attacked and killed after eating dinner at an integrated restaurant.

King returned to Chicago later that week. Devastated as he arrived in the city, King explained, "I get so tired and weary." He then canceled a second event at the University of Chicago because of "an attack of hiccups," according to the *Boston Globe*.[103] One can imagine how bad he must have been feeling to make this public. King had struggled with hiccups, depression, and physical exhaustion for years. Here again, his health was low. By 1965, King's schedule was "almost unbearable." He told reporters he was sleeping four hours a day (and often it was less), which was taking a toll on his body. He was barely home.[104]

The Kings with their four young children had just moved into a modest house on Sunset Street in the Vine City neighborhood of Atlanta. "My father really struggled with the whole notion of owning anything," his daughter Bernice King later explained, so the first year they rented. Martin's anticapitalism had been evident when Coretta met him, but as his movement leadership grew, "money and material success meant less and less to him." He used to devote himself to sharp dressing, but over the years, he "discarded that view completely."[105] With his speaking engagements, he brought in about $200,000 a year but only allowed himself an income of $10,000 to $12,000 a year. The vast majority of his income went to the movement, which she understood and agreed with. But she worried about how they would survive if the unthinkable happened and privately thought they might set aside $20,000 of the $54,600 award from the Nobel Prize in an account for the kids' college. But he gave the entire sum to the movement. (Harry Belafonte would ultimately step in to help with college expenses.) She wanted the economic security of owning the house and ultimately convinced him. So in 1966, they bought the house. In a rare move for the 1960s, the deed was put in her name.[106]

Having seen the level of organizing in Chicago for years and the city's complete intransigence, King knew that the odds for their campaign weren't great. But he refused to be cowed by the "paralysis of analysis."[107] Some accounts have wrongly argued that King and SCLC saw Daley as an ally. They did not. As Al Raby explained, they understood Daley's tremendous power; if they forced his hand, Daley had the clout "to implement that decision politically." [108] And so they announced their decision.

So, even as SCLC continued the voting rights campaign in Alabama, King was also preparing for its Northern work. On March 25, when the second Selma-to-Montgomery March made it to Montgomery, King declared, "Let us march on segregated housing until every ghetto of social and economic depression dissolves. . . . Let us march on seg- regated schools." [109] One week after speaking those words in Mont- gomery, at a rally in Baltimore on April 1 and then at an SCLC board meeting the next day, "in spite of strong opposition on the board," Coretta explained, "Martin proposed that SCLC expand its activities to the North and West. 'You can expect us in Baltimore, Philadelphia, Detroit, Los Angeles, and Chicago,' " she reported him saying.[110] Yet most biographers miss the timing of this decision, perhaps because it seems out of place in the crescendoing story of the march toward the Voting Rights Act.[111]

The announcement that King was coming to Chicago shook the city. "An almost perceptible shudder shook the privileged areas of our city and seats of power," reported the *Defender*.[112] White Chicago was not pleased. Nor were some of Daley's closest Black allies—like Rev. Joseph Jackson, president of the National Baptist Convention, who said Chicago did not need the help of outsiders, particularly when it had "friends" like Daley and Willis.[113] The *Chicago Tribune* took note on April 2 of King's decision to base a campaign in the city and over the month editorialized against him.[114] On April 7 the paper blasted the "offensive" call for Willis's resignation, calling it "fanat- icism." The board should be considering the "desires of Chicagoans who do not belong to the 'civil rights' groups and who do not be- lieve in conducting government by demonstration in the streets." [115] On April 18, the *Tribune* reprinted a *National Review* op-ed comparing King to Marxist philosopher Friedrich Engels, claiming King favored a "program of government by force and terror." [116] And its April 24 editorial lambasted King as a troublemaker who was now bringing his "anarchy" to the North.[117] Despite massive protests, the board gave Willis another four-year contract.

But King moved forward, as did many of his colleagues. They continued people-to-people tours that spring, meeting with various Northern movement activists in Boston, Chicago, Cleveland, Los An- geles, and Philadelphia. But Chicago was calling them. In Syracuse,

New York, in April, King told an audience that school segregation in the North was one of the most pressing issues facing the nation and described CCCO's campaign to get rid of Willis "as significant a campaign as ever organized."[118] In May, Ralph Abernathy came to Chicago to address a convention of two thousand people, vowing that they wouldn't stop until there was "integration in every school in Chicago" and would use rent strikes as a "chief weapon" to attack slum housing.[119] Despite his initial opposition, Hosea Williams began suggesting the use of SCOPE volunteers (a national voter registration drive he was spearheading) for Chicago as well.[120]

Other colleagues of King, notably Bernard Lafayette, had moved to Chicago years earlier. Lafayette got his start in Nashville, Tennessee, in SNCC and was hired in 1963 by the American Friends Service Committee (AFSC) to bring the ideas and practices of nonviolent direct action and conflict resolution to local teenagers. Lafayette had two years on the ground before the SCLC's formal campaign. James Bevel had been hired by the West Side Christian Parish and moved to Chicago in the summer of 1965.

Dorothy Tillman was only eighteen when she moved to Chicago to do youth organizing for SCLC. Tillman had grown up in Montgomery and took part in the march over the Edmund Pettus Bridge before moving to the Windy City in the fall. She underlined how much strategy the Chicago campaign had: "it wasn't haphazard." Part of King's talent was that he surrounded himself with a group of organizers, listened, and didn't make decisions on his own. "One thing that people don't know about Dr. King is that the discussions and decisions included the field staff. . . . Dr. King was a very good listener. He cracked a lot of jokes. . . . But when it came to Bevel and the field secretaries, we had some serious talk. He listened."[121]

On June 23, to try to destabilize the campaign, Willis announced that he would retire the next year, when he turned sixty-five. The Board of Education hoped to take that issue off the table and make the movement less "viable," according to Raby.[122] But they were not cowed.

In July, King came to the city for three days of action to kick off the Chicago Freedom Movement (CFM). He gave twenty speeches and marched through the Loop. "I have found the North no better than the South," King thundered.[123] Thirty thousand people marched through the Loop. Juanita Abernathy observed the power of tens of thousands to highlight the city's segregation: "For Chicago to have a decent image, they're going to have to clean house."[124]

King spoke to residents in front of the Robert Taylor and Altgeld Gardens projects and then ventured into one of Chicago's richest suburbs, Winnetka, Illinois, to draw attention to the North Shore Summer Project. The project, modeled after Freedom Summer in Mississippi, sought to open up housing in Chicago's exclusive, nearly all-white suburbs to Black buyers and renters. It was the brainchild of a group of white Chicago women who had gone to Mississippi in the summer of 1964 and come home changed. A suburban mother of five, Henrietta Moore had realized that the problem wasn't just in the South but also in her own segregated white suburban community. So they spent the summer trying to change it—and invited King to help highlight the problem. But King's appearance, according to historian Mary Barr, "seemed to appease residents more than challenge them." Many gave him a standing ovation in the town square, but not a single home was sold or rented to African Americans in this Chicago suburb that entire summer.[125] These liberal suburbanites were proud that King had visited them, but most had no interest in changing their own communities. King was also picketed and called a Communist for his open-housing stance during this visit.[126] So the movement faced various forms of white resistance as it prepared to launch an even more audacious campaign against Chicago's slumism.

To kick off the campaign, King reinterpreted the story of Northern migration as one of promise and then deep betrayal: "We sang *Going to Chicago* until there were as many of our people in Chicago as Mississippi. Now we see the results. Chicago did not turn out to be a new Jerusalem . . . but a city in dire need of redemption and reform." [127] Black migrants had come with hopes and plans and instead found a new Egypt. As they prepared to double down in Chicago, the pharaohs they would have to take on included not only the most powerful mayor in America, but President Lyndon Johnson himself.

Act III

1965–1966

King spoke at many rallies and organizing meetings to end slums in Chicago in 1965 and 1966.

7

Police Brutality in the North
Is Rationalized, Tolerated,
and Usually Denied

King Takes On White Shock After Watts

The ways that many Northern whites continued to deny Black suffering and preserve their own segregation haunted King.[1] At the beginning of August 1965, alongside the signing of the Voting Rights Act, King met with President Johnson and then forwarded him a set of proposals to address "increasing segregation" in the North. "The ghetto is being intensified," King stressed, "rather than dispersed."[2] The proposals included: cutting off federal funding—as the Civil Rights Act required—to school districts that practice "de facto" segregation; extending an executive order against housing discrimination to include private lenders as well as the federal government; taxing landlords and passing statutory codes to make ownership and operation of slums less profitable; and establishing large public works and job training programs to address Black unemployment (particularly in the face of deindustrialization and automation). In other words, despite the jubilation around the Voting Rights Act, King had well-defined proposals, alongside many other activists, to deal with Northern racism. He knew the enormity of the task undone. But Johnson, Congress, Northern mayors, and many Northern whites continued to choose to ignore them.

Warning about the potential for uprisings, King was up front with Johnson at the beginning of August about what it would take to avoid them. Los Angeles mayor Sam Yorty, on the other hand, had just bragged to the US Civil Rights Commission that his city had "the best race relations . . . of any large city in the United States."[3]

Five days later, on August 11, LA police pulled over a twenty-one-year-old Black man for drunk driving at 116th and Avalon, near the

Watts neighborhood. Marquette Frye and his brother Ronald, who had just returned from the air force, had been out celebrating. Marquette had grown up in Wyoming before moving to California in 1957. He contrasted how much more segregated and policed LA's schools were: "When we came to California, we got into an all-Negro school. . . . I made A's and B's back in Wyoming. But here I kept getting suspended for fighting."[4] Frye ended up dropping out of South LA's deeply segregated Fremont High School.

Police pulled Frye over about a block from his home. When officers began beating Marquette and his mother (who had arrived on the scene), a gathering crowd got angry and began throwing rocks and bottles. A sea of twenty-six police cars descended, sirens blazing.[5] This massive police onslaught further incensed the growing crowd, and Watts erupted into six days of rebellion, looting, and fires.

The uprising was, in part, a commodities riot, as people looted stores for basic needs. More than half of the African Americans living in South LA lived below the poverty line, one in three was unemployed, and median income in South LA had *declined* from 1959 to 1965.[6] While public officials likened the rebellion to Black people burning down their own neighborhood, the uprising was more targeted than officials suggested. Aimed at commercial interests like banks that charged Black people high rates, grocery stores that marked up prices and sold rotten food, and pawnshops that preyed on poor people, most housing, schools, and libraries were untouched. So were many Black businesses, white businesses that gave Black people credit, Simon Rodia's artistic Watts Tower, and the Urban League's Watts project—as King would later point out.[7] In other words, rioters had largely spared institutions that served the Black community.

In response, the police cracked down on Black Angelenos at large. The city announced a curfew that covered *only* Black LA—an area the media began calling "Watts," although it covered the neighborhoods of Watts, Central, Avalon, Florence, Green Meadow, Exposition, and Willowbrook. That this swath of more than 250,000 residents (which represented more than 75 percent of Black people living in LA County) could be effectively cordoned off from the rest of the city was testament to the degree of LA's segregation. Cynthia Hamilton, a high school student at the time, explained how the city used the uprising "to quarantine the entire community."[8] The law enforcement response to the uprising—comprising the LAPD, California Highway Patrol, and National Guard—was bigger than the force Lyndon Johnson had used to invade the Dominican Republic four months earlier.[9] Marnesba Tackett noted how police came in shooting many people in the back or with their hands up.[10] Tens of thousands of people were on the streets during the uprising. By the end, thirty-four people were dead and more than one thousand injured—most at the hands of law enforcement.

The head of LA's NAACP, Celes King III, a bail bondsman, posted bond for hundreds of people, risking his business by eliminating the standards usually used to agree to post bail. "The community was, I would say, generally supportive of the blacks that were the so-called rioters," he explained.[11] A UCLA study found that 58 percent of Black Angelenos in the curfew zone, even those who didn't approve of the property damage, felt that positive results would follow the riot. And 64 percent thought the attack was deserved.[12]

But many white Angelenos—residents, politicians, local media like the *Los Angeles Times*—and much of the nation professed shock. Such claims of surprise framed Black anger as unwarranted and out of nowhere. Refusing to look inward and acknowledge years of nonviolent movements against the city's endemic segregation that they had ignored and disparaged, they blamed Communists, Black activists, ghetto culture, and King himself for the breakdown in "law and order." Proclaiming California a "state without racial discrimination," Governor Pat Brown, who was vacationing in Greece when the riot happened, flew home immediately, informing reporters that "nobody told me there was an explosive situation in Los Angeles."[13] Brown's lie was outrageous—but reporters did not call him on it.

Years of movement demands, meetings, and nonviolent demonstrations around police brutality, housing and school segregation, and job discrimination had been ignored. King's own warnings had been dismissed. In a June 1963 television interview, King outlined how unemployment and housing segregation in the North were "growing every day." He continued, "These communities can explode into a terrible racial nightmare if something isn't done, and I think it can be warded off."[14] Three months later, in a September 1963 *New York Times* op-ed, he talked about the urgent need for progress around police brutality, voting, and unemployment. "We can deal with it now or we can drive a seething humanity to a desperation it tried, asked for and hoped to avoid."[15] In his 1964 book *Why We Can't Wait*, King emphasized police brutality as a national problem: "[A]rmies of officials are clothed in uniform, invested with authority, armed with the instruments of violence and death and conditioned to believe they can intimidate, maim, or kill Negroes with the same recklessness that once motivated the slaveowner." Indeed, just as the uprising was taking place, the *Los Angeles Times* published a long piece on King's plans after the Voting Rights Act, where he warned that "ghettos in cities like Los Angeles, Chicago, New York, and Washington are racial powderkegs" if substantive programs weren't undertaken.[16]

King stressed that there was no way to separate California's "vote for ghettos" in Proposition 14 the previous November from what ensued on the streets of South LA nine months later. Black psychiatrist Alvin Poussaint, interviewed three days after the rebellion, agreed.[17] White Californians had sent a decisive message about their commitment to segregation. But the city's mainstream newspapers, along with much of the national media, amplified white "shock" and did not hold city leaders and residents accountable for their years of intransigence to Black grievances around schools, housing, jobs, and policing. Black Angelenos had built nonviolent movements for years but were now cast as naturally violent and angry—"terrorists," the *Chicago Tribune* called them.[18]

The *Los Angeles Times* didn't have a single Black reporter on staff before the uprising. Instead, well-known white writer Theodore White described the "open and easy tolerance" of the city where Black people had made "spectacular progress."[19] The paper doubled down on the importance of the police, who "are doing their job and doing it well."[20] They refused to acknowledge the systemic injustice endemic to the city or that the police were part of the problem. Describing Los Angeles as a "civilized" city, the editors called for "an increase in the size of the police force."[21] While endorsing dialogue between the Black community and the police department, they downgraded Black concerns: "It is likely that Negro complaints hinge more around their resentment of alleged police attitudes and procedure, than outright brutality."[22]

King was angry at this willful shock. "If Mayor Yorty had listened to me, there would have been no Watts," he later observed.[23] This is not to say that King was not unnerved and saddened. He felt deeply responsible for not doing enough to prevent the uprising. As Coretta repeatedly observed, he was his own deepest critic. He had known how catastrophic Proposition 14's passage would be, and yet it had passed. Alongside a phalanx of activists, he had highlighted the pattern of segregation and police brutality for years, and still it continued unabated. He should have done more. He needed to do more. Even though King had been in LA more than fifteen times in the past decade calling out problems in the City of Angels, city officials had paid little attention to the urgency around police brutality and housing and school segregation in LA. He needed to do more.

When the uprising broke out, King was speaking in Puerto Rico, but he cut his trip short. While order needed to be restored, he stressed, "police power can bring only a temporary halt. Better housing and economic conditions and opportunities for Negroes" were what was needed to solve the problem.[24] King wanted to travel to LA—and had been asked by some Black Angelenos to come. But Bayard Rustin and some Black leaders warned about associating with rioters.[25] Governor Brown told reporters, "I prefer we handle this ourselves. . . . I think [King] is a great man but I don't think this is the time for civil rights demonstrations."[26]

But King decided it was precisely the time he needed to be there. Martin was "intuitively sympathetic to blacks who rioted," Coretta explained. He understood the frustrations of their grievances long unanswered.[27] Brown was "tragically misled," King emphasized, "if he thinks my only role is to lead civil rights demonstrations."[28] Six days after the uprising began, King traveled to LA to assess the situation, talk with Black people, and stress to as many levels of white leadership as he could the context for what had happened. Many journalists disingenuously cast it as King's first real visit to Black LA—as have many of his biographers—but King himself was clear: "I had visited Watts on many occasions and received the most generous of acclamations."[29]

Martin "sought to impress upon the Establishment the fact that the people had legitimate complaints," Coretta Scott King explained. "The solution was not to quell riots and return to business as usual but to ensure economic and political equality."[30] Interviewed on his arrival, King emphasized to reporters the depth of public action needed to address the situation: "Out of the ashes of this crisis we have the opportunity to deal with the housing problem, to build better schools, to deal with the police problem and perhaps make Los Angeles a model community."[31] While reiterating that "violence is not the answer to social conflict," King stated his desire to work with the mayor and other LA officials "in proposing programs for the eradication of those problems relating to housing, schools, jobs, and police behavior that were directly or indirectly related to the disorder."[32] Only a massive program of change would restore Black people's faith.[33]

King's compassion was evident for the dehumanizing conditions people had been forced to endure, as he stressed the city and state's responsibility for maintaining racial injustice in housing, schooling, jobs, and police brutality. Repeatedly over the next few years, King quoted Victor Hugo's *Les Miserables*: "If the soul is left in darkness, sins will be committed. The guilty one is not he who commits the sin, but he who causes the darkness." At a press conference, King underlined the larger societal responsibility for the uprising—including himself in the castigation: "By acts of commission and omission, none of us in this great country have done enough to remove injustice. I there-fore humbly suggest that all of us accept our share of responsibility for these past days of anguish."[34] King had highlighted the city's systemic racism long before these events, but a tsunami of reporters now de-scended on him and reported it as new—perhaps because they hadn't wanted to pay attention before Watts erupted. As Black LA bookstore owner Alfred Ligon explained, "It was only because of the uprising that they became interested in the blacks [here]."[35]

King had gone to Watts to meet with people, to listen to their griev-ances and be with them in this time of need. While the *Los Angeles Times* headlined the "heckling" the civil rights leader received, this was but a tiny fraction of people; *Jet Magazine* wrote "the cynics were drowned out by cheers and applause" with young people both speaking and lis-tening.[36] King described the reception as "marvelous," particularly be-cause "I had heard so many people didn't want me to come."[37]

Most biographers cite Rustin's description of King being "undone" after his visit to Watts. How that is typically framed is that King had realized the urgency of Northern problems.[38] They don't mention the scores of visits and protests King had made in the city in the preceding years (or the fact that Rustin had not joined him in those). Being un-done is also a recognition of the measure of societal disregard for Black suffering. He, like so many Black Angelenos, had decried LA's racism over and over, protested over and over, and people in power hadn't lis-tened, never mind acted. King was undone by that indifference. On top of it, his conscience haunted him. He felt he hadn't done enough.[39]

The contentious meeting King did encounter was a three-hour session with the mayor and the police chief, along with Rustin and other civil rights leaders in the city. King reiterated the riot's context: long-standing Black grievances around schools, housing, jobs, and po-licing, highlighted for years to no avail, had pushed people to a break-ing point. He called for a civilian complaint review board—as he had in New York a year earlier—to provide oversight over the police, and Chief Parker's resignation. But like in New York, the suggestion was angrily shot down. Complaining of "unfounded charges of police bru-tality," Mayor Yorty accused King of advocating Black "lawlessness" and said Los Angeles "would not stand" for Parker's resignation. He maintained that there was "no reason to find fault in law enforce-ment."[40] King wanted to meet with Black people who had been jailed for "rioting" (over four thousand had been arrested just for curfew vi-olations) but Yorty and Parker refused.[41] The LAPD further punished people by upping the bail requirement by $3,000, making it impossi-ble for many people to make bail and thus affecting their work and their families.[42]

King grew angry, criticizing the mayor for being "insensitive to so-cial revolution" and overlooking police abuses and the oppressiveness of the city's segregation. Relegating the uprising to a "criminal element was a dangerous fantasy,"[43] King emphasized, and he highlighted the damage of California's approval of segregation and ghettoization with Proposition 14's passage. But Yorty and Parker denied LA's segrega-tion. "That's no indication of prejudice," they claimed. "That's per-sonal choice [in terms of where people live]."[44] Rustin had never seen King as confrontational as he was in this meeting. And even though King kept his cool, Rustin and King were "completely nonplussed" by how rude and aggressive Parker and Yorty were.[45]

Telling reporters afterward he had called for a CCRB, a shaken King repeated that Parker should be removed as police chief immediately. Highlighting the city's deep economic inequities, King noted how city leaders denied that poverty or police misconduct had contributed to the uprising.[46] City leaders were trying to shirk their own responsibil-ities, "particularly the explosion of accumulated frustrations that have been developing over the years [around] housing, schools, jobs, and police behavior." Amid "luxury living for whites," King underscored the poverty many Black Angelenos lived in—calling the uprising "a class revolt of the underprivileged against the privileged."[47] With dev-astating clarity, King laid the cause of the riot at the feet of white public officials, particularly Yorty, saying he hadn't found any statesmanship or creative leadership in the city around civil rights. He was sorry that Yorty found charges of police brutality "ridiculous" but cited "a unan-imous feeling" among Black people about police brutality. "You don't solve problems by keeping them under the surface."[48]

Yorty overheard the last part of the press exchange and told report-ers that King's visit was "a great disservice to the people of Los Ange-les and to the nation." He made clear that King "shouldn't have come here." [49] Two days later, Chief Parker attacked King's call for a CCRB as an attempt "to break the will of police." The riot showed the need for more and stronger policing, Parker stressed; "next time they'll burn our whole city down." [50] Yorty flatly refused to remove Chief Parker, saying he "wouldn't even accept Parker's resignation if he were to resign." [51] Instead, the mayor claimed that charges of police brutality were part of an international Communist "big lie" to discredit law enforcement. [52] To Yorty, Parker, and many white residents, the problem was not too much policing but too little.

The *Los Angeles Times* gave ample space to Mayor Yorty and Chief Parker—who lambasted the "big lie" of police brutality and likened the rioters to "monkeys in a zoo." [53] They interviewed few Black activists and ignored the long movement challenging police brutality and calling for Parker's resignation. As writer Maya Angelou, living in LA at the time, observed, reporters who descended on Black LA maintained a familiar set of cultural stereotypes in their coverage, allowing readers "to hold onto the stereotypes that made them comfortable while congratulating themselves on being in possession of some news." [54] Nonetheless, the *Los Angeles Times* would win a Pulitzer Prize for its coverage of the uprising. In many ways, the *Times* would provide the template for covering the uprisings that took place over the next few years: "surprise" at the uprising and alarm at Black anger, followed by "discovery" over the coming months of patterns of inequality in the city (which had been pointed out for years by local activists and King himself), with little to no acknowledgment of years of Black organizing and grievances before the uprising, and then calls for increased police. [55]

Five months earlier, Yorty had proclaimed King always welcome in LA. [56] But as King would observe time and again, leaders like Yorty embraced him so long as they could cordon off his work in the South, and reacted angrily when he dared highlight their own city's problems and the consequences of their own inaction. King also met with Governor Brown, telling him of the "unanimous feeling that the chief of police of this city is insensitive to the social demands of this hour and that there is police brutality." [57] Pressing Brown to actually visit Watts, King again called for a CCRB. [58] Brown stuck by his belief that California had no systemic racial discrimination, and that the riot was *not* the result of civil rights issues. He unequivocally refused to create a CCRB. Defending Parker—"I don't believe he has the slightest bit of prejudice in him"—the governor then bizarrely claimed the police chief's zeal for policing could be mistaken for prejudice.[59]

Criticizing police conduct was politically anathema, and condemnation rained down on King, as it had on the activists challenging LA's pattern of police brutality. He received many letters from white Californians angry at him over the rebellion and telling him he was playing into "communist's tactics in crying 'Police Brutalities.' "[60] The *Los Angeles Times* editorialized, "Los Angeles, however, is not Birmingham or Selma. Police Chief William Parker is not Bull Connor or Jim Clark."[61] Increasingly, white journalists and columnists used words like *arrogant* and *pompous* to describe King in these years.[62] Such charges served to displace King's criticisms of the city's injustices; commentators who might have looked favorably on King's bold condemnations of Birmingham's racism found it problematic when trained on LA.

Despite Rustin's crucial assistance during the visit to Los Angeles, their politics were starting to diverge. Back in February, Rustin urged the movement to move from "protest to politics" to appeal more effectively to the halls of power. He cast King's decision to build a campaign in Chicago as folly.[63] King disagreed. He saw even more clearly how confrontational protest was essential. The uprising and meetings with gaslighting city officials reinforced the need for the broad Chicago campaign they had kicked off the previous month.

But such hostile treatment by public leaders, who professed to be friends, was also exhausting and devastating. The idea of speaking truth to power is a much-praised notion, and sometimes it seems King came naturally to it. He did not. Increasingly over his shortened life, he had more access to the powerful than most. And so King made himself do it again and again to live with himself and his responsibilities. But to be "scorned and abused by many in high places," as Coretta put it, took a deep personal toll. He hated personal conflict. His refusal to tone himself down or, conversely, to get so despairing that he stormed out required tremendous fortitude and bravery.[64]

Disturbed by his meeting with Yorty and Parker, King alerted President Johnson to the problem. Johnson was eager to talk about his War on Poverty solutions, but King broke in:

That's all right. But in my meeting with Police Chief Parker and Mr. Yorty—Mayor Yorty—I just felt that they are absolutely insensitive to the problem and to the needs, to really cure the situation. . . . I'm fearful that if something isn't done to give a new sense of hope to the people in that area—and they are poverty-stricken—that a full-scale race war can develop here. And I'm concerned about it, naturally, because I know that violence . . . doesn't help.[65]

War on Poverty money was crucial, King told Johnson, but not sufficient. The racism and segregation of LA's policing, housing, jobs, and schools needed to be addressed head-on, and Yorty and Parker were key obstacles.

But this is not what Johnson wanted to hear. He wasn't interested in taking on Northern Democrats and the structural racism they maintained. Wanting more praise from King for what he was doing, Johnson spurned King's advice on LA, his aides reported to the FBI.[66] The approach Johnson favored was a mix of self-help programs like adult education and youth recreation to remediate Black culture, expanded law enforcement, and increased expenditures on advanced military equipment, as historian Elizabeth Hinton has documented.[67] Johnson also wanted John McCone, who had stepped down as CIA director in the spring, to head a commission Governor Brown was putting together to study the riot's causes.[68]

While the media swarmed around King, they largely heard what they wanted.[69] Reporters constantly badgered him on the fact that many Black Angelenos didn't see him as their leader, even though King himself was *not* portraying himself as such. Many journalists and subsequent biographers quoted an encounter between King and some young rioters to illustrate the supposed divide between him and young Black Angelenos. "We won," these young men told King, "because we made the whole world pay attention to us."[70] But this reads much differently in the context of a decade-long struggle in the city against school and housing segregation, job discrimination, and police brutality that had garnered little change.

When he returned home from Watts, Martin told Coretta that what struck him the most "as he walked the streets those terrible nights, the people, young and old, would gather and listen to him thoughtfully and sympathetically."[71] But exaggerating a divide between King and young Black Angelenos was a convenient framing for reporters and commentators eager to avoid addressing the city's pervasive and devastating inequality and cast urban Black people as alienated, reckless, and bent on "destroying their neighborhoods."

The willful denial of systemic issues with policing in Los Angeles after the uprising signaled the embrace of a law-and-order politics that would prove politically ascendant in the state over the coming years. While often associated with Ronald Reagan's election to governor in 1966, it had bipartisan support from liberals like Yorty and Brown before that. While California is often associated with the more radical side of the 1960s, what the white liberal reaction to the Watts uprising sharply revealed was the other side of California's political identity. The doubling down on a racially driven, law-and-order politics would bring Reagan to the governor's office, increased policing to the streets and schools of Black LA, and California as an early harbinger of US carceral politics. Richard Nixon would carry the state in 1968.[72]

Returning from LA, King contextualized the uprising in his *Amsterdam News* column: "At a time when the Negro's aspirations were at a peak, his actual conditions of employment, education and housing were worsening." A driving factor among the hundreds of Black Angelenos he had talked to were "serious doubts that the white community is in any way concerned or willing to accommodate their needs." Condemning the "blind intransigence" of public officials, he warned that treating the uprising as "merely the result of an irresponsible criminal element is to lead the Watts community into a potential holocaust."[73]

A week later, Brown announced a commission to study the riot's causes, naming McCone to head it. Brown made clear that Los Angeles had no legal discrimination; the "riot took place in a scene of broken families and broken hearts, of lonely children and aimless adults, of frustration and poverty."[74] The report that came out in December replicated this blindness. "A Negro in Los Angeles has long been able to sit where he wants in a bus or a movie house," the report proclaimed, "to shop where he wishes, to vote, and to use public facilities without discrimination. The opportunity to succeed is probably unequaled in any other major American city."[75] Rather, the McCone Commission found that Black Angelenos needed "attitudinal training" and also blamed civil rights activists for creating the climate leading to violent riots.[76] The commission largely attributed the uprising to Black pathology and a "dull devastating spiral of failure that awaits the average disadvantaged child." Advocating more remedial programs, the commission blamed "unprepared and unready" Black students: "the very low level of scholastic achievement we observe in the predominantly Negro schools contributes to de facto segregation in the schools. . . .

We reason, therefore, that raising the scholastic achievement might reverse the entire trend of de facto segregation."[77] Proclaiming that fixing Black culture would fix segregation, the report also whitewashed the Board of Education's and LAPD's actions more broadly.[78]

This culturalist framing came to dominate much of the long-form journalism in the uprising's wake. Lengthy articles intertwined searing portraits of poverty and racism with titillating accounts of the seamy underbelly of ghetto life.[79] Renowned novelist Thomas Pynchon took "A Journey into the Mind of Watts" in a celebrated *New York Times Magazine* piece on the uprising's one-year anniversary.[80] The piece voyeuristically traveled to "the heart of L.A.'s racial sickness . . . the coexistence of two very different cultures: one white and one black." According to Pynchon, "black culture is stuck pretty much with basic realities like disease, like failure, violence and death, which the whites have mostly chosen—and can afford—to ignore"; Black kids in Watts, he wrote, "are so tough you can pull slivers of it out of them and never get a whimper." Such a culturalist approach treated Black urban communities as a problem to be studied, evaded institutional sites of racism, otherized Black youth, and helped reinforce a language of racial difference framed through cultural deviance.

So in November 1965, when King took to the pages of the *Saturday Review*, he knew firsthand how many white Californians who saw themselves as open, fair, and friends of the Southern movement had brushed off local Black movements and repeatedly countenanced segregation, job inequities, and police brutality at home. Mayors like Yorty and Wagner exhibited "blindness, obtuseness and rigidity" while Mayor Ivan Allen Jr. of Atlanta and many other Southern public officials, "with all their conflicts, came much further in human relations than Northern mayors."[81] King denounced the two-facedness of Northern white leaders who "sat on platforms with all their imposing regalia of office to welcome me to their cities and showered praise on the heroism of Southern Negroes. Yet when the issues were joined concerning local conditions, only the language was polite; the rejection was firm and unequivocal."

The year before, in an interview with writer Robert Penn Warren, King challenged Warren's framing of the "random and uncontrollable" riots in places like Harlem. They weren't random; if city practices had shifted and patterns of police abuse were addressed, these uprisings wouldn't occur.

[T]he only answer to this problem is the degree . . . [and] speed in which we move toward the solution of the problem. If the Negro feels that he can do nothing but move from one ghetto to another and one slum to another, the despair and the disappointment will be so great that it will be very difficult to keep the struggle disciplined and nonviolent.[82]

King bore down on the differential outrage around police brutality in the South versus the North: "As the nation, Negro and white, trembled with outrage at police brutality in the South, police misconduct in the North was rationalized, tolerated, and usually denied."[83] While Bull Connor's violence was blasted across the nation, most Northern police brutality and racist, repressive police chiefs like William Parker were not exposed by the mainstream press, only the Black press.[84]

A War on Crime, Not Segregation

Like McCone, President Johnson had pivoted toward crime and Black cultural dysfunction as the most urgent problems facing Black urban America. Earlier that year, in March, a week after he sent the Voting Rights Act to Congress, LBJ had introduced a "War on Crime." Casting crime as an epidemic facing the nation, Johnson initiated a new federal role in local law enforcement, calling urban policemen the "frontline soldier" and building a weapons arsenal for their use.[85] In June, armed with ammunition from New York senator Daniel Moynihan, the president gave the commencement speech at Howard University declaring the "next and more profound stage of the civil rights struggle" was not tackling job discrimination or housing and school segregation but "the Negro family structure."[86] Similar to LA's Board of Education and Chief Parker, Johnson claimed that problems in education, housing, and jobs were rooted in Black community responses. It was Black crime and family structure that needed urgent attention.

King countered this framing: "In the United States, [the Negro family] has lived in a man-made social and psychological jungle which it could not subdue. Many have been destroyed by it. Yet others have survived and developed an appalling capacity for hardships. . . . What is required is a recognition by society that it has been guilty of the crimes and that it is prepared to atone."[87] But, following the Watts rebellion, the Johnson administration saw increasing police patrols and providing advanced weaponry for police as the *best* short-term measure to address uprisings.[88] In the next three years, the federal government allocated $30 million to local and state police that modernized and armed police departments, including providing military-grade weapons, steel helmets, three-foot batons, armored vehicles, and tear gas, which would drastically escalate the number of people incarcerated.[89]

King knew what was needed was societal redress, jobs programs, and federal action on school and housing segregation. In July 1965, Chicago parents with the CCCO had filed a complaint with the US Office of Education stating that the Chicago Board of Education had violated Title VI of the 1964 Civil Rights Act—which gave the US Department of Health, Education, and Welfare (HEW) the power to withhold federal funds if school districts continued to segregate. In an August speech, King emphasized the urgency of enforcing the Civil Rights Act against school districts across the country, including Chicago and Milwaukee. Then, following his conversation with Johnson after visiting Watts, he again reiterated the paramount importance of the act's enforcement in Northern school districts as well as Southern.

Chicago stood to lose over $30 million. The federal government requested a host of information from the city: racial head counts of students and teachers, per-pupil expenditures in schools, average class size, student-teacher ratios, and the method of assigning teachers. HEW sent a team of investigators, but Willis and the Board of Education did not comply.[90] Willis had long refused federal requests for information. Also, HEW had learned that Willis intended to use the federal money to aid middle-class white districts and build more Willis wagons.[91] As a result, on October 1, Assistant Secretary of Education Francis Keppel withheld those $32 million in federal funds, finding the Chicago school system was in "probable non-compliance."

King telegrammed President Johnson praising the decision and the importance of enforcing the Civil Rights Act against Northern school systems.[92] Al Raby and many Black Chicagoans celebrated; this federal decision underscored what they had known for years—"that the board was flagrantly in violation of the federal requirements."[93] But most white Chicagoans were apoplectic at HEW's decision. Their taxes gave them the right to "their" schools, and, much like their Southern counterparts, they didn't want the federal government meddling. Willis called the action "illegal, despotic, alarming and threatening."[94] The *Chicago Tribune* slammed "federal interference," calling the decision "outrageous" and "based on unspecified and unproven charges

of 'discrimination' against Negro pupils."[95] Illinois Republican senator
Everett Dirksen and Chicago Democratic congressmen Dan Rosten-
kowski, John Kluczynski, and Roman Pucinski—all of whom had supported the Civil Rights Act the year before—opposed its enforcement
in Chicago.

Incandescent with rage, Mayor Daley got on a plane to confront
President Johnson directly. Daley was so unrelenting in his arguments
about why the money had to be restored, according to Johnson, that
the president was late to meet the pope.[96] Johnson and Daley were
friendly, and Johnson understood Daley's importance to his planned
reelection campaign. Additionally, the national media coverage of
HEW's decision didn't highlight the systemic segregation, decrepit
overcrowded schools, and deep inequality of Chicago's schools or
the fact that the city had refused to provide information to the federal government. In contorted language, the *New York Times* described
it as "complaints of school segregation" that prompted HEW's action
while one United Press International (UPI) reporter described "the appearance of segregated public schools."[97] Such problematic national
coverage of HEW's decision minimized Chicago's school segregation,
aided Daley, and sounded the death knell for federal intervention into
a Northern school system.

Johnson, concerned about Daley's political reach and not worried
about a media backlash, summoned Keppel to the White House and
told HEW to settle the issue.[98] *Less than a week* after it had withheld
funds, HEW capitulated and released the $32 million to Chicago. In-
stead of continuing to investigate the CCCO complaint, they put the
Chicago Board of Education in charge of investigating it themselves.[99]
The political pressure was out in the open. King was furious about the
return of the money, making clear, "The act is not worth its salt if the
government won't enforce it."[100]

Keppel was not some minor federal bureaucrat—he was one of the
faces of Johnson's new approach to civil rights and economic justice.
Days later, he was featured on the cover of *Time* magazine. But he had
mistaken the Civil Rights Act as something to be enforced against segregated schools *across* the entire nation.[101] According to Daley's biographers, Daley didn't just want Chicago's funding restored; he wanted
Keppel punished and a message sent to anyone who dared take on
his segregation. So Keppel was "quietly removed to a position where
he could do no further harm." He would later explain, "In effect I was
fired."[102] Daley, Willis, and the white families who supported Chicago's

segregated schools emerged victorious. The *Chicago Tribune* rejoiced.[103] Raby, like many Black Chicagoans, was "absolutely astounded that Daley was able to evidently call Johnson directly and have Keppel called on the carpet, and those resources re-established." [104]

Every potential "proper channel" to address the city's school segregation had not worked. Black Chicagoans had tried to go through the Board of Education and to the mayor's office. They had done studies, marched, picketed, kept their kids out of school, sat in, blocked the Willis wagons, filed suit, attempted to use the Civil Rights Act's provisions, and now the president of the United States had failed them.

Keppel had done what many Black Northerners and King had been demanding for years—to bring the federal government's power to bear on Northern segregation. The 1964 Civil Rights Act was now the law of the land and HEW had briefly taken up its enforcement across the country. But Johnson deliberately halted that in its tracks, allowing school segregation to persist in Chicago and other Northern cities.[105] If Chicago's segregated schools had been brought to heel in 1965, then Los Angeles, Boston, New York, and many other segregated school systems likely would have faced intervention in the coming years. But that didn't happen.

In his *Amsterdam News* column, King criticized how white Americans wanted to "rest on their laurels" with the passage of the Civil Rights Act and Voting Rights Act when the North had been "neglected during this entire period of change." He made clear that "laws passed for the Negro's benefit are so widely unenforced it is hard to call them laws." [106] Given how untouched most Northern segregation remained, King saw they would need to escalate the scope of their demands and their tactics of disruption. He would move to Chicago to do it.

8

Warrior Without a Gun

The Kings Move to Chicago

The Kings had lost patience with the ways that many Northern whites celebrated the Southern movement but gaslighted local Black grievances while the federal government propped up Northern segregation.[1] "The North is not the promised land," Coretta Scott King made clear.[2]

The Watts rebellion would define reporters'—and thus much of the country's—reactions to the Chicago campaign, even though the campaign was initiated *before* the Watts uprising, announced in April 1965 and kicked off in July. Even the *New York Times* in early July had run a sizable, if inaccurate, article on King's campaign in Chicago for desegregated schools and housing. But the robust local movement that led to his coming to Chicago, King's many stands against Willis and Chicago's segregation over the previous years, and the intransigence of white Chicago were left out of the story.[3]

As they launched the CFM in July, King proclaimed, "When a man cannot get a good job and good wages, he is a slave. When he cannot get good, substantial housing, he is a slave. When a man cannot get integrated education, he is a slave. Before I'll be a slave, I'll be buried in my grave. We are eternally through with racial segregation."[4] King offered a prayer for Chicago that city leaders "respond to the legitimate discontent . . . with creative and imaginative programs which will rectify the injustices of the past." Like their Southern counterparts, many white Chicagoans needed to "atone for the sins they have perpetrated on their colored brethren."[5] To cut through the self-delusions of many Chicagoans, the distortions of the white media, the duplicity of the Daley machine, and the complicity of Congress and Johnson, the Chicago Freedom Movement would build an audacious campaign—and King would put himself and his family on the front lines to expose the structures that sustained Northern racism.

One of the greatest myths about King's work in the North—and the Chicago campaign in particular—was that it lacked concrete proposals. Journalists, politicians, and Northern whites and even subsequent historians favored this take, positing it as more difficult to address Northern segregation. For years, white Northerners had cast their segregation as a product of personal prejudices, housing choices, and cultural differences—more amorphous and accidental, rather than systemic and deeply changeable.

King and the CFM aimed to destroy that dangerous idea. By building on campaigns Black Chicagoans had already been organizing to expose the many policies and institutions that maintained and profited from the slums, their campaign sought to break through Daley's "tokenism"—the repeated denial of a structural problem accompanied by a few quick fixes (a recreation center built or an apartment building fixed to code). The CFM had wide-ranging targets and a variety of proposals to address the forces that maintained the city's devastating segregation and "slumism." But many Northern politicians, local, state, and federal, didn't want to act.

Relatedly, many historians have been consumed by the infighting and tensions within the Chicago Freedom Movement. This is not to downplay those tensions; there were tensions between SCLC and some community leaders, as well as within SCLC itself about the best approach. But ideological and personal disagreements were widespread in movements in Albany, Birmingham, and Selma—and they have not eclipsed the story. The focus on the tensions also cannot be separated from the white media narrative on Black division that dominated the way the Chicago campaign was covered, the role Daley and perhaps the FBI played in stoking those tensions, and culture-of-poverty ideas, which framed Black Northerners as angry, unorganizable, and different from good Southern Black people.

In July 1965, King kicked off the new chapter of the Chicago campaign with twenty speeches over two days across the city, speaking at two of the city's largest housing projects, the Robert Taylor Homes and Altgeld Gardens.[6] The *Defender* captured the diversity and enthusiasm of the crowd that turned out: "The look of bright-eyed wonder and anticipation lighting the faces of young and old alike were only a few of the ingredients blended into a rousing West Side street rally to greet and hear Dr. Martin Luther King."[7]

Activists had commenced daily marches to City Hall against school segregation in July. King joined one on Monday, July 26. Ralph

Abernathy was predicting ten thousand would march, snarling traffic downtown. But the crowd burgeoned to thirty thousand.[8] A predominantly Black throng marched through downtown—again challenging Willis's policies and demanding a quality education for Black students. King, sick with bronchitis, still marched, emphasizing that "years of indifference and exploitation . . . could grow more serious and ominous" unless city leaders acted.[9] The CFM's message was clear: Chicago was no promised land and it was long past time to address that.[10]

But when the *New York Times* covered it, the story shifted. Chicago's racism was framed in qualifying terms, describing "policies are branded pro-segregationist" with no details about the actual policies and the overcrowded, underfunded, segregated nature of Chicago's Black schools.[11] The *Chicago Tribune* reproved King for "encouraging a mood of lawlessness among Negroes."[12] Many news outlets helped sow the myths that have continued to define the story of King's work in Chicago. Amplifying division, they framed the host of movement demands as lacking focus and treated Chicago racism as not real segregation like the South's (people just preferred to live with "their own kind" in Chicago). In many ways, the media echoed the incredulity of most white Chicagoans. "We are not Birmingham. We are not Selma. We are Chicago," they would say.[13] *How dare he bring his movement here?* Privately, Daley raged, calling King "a dirty son of a bitch, a bastard, a prick . . . a rabble-rouser [and] a troublemaker."[14]

Having learned from movements in Chicago, Los Angeles, New York, and elsewhere, King brought a deep understanding of the Windy City's structural racism. It was not passive. It was not some indignities Black people had to endure. It was structural violence and continually reinforced segregation. Thus the freedom dreams of the Chicago Freedom Movement were deep and wide—to expose the various areas of injustice and illustrate that the deeply inequitable ways in which the city functioned could be concretely addressed and remedied.[15]

One such issue was environmental racism. Before it even had a name, community members had begun to identify environmental issues brought on by racism.[16] Bernard Lafayette had begun working with students from John Marshall High School in the summer of 1964. A young mother at a community meeting sounded the alarm. Both her kids started having serious symptoms of lead poisoning—one with a swollen abdomen and the other paralysis in one arm.[17] So Lafayette and fellow AFSC volunteers David Jehnsen and Tony Henry organized students to investigate childhood lead poisoning in the neighborhood.[18]

That summer of 1964, the students gathered over six hundred urine samples, resulting in the discovery and treatment of four definite cases of lead poisoning. When Lafayette pressed public officials, asking why the city wasn't screening children for lead poising, one public health official replied, "If we did that, the hospitals would be full." [19] Lafayette was astonished by the baldness of their reply—the city knew there was a problem; it just didn't want to address it. Under pressure, in December 1965 the city finally moved to use War on Poverty money to create a testing program similar to the students'. In the next two years, 68,744 Chicago children were screened, and 6 percent were found to have dramatically high rates of lead, 50 micrograms per liter. [20]

But testing was not enough—community activists wanted to stop the poisoning, which meant taking on slum housing. The dangers of lead paint were well known. New York City had banned it in 1960. That year, the *Chicago Defender* had exposed 108 cases of lead poisoning from substandard housing. [21] The Chicago Board of Health warned that the disease was "of epidemic proportions." [22] In 1961, the *Defender* doubled down the efforts of physician Dr. Joseph Greengard to coalesce public attention around the problems of lead paint in slum housing. The "real hazard," Greengard told the City Club, lay in "segregated slum areas where masses of poor people live in old, dilapidated buildings." [23] These old buildings had lead paint that was chipping off, creating dust and paint chips. Moreover, because lead paint is sweet, children would often put chips in their mouth or chew on windowsills (particularly if they were hungry). But the Daley administration was unwilling to hold landlords accountable.

As the city's testing program revealed the scale of the poisoning, community outrage spread and the Citizens Committee to End Lead Poisoning was founded in 1965. Quentin Young, one of the founders of Chicago's Medical Committee for Human Rights (MCHR), was involved in these community efforts. [24] MCHR had been founded the previous year to help take on Mississippi's system of Black disfranchisement and poverty. The committee quickly realized that health issues were not just a facet of Southern Jim Crow but nationwide, leading to the creation of Chicago's chapter. King then hired Lafayette to help plan and execute SCLC's campaign against Chicago's slums. [25]

This linking of targets reflected the breadth of King and the CCCO's approach to Chicago's racism. The CFM challenged segregated and decrepit schools *and* housing, health hazards *and* union discrimination, political machines *and* the need for parks and pools, *and* abusive law enforcement *and* Black political power. Yet in August (just after the Watts uprising), the *New York Times* ran a piece claiming that law and national policy had already taken care of most of the country's inequality and King and the SCLC were now "groping" for targets. Midway through the piece, King was quoted talking about the scale of the programs and policy needed "to bring an end to the ghetto through powerful programs to end housing discrimination, get better jobs for Negroes, and end de facto segregation in public schools." [26] The *Times* neither acknowledged that King had long been challenging these aspects of American racism nor indicated that King's calls for broad policy change refuted the piece's framing itself.

The direct action continued. On August 2, Dick Gregory led a three-and-a-half-hour march through the Chicago Loop, first to City Hall and then to the mayor's home on the South Side. As Gregory explained, "First we will go over to the snake pit [City Hall]. When we leave there, we will go to the snake's house [the mayor's home]. Then, we will continue to go to the mayor's home until he fires Ben Willis." [27] In late August, faced with continuing opposition from some colleagues, King trumpeted the robustness of Chicago's movement to his SCLC advisors: "Chicago is on fire with a nonviolent movement. They want us to come in September. We must not ignore their call." [28] Raby stressed to King how they wanted him and the SCLC back in the city for "an extended period of time." [29]

Chicago was emblematic of the many facets of Northern segregation, as Birmingham had been of Southern. So King saw the CFM as "the test case for the SCLC and for the freedom movement in the North." Some have interpreted this statement to mean that this was the first organized nonviolent movement in the North or King's first time protesting Northern inequality or that Chicagoans were previously disorganized and alienated. It was none of these. What King and the SCLC were attempting to do was to bring more people, power, and attention to a movement that had been going on in the city for years.

But he knew the difficulties they faced: "Egypt still exists in Chicago but the Pharaohs are more sophisticated and subtle." [30]

The Kings Move to Chicago

A group of SCLC organizers who had cut their teeth in the South—including Jim Bevel, Bernard Lafayette, Jim Wilson, James Orange, Dorothy Tillman, and Lynn Adler—were already living in Chicago as King

traveled to the city repeatedly throughout 1965. They had been can-
vassing the neighborhoods, getting a sense of the decrepit conditions
and beginning to build trust with the city's gangs.[31] Moving to Chicago
in 1963, Lafayette was struck by "a sense of sadness" in Chicago's ghettos, the broken glass on the streets a metaphor of the ways in which
Black lives were broken and left to wither by a hostile city machine. He
worried whether the situation could be changed. "But we had to have
hope because there was no alternative." They prioritized organizing
with gang members, according to Lafayette, to cultivate these young
men's political leadership and "redirect them from confrontation with
the police where we knew they would get killed."[32] The strategy, the
planning, and the months and years of groundwork of the Chicago
campaign, Tillman lamented, have been missed by many writers. "We
studied where we were going and how we were going to do it. It was
not loosey-goosey, it was not just about marches, it was strategic."[33]

King was prioritizing working with young people in Chicago—and
had wanted the eighteen-year-old Tillman's assistance. And so Tillman
moved to the city in the fall. Tillman would go on to work in Chicago's
westside ghetto and with many of the girl gang members.[34] A huge
man at six foot three, three hundred pounds, James Orange focused
on gang organizing, taking a number of beatings from gang members
to demonstrate his nonviolent discipline. Clearly committed to the importance of cultivating their leadership in the struggle, he came to be
deeply admired by these young men. Orange was also an early draft
resister; when he received his draft notice in 1963, he "told them to take
me off their mailing list because I wasn't interested in going to war."[35]

The federal government's indifference to Chicago's segregated
schools and the speedy return of the $32 million and punishment of
Francis Keppel in October sent a chilling message about Daley's power
and the lack of federal will to enforce the Civil Rights Act in the North.
King bore down on this disparity, condemning the "feeble and ane-
mic enforcement . . . trifling with life and death issues with unfeeling
clumsiness and opportunism."[36] With Johnson siding with Daley, the
challenge of the Chicago campaign became even more evident.

With the urging of some of his staff, King had decided he needed
to move to the city. In December 1965, King began to publish a series of "My Dream" columns in the *Chicago Defender* in preparation
for the escalation of their campaign. His first column castigated the
self-righteousness of Northern liberals who refused to face their own
racism; "as the South has slowly, reluctantly begun to turn to face her

destiny, the rigidities of Northern discrimination and segregation have stiffened."[37] These columns were picked up by other Black newspapers, including the *Amsterdam News*, the *Los Angeles Sentinel*, and the *Pittsburgh Courier*, but by no mainstream white ones. The *New York Times* covered King's new column but apparently did not consider the possibility that it could also run these columns and completely missed that King had been writing a biweekly column in its hometown *Amsterdam News* since 1962.[38] FBI surveillance seems to indicate that King understood the importance of a direct media voice to Black Americans since there had been so much problematic coverage.[39]

In early January, King, the SCLC, and the CCCO held a somewhat clandestine meeting in a hotel near the airport to explore the variety of fronts they wanted to attack—alongside schools, they would focus on housing, jobs, and political education. King wanted to "smash slumlordism" and organize *with* poor Black Chicagoans, not for them. But the press found out and questioned why he was moving to the city. "You can't really get close to the poor without living and being near them," he explained to the *Defender*. Despite criticism of this as a stunt, he asserted the need "to be right here with the people."[40]

The plan was that he and Coretta would move to Chicago in January and bring the children after school was finished in the summer. Because the Civil Rights Act required school desegregation or else districts would lose federal funding, and with the federal government's oversight in the South (though not Chicago), Atlanta had begun desegregating its schools. Coretta had succeeded in getting the two oldest kids into one of the best schools in Atlanta, the Spring Street School, in the fall. The Abernathy kids went too.

Shortly before leaving for Chicago, Martin and Coretta attended a school program called "Music That Made America Great" where students sang various songs from different immigrant groups. There was not a single African American song, and the program ended with everyone singing "Dixie." The Kings were stunned, Martin later writing, "I wept for my children who, through daily miseducation, are taught that the Negro is an irrelevant entity in American society. I wept for all the white parents and teachers who are forced to overlook the fact that the wealth of cultural and technological progress in America is a result of the commonwealth of inpouring contributions."[41] The teaching of Black history would become a demand of the Chicago campaign.

After years of visits and months of sustained organizing, in January

1966, King and the SCLC joined local organizers like Al Raby to launch the next stage of the Chicago Freedom Movement (CFM), targeting "institutionalized discrimination" in housing, schools, and jobs in the city. Not mincing words, King would describe it as "our organization's first sustained Northern movement directed against public and private institutions which over the years, have created infamous slum conditions directly responsible for the involuntary enslavement of millions of men, women and children."[42] But he made clear that this came after "two years . . . [of] a conscientious and creative attempt to dramatize the evils of Northern segregation."[43] Their goals were "federal, state and local—targeting both public and private institutions." They would *not* focus on a single issue in the slums but "target each and every issue" because they knew Northern politicians favored "accommodation . . . in some token manner"—one housing project was integrated or a few jobs opened to deflect the systemic critique and broader change. To thwart this strategy, the CFM would take on the constellation of issues from housing conditions to welfare to lead poisoning to lack of recreational opportunities that made the slums.[44]

This structural racism and the city's segregation also required federal intervention. Therefore "our work will be aimed at Washington," King declared.[45] They needed comprehensive legislation to meet the problems of slum life across the nation, specifically federal fair-housing legislation.[46] Chicago was a "prototype" of Black ghettoization across the country. Part of the CFM's power, according to SCLC organizer Jesse Jackson, was that the organizing infrastructure built by Chicago activists "did not exist anywhere else."[47] The CCCO's "Get Rid of Willis Campaign" was "as significant as any campaign ever organized in this country," King stressed. "A similar campaign in Fort Wayne, Indiana, or Lexington, Kentucky or Atlanta, Georgia would have indeed met with an unparalleled success in the area of school desegregation but before the Goliath of Chicago, their efforts made only limited impact."[48] The Goliath of Chicago, King understood, included the powerfully racist Daley machine, business interests that profited from it, a national media that allowed for Northern segregation, and a federal government that had so far refused to take substantive action.

If the national press had focused on what King was actually saying, they would have heard a pointed analysis of the dynamics driving the city's systemic racism and a searing indictment of the conditions people were being forced to live in. King reversed the Cold War idea of racism being a Southern anachronism and the North as fair and open.

Instead, Chicago was a place of "repudiated dreams" where those who generations ago sang "going to Chicago . . . now sink into the depths of despair."[49]

On January 23, the Kings moved into a ninety-dollar-a-month, four-room "typical ghetto apartment" in North Lawndale at 1550 South Hamlin Avenue. (This was the average rent in North Lawndale, or "Slumdale" as it was known.)[50] Chicago's slums were huge. The Chicago Freedom Movement had made the deliberate choice that the Kings should live on the West Side. Chicago's West Side ghetto was newer and conditions even worse than the South Side, the city's other even larger, segregated Black ghetto. About 250,000 Black people were clustered on the West Side; many were Southern migrants.[51] Ralph Abernathy was struck by how massive these Black neighborhoods were, as they drove through the South Side. "[W]e saw more slum blocks. And more. And more. . . . 'That's nothing,' Jesse said. 'Wait till you see the West Side.' "[52]

The Kings understood the significance of what they were trying to do. He wanted this community base: "I believe there is only one dignified, sincere, effective method of working with the poor who exist from day to day in wretched and miserable conditions. You cannot work over them. You cannot work around them. You cannot work for them. You must work with them."[53] At the heart of the decision was a religious conviction to be among the poor. King had not moved to Birmingham or Selma during those campaigns. But what he was trying to do here was different, by attacking the intertwined structures of racism and poverty and living among people most affected. It was about proximity to people's lives and suffering. But this would be an exhausting choice. He was still pastoring at Ebenezer in Atlanta, where the kids were finishing out the school year; Coretta moved with him initially but then visited occasionally until school ended in Atlanta. He went back and forth, committed to spending two or three days a week in Atlanta fulfilling those duties, then residing in Chicago's slums the other half.

Many landlords did not want to rent to King, fearing their building conditions would be exposed. So the CFM had to use the name of an SCLC staffer to rent the apartment.[54] But word soon leaked out that the Kings were the new tenants, and their white absentee landlord sprang into action. A phalanx of workmen—four plasterers, two painters, and two electricians—worked furiously the weekend before the Kings moved in to bring the decrepit apartment up to code or at least to address the most glaring violations.[55] (The building had been cited back in October with many code violations. But it took King's arrival to motivate the landlord to abide by the law.)[56]

The upgrade of the Kings' apartment demonstrated that changes could happen, if landlords summoned the will to do so. Like in Montgomery, the sense of possibility grew. As one of his neighbors observed, the rehab of the Kings' apartment showed "it can be did." Slum conditions could be fixed.[57] The *Chicago Defender* trumpeted, "It wasn't the plan but . . . Dr. King Shows How to 'Cure' a Slum: Eight Workmen Do Whirlwind Job of Repairing Westside Walk-up."[58] An eight-year-old kid who lived in the building celebrated: "Now maybe we'll get some heat in our rooms."[59] Another tenant reported they had fixed her radiator, and "All I can say is thank the Lord . . . he decided to move here."[60]

People joked with some seriousness that maybe King could keep moving to different apartments to improve other buildings. As they moved in, King made clear the job was "not just in this building but in the whole slum operation. We will be organizing tenant unions to end slums . . . rent strikes if necessary."[61] Tenant unions and rent strikes were a key "network of protection" for renters to assert their economic power and collective needs.[62]

The building's upgrades only went so far. Coretta described the building hallway's dirt floor and the overwhelming smell of urine. The heat and refrigerator didn't work. "As we became friendlier with our neighbors and were invited into their apartments, we learned that, as bad as our accommodations were, others had it even worse."[63] The food sold in nearby stores was often of poor quality that had been rejected in more prosperous areas in the city. Rats were plentiful, often making their way into people's apartments. The Kings later found out that in the all-white, working-class neighborhoods of Gage Park, South Deering, and Belmont Cragin, whites paid an average of less than $80 for five-and-a-half-room modern apartments. Working-class Black Chicagoans were both paying more for rent and living expenses and getting smaller, more decrepit units than their white working-class counterparts.[64] Coretta and Martin knew the South and had traveled through parts of the colonized world, but still the conditions were shocking. "In all my life, I had rarely seen anything like the conditions we faced in Chicago," she reflected. "The level of poverty called to mind our travels through Bombay a few years before."[65] The parallels to colonialism—the racialized impoverishment it produced—were on both of their minds.

The Kings were not new to the realities of colonialism. They had visited Ghana and Nigeria in 1957 and India in 1959. Shortly after Algerian independence was achieved on October 13, 1962, King met with President Ahmed Ben Bella, who underlined the "close relationship between colonialism and segregation." [66] And Scott King had worked with many anticolonial activists through her WSP work. They saw Chicago's segregation as a form of domestic colonialism: profit was made from Black immiseration, many ghetto jobs from sanitation to teaching went to outsiders, law enforcement contained the Black population, and a cadre of Black people were elevated to high places to act as a buffer for this deep inequality.

King described the slums as a "system of internal colonialism" where police and the courts acted as "enforcers." [67] In his *Chicago Defender* column in early February, he expounded on the domestic colonialism that characterized Chicago's Black ghettos. "Every condition exists because someone profits from its existence. . . . [I]n a slum, people do not receive comparable care and services for the amount of rent paid on a dwelling. . . . They pay taxes but their children do not receive an equitable share of those taxes in education, recreational and city services." [68] Black workers were relegated to the bottom rungs—"the legion of the damned in our economic army." [69] Thus the movement took on the violence of poverty, segregation, and political powerlessness together. Shortly after moving to Chicago, King attended a lunch in New York City at the United Nations sponsored by sixteen African nations. There he spoke about the "domestic colonialism" within the United States, singling out Chicago, Harlem, and Los Angeles. [70] While many white Chicagoans minimized the problem, King referred to Chicago as the "capital of segregation in the North" and compared Chicago's internal colonialism "to the exploitation of the Congo by Belgium." [71]

That first night they moved to the city, King held a hearing where neighborhood residents could testify to the issues they were facing. Five hundred people packed into a neighborhood church and laid out the rampant inequalities in schools, municipal services, housing, and outdoor space they faced in the city. It was a gut-wrenching list. At the end, King spoke heavy with emotion: "Many things you said tonight I heard in the same kind of session out in Watts. I say to the power structure in Chicago that . . . if something isn't done in a hurry, we can see a darker night of social disruption."[72] Reporters furiously transcribed his words. This was a message he would return to in Chicago—that Black people had challenged these injustices for years but they had not been addressed. If the same deafness to Black grievances continued in Chicago as they had in LA, there was a rising danger that a similar uprising would occur.

The conditions people were being forced to live in were horrendous. Many had such little money, "I don't know how they managed to eat," Coretta explained. Sometimes people would be embarrassed in front of the Kings by the conditions they were being forced to live in, which further pained both Martin and Coretta.[73] Rats as big as dogs, no sanitation pickups, cockroaches, many places without heat, everyone crowded around their gas stove if they were lucky enough to have one, these were the conditions of Chicago's West Side slums, white SCLC field staff worker Lynn Adler recalled. Adler had been a student at the University of Pennsylvania before going South to work in Selma; seeing the need to be fighting in the North, she was recruited by James Bevel to come to Chicago.[74] Living on the West Side, the Kings—as well as the SCLC field staff—were accessible. "A close identification with the people in the neighborhood" developed through living there.[75] So people would come by to share the horrifying conditions they were facing but also to eat, joke, and be in community with them.

Gang Alliances, Friendships, and Movement Building

The very first night the Kings moved into their apartment, six members of the Vice Lords gang came by to meet them. Coretta was wary at first but they "extended such a warm welcome . . . and offered their protection. They came by from time to time to visit . . . it was a great feeling you know, knowing that these people really cared and that they would, they would be there whatever we needed."[76] Lawrence Johnson, leader of the Vice Lords, explained that the first time they went by the Kings' it was a show of power. The "great civil rights leader was in Chicago, and in our 'hood, on our turf! . . . It was basically determined that the guys with rank would go."[77] Many gang members were initially like "we don't want to turn the other cheek," according to Dorothy Tillman, but "we worked with them."[78]

The Vice Lords ended up going over to visit the Kings' apartment often for continued conversation and debate. "There were a lot of conversations on the back porch as well as in the hall," Johnson explained.

"We had ideological struggles—well you could call them respectful arguments . . . you couldn't help but to fall in love with him, to admire him, want to protect him."[79]

You couldn't help but fall in love with him—this is not the way interactions between Dr. King and Chicago gang members have often been portrayed. Yet it was a deep and reciprocal compassion. Martin and Coretta felt in community. "They were so happy to have us there," Coretta said. At first, some of the gang members did not want any white people around—and the Kings had white colleagues coming by their apartment. But over time, they said, "Well, Dr. King, we'll accept anyone if you recommend them."[80]

Coretta described how another night a member of the Blackstone Rangers dropped by, and Martin had just ordered some barbecue and invited the young man to join him. " 'Are you Reverend Martin Luther King, Jr. . . . Are you really?' " the young man asked. "You don't mean that this cat's been up there in Washington, eating with Presidents, eating filet mignon steak and here he's sitting down here eating barbecue just like me. And of course we really knew then we had it made because he saw Martin as another human being." These gang members "would do everything they could to protect us."[81]

According to Blackstone Ranger leader Jeff Fort, many people questioned why King wanted to recruit gang members, but King understood the numbers of young people in gangs and how organized they were. While others saw a problem, King saw a "wealth" in street organizations. The civil rights leader wanted to "change how the government was treating his Black and poor people [and] he wanted to change the violence that Black people were inflicting upon themselves." King understood the interrelation: "It was almost like Dr. King wanted to get in between all violence with his hands." They grew to love this "warrior without a gun" and King became like a father figure to Fort.[82] Even if they didn't always agree, two factors garnered respect from a broad swath of gang members, according to Fort: King's commitment to stand up for the fate of "all oppressed people" and the fact that he "stood on it." A "smart tongue" was not enough; Dr. King displayed the courage and ability to back it up.[83]

From the beginning of the twentieth century, Chicago had a long history of white gangs, like the Hamburg Club the mayor had belonged to.[84] Faced with the violence of white gangs and the city's segregation, many young Black, Mexican, and Puerto Rican Chicagoans turned to their gangs for community, protection, and to participate in the informal economy.[85] As Black and Latino migration to the city soared, community solidarity and protection became paramount given the city's deep segregation, ringed with violent white neighborhoods. Chicago's West Side and South Side Black communities became home to a number of gangs, including the Vice Lords, Blackstone Rangers, and Gonzato Disciples. As the number of Black and Latino gangs increased, they became a police obsession. Daley had campaigned for mayor in 1955 promising that he would add two thousand cops to police the gang problem. This didn't happen when he got to office, but the cops added to the force over the next decade further harassed Black and Latino youth, which then increased the need for protection, which then furthered growth in gang membership.[86]

The Vice Lords were among a number of Chicago gangs that were already thinking politically, even before King moved to the city.[87] An extensive article in the *Chicago Defender* on the city's Black gangs in September 1965 documented this growing political awareness among many gang members that bad housing, schools, and jobs must be corrected.[88] Orange, Lafayette, and Rev. Al Sampson had already spent months working with gang members in the city, seeking to build a unity coalition and political leadership among the city's gangs.[89] The SCLC, according to Lafayette, saw gang youth "not as a menace to the community but as a resource." [90]

From the very first night when the Vice Lords came by, King had a fair amount of contact and affection from many of the neighborhood's gang members. Two days later, they gave him a tour of the neighborhood.[91] It was freezing cold, but that didn't thwart his tour guides or the neighborhood response. According to one reporter, "windows were shoved open and left open as long as King and his entourage remained in view." [92] King's work with gang members was repeatedly disdained by city officials, the media, and even some in SCLC. In doing so, King departed from respectability politics, political theorist Brandon Terry explains, to the "consternation of many. Transgressing the norms of a Southern Baptist preacher, [s]uch efforts, which have been obscured in King's legacy, sit provocatively alongside the work of the Black Panthers and Nation of Islam." [93]

Along with some of the other SCLC field workers, King spent a great deal of time with young men from Chicago's South Side and West Side gangs. His relationship to them, according to Rev. Eric Gerard Pearman, who grew up on Chicago's South Side and worked with many of these gangs, was marked by "compassion, understanding, warmth, honesty, openness, and direct accessibility in listening and talking with them." Because of that accessibility and honesty, "Brother King won much praise and respect from Chicago's African American street gangs."[94] He came to know each of the street organizations and their leaders.[95] According to Chicago CORE leader Bob Lucas, King spent most Friday nights negotiating with leaders of street gangs to keep the peace and talking through ideas with them. King spent hours listening to these young men talk about Chicago's corrupt politicians, abusive police, apathetic preachers, and the ways they were mistreated by the system.[96] They discussed the conditions they faced in the city—and King was eager to get their analysis. Many young men, Fort recalled, would get nervous and talk very fast when King asked for their analysis of the various oppressive conditions they faced. Slow down, he would say, take your time and explain; I am listening.[97]

One young man told him, "You know I've been in the basement all my life and I've been trying to get out of the basement but I'm still there."[98] These young men had a political analysis of their lives and the city that they discussed with King. These conversations led many gang members to respect him a great deal. "The only person we have faith in is Dr. King," one gang member explained. King would sit around late into the evening talking with them and occasionally playing pool.[99]

Another Vice Lord explained, "We were labeled a gang but we always considered ourselves protectors of the community."[100] So they saw their mission to protect King as well. Over time, Coretta explained, many of these gang members became "very protective towards him. . . . We never encouraged their protection though we understood they were always around."[101] Johnson and many other gang members "thought we could protect him better than the Chicago Police Department. I think he thought that too."[102] They also came to admire and trust him more, according to Fort, because of the time he took to be with Coretta and his family.[103]

These discussions weren't, as King's treatment of ghetto youth is often stereotyped, some sort of just-say-no sermonizing. It was serious discussion of structural racism, political strategy, and the urban political economy of the city. These young men liked talking to Dr. King, even if he held different ideas from them, because he was committed to them and to challenging injustice around them and because he talked about ideas and strategy *with* them. He didn't leave when they challenged him, which furthered their trust that he

was listening.[104] Fort underlined what a good listener King was. "He
was very attentive. . . . Dr. King used to say something like 'go ahead'
after every point you made to him. . . . He never interrupted you
while you were speaking."[105] Ten to twenty years older than them,
King liked talking to these young men, even if they held different
ideas from him, because he saw their potential for leadership and action in the struggle. These discussions weren't all about nonviolence.
They were waging war against slumism, against the forces of racial
capitalism and a legal system that criminalized Black ghetto dwellers
rather than those who perpetuated the injustice. Grappling with how
the city, its economy, law enforcement, and municipal governance
worked, and how they might be challenged, required analysis. King
was thinking deeply and so were many of these young men.

Doris Crenshaw, who had become active as a preteen in Rosa Parks's
Youth Council and then the Montgomery Bus Boycott, joined the efforts
in Chicago after college. She talked about how afraid Black people were
in Chicago and the kind of repression leveled against those who took
a stand. One reason the CFM centered part of its organizing with gang
members was that they were not afraid. "They were who we talked to
a lot. A lot of the other people were afraid to be bothered." The climate
of fear in Chicago was intense—Daley's power and many levers of punishment he could deploy, the police and the hostile sundown towns
that dotted the metro area made Chicago worse than Montgomery,
Crenshaw felt.[106]

Gang members in Chicago were hardly unusual in terms of Black
people, South and North, who believed in self-defense. Many activists
from Rosa Parks to North Carolina NAACP leader Robert Williams
were committed to self-defense—as were many of King's parishioners. As SNCC's Stokely Carmichael explained, "[B]y 1963, I would
say ninety percent of your field staff in SNCC were carrying guns.
Of course, not publicly, but . . . field staff in Alabama and Mississippi
were definitely carrying guns by 1963." [107] Some of these gang members pointed to the hypocrisy of public officials telling them not to
use violence while the US waged war in Vietnam, the Dominican Republic, and other places across the world. King heard their point and
then echoed it sharply the next year at New York's Riverside Church:
"I knew that I could never again raise my voice against the violence
of the oppressed in the ghettos without having first spoken clearly to
the greatest purveyor of violence in the world today—my own government." [108] He wasn't going to be a hypocrite. If he was going to argue

that using guns didn't make sense in Chicago, he needed to say to the government that it shouldn't be using them in Vietnam either.

Some of King's advisors were not on board with this gang outreach. They hadn't wanted him to live in Lawndale and didn't like these "gangbangers." But King persisted against these colleagues' respectability politics. In his many talks with these young men, King highlighted the power they were trying to build to "get the largest political machine in the nation to say yes when it wants to say no." [109] He also talked about the rationale of nonviolent direct action, in a situation where police weaponry far exceeded theirs. King and Bevel showed some of the young men footage of the Watts rebellion, explaining that in the uprising thirty Black people had died mostly at the hands of law enforcement—and the cops remained in power, with more latitude and weaponry. [110]

King's many experiences with police abuse and harassment was a point of commonality with the gang members he spoke with. Sharing his own police encounters, King was deeply concerned with theirs. King knew, like they did, violence at the hands of the police. King saw how police often functioned as "enforcers" to keep Black people in line; his own experience demonstrated they would mess with you to demonstrate their power and mess with you more if you crossed "the line." One Vice Lord explained, "Down South they have white sheets on but in Lawndale they have blue." [111] King worried about what the police would do to these young men.

King also challenged public narratives of personal responsibility. When a white woman wrote King saying that Black people should take pride and sweep the streets to clean up their own neighborhoods, he made clear, "That's the job of the sanitation department." [112] He wasn't trying to get these gang members to pick up litter; he wanted them to organize for community empowerment to demand better sanitation services, schools, and housing for their communities. One Vice Lord explained the changes this wrought in the city: "[F]rom 1965 to 1967, we stopped gang wars and started to build a new kind of Vice Lord Nation. . . . Between 1967 and 1969 we opened several businesses and community programs. The police never thought they would see the day when we put our minds to do something like that." [113] The Vice Lords and Blackstone Rangers moved from calling themselves a "gang" to a "nation." [114]

King also saw these young men's growing loyalty to him and its potential for organized community power. The Blackstone Rangers often served as nonviolent marshals for many of the marches and demon-strations, meeting with him before each march so King could give them instructions. Lafayette underscored these gang members' role in giving organization to the marches, maintaining order, and providing a wall of protection.[115] Despite this important work, according to histo-rian James Ralph, SCLC's work with gang members attracted negative attention from both the city and the media.[116] City officials saw it as "inciting" and the media claimed, at times, that King was naïve in this work and, conversely, that these young men disdained him.[117] The FBI was also alarmed, particularly as Chicago's gangs started to make alli-ances in 1966 and grow more political.[118]

Thus the reality of King's life in Chicago was much warmer than the "stunt" portrayed in the media.[119] According to one observer, the Kings' apartment was often full to the rafters: "People swarm in and out. . . . Little kids come in just to look at him." [120] As SNCC's Judy Rich-ardson explained, while SNCC had criticisms of SCLC's organizing and King (sometimes calling him "de Lawd" behind his back), King differed from many of his SCLC colleagues: "[He] *liked* people. . . . You could drop him down in any circumstance. He could be in that com-munity. He could relate to it, and they could relate to him." [121]

In February, the *Chicago Defender* praised the "great psychological ef-fect" King's efforts were having on the Black community—enlarging the sense of possibility for change. Characterizing his determination as "inflexible as an oak tree," they celebrated King's "remarkable abil-ity to unveil the issues in their stark nakedness and to dramatize the means for mass action has made converts out of cynics who saw no way out of the dilemma that confronted them." [122] *Ebony* magazine ran a substantial piece in April 1966 demonstrating Chicago's Black com-munity's wide embrace of King: "Apart from some isolated instances, generally regarded as the work of pranksters or crackpots, it is becom-ing increasingly clear that Dr. King's Chicago venture is welcomed by nearly everyone in the communities directly affected." [123]

Welcomed by nearly everyone. This challenges the ways many histo-rians have centered Black discord with King's approach. This didn't mean that no one had questions or criticisms; many did, just as peo-ple in Albany and Birmingham had. But looking more closely at the Chicago campaign reveals the extent of the relationships King built in Chicago and how the focus on Black division has been driven partly by cultural stereotypes about Northern Black communities popular at the time to rationalize Northern school and housing segregation.

As Coretta had long realized, one of King's greatest gifts was the ways he helped people feel their own power. This had been true in Montgomery, and it was true in Chicago. It wasn't "maybe King can fix this." Many different kinds of people from gang members to church mothers to public housing residents felt a reinforced sense that the conditions they faced were unacceptable and an enlarged possibility of their own action. The status quo was unacceptable, and they were the people to take action.

Taking On the Policies and Practices That Maintained Chicago's Slums

In his *Chicago Defender* column, King played with Langston Hughes's question "what happens to a dream deferred?" He challenged the passive voice that many preferred that masked the patterns of exploitation.

> [T]hese dreams were not deferred, they were denied and repudiated by vicious though subtle patterns of exploitation. So the dreams do not "dry up like raisins in the sun." They decay like sun-ripened oranges that are devoured by worms and birds until they fall to the ground making a rotting mess.[124]

Worms and birds. From landlords to school officials, white Chicagoans were devouring Black life chances. Part of what King was trying to do was to insist people see it—and not look away.

A day after they moved in, King spoke at the University of Chicago and took issue with the Moynihan Report. Officially titled *The Negro Family: The Case for National Action*, the report was commissioned by Assistant Secretary of Labor Daniel Patrick Moynihan and focused on Black poverty in the United States. Johnson had previewed it back in June at his Howard commencement speech. The report framed the greatest problem facing Black people as not the structures of inequality endemic to American society but rather pathologies that had taken root within Black culture and the Black family in response. King, on the other hand, maintained that the main cause of Black family instability was economic. He advocated for extending the minimum wage to workers left out of its protections, raising it significantly, and expanding federal aid for Black families. Without naming Moynihan's study explicitly, he talked about how such theories would be used "to justify neglect and rationalize oppression" and emphasized how they had come to Chicago to fight for a fair chance. "No one in all history had to fight against so many psychological and physical horrors to have a family life." [125]

Two days later, King informed the press that they were serving notice on landlords to make needed—and often legally mandated—maintenance or else they would lead a rent strike. [126] Like the building the Kings had moved into, most buildings in Chicago's Black neighborhoods had dozens of city code violations to which the city turned a blind eye. Chicago had some of the nation's most developed building codes in the nation but largely enforced them politically, not to remedy conditions but to punish people who bucked the machine. Landlord and city negligence went hand in hand in maintaining the horrifying living conditions many Black Chicagoans were forced to endure.

Within weeks of the Kings moving to the city, the CFM announced plans for a Union to End Slums, seeing "the interconnection between poverty and poor housing, poor-quality food in the stores, lack of employment, and more." [127] This wasn't about a few bad landlords or realtors—but systematic practice aided and abetted by the city and federal government.

Then, in early February, Andre Adams, a baby two days shy of his first birthday, was chewed to death by a rat. The one-year-old was also severely malnourished, weighing only 5 pounds, 8 ounces when he died. West Side parents rose up in anger. These inhumane conditions—starvation, rats, buildings without heat—were "why we're here fighting in the slums of Chicago," [128] King trumpeted, underscoring that Adams's death was "as much of a civil rights tragedy as the murder of [Viola] Liuzzo" after the Selma march. "We don't have wall-to-wall carpeting . . . but wall-to-wall rats and roaches." [129] King was sickened by the "slow, stifling death of a kind of concentration camp life" of Chicago's slums and hated the ways many Americans just looked away. [130] Indeed, Adams's death garnered little national outrage, nor subsequent attention by King biographers, despite how much such horrors haunted King and spurred the CFM's organizing. [131]

Shortly after, a group of families came to the Kings' apartment to ask for help addressing the inhumane conditions of their building—the lack of heat, hot water, and proper sanitation, along with plentiful rats. "They were very concerned that they had to continue to live this way," Coretta recalled. [132] King then went to the building himself, according to Andrew Young, and found "one place had no heat; it's still sixteen degrees outside and they had a new baby wrapped in newspaper and a bath towel." [133] Some of the residents had to stay up at night to protect their children from "rats as big as cats."[134] Outraged, King and the SCLC decided to organize a tenant action at that building, 1321 S. Homan Street, where the five families, including twenty-three children, lived. They would collect the rent themselves, place it in a trusteeship, and use it to pay for much-needed repairs.

The press photographed the Kings, Raby, and others cleaning up the building.[135] Part of why they did this was to expose "how bad the slum conditions were" and the "exorbitant rents for what they were getting."[136] They wanted to make the nation face these injustices. Filing a complaint with the Housing Authority, they used $889 of the rental money to fix the building's electrical system and $150 for coal to get heat into the building.[137]

But that was not how the *Chicago Tribune*, the *New York Times*, or other national outlets presented the story. They did not highlight the horrible conditions the landlord kept in the building nor that the money had been used to fix the furnace so tenants had heat in the dead of winter. The *Tribune* cast the trusteeship as a criminal act and "invasion of the property rights of others."[138] *Time* magazine published a piece by a Black judge lecturing King on "theft."[139] Multiple articles in the *New York Times* and other news outlets focused on the building "seizure" but glossed over the actual conditions of the building, including families living without heat in the dead of winter, rats in apartments, and compromised sanitation. Instead of covering the illegality of such building conditions and city corruption that allowed landlords to get away with scores of code violations, the *Times* portrayed the landlord, an elderly man, as the victim—and King's tactics as mean and violent.[140]

The landlord took King and the SCLC to court, and the city's welfare office went after the tenants for not paying rent. They withheld rental allowances for three families and threatened to evict all five.[141] King defended their action as the "highest moral right, the right of tenants to live without threat to their health and lives."[142] While the mainstream white press largely ignored the building's inhumane and illegal conditions, the trusteeship prompted the *Chicago Defender* to send a reporter to live with one of the families, the Townes, for a time to report on the building's horrifying conditions.[143] The Townes praised the SCLC takeover of the building.[144] Their place had been overrun with rats, which congregated *every* night in their kitchen, the *Defender* reported. It was sickening. King's efforts finally led to a city rodent-control team coming to block up the holes in the building, so now the Townes could hear the rats scratching in the walls but no longer had them all over their kitchen.[145]

A court order finally put a stop to the trusteeship but did *not* find King guilty of a crime. The judge appointed a receivership and ordered the absentee landlord to bring the building up to city code—the building had twenty-three violations—or face imprisonment.[146] In March the landlord was given one more month to fix the violations. The tactic had worked. Simultaneously on the South Side, two families sued their landlord for not keeping the building up—the *Defender* said this was the first time such a suit had been tried, and this judge too ordered a receivership hearing.[147]

Now the CFM hoped to scale it up, as it took on the scores of decrepit buildings across the city. Bevel, Lafayette, Adler, and others leafleted buildings and knocked on doors on the West and South Sides: "If your building is uninhabitable, call a meeting and call this number. And if you want, we'll come and tell you how you can make a difference." They would hold meetings, learning how many buildings were unlivable places that were not maintained at all. They worked on tenant organizing, urging people to engage in rent strikes to protest and put their rent in escrow to pay for the repairs they needed. Despite the awkwardness of showing up on people's doorsteps (and being interracial groups at that), Lynn Adler explained that they were "surprisingly welcomed" by most of the Black tenants. People were so frustrated by their living conditions that they were willing to do anything to get some change.[148]

They then asked a University of Chicago law student, Bernardine Dohrn, to investigate who the biggest slumlords were in the city. This proved impossible. "We had to look Dr. King in the eye" and say we failed, Dohrn recalled. There was no way to identify the owners because "they were held in blind trusts and holding companies" to obscure the ownership and therefore any accountability. But organizers persisted. They got lawyers to defend the eviction cases by taking pictures to demonstrate that city ordinances were not being followed and then packed the hearings with people.[149]

At the top of the system was Mayor Daley, who responded to King's pressure by feinting toward reform, while playing the mainstream media like a fiddle. A week after Andre Adams's death, the city filed suits against sixty slum landlords—asking for receiverships in fifty-seven to collect rents to make needed repairs and gaining much favorable press.[150] There is no way to separate the city's action around these sixty buildings from the campaign King and CCCO were waging. But the media played Daley's hand by making it seem like the city was proactive and committed, while ignoring the thousands of buildings not being attended to.

In Daley's political machine, building codes were enforced when politically useful or politically damaging—and largely ignored in Black neighborhoods. Daley had no intention of giving up that tool. While in King's Southern campaigns, outlets like the *New York Times* and *Washington Post* investigated the claims of Southern public officials, with Daley they largely took his word.[151] In mid-February, Daley and city administrators announced a campaign for the "elimination of the slums by 1967" and hiring of fifty new housing inspectors. Daley denied that King and the SCLC's campaign swayed their decision and Cook County director of public aid Raymond Hilliard sneeringly instructed King to inspire Black Chicagoans "to put the full force of their deep pride and responsibility for their homes."[152] But again, these inspectors were hired because the Chicago Freedom Movement's exposure was working.

The trusteeship—and abysmal conditions in many other buildings—inspired other rent strikes.[153] Some buildings didn't have running water or heat; in others the electrical systems were so decrepit that kitchens became fire hazards. In April, three children and their great-grandmother died in an apartment fire in a building with 136 code violations.[154] This intensified community outrage and redoubled the struggle against these conditions. Forty-six percent of Chicago's Black people—nearly half—lived in substandard conditions, King made clear. King described the "political servitude" Black Chicagoans lived under and the "ghetto tax" Black Chicagoans paid where Black people had to spend *more* to live in decrepit ghetto housing and for substandard food and other retail goods. Many businesses were gaining tremendous wealth from trapping Black people in these slums. "You can't talk about ending the slums without first saying profit must be taken out of slums," King explained. That meant—like it had in Montgomery and Birmingham—taking on the economic elites of the city. But in Chicago, the second-largest city in the country, he knew that was "dangerous ground because you are messing with . . . captains of industry."[155]

The housing campaign the Chicago Freedom Movement pursued

had a dual strategy—partly it was about opening housing in neighboring white communities and suburbs that ringed Black ghettos but
equally it was about making concrete changes in those ghettos as well.
There were tensions in SCLC between these two different prongs. As
King told Levison who had criticized the trusteeship, "[N]o matter how
much open housing you have, you'll not get all the poor people out of
the ghetto immediately. You have to make life livable for those who will
be in the ghetto." [156] Tenant and rent strikes—and the political pressure
they built—were key, marshaling collective power and challenging the
idea that the conditions were the fault of the people who lived there.

As Coretta had articulated from Montgomery onward, part of Martin's gift was to show, by example, that such conditions were an affront
to God and that people themselves had the ability to take action. She
told a group of wealthy liberal Chicago women that all of them had to
be willing to pay a great price in order to address the city's inequality. During a radio interview, a white student, Paulette from Chicago,
who'd been arrested the previous year in the Willis demonstrations,
called in to ask Dr. King "what tangible we had done." Her friends
were dismissive, and she felt "more [was] done in the South." Taking
the question very seriously, King provided a multipronged answer. He
began with the transformative power within herself by taking action
in the first place. Then he went on:

> You did accomplish something and I hope you won't be
> discouraged. . . . [T]he movement last summer while not bringing
> immediate tangible results did bring the whole question of seg-
> regation in the schools, inadequate schools out in the open. . . . If
> there had not been a movement last summer, the conditions in the
> schools would continue without anybody raising a question or
> raising a voice against it. . . . I'm sure the movement itself created
> the atmosphere which finally led to the removal of Mr. Willis . . .
> so that itself was an accomplishment. Often you are accomplish-
> ing much more than you can see at the moment because you are
> at the heart of the situation. . . . Many of the things we are going
> to be able to do now . . . [are] because the atmosphere was created
> last summer for a building of a vibrant movement to end discrim-
> ination, injustice, slum and slumism in the city of Chicago.[157]

This was King's philosophy on how change happens—a community in motion, just like in Montgomery, had exposed injustice and

enlarged what people imagined could be challenged. Many Black Chicagoans wrote the *Defender* to say how the CFM was altering their imagination of the possible.

Meanwhile, the *Chicago Tribune* seethed—running editorial after editorial through winter and spring condemning various aspects of the campaign. The paper editorialized against King's determination to challenge slumism as "absurd . . . there are no forces dedicated to maintain them." They called King's charges that "the police are little more than enforcers of the present system of exploitation" "hogwash"—"stale rhetoric carried over from his speeches in Alabama."[158] And they admonished him to concern himself with the dysfunctions of Black families. Family stability, not job discrimination, was the real issue. Black economic problems, the *Tribune* claimed, "do not arise by white malice or discrimination but are occasioned by the acts of omission or commission by Negroes themselves," so King should concentrate his efforts on "promot[ing] family stability to members of his own race."[159] The *Tribune*'s disdain in 1966 for Black organizing (and its tendency to refer to King in headlines by his first name) could be mistaken for the *Montgomery Advertiser* in 1956.[160]

While many white Chicagoans suggested King should return to the South where the real problem was, some saw the injustices.[161] Appalachian-born Peggy Terry was one. Terry, whose father had been in the Klan, had grown up in Montgomery; the bus boycott and King's arrest opened her eyes to a different reality. She moved to Chicago; outraged by the conditions working-poor white people were living in, she began organizing her neighbors in Chicago's Uptown neighborhood to engage in rent strikes and welfare protests. Seeing how the deceptions of racism prevented interracial solidarity of the poor, she connected with CFM's campaigns to increase Black and white poor people's power. She was inspired by King's tenant organizing: "Where else could poor white trash be accepted by a Nobel Prize winner?"[162]

Continuing the Fight Against Daley's Racist Machine

Chicago's inequality had a face, King made clear. He listed twelve facets of Chicago society that contributed to Black exploitation in the city: an unequal educational system, the building trades unions, real estate boards, slum landlords, banks, the welfare system, the Federal Housing Administration, the courts, the police, the political system, the city administration, and the federal government. This damning indictment laid the structural inequality that Black Chicagoans faced on a bevy of people from landlords to city officials to union leaders who maintained it. King saw the key role law enforcement played in this system, depriving poor Black Chicagoans of the "status of citizenship in order that they might be controlled and 'kept in line.' "[163] The courts, King wrote, "are organized as tools of the economic structure and political machine."[164] So was the policing of welfare recipients. Chicago was a "system in many ways more resistant to change than the rural South."[165]

Chicago's school segregation extended to its teaching force, with disproportionately few Black teachers and very few Black administrators hired in CPS. Many Black schools were being run by people who didn't see Black children as worthy of educational excellence. The CFM began organizing to take on school leadership and push for community control of schools. One target was Principal Mildred Chuchut of Jenner Elementary School. Jenner served Black children from the Cabrini Green housing project, and Chuchut treated her Black student body harshly and dismissively. Parents challenged her dictatorial style toward their children. In January, 95 percent of students stayed out of Jenner for three days as parents called for Chuchut's removal and protested the transfer of a teacher critical of Chuchut.[166] The SCLC and CCCO joined the effort. "Jenner is but a single and bitter example of the system's insensitivity and failure to educate," King proclaimed at a large rally in February.[167] Describing Jenner as a "fortress of non-understanding, non-education and non-communication," he noted how its boundaries were "clearly gerrymandered to contain the burgeoning Near North Negro community" and urged the Board of Education to take decisive action.[168]

In April, parents again kept their kids out of Jenner for five days—this time with the backing of the city's civil rights organizations.[169] They set up Freedom Schools as well as a Freedom School Health Center where doctors, nurses, and dentists from the Medical Committee for Human Rights gave scores of children blood, ear, eye, dental, and urine tests.[170] The city reported 85 percent absenteeism. That night, King addressed the crowd of four hundred parents and other supporters: "Nothing is more irresponsible and ridiculous than to allow our children to be packed into overcrowded, segregated and otherwise inadequate schools for all of their young lives."[171] *Ridiculous*, he extolled; poor Black parents were worthy of the same parental say and should not have to put up with having their children treated this way. He pledged the movement's support in the event the city made good on its threats to jail parents, saying he would join them in jail, if necessary.

Daley decried the boycott and the city sent truant officers to threaten boycotting families.[172] But ultimately, given increasing public pressure, Chuchut was transferred to another school. The movement had gained another victory.[173] In late May, at a conference of Baptist ministers in New York, King pressed the urgency of enforcing *Brown* across the US. Northern schools are "as well and completely segregated as any in the South—just as if the law had never been written." He bore down on the extent of the problem: "92% of students in Chicago attend schools where 90% of the students are of the same race." [174]

Battling Daley's machine meant contending with the mayor's Black elected allies. Daley's retinue of Black politicians (six aldermen and Congressman William Dawson) and cadre of Black ministers provided a buffer between the city's power structure and a restive Black community. Congressman Dawson had denounced King's efforts in the city: "What does he mean coming here to tell us our citizens are segregated? Chicagoans know what's best for Chicagoans." [175] Known as the "Silent Six," these six Black aldermen, according to CCCO co-founder Edwin Berry, "simply carried out Massa Daley's orders, for what he wanted done on the plantation," praising Willis and discrediting Black activism.[176] King called it "plantation politics"—Black people voted for Black people who served the mayor's interests, not the voters'. For Bernard Lafayette from Tennessee, this class of Black overseers felt new: "most Black people I know, you know, wanted to be free." [177]

For Dorothy Tillman as well, Daley "ran a great plantation" and the Montgomery-born Tillman was unnerved by the ways the Black political class "told us to go back down south where we came from." [178] The mayor's cadre of Black politicians and clergy were given some personal benefits and then interposed between City Hall and the Black community as a massive, near-insurmountable barrier to change. "We were rejected by most of the black leadership," Tillman explained. "Dr. King said that Daley's plantation was worse than the plantations in Mississippi. He'd say, 'Those Negroes were in deep.' " [179]

Daley's machine was so threatened by any independent Black political organizing that it had long employed various tactics to neutralize it. A decade earlier, following the NAACP's campaign to expose the lynching of Chicago teenager Emmett Till in Mississippi, they organized to unseat Chicago NAACP leader Willoughby Abner. Abner's continued service was deemed not beneficial to Daley (even though the Till organizing focused on Mississippi), Raby explained, "so they had Dawson organize an effort to take over the NAACP, and literally he called out every precinct captain, had them take out membership in the NAACP, checked them off as they walked through the meeting that was gonna vote on the presidency, and voted Willoughby Abner out of office . . . [and] took over the control of the NAACP locally here in Chicago." [180] This takeover meant Chicago's NAACP largely stayed away from challenging the city's segregated schools in the late 1950s and 1960s.[181]

Daley's machine was so far-reaching that clergy who supported it were able to buy city lots for one dollar to build church parking lots and access federal social service money. Those who opposed it or took the movement's side got parking tickets on Sundays, visits from city health inspectors, permit denials, and other forms of municipal harassment.[182] Put simply, city codes existed as political tools to be leveraged. According to Rev. Clay Evans, "Many ministers who were with us had to back off because they didn't want their buildings to be condemned or given citations for electrical work, faulty plumbing or fire code violations." [183] Evans was severely punished for his movement work; his new church building was held up for seven years for code violations.[184] Many Black churches worried about even hosting a meeting, because pastors feared the consequences of crossing the mayor.[185] The SCLC had to locate its office in a white church, Warren Avenue Congregational Church, pastored by Rev. William Briggs, which became a meeting spot and hangout place; even many gang members would come by. [186]

One of King's biggest foes in Chicago was National Baptist Convention president Joseph H. Jackson. Jackson had known King's father and initially supported the bus boycott but quickly pulled away, seeing King as a threat to his leadership of the NBC. In 1961, King broke with them to form the Progressive National Baptist Convention. Jackson took to referring to King as a new breed of "hoodlums and crooks in the pulpit." Jackson and many other Black ministers in Chicago spoke out against King and the CFM, forbidding even leaflets of King's events in church and blocking access for movement events to many Black churches.[187] Calling Daley and Willis "true-hearted friends of Black people," Jackson cast the movement as "not far removed from open crime." [188] Thus Rev. Jackson provided tremendous cover for Daley, Willis, and "the fine citizens" who sat on Chicago's Board of Education.[189] Accusing King of waging a "militant campaign against his own denomination and his own race," Jackson denounced the movement's tactics as unnecessary and unwanted and praised ongoing city efforts to improve conditions.[190] But King refused to be thwarted by this: "I don't believe Dr. Jackson speaks for the Negroes in this country." [191]

To further obstruct the movement, Daley's Black surrogates created the Interracial Committee of 100 to oppose King and CFM. The media lapped it up, delighted to feature Black people speaking out against King, and portrayed it like a local civil rights group (even though it had little constituency).[192] Much of the mainstream media, already poised to see Northern racism differently than Southern, were captivated by these Black men who spoke out against King. It contributed to a "feeling of powerlessness" greater "than I ever saw," SCLC's Hosea Williams confessed a month into the Chicago campaign.[193]

Daley counted on Black political servitude and was particularly threatened by the CFM's attempts to get more registered voters. Urging voter registration, King stressed the need for candidates to earn the Black vote, rather than own it.[194] This capture of the Black vote had dire consequences because the city administration then refused "to render adequate services to the Negro community. Street cleaning, garbage collection, and police protection are offered menially if at all." [195] According to Chicago CORE president Bob Lucas, Black precinct captains would threaten people that they would lose their public housing or their welfare if they didn't vote for the Daley-approved Democratic ticket.[196] West Side organizer Nancy Jefferson described how Daley had Black people snitch on their neighbors. Daley "had spies in every floor to see who was participating [in the movement]. . . . He owned the system." Jefferson had just put in a new kitchen but, given her activism, city inspectors sent her a seventeen-page list of violations. The level of political retribution was so extreme, Jefferson said, that it seemed almost unbelievable to those outside the city—and thus was missed by nearly everyone who covered the Chicago movement. "You could never think of that was going on down during the time King was here." [197]

Opposing Daley was thus extraordinarily costly, given all the levers of local administration that could be exercised against those who sided with the movement. These municipal practices could be changed, King emphasized, but they needed to build power independent of the machine. Chicago's police also harassed the SCLC field staff and CFM activists, following them, pulling them over repeatedly, and using racial epithets (including calling the white staff "nigger lovers").[198]

On March 23, they held another hearing where community residents testified to the hardships experienced living in the slums.[199] The next day King, Raby, and other clergy met with Daley—the first time the mayor met with King since the campaign had begun. The meeting lasted four hours. King initially was going to let Raby do the talking. When Raby started criticizing ward politics and the lack of community accountability, Daley tried to shut the conversation down entirely. Then King stepped in and spoke for nearly twenty minutes about how the mayor needed to grant some of their demands or rising frustrations around the enduring level of segregation in housing, schools, jobs, and city services could spill out into violence. "If Mayor Yorty [of Los Angeles] had listened to me," King made clear to Daley, "there would have been no Watts. He declined to listen and Watts resulted."[200]

Unmoved, Daley blamed the problems of schools and housing on Black migrant behavior that "did not originate here but came from the various Southern states."[201] Like many white Chicagoans, Daley instinctively reached for cultural explanations for the city's inequities in jobs, housing, and schooling. Black kids' work habits, attitudes, and home situations were what needed fixing. But King countered that the "incredibly bad slum schools" and lack of jobs were what impacted Black youth. King castigated these cultural explanations for obscuring "life-long patterns of exploitation which can only be described as our system of slavery in the twentieth century."[202] Young Black men like Blackstone Rangers leader Jeff Fort, according to teacher Timuel Black, were often pushed out of school while young white guys were counseled and given more opportunities for remediation and redemption.[203]

The Chicago campaign was not popular with many SCLC donors. Harry Belafonte had the idea to turn to European sources, and in late March, King and Belafonte set out for Paris and Stockholm. King's father opposed this European fundraising, worried that it would seem unpatriotic and anger white liberals, but Belafonte pushed forward.[204] When the US State Department tried to shut their Paris event, Belafonte found a new venue. King told the 4,500 Parisians who gathered about their campaign in Chicago to end slums and "create national legislation to rid our cities of these forces of oppression."[205] The reception and fundraising proved tremendous.

By April, Daley had used his patronage in the Black community so effectively that when he said it was time for King to return to Georgia, all of Chicago's Black aldermen agreed.[206] Claiming King was "jealous of the things we have managed to get done," Daley accused King of just trying to grab power: "we have no need to apologize to the civil rights leaders who have come to Chicago to tell us what to do."[207] Daley tried to portray King's challenge to the machine as a partisan effort to benefit Republicans (despite knowing this wasn't the case), and a number of journalists picked up this argument, writing articles about King's campaign helping Republicans.

Many whites in Chicago and across the country felt that enough was enough. The country had passed a Civil Rights Act and Voting Rights Act. What more did Black people want? King devoted a whole column in March to taking on white liberals who questioned when Black people would be satisfied. "We do not want to return to normal," King underscored.[208] At city hearings King called Chicago a "slum colony" and stressed that "to be poor and Negro in America is to be powerless . . . to be governed by the police, housing authorities, welfare departments without rights and redress."[209]

Jobs!

> Keep a slice of the "bread" in your community.
> —Operation Breadbasket slogan

Tenant organizing, rent strikes, and organizing around Chicago schools were only part of the movement's portfolio. With Black unemployment in Chicago double the rate of whites, another arm of the CFM took on discriminatory hiring practices.[210] Operation Breadbasket, begun in Atlanta in 1962, sought to harness Black economic power to pressure companies to change. Modeled on "Don't Buy Where You Can't Work Campaigns" of the 1940s, they identified businesses selling products or services to Black people yet not employing Black people or restricting them to menial positions. Breadbasket organizers first attempted to "negotiate a more equitable employment practice," but if that didn't work, they would boycott that business or establishments that sold their goods.

Now they were bringing it to Chicago. As King announced in January, Black Chicagoans had the buying power to make the difference between profit and loss in almost any business, but many businesses "deplete the ghetto without returning to the community any of the profits through fair hiring practices."[211] Jesse Jackson directed the Breadbasket effort, initially targeting five dairy industries. Both Black and white clergy helped spread the word. Milk sellers were particularly vulnerable to this kind of pressure; if their perishable product didn't sell quickly, their losses would stack up. Three of these businesses negotiated to add jobs for Black applicants immediately and the remaining two did so after the boycotts began.

Next, Breadbasket took on Pepsi and Coca-Cola bottlers, and then supermarket chains and construction jobs. Because of their pressure, Jackson described how two Black contractors built the National Tea Supermarket at Forty-Seventh and Calumet and how they got rules changed to support minority-owned banks.[212] King would periodically attend Breadbasket's weekly Friday afternoon meetings. In 1967, King proclaimed Operation Breadbasket their "most spectacularly success-ful program," responsible for 2,200 new jobs for Black Chicagoans in eleven months.[213]

The movement prepared for even more confrontational tactics. King, Bevel, Lafayette, and others had been working for months to build capacity for demonstrations from gang members. In May, Bevel met with four hundred gang members in Woodlawn to get their help to "close Chicago down" if their demands weren't met. He criticized them for playing Daley's game by "fighting each other while he gets free."[214] "You have to be ready to go to jail and stay there," Bevel told the young people gathered; many, according to the *Chicago Defender*, had already been in jail. He called for three thousand teenagers to join them in June, floating an idea to close down the Dan Ryan Expressway by lying down on it.[215] In early June, King and Raby joined welfare recipients on a panel highlighting the "inequities" in welfare adminis-tration and the ways welfare officials policed welfare recipients' homes for evidence of wrongdoing.[216]

SCLC's Chicago campaign, learning from previous mistakes, had committed to a different kind of organizing and a wide field staff in Chicago. Arkansas-born Jimmy Collier, who moved to Chicago in 1961 to attend junior college, helped instill a new grassroots approach for the CFM. Along with SCLC field staffer James Orange, they were "on the streets—James, Eric, me and my guitar. We contacted gangs like the Vice Lords and the Blackstone Rangers. We knew if we could get young people involved it would draw their parents. . . . They liked music though. I could make up a song on the spot about what-ever, and they liked that. Dr. King liked that too. The music had a real role."[217]

Collier crafted songs like "Lead Poison on the Walls," "Rent Strike

Blues," and "Everybody's Got to Live" that spoke to the realities that Northern Black people faced. Like songs used in the Southern movement, Collier took contemporary songs and added new words. He riffed on Curtis Mayfield's "Never Too Much Love":

> I like to drink whiskey, I like to drink wine.
> I'd like to have some now, but I don't have time.
> I have to fight for my freedom, got to fight for it now,
> Come and join with Dr. King and we'll show you how.[218]

Many of these young men started to see their own capacity to advocate for their communities' needs.[219] Still, there was much resistance. At one meeting with the Blackstone Rangers, when the young men didn't want to sing, the three-hundred-pound Orange bellowed, "You think you're too bad to sing? Well I'm badder than you so we're going to sing." So they all sang.[220]

At one mass meeting, some young men booed King. He would say it was the only time he was ever booed by Black people. At first he was demoralized, but then he contextualized it: "I had urged them to have faith in America and in white society. Their hopes had soared. They were now booing me because they felt that we were unable to deliver on our promises. They were booing because we had urged them to have faith in people who had too often proved to be unfaithful."[221]

A New Civil Rights Act?

By the spring of 1966, the Chicago Freedom Movement had decided to prioritize local and federal action around housing inequality. Interviewed in Toronto in May, Scott King stressed that despite the difficulties, "we are so excited about what we are doing."[222]

In mid-March, King had joined other civil rights leaders in Washington to meet with President Johnson about new civil rights legislation that included prohibitions for housing discrimination. Johnson had announced it two months earlier in his State of the Union address. At this meeting, the president told them his plans for a new civil rights bill that would attack discrimination on juries, enact greater penalties for people who attacked civil rights workers, give the federal government the ability to go after school districts that weren't desegregating, establish penalties for inciting a riot, and, perhaps most importantly, prohibit discrimination in the sale or rental of housing. Johnson was clear that day about the importance of tackling housing discrimination in proposing the bill: "Negro ghettos indict our cities North and South. As long as the color of a man's skin determines his choice of housing, no investment in the physical rebuilding of our cities will free the men and women living there."[223] Attorney General Nicholas Katzenbach warned that the housing provision would be "particularly difficult" to get passed through Congress but claimed Johnson would push for it.[224]

King took the message for federal change on the road. In Texas in March, he called for national action, saying, "The ghetto in the North is not being dispersed; if anything, it is being intensified."[225] In Michigan, King highlighted the need for national action to address slums, for instance, cutting off federal funds to areas practicing housing discrimination.[226] Not to be outflanked, Daley announced at the end of May that he had secured a large government loan through the US Department of Housing and Urban Development (HUD) to renovate five hundred apartments. He vowed that the slums would be eliminated by the end of the decade.[227] One of the Daley administration's tactics was to make it seem like he was already doing the things the movement was asking for so there was no need for King, who "evidently doesn't know what's been going on."[228] But five hundred apartments in a city of one million Black people was a drop in the bucket.

President Johnson came to Chicago to speak at a Democratic Party fundraiser on May 17. The date coincided with the twelfth anniversary of the *Brown* decision. Raby had wired the president criticizing HEW's decision not to enforce the Civil Rights Act in Chicago and asked for a meeting. He called Johnson's visit an "especially appropriate time to address attention of your office to Chicago school system's oppressive practices of school segregation."[229] But Johnson did not meet with them. The SCLC—and its Student Union Organizing committee—had called for a school boycott for that day. In three "all Negro high schools" and one elementary school, as the *Chicago Tribune* un-self-consciously reported, students stayed out of school to mark the anniversary and Chicago's enduring segregation.[230] So twelve years after the Supreme Court had ruled school segregation unconstitutional and two years after the Civil Rights Act had tied federal funding to school desegregation, schools in Chicago were relentlessly segregated, the movement highlighted it, newspapers described them as "Negro schools" without any hint that this should be changed, and the president refused to intervene.

On June 1 and 2, Martin and Coretta Scott King went to Washington for President Johnson's two-day Conference on Civil Rights. Many historians have noted that King was sidelined at the conference, and attribute it to King's growing dismay about Vietnam. Equally salient was that King was leading a civil rights fight in a place that Johnson wasn't interested in disrupting. Both Roy Wilkins and Thurgood Marshall, Johnson's preferred Black spokesmen, disparaged King's ongoing campaign in Chicago as unnecessary diversions from the real work they were doing through the law.[231]

King complained privately to advisors on how disrespected he felt, and some suggested he leave after the first day, given the way he was being treated. But he stuck it out.[232] He had grown used to this kind of disdainful treatment when he highlighted Northern racism. Here it was from the president as well. It took its toll—but he wasn't going anywhere.

9

One Day That Man Wants to Get Out of Prison

The Organizing Deepens but So Does White Resistance

On May 25, 1966, the violent face of Chicago's racism reared its ugly head. A seventeen-year-old Black teenager named Jerome Huey set out for a job interview in Cicero, Illinois, a suburb of Chicago. Huey dreamed of becoming an engineer and was attending Wright Junior College, but he needed extra money to help his parents with their struggling grocery store. On his way back from the interview at a freight-loading company in Cicero, four white teenagers attacked him with a baseball bat, smashing his head so hard that his eyes came out of his skull.[1] Huey's sixteen-year-old sister recalled visiting him in the hospital and finding her brother unrecognizable from all the injuries. He died two days later.[2] He had been lynched in plain sight.[3]

Cicero was well known to Black Chicagoans as a sundown town, a place where Black people worked but couldn't live.[4] As one Vice Lord explained, "We could clean their houses and sweep their streets but when it got dark we had to leave."[5] When a Black family, the Clarks, had tried to move into Cicero in 1951, the police had prevented them. Even after the Clarks got a court order allowing them to move in, local white people rioted for three days and burned all their belongings.[6] No white people faced any punishment for this violence—instead, Harvey Clark himself was indicted for inciting a riot, as were his real estate agent, landlady, and lawyer.[7]

For most white Chicagoans, Huey's murder hazarded little concern. While horrible, the white hoodlums who beat Huey to death had little to do with them.[8] Like so many white Southerners who distanced themselves from the Klan, these white Chicagoans preferred political and economic means to maintain segregation, distancing themselves from those "ruffians" who used violence to maintain segregation. And again, the national media and public officials looked away. As Ralph Abernathy would later observe, "When you attacked Mississippi, New Yorkers and San Franciscans felt good about themselves. When you attacked Chicago, everybody felt uncomfortable. So the press backed off."[9] Northern racial violence was viewed as unfortunate and aberrational, not revealing of a racial sickness like in the South.

Huey's death chilled Black Chicago. It revealed the lengths white Chicagoans would go to "protect their neighborhood"—underscoring the urgency of what the CFM was trying to do. For King, the hypocrisy was outrageous; Huey had been killed just two and a half miles from his apartment for being a Black person in a white Chicago neighborhood, and yet most white Chicagoans, including the mayor, and many across the country, denied the city's segregation. White sundown neighborhoods like Cicero dotted the metro area. According to the 1960 census, in the white South Side neighborhoods of Gage Park and Marquette Park, *only seven* of the one hundred thousand people who lived in these neighborhoods were not white.[10]

In 1955, after her son had been lynched in Mississippi, Emmett Till's mother had opened her son's casket to "make the world see what they had done to my son." The CFM would do the same to try to force the city and the nation to face the violent as well as bureaucratic, political, and economic forces that kept Chicago definitively segregated and extremely unequal.

There have been a litany of explanations about what made Chicago's racism so difficult for King's Chicago campaign to overcome: the targets were too broad or not broad enough; organized nonviolence was unpopular or too militant, King was not an organizer, the SCLC was out of its depth, King was naïve, Black Chicagoans were not on board.[11] But common among nearly all of them is the idea that there weren't the clear villains and violent white resistance like in the South to move the nation. But that is simply not true. As Huey's death brought home, violence was always a part of Northern segregation. Open housing was "the best issue in the North . . . to really create a movement," CORE's Bob Lucas explained, because whites of all economic levels were willing to use any means necessary to prevent it. Lucas believed King wanted "to show the rest of the country, the rest of the world how racist the North, how racist Chicago was."[12]

They faced a clear villain in Mayor Daley, his machine, the police, and the white constituency and businesses that supported his segregationist reign. Daley lived in an all-white neighborhood and sicced the police on Black protesters who marched on it. But his villainy was portrayed very differently and his word given much more credence than, say, a Bull Connor or a George Wallace around issues of race. Daley was, as Harry Belafonte explained, "the well-honed benevolent racist," tied to Democratic power in Washington and to President Lyndon Johnson himself.[13]

Perhaps because it happened in Chicago and not Mississippi, the lynching of Jerome Huey has become a footnote in the histories of King.[14] Indeed, the decision to engage in open-housing marches in Chicago in 1966 is often framed as a strategy (good or bad) that the movement turned to for media attention and a tactic (valiant or misguided) to try to get some Black families into these white neighborhoods. It was much, much more than that. Black life mattered in Chicago as well as Mississippi—and there should be no place, King believed, that Black people could not go. The movement would put their lives on the line to open the casket of Chicago's racism and try to make the world see.

Building a Multiracial Coalition and King's Long-standing Commitment to Puerto Rican Organizing

Over the course of the spring, the CFM had been developing alliances with the city's Puerto Rican community to take on the Daley machine. Though most accounts of King's work put his multiracial organizing and Latino alliances with the Poor People's Campaign, these alliances began much earlier.[15] King had become familiar with the similarities of discrimination, segregation, and inequitable treatment that Blacks and Puerto Ricans encountered with New York's 1199 strikes from 1959 onward. They had gotten to know Gilberto Gerena Valentin there, recruiting him to organize thousands of Puerto Ricans for the March on Washington. King had traveled to Puerto Rico twice: first in 1962, then in the summer of 1965. So Chicago would not be the first time King saw the need for a "united front" of African Americans and Puerto Ricans.

"The prospect of establishing a rainbow coalition," Coretta explained, "excited Martin."[16] King called for a summit meeting of Black and Puerto Rican leaders in the city to launch a combined effort to "totally free all minority groups"; Puerto Ricans would "help spearhead" the movement.[17] The segregation Black people faced in Chicago was replicated in the segregation Puerto Ricans and Mexicans faced. Raby highlighted the commonalities between Chicago's Black and Latino communities: "They, as we, are without job opportunities, without community services, without proper representation and without the specialized education facilities they need." And so "we joined hands with them."[18]

This united front would extend to Latino gangs as well. In May, Jesse Jackson and James Bevel had organized a South Side "leadership summit" for over 250 Blackstone Rangers; in early June they held one on the West Side for the Vice Lords and Cobras.[19] Then, on June 11, 1966, SCLC convened a bigger summit—the Turfmasters First Annual Conference—bringing together two hundred gang members from eighteen different gangs in the city—Black, white, Native American, Mexican, and Puerto Rican, representing more than two thousand members (including some girl gangs).[20] The all-day meeting aimed to get gang members "to try out a new weapon—nonviolence—and to examine the extent to which gang members were thinking and could advocate about the larger community." They wanted to end violence between gangs that was leading to dozens of gun deaths of Black young people and turn these young men's energy and vision to advocating for their community needs.[21]

Together that Saturday, over food and coffee at the Sheraton Hotel, King and other SCLC organizers mapped out the power of nonviolent direct action and a united-front strategy with these young men and a smattering of young women. They discussed commonalities facing poor Black, Latino, and white Chicagoans and the organized power they needed to develop to take on the largest political machine in the nation.[22] They outlined these young men's skills and started to make concrete plans of action. Some of the men had served time in prison or dropped out of school but all, according to the *Chicago Defender*, "agreed that they possess experience and skills that could be used to help create better communities."[23] The Vice Lords already had a plan to "set up our own agencies for jobs, health, information and recreation," to encourage kids to stay in school, and to support young people getting out of jail with jobs and support.[24] They created a council consisting of two members of each gang with committees around housing, health, education, employment welfare, and recreation.[25]

James Orange was in awe: "Those guys just sat down and started talking about working together. From that period on, we worked with those guys."[26] Gonzato Disciple Darris Williams described King as a "heavy stud" and hoped that working in concert would lead to "a better deal now" for their community needs. Another Disciple called the meeting "a big success."[27]

One key issue these young men faced was police brutality. Chicago's police were notorious and had grown even more punitive toward the Black and Latino communities in the 1950s and 1960s—engaging in petty arrests, "constant shakedowns," and an "avalanche" of police brutality after 1963, according to historian Simon Balto.[28] From 1957 to 1968, arrests of Black people increased 65 percent and misdemeanor arrests skyrocketed by 165 percent.[29] The CPD helped maintain borders between "white" and "black" neighborhoods. Members of the American Civil Liberties Union (ACLU) were on hand that day; the executive director of Chicago's ACLU, Jay Miller, encouraged the young men to document incidences of police brutality, including witnesses, to be used to build cases against the police.[30]

These efforts and fledgling alliances would lay the groundwork for what Fred Hampton, Bobby Lee, and others in Chicago's Black Panther Party would deepen a couple years later through alliances with the Blackstone Rangers, the Young Lords, and Young Patriots Organization.[31] Hampton would attribute the race/class approach he pursued to King's influence.[32] A multiracial coalition had the possibility to change power relations in the city. Indeed, there is no way to understand why Daley and the CPD, along with the FBI, saw Fred Hampton as such a threat without understanding the power of this kind of interracial organizing. And it had roots in the CFM.

Just one day after the summit, on June 12, a three-day uprising flared after police shot a Puerto Rican man named Aracelis Cruz. Mayor Daley had declared the previous week Puerto Rican week and the city's first Puerto Rican parade took place on June 11, but area aldermen had sternly warned Puerto Rican organizers not to invite *any* civil rights speakers.[33] The day after the parade, a fight broke out between a landlord and a tenant. When the police arrived, Officer Thomas Munyon chased twenty-year-old Aracelis Cruz and another friend down an alley. Munyon shot Cruz dead.

A crowd of Puerto Ricans assembled to protest the police. More police were called to the scene, and they turned dogs on the protesters. A twenty-year-old bystander named Juan Gonzalez was bitten by one of the dogs, further inflaming the crowd.[34] Police shot into the crowds of Puerto Rican and Black Chicagoans who were protesting.[35] Dozens of squad cars arrived and "police poured out. They were everywhere. They had dogs, they had helmets, and they were beating the hell out of everyone on the street."[36] By now thousands of people had gathered, throwing cans and bottles at the officers and overturning police cars. As the Division Street uprising continued, Chicano community organizer Obed Lopez reached out to SCLC to send observers to "witness what was taking place."[37] Lopez had been working with SCLC, and SCLC quickly responded.[38] With Bevel's help, the SCLC began documenting cops beating many young Latinos.[39]

Despite the police abuse, many Puerto Rican Chicagoans felt the uprising helped solidify a sense of Puerto Rican identity and community. "We didn't know how many of us were here," explained Mirta Rodriguez, a bilingual educator who helped establish the Puerto Rican educational organization ASPIRA in Chicago, "and all of a sudden because of the riot we find out we're a good number . . . that was the call."[40] King saw the uprising as indicative of the oppressive conditions poor Latinos and Black Chicagoans faced in the city. But Daley blamed it on "outsiders" who were instigating trouble.[41]

Two weeks after the uprising, on June 28, more than two hundred Puerto Ricans, Chicanos, African Americans, and other allies marched from Humboldt Park five miles through the Loop to City Hall to protest police brutality.[42] They had reached out to King to speak, but he was not back in the city. After the march, and inspired by the Chicago Freedom Movement, Puerto Rican and Mexican Chicagoans formed the Latin American Defense Organization (LADO) to press for community needs, which immediately came under the suspicion of Chicago's police.[43] The Black–Puerto Rican solidarity would continue throughout the Chicago campaign, helping to deepen King's thinking for the multiracial Poor People's Campaign and laying the seeds for the rainbow coalition a few years later between the Chicago Black Panthers and Young Lords.

With Jerome Huey's murder in Cicero and then the Puerto Rican uprising, things were heating up in Chicago. The CFM was planning a massive rally at Soldier Field and marches into Chicago's sundown neighborhoods. But in mid-June, King was forced to leave Chicago after the shooting of James Meredith. Having fought to desegregate the University of Mississippi in 1962, Meredith had commenced a solo 220-mile March Against Fear in Mississippi on June 5 to challenge the terror across the state around registering to vote, despite passage of the Voting Rights Act. The very next day, he was ambushed on the highway; he survived the injuries but could not keep going. SCLC, SNCC, Fannie Lou Hamer, Stokely Carmichael, the Deacons for

Defense, King, and local Mississippi activists decided they needed to continue Meredith's March. King made arrangements for eight gang members working with them (chosen by the gang leaders from the conference) to join the Meredith March.[44] Gerena Valentin and a contingent of thirty Puerto Rican activists from New York joined them in Mississippi as well.[45] King connected people, north and south, into the broader fight against injustice.

King marched alongside many SNCC activists, including Carmichael himself. According to historian Peniel Joseph, "Carmichael credited the time spent in Mississippi for turning the grudging respect many in SNCC felt toward King into open admiration." Carmichael "marveled at King's courage in the face of threats, hecklers, and law enforcement" along the route.[46] King's courage stuck with Carmichael, as did King's deep love of Black people. Carmichael would later say, "I'm always scared. Sometimes when I'm in a march or the cops have hold of me, I'm crazy with fear."[47] Along the route, after being arrested in Greenwood, Carmichael proclaimed, "This is the twenty-seventh time I have been arrested. I ain't going to jail no more. We been saying freedom for six years and we ain't got nothin'. What we get to start saying now is Black Power!"

The mainstream media would get obsessed with the calls of Black Power on the march, overplaying the differences between King and the SNCC radicals. While King did not like the phrase's "connotations of violence and separation," he well understood the frustrations of Black people who were "taunted by empty promises, humiliated and deprived by the filth and decay" of America's ghettos.[48] He liked the concept, not the slogan. According to SNCC's Judy Richardson, he was careful not to criticize SNCC and the ideas its members were trying to promote.[49] As they were marching, Stokely said, "Martin, I deliberately started the Black Power thing to get you committed to it." "That's alright," Martin said smiling. "I've been used before. One more time won't hurt."[50]

This media obsession would become another way to downplay and disregard what was happening in Chicago. It pitted Carmichael against King for the rest of his life, missing the love and respect between them. Key to Carmichael's admiration was King's love for Black people—not just respectable Black people or churchgoing Black people, but Black people. And "because he loved our people, he would not compromise or . . . become corrupted."[51]

From Tougaloo to Jackson, Coretta and their two oldest children,

Yoki and Marty, joined them. In Jackson, Mississippi, at the end of the Meredith March on June 26, King spoke before a crowd of twenty-five thousand and declared how over the past three years he had seen his dream "turned into a nightmare." [52] The nightmare he was talking about was *not* Black Power but the many flavors of white resistance they were encountering in Chicago.

Nailing the Demands to the Door: The Chicago Freedom Movement Goes Wider and an Uprising Occurs

After the Meredith March, the whole King family returned to Chicago. "It was very good for my children," Coretta observed, "who had never experienced poverty." The Kings were determined the kids not be spoiled or feel separated from other children who did not have decent housing or food as they did. [53] As Martin explained, "They cannot be what they are to be until these children can grow up to be what they ought to be." [54] The Kings were trying to parent in socially conscious ways.

Still in Chicago, there was little for the children to do except go "and play in the black dirt." No greenery or close-by parks or pools were available to Black children—and when Coretta tried to keep the kids inside, "tempers flared, there were shouting and pushing matches." [55] Like many of their neighbors, the lack of summer recreational spaces where kids could play was a problem. Hot and crowded, without parks and pools to use, the kids grew restless and frustrated being cooped up. The Kings understood anew the ways ghetto conditions wore people down. [56]

Months into the Chicago Freedom Movement's campaign, the media were still refusing to investigate the depth of the city's inequality or cover the broad-based movement with the seriousness of the Birmingham campaign. King, Andrew Young, and other SCLC organizers thought marching would "empower" the community given how many parts of the city were "no-go" territory for Black Chicagoans, as Huey's murder in Cicero had devastatingly shown. [57] And so SCLC decided to march into white neighborhoods. Targeting white realtors and homeowners to dramatize the degree of segregation of the city, they hoped to break the fear Chicago's white neighborhoods imposed and ideally bring the media's eyes with them. [58]

On July 10, 1966, more than thirty-five thousand Chicagoans—perhaps as many as sixty-five thousand, as King said later—braved the

98-degree heat for a rally at Soldier Field and march to City Hall to publicize their demands.[59] Mahalia Jackson sang, as did Coretta Scott King, Stevie Wonder, and Peter, Paul & Mary.[60] Comedian Dick Gregory spoke, as did CORE head Floyd McKissick, who called for Black Power, which he said was not about violence but economic and social progress through Black unity.[61] Many Puerto Ricans joined the march that day as well.[62]

Members of the Blackstone Rangers, Gonzato Disciples, and Vice Lords turned out.[63] Some carried Black Power signs, including ones picturing a shotgun saying "Freedom Now." After hearing one of King's lieutenants say they didn't need gangbangers because "they weren't going to do nothin' but disrupt the rally," a group of Vice Lords, Blackstone Rangers, and Gonzato Disciples walked out. That night, according to one of the Vice Lords, a handful went to meet with King. King made clear that "he didn't know who made the statement but he did need us."[64] Many books mention tensions with gang members at this Soldier Field rally—some reducing it to a civil rights–Black Power divide.[65] But very few accounts follow what King did next—which was to meet with these young men that evening at his apartment, listen to them, apologize for the hurtful statement, and underline that this was *not* what he believed.

The air was hot and electric that Sunday at Soldier Field. "We will no longer sit idly by in agonizing deprivation and wait on others to provide our freedom," King proclaimed:

> We are here because we're tired of living in rat infested slums and the Chicago Housing Authority's cement reservations . . .
>
> We are tired of having to pay a median rent of $97 in Lawndale for four rooms while whites in South Deering pay $73 for five rooms . . .
>
> We are tired of inferior, segregated and overcrowded schools which are incapable of preparing our young people for leadership . . .
>
> This day, henceforth, and forever more, we must make it clear that we will purge Chicago of every politician, whether he be Negro or white who feels he owns the Negro vote rather than earns the Negro vote.[66]

King promised to withdraw "our money en masse" from any bank that didn't have a nondiscriminatory lending process and any company that didn't employ "an adequate number of Negroes, Puerto Ricans and other ethnic minorities in higher paying jobs." He extolled "black is as beautiful as any color." The federal government, the Supreme Court, and the mayor "will only respond when they realize we have a powerful determination to be free. . . . So we must go out with grim and bold determination to free ourselves."[67] *Grim* was not a usual word for King—but reflected the gut-wrenching conditions Black Chicagoans were living under, alongside the bravery it took to keep fighting and not lose hope. King promised to take their demands to City Hall, and if Daley wasn't there, "we'll tack them on the City Hall door."[68]

The *Defender* described a forty-car motorcade of dignitaries arriving to the rally and King leading the march to City Hall.[69] King was so weary, historian James Ralph documents, that he decided to ride "in an automobile (air-conditioned, his critics carped)," leading over five thousand followers on a mile-long trek to City Hall.[70] An ambulance trailed behind picking up eleven people from heat exhaustion.[71]

The Kings had planned for the three older children to get out and march with them, but three-year-old Bunny wanted to march too. King said yes, and they all got out and marched. It would be the only time the whole family ever marched together, Coretta explained.[72] Bunny got tired and had to be carried half the distance on Andrew Young's and Bernard Lee's shoulders, her head bobbing along atop the march, Coretta recalled.[73] They marched through the Loop to City Hall "like a huge tidal wave," as one activist described it.[74] People sang freedom songs and chanted "Mayor Daley Must Go."[75] When they arrived, King and Raby taped the six-page, fourteen-point list of the movement's demands to the door.

The demands laid out a detailed blueprint for addressing the city's inequities. After months of discussion and disagreement within the CFM, they had formulated these clear-cut ways to address the city's structures of racism. They included:

- school desegregation and enforcement of the 1964 Civil Rights Act regarding the complaint against the Chicago Board of Education
- a civilian complaint review board to monitor the CPD
- a bargaining union for welfare recipients and ceasing of home investigations
- increasing the supply of housing options for low- and middle-income families

- rehabbing public housing amenities
- a $2 state minimum wage
- increased garbage collection and building inspections
- requirements that precinct captains live in the voting district
- data published on how many Blacks, whites, and Latinos worked at all city departments and places the city contracted with, and
- federal supervision of nondiscriminatory granting of loans by banks and savings institutions[76]

A few days earlier, King had also called for a course of Black history taught in all Chicago schools, expanded health services, and the expansion of mass transit to O'Hare Airport and the Northwest side so all Chicagoans had access to jobs and housing there.[77] The CFM made it clear: a set of policy changes, programs, and oversight was needed to unravel the decades of segregation, discrimination, and policy inequity. It could be done, it must be done—and they spelled out how and where to begin. The spirited rally, march, and fourteen urgent demands tacked on to the City Hall door, the *Defender* reported, evidenced an organized movement, bigger than Birmingham, that was taking on Chicago's terrifying injustices with definitive suggestions.[78]

The heat that day was merciless and the turnout below the 100,000 they had hoped for.[79] Rev. Joseph Jackson had played a role in diminishing the numbers, urging members of Black Baptist churches around the city not to attend. A *Chicago Tribune* editorial leapt on the low numbers. "Marches and demonstrations have become tiresome, and the Rev. Mr. King's rhetoric about 'filling up the jails of Chicago to end slums' is becoming stale. . . . Hot air on a hot day seemed just a little too much. . . . We suppose that 'civil rights' spokesmen will engage in these charades just as long as there are publicity and a chance of passing the hat."[80] Along with the *Tribune*'s derision came counterprotests. Later that night, the demands were taken down and replaced by a sign reading "Support the police."[81]

To steal the movement's thunder, two days before the march, Daley had announced he would meet with King the day after it. He then fed the media all sorts of statistics to position himself as the solution, and thus King was unnecessary and out of touch with what the city was doing. The next day, in the three-hour meeting with Daley, King restated the demands, but Daley was largely disdainful, claiming that the city had the best anti-slum program in the nation. When King and

Raby highlighted the need for a CCRB, Police Superintendent Orlando Wilson claimed that would only hamper attempts to root out police abuse.[82] Back and forth it went, and nothing resulted from the meeting. Raby characterized Daley's response: "There was no need for Martin, and that Martin should go someplace where he was really needed."[83]

Talking to the press afterward, Daley was dismissive, claiming the movement had no solutions: "We asked them, 'What would you do that we haven't done?' They had no answers. I asked for their help and suggestions, and they frankly said the answers were difficult."[84] Daley disparaged King's knowledge of the situation, saying "he doesn't have all the facts on the local situation. After all, he is a resident of another city."[85] King, on the other hand, was visibly frustrated. He told reporters he didn't think Daley understood "the depth and dimensions of the problem we are dealing with" and had only made "surface changes, and the Negro community can no longer live with token changes."[86] The CFM had a host of clear ideas for change, but the mayor refused to implement any of them. He also highlighted the pressure on city workers *not* to participate in the movement. When asked if there would be more meetings with the mayor, King said, "The time for meeting is over. . . . There will be marches and there will be mass jailing."[87]

The next day, July 12, was another blazing 98-degree day in this weeklong heat wave. Yet on the West Side, the police turned off an open fire hydrant. Police rarely turned off the fire hydrants in neighboring white neighborhoods. With few pools available to sweltering Black children in this and other segregated neighborhoods, the racism was unmistakable.[88] One pool that served West Side Black youth had been torn down to make way for an expressway. The closest beach had been closed by public health officials due to pollution.[89] The lack of public green space and access to water for Chicago's Black community had long been an issue.

When the cops turned off the hydrant, some Black kids started shouting back. "Why didn't the cops turn off hydrants in white neighborhoods?" one kid asked.

"We run this. You niggers don't run nothin' around here," a cop barked in response.

Shortly after the police left, another kid announced, "If they can keep theirs on, we can, too," and two teens opened the hydrant again to give their neighbors some relief. The police descended, arresting them and beating the kids indiscriminately. People responded to the arrests by throwing rocks and bottles at the police car. Thirty squad cars descended on the angry crowd and a half dozen teenagers were beaten till bloodied by the police before being arrested.[90] This further incensed the crowd and people continued throwing rocks and Molotov cocktails and smashing store windows and cars.

Hearing about the fire hydrant incident, King went to the 12th District police station with singer Mahalia Jackson to negotiate the release and post bail for the six battered teenagers. The young people then went with King to Shiloh Baptist Church to an impromptu meeting. Nearly one thousand restive young people, many of them gang members, came that night, deeply upset by the events of the day.[91] The teenagers talked about police brutality, the lack of outdoor space open to them, and the ways they were treated by city authorities. King was angry: "[S]ome of our brothers in Chicago tonight faced serious police brutality. They were arrested unnecessarily and they were victims of the system that exists in this city."[92] King lambasted the paucity of Daley's token reforms: "It's like improving the food in prison. One day that man wants to get out of prison."

The next day, exhausted, Coretta Scott King addressed an integrated meeting of women at the YWCA, asking the one hundred gathered to sign a statement supporting the proposals the movement laid out. At first many of the women were scared, fearing for their husbands' jobs. "What are you afraid of?" she countered. "The time comes when we have to make a decision."[93]

Meanwhile, the uprising continued, as did the massive police crackdown using tear gas and machine guns.[94] King and his staff worked the streets continuously, trying to prevent further violence. King, Young, and Raby drove around talking to young people: "We understood their frustration. We were trying to address it and find avenues for that energy, and frustration, and anger to be channeled in a constructive way. And that, that the most dangerous situation was that the police would overreact, and they would in fact be physically hurt, or damaged, or end up in jail."[95] King canceled a trip to Switzerland because he felt responsible to stay in Chicago.[96] One Vice Lord member praised King for his work on the street all through the night. "All the other 'leaders' were in bed."[97]

The national media coverage of the uprising was wide and hysterical, far outpacing the kind of attention the movement had been trying to get for months about Chicago's inhumane slum conditions. Daley asked the governor to mobilize the National Guard and four thousand members of the National Guard descended on the West Side on

July 15.[98] One witness said there was so much shooting it "sounded like . . . a movie." [99]

Daley laid blame for the uprising on the movement itself. "You can't charge it directly to Martin Luther King," Daley told reporters, "but surely some of the people that came in here and have been talking for the last year on violence and . . . instructing people in how to conduct violence. They are on his staff and they are responsible in a great measure." [100] Criticizing SCLC's work with gangs, Daley declared, "Someone has to train these youngsters." [101] So did Daley ally Rev. Joseph Jackson. "I believe our young people are not vicious enough to attack a whole city. Some other forces are using these young people." [102]

King was furious, particularly given the work they had done to keep the uprising from spreading. If we hadn't been there, he told a reporter, "it would have been worse than Watts." [103] He marched into City Hall and insisted on meeting with Daley. Daley finally agreed to sprayer attachments on fire hydrants to be installed, police and park officials to ensure all Chicagoans could access all public parks and pools, and the erecting of more pools in the neighborhood of the uprising.[104] Rather than meet the movement's demand for a civilian complaint review board, however, Daley chose instead to appoint a twenty-three-man, police-run review board to investigate the situation, claiming defiance of the law was increasing in the city.[105]

King was deeply frustrated. They'd met with Daley on July 11 but gotten nothing. Then the uprising finally produced some movement from Daley, but this sent the signal "that not peacefulness but violence will bring the granting of demands." [106] King would return to this theme again and again in interviews; Northern white power structures often planted the seeds for riots, and then *only* after uprisings— not nonviolent protest—were willing to grant any demands.[107] On top of it, the larger segregation remained in place.

The White House was worried about the uprising. So the night of Friday, July 15, the Department of Justice's John Doar and Roger Wilkins arrived at King's apartment around midnight and found it packed with Vice Lords, Roman Saints, and Cobras. There was no fan or air-conditioning and King was sitting on the floor with the young men. Over the next four hours, they watched, in awe, the conversation that ensued about the strategies and philosophies of nonviolence, of experiences with the police, and of what was happening in Chicago.[108] The relationship that King and some of his field staff had been building over many months bore fruit. A leader of the Roman Saints, Richard

"Peanut" Tidwell, convinced his fellow members to go out with him and help to calm people. It worked. The uprising ended not because of the National Guard, or the CPD, or Daley's leadership but because of the leadership that these young gang members marshaled and the relationship they had forged with King.[109] At the end of the uprising, the police had killed two people, including a pregnant fourteen-year-old, injured eighty, and arrested more than four hundred.[110]

This wasn't the first time an uprising had erupted in the middle of an SCLC campaign. Three years earlier, the day after the Birmingham Agreement was reached, white segregationists angered by the agreement bombed King's brother's home and the Gaston Motel, where King and the SCLC were staying. After state troopers moved in and brutalized protesters, more than two thousand African Americans gathered outside the damaged motel, throwing rocks and bricks, looting commodities, and setting a nearby grocery store on fire.[111] The day after the uprising, President Kennedy endorsed the Birmingham Agreement. On some level, Kennedy had recognized that African Americans had reached an understandable breaking point, and he needed to take action. In Chicago, there would be no such presidential pressure, even though the community was similarly at a breaking point. "The people didn't want to riot. They wanted their rights," one Vice Lord underlined.[112]

Praising Daley regularly and frequently inviting him to the White House, Johnson wasn't interested in challenging the most powerful mayor in the country.[113] The only recorded call Johnson made during the crisis in Chicago was to Daley, not King, on July 19.[114] Daley lambasted King. "He's a goddamn faker," Daley told Johnson. The movement organizing was "subversive" and "the most dangerous thing we have in this country," Daley reported to the president. SCLC, according to Daley, "has become an extortion in all the big cities" and he was exceedingly worried about gangs getting politicized and involved in poverty programs. Daley painted himself as the real friend to civil rights and praised Johnson's work.[115]

Johnson asked hopefully, "What shape do you have King in? Is he about ready to get out?" Daley disparaged the idea that King was about civil rights and claimed the reverend was just playing politics when he pushed for different precinct captains. Saying he would consult with FBI director Hoover, Johnson told Daley that he felt about "this whole outfit about like you do." Indeed, the FBI had also grown worried about King's activities in Chicago and had developed a "probationary

racial informant"—a young Black staff member at an allied organization who provided the Bureau information.[116]

Daley portrayed King as ungrateful and disloyal to his benefactors
like Johnson: "I'll be damned if we let anyone take over themselves the
running of the city." LBJ agreed, "You're just about as right as can be
and I'll support you." [117]

10

Never Seen Mobs as Hostile . . . but the Nation Turns Its Back

The Chicago Freedom Movement had spent months organizing tenants. The push for rent strikes and tenant unions to improve living conditions started to bear fruit. In July, after several weeks of picketing, demonstrations, and rent withholding, a union of 1,500 tenants in the nearly thirty buildings managed by the real estate firm Gondor & Castalis was recognized to bargain for all the tenants. Their first demand simply insisted that Gondor & Castalis fix all the code violations in their buildings.[1] In August, the Federation of Tenant Unions (with the help of the AFL-CIO) had organized several thousand Chicago renters to engage in rent strikes, which succeeded in negotiating better rental agreements for three thousand additional tenants. One white real estate broker termed it "the beginning of a very serious revolution."[2]

According to Bernardine Dohrn, Muhammad Ali joined one of the anti-eviction protests. Yet another family was being evicted and officers had strewn their belongings outside the building. "He walks over, picks up a couch, walks right by the sheriff, and starts climbing the stairs. So every one of the 200 people walk over, pick up a piece of furniture, and climb back up the stairs; another great kind of creative disruption."[3] They didn't have to stand for this mistreatment.

The CFM had won some key local victories, but widespread change was still needed. Even after Jerome Huey's lynching, Daley continued to claim "people just chose to live where they were." The movement determined, according to Raby, that they were not going "to be frightened out of those neighborhoods."[4] To break this color line, in late July and August, the CFM began holding open-housing marches into the all-white South Side neighborhoods of Gage Park and Marquette Park and picketing real estate agencies, the front lines shielding these neighborhoods from Black renters. A white sociologist, Richard Murray, selected these working-middle-class "brickthrowing" neighborhoods for the marches because the segregation was intense, the rents were similar, and the properties serving working-class white Chicagoans were better maintained. (Murray did not choose the white upper-middle-class suburbs where he lived, which were also segregated.)[5] Some in the SCLC field staff worried that these marches might be flashier but they would take energy away from the tenant organizing they'd been working on for months.

These all-white neighborhoods, Marquette Park in particular, were places where Black people did not go. Marching into them was terrifying. For Doris Crenshaw, who'd grown up in Montgomery and taken part in the bus boycott as a teen, Chicago was "more brutal."[6] Huge crowds of angry white people of all ages met the marchers. Young white men carrying baseball bats and waving Confederate flags and Nazi symbols threw rocks, bottles, and eggs. They chanted "Nigger Go Home" and "We Want King" and sang a little ditty:

I wish I were an Alabama trooper.
That is what I would truly like to be.
I wish I were an Alabama trooper.
'Cause then I could kill the niggers legally.[7]

White families came out of their houses to join the growing masses. They turned on fire hydrants and hoses (despite the fact that just weeks earlier, Black kids had been arrested for doing the same thing). They tossed cherry bombs and fire crackers, threw feces, dropped firecrackers from trees, and tore out women's earrings.[8]

While the marchers were majority Black, many committed white people, including Peggy Terry and others in Jobs or Income Now (JOIN), marched as well.[9] The neighborhood residents attacked both white and Black marchers. When a rock hit a white nun marching, the crowd cheered. According to one marcher, "White persons in the line of march were targets of special abuse as the residents— especially older women—spat at us and called us 'traitors, communists, white niggers.' "[10]

On July 31, the white mob set fifteen cars on fire (including Rev. Addie Wyatt's), destroyed other cars, and pelted marchers with bricks and bottles for eighteen blocks as they marched back from Marquette Park to the Black community. At least twenty-five people were injured, including Jesse Jackson.[11] The police stood by and watched as the marchers were attacked. Members of Chicago's Medical Committee for Human Rights tended to the wounded.[12] At one point, the police offered to put the marchers in police cars, but activists didn't find that offer appealing. The television news revealed how large numbers of police vans "with a very large contingent of police," according to Raby, "simply sat and waited until everything was over."[13]

"Cops laughed and joked with persons who threw bricks at Negroes," Raby observed, even though police officers had also been injured by these white mobs.[14] Despite the violence and the burning of two dozen automobiles, police made few arrests. In fact, the *Chicago Defender* reported, police pretended to arrest white rioters, only to take them around the corner and "turn them loose."[15] King slammed the lack of police protection of these peaceful marchers. "It is clear that the police were either unwilling or unable to disperse the riotous mob that brutally attacked Negroes and whites who had come to the community to seek open housing in compliance with the law." Again he called for a civilian complaint board to review police conduct. Again they were denied. It was later discovered a special unit of intelligence detectives from the Chicago Police Department (a unit supposedly created to fight organized crime) was dispatched to write down the license plates of every marcher's car to try to show Communist sympathies or other unsavory ties of civil rights activists (but not the white mobs).[16]

Nazi Party leader George Lincoln Rockwell was so inspired by the white mobs in Marquette Park that he came to the city, holding rallies and marches in August and September. The rabid segregationism of Chicagoans would lead to the establishment of the National Socialist Party (Nazi) headquarters in Marquette Park by local leader Frank Collin.[17] The *Chicago Tribune* and *Chicago Sun-Times* were largely uncritical of the white mobs; it was the Black marchers who were "asking for trouble" by marching in these neighborhoods.[18]

On Friday, August 5, King, Raby, a number of the gang members, and eight hundred others marched through Marquette Park headed to Gage Park. Nancy Jefferson marched too, "absolutely scared to death . . . you knew that the White police was not going to protect him or us."[19] Gang members served as marshals in many of these open-housing marches, according to Lafayette, because of their "discipline and courage. And they had no problem following directions because they were organized in that way."[20] Some Blackstone Rangers wore baseball gloves to catch the bottles and rocks being thrown at them.[21] They decided to pair gang members from different gangs together so "they got to know each other."[22] This cross-gang organizing led to a temporary truce.[23]

They were marching on three realty companies that day—Mark Realty, Rio Realty, and Halverson Realty. Seven thousand white residents turned out to oppose them.[24] When they crossed Ashland Avenue into Marquette Park, they were greeted with screaming mobs of men and women. Andrew Young talked about how scary it was. "Now in the South, we faced mobs, but it would be a couple of hundred or fifty or seventy-five. The violence in the South always came from a rabble element. But there were women and children and husbands and wives coming out of their homes [and] becoming a mob—and in some ways it was far more frightening."[25] King noted how "swastikas blossomed in Chicago's parks like misbegotten weeds."[26] People chanted "Kill Coon King" and called for a knife in King's back.

Then a rock "as big as a fist" hit King on the back of his head.[27] Dazed, he sank down to the ground, at first believing he'd been shot. Some whites chanted, "Kill him, kill him." Still, he got up, brushed off his head and neck, and continued on saying: "Oh, I've been hit so many times I'm immune to it."[28] He dodged a knife thrown at him, which hit the neck of another marcher.[29] They continued on, many marchers with blood running down their faces as they tried to shield King. Another rock hit Raby, and rocks hit dozens of other marchers.[30] Raby talked about how angering it was to "have the mayor to say that the marchers were causing the problems rather . . . [It] reinforced what we already knew, that the mayor of the city of Chicago was giving the leadership to maintain racial segregation in Chicago."[31]

Given the level of violence and police misconduct, King praised the gang members who had joined the marches for not returning the violence being directed at them. "After the first two or three marches . . . they saw who the enemy was." These young men realized that each other was not the problem, the white power structure was. "I saw [gang members'] noses being broken and blood flowing from their wounds and I saw them continue and not retaliate, not one of them, with violence."[32] These gang members, according to Lafayette, "felt a sense of responsibility."[33]

Blackstone Rangers leader Jeff Fort called a meeting of leaders of the city's gangs that night to discuss the violence and hostility they'd encountered. They questioned the value of the marches and were fed up with being the targets of violence. On top of it all, they had seen themselves as King's protectors, and he'd gotten hit. King came to the meeting and listened while they vented about the horrors of the previous days. According to Rev. Al Sampson, who also attended the meeting, King listened for a while. Then he asked a question: "If a building was burning down and you had the ability to save it, what would you do?"

The young men were annoyed with the question.

King asked again.

They grew angrier with what seemed like a leading question. "Mothafucka don't fuck with us," they told King. "Everybody know you use water to put the goddamn fire out."

He asked again. They pushed back angrily, not mincing words. Then King responded, "Water is an option, my brothers, 'cause you don't put out a fire with fire." Then he told them that *they* represented the water of "our people, the sustenance of life." [34] *They* were the water. It wasn't just about the tactic. It was their power, their leadership, their refusal to accept the kinds of inequalities their communities faced, and their willingness to stand up and challenge these injustices. The next day, even more Blackstone Rangers "were out there catching bricks with us," so many that they were able to have three demonstrations that day, further taxing the police and the city's reputation. [35]

King too was outraged by the violence, telling reporters he had "never seen—even in Mississippi and Alabama—mobs as hostile and as hate-filled as I've seen here in Chicago." [36] He had faced mobs, marched through police hoses and dogs, had his house bombed, been brutalized by the police, and yet he attested that he had *never* met anything like these Chicago mobs. "I think the people from Mississippi ought to come to Chicago to learn how to hate," King said afterward. Harry Belafonte called it "the worst single experience Dr. King ever had." [37]

A year before, when violence rained down on unarmed marchers on Selma's Edmund Pettus Bridge, President Johnson had been moved to action, addressing the nation eight days later and instructing his advisors to begin drafting the language for the Voting Rights Act. Here with violence raining down on unarmed marchers in Chicago, the president was silent. With mobs of thousands of white Chicagoans bearing swastikas and yelling "Kill him, Kill him," with dozens of people injured and a brick having hit King, with the numbers of incensed white Chicagoans on the street in far greater numbers than what movement stalwarts had seen in the South, President Johnson remained silent.

Johnson had a new civil rights bill he was allegedly trying to get passed through Congress that targeted housing discrimination. He could have used this violence like he had the year before with the Voting Rights Act to highlight the urgency of congressional action. "The myth of the racist South and the moderate North lay crumpled once and for all," the *Los Angeles Times* observed, "amid the white hurled stones and shattered bottles in the Chicago street." [38] This had given Johnson an opportunity to underline the urgency to pass the 1966 Civil Rights Act. But Johnson would do no such thing.

One of the young marchers was NAACP youth chapter leader Fred Hampton. Seventeen years old, Hampton had just finished high school; in a couple of years, he would head up the Chicago Black Panther Party. That summer he was working at the Corn Products plant and was impressed by its union head, Bill Taylor. Taylor and Hampton went on a number of the marches. According to Taylor, "Fred was enthusiastic for awhile but in Jefferson Park, a heckler spit in the face of a woman with us. After that, Fred told Dr. King that he couldn't keep marching for nonviolence in the face of the violent mobs around them." [39] Still Hampton continued to speak of his "great respect" for King and would take up the challenge of uniting and further politicizing the city's gangs with the Black Panthers and the work of multiracial organizing with the Young Lords and Young Patriots. [40]

The marches continued. On August 14, 1,200 civil rights activists marched through four different all-white neighborhoods—Jefferson Park, Gage Park, Chicago Lawn, and Bogan. Part of the movement strategy was to march on multiple neighborhoods and realtors at once in order to tax city and police resources. White residents threw bottles, cans, and firecrackers and attacked cars. Two people were hurt when their car was tipped over and set on fire. [41] On August 16, they picketed First Federal Savings and Loan along with the Board of Realtors, the Department of Public Aid, City Hall, and the Chicago Housing Authority to expose the variety of institutions that supported housing discrimination. [42]

On NBC's *Meet the Press*, the interviewer was surprised by King finding "more hatred among white opponents in Chicago than you have encountered in the Deep South." King bore down: "For years the hatred existed beneath the surface in northern communities and as I said earlier, it's coming out now." [43] The interviewer tried to justify the white preference to not "want a Negro for a neighbor, as evidenced in

the resounding victory of Proposition 14." But King countered, drawing the comparison to Southern lunch counters.

> It's quite true that there are many people who are against open
> housing. . . . This does not mean that we don't go all out to end
> housing discrimination. It may be true that in the South many
> white people do not want Negroes to eat at lunch counters. . . . But
> this did not stop the nation from having a conscience so aroused
> that it brought into being a civil rights law as a result of our move-
> ment to end this. . . . [P]eople will adjust to living next door to a
> Negro once they know it has to be done . . . [and] the law makes it
> clear and it's vigorously enforced.[44]

Time and again, King resisted the tendency to normalize Northern racism, directly comparing Northern and Southern "preferences"
for segregation.

King's family had returned to Atlanta and so Coretta had to explain to the children that their dad had been hit by a brick. "They
were calm," she said. "They had come to expect it."[45] In addition to
being the primary caregiver, Coretta was the one who helped the
kids understand what was happening and the dangers they faced.
She also continued to bolster Martin's spirits amid Daley's nastiness,
intransigence, and mounting violence. Publicly, his role was often to
expand people's sense of the possible and underline what they could
accomplish. She played that role for him privately, urging him forward in Chicago.[46]

Violence was not the only form of opposition King encountered.
Aiming to diminish one of the most effective weapons the movement
had, Daley went to court for an injunction to limit the size and hours
of the marches. Seeking to tie the movement's hands, Daley alleged
there had been an uptick in crime in the city—that the movement
was harming the public safety of the city because it was diverting police resources. Police commissioner Orlando Wilson agreed,
saying that crime "can be expected to continue as long as we have
these demonstrations."[47]

Daley's machine had wide tentacles. Religious leaders proved unwilling to challenge their own racist flocks. One of the people now
pressuring King to stop marching was Chicago's Archbishop John
Cody. Cody had supported the July Freedom Rally but was no progressive and did some of the mayor's bidding.[48] The FBI, worried about

King's appeals to Cody, paid the archbishop a visit and shared some of their "findings" on King. Cody told the FBI he found King "glib."[49] Now, faced with a huge backlash among parishioners for his support of the July rally and open white violence, the archbishop took up Daley's position: the marches were causing the problem so they must stop. "It is truly sad, indeed deplorable that citizens should ever be asked to suspend the exercise of their rights because of the evil-doing of others," the archbishop noted. "However in my opinion and the opinion of many men of good will, such is the situation we find ourselves in." Cody cited the fears of the police and city officials that the marches would result in serious injury or loss of life, despite acknowledging it was whites who were "guilty of violence and lawlessness."[50] In other words, Black people needed to stop, because white Chicagoans weren't about to and shouldn't be forced to.[51]

Joining the public call to end the marches was Robert Johnson of the United Auto Workers. Behind the scenes, UAW head Walter Reuther called King. While the UAW had supported SCLC's efforts in the South, in the North its support grew wobbly. Reuther thought they should stop the marches.[52] So did national NAACP head Roy Wilkins. Wilkins for years had critiqued King's direct-action tactics, particularly in the North. And mainstream newspapers loved to provide Wilkins a platform to do this. On August 15, the *Los Angeles Times* ran an op-ed by Wilkins saying that while protest was deeply American, these marches were an "unsuitable tool" that reduced it to a "dirty racial conflict on the lowest level."[53]

Perhaps most devastating, Vice President Hubert Humphrey jumped on board saying the marches had gone too far: "The Archbishop's call not only merits support but it is of urgent necessity that it be respected and responded to effectively." Rather than condemn the immense violence being perpetrated on Black marchers who aimed to break Chicago's color line, Humphrey implied the problem was on both sides: "people are sick and tired of violence and disorder."[54] Akin to holding John Lewis and the marchers responsible for the Alabama troopers who attacked them in Selma, Humphrey urged Black people to stop the trouble they were causing. Speaking in Indianapolis in August, President Johnson in veiled terms also criticized the marches. "There are ways of protesting that any civilized society can tolerate. There are also ways of protesting that are unacceptable. The ballot box, the neighborhood committees, the political and civil rights organizations—these are the means by which Americans express their resentment against intolerable conditions . . . but not to rip it apart." [55]

Raby and King announced the marches would continue.

Negotiations, an Agreement, and the Mayor's Duplicity

The marches finally forced Daley to the table. He wanted them over with, and on August 17, the mayor and his men convened with representatives of the real estate industry, King, and members of the Chicago Freedom Movement. There had been debate within the CFM about whether to participate in the meeting and whether Daley could be trusted.[56] But they decided they needed to try.

Daley and the Real Estate Board pressed for a moratorium on the marches. They were not to blame for housing discrimination, it was private prejudice; as Real Estate Board member Arthur Mohl claimed, "We are not the creators, we are the mirror." King countered: "All over the South I heard the same thing we've just heard from Mr. Mohl . . . that they were just the agents . . . but we got a comprehensive civil rights bill and the so-called agents then provided service to everybody . . . and the same thing can happen here." [57]

King, Raby, Young, and Bevel grew increasingly frustrated. Finally, King declared,

Let me say that if you are tired of demonstrations, I am tired of demonstrating. I am tired of the threat of death. I want to live. I don't want to be a martyr. . . . A doctor doesn't cause cancer when he finds it. In fact we thank him for finding it. . . . Our humble marches have revealed a cancer.

They were tired of being treated as the problem. "If we hadn't marched, I don't think we'd be here today. No one here has talked about the beauty of our marches, the love of our marches, the hatred we're absorbing." [58] Under tremendous pressure, King, Raby, and the Chicago Freedom Movement refused to relent.

Two days after meeting, the CFM called for visits to at least one hundred realtors in white West Side neighborhoods. "The real estate people indicated in our meeting on Wednesday that they wanted to do something about open housing," King explained. "We want to see if they're serious. Some people have high blood pressure when it comes to words and anemia when it comes to action." [59]

But that same day, Daley succeeded in getting a temporary injunction limiting the CFM's operations to a single march of five hundred people per day, not during morning or evening rush hours or at night. The judge, an elected Democrat beholden to the machine, granted Daley's request. A twenty-four-hour notice would have to be given as well. The *Chicago Tribune* celebrated the decision.[60]

King blasted the injunction as "unjust, illegal, and unconstitutional." Declaring it "a very bad act of faith on the part of the city," he said that they might consider violating the injunction, as they had in some places in the South, but they agreed to abide by the injunction until the next summit meeting on August 26.[61] Abernathy would later say that their decision to abide by the injunction was a grave error.[62] So would CORE's Bob Lucas, who believed breaking the injunction could have "rallied thousands of black people in this city and perhaps across the country."[63]

On August 21, they announced a march into white communities outside the city limits where the injunction didn't apply. And they declared they would march August 28 on Cicero, where Jerome Huey had been killed three months earlier. Cicero had seventy thousand residents—and not a single Black resident.[64]

The *Chicago Tribune* continued to condemn the movement. On August 22, it editorialized about seven "outside" leaders causing "disorder" in the city: Martin Luther King, Andrew Young, James Bevel, Jesse Jackson, George Lincoln Rockwell of the American Nazi Party, Charles Lynch of the National States Rights Party, and Evan Lewis of the KKK.[65] In plain language, the *Tribune* equated King with the Klan.

Daley understood the kind of violence and visuals that could come out of a march in Cicero. And so on August 26, at a second meeting, Daley laid out an agreement to lobby for more open-housing legislation, build scattered-site housing projects, make mortgages available regardless of race, and make an amendment to the injunction against marching to allow for school and employment protests. This represented a marked change by the mayor and a substantial win. King, Raby, and the CFM decided to agree. King explained the significance of what they had accomplished, saying, "They said you can't fight City Hall; you better go back down South,"[66] and cast the agreement with Daley as "the most significant program ever conceived to make open housing a reality."[67] And it would have been if Daley had enforced it.

The *Chicago Defender* praised the agreement and the significance of its provisions, making clear how much pressure and how many marches (despite how many times the city had criticized them) it had taken to get the city to negotiate.[68] Raby also explained the decision to call off the Cicero march in light of activists' exhaustion:

> I had had the experience in 1965 of marching until the troops were exhausted and totally dissipated. One of the considerations . . . in negotiations is, where is the point where you've maximized what you can get? . . . We made the best one we could as honestly as we could, with all the suspicions that were shared by those of us who were criticizing us.[69]

Even amidst the announcement of the agreement with Daley, there were well-founded fears about whether the city would actually enforce it. CORE's Bob Lucas, who also attended that meeting, felt King was "very ill advised about some of his own colleagues" who then led him astray.[70] Many Black Chicagoans—including Lucas and Chester Robinson of the West Side Organization, who had been key to the CFM—vehemently disagreed with the decision to agree and call off the Cicero march.[71] They did not trust Daley and felt the agreement had no enforcement provisions.

Lucas decided to go forward with the Cicero march without King. He and King talked; as Lucas summarized, King didn't want them to march but still gave him his blessing and wasn't bitter that they decided to go forward with it.[72] Nearly five hundred people, including Peggy Terry, marched and faced off tremendous ugliness. The governor deployed two thousand members of the National Guard. White people yelled "niggers" and "the zoo wants you back" while throwing bricks, bottles, and firecrackers. While he didn't march, King spoke to a student group that night and made clear he understood the severity of the problem. "Some astronauts walked in outer space and you can't walk the streets of Cicero."[73]

King's decision not to march might have been the wrong one. He came to regret it.[74] The pressure had been getting to Daley, and now that pressure was alleviated. But short of King getting killed in Cicero, there is not a lot to suggest that violence exploding at the march would have made President Johnson, the US Senate, or the national media any more willing to hold Daley's feet to the fire or insist on the urgency of passing fair housing legislation. King described the summit agreement to his Ebenezer congregation as "the first step in a thousand mile journey."

The Federal Government Fails the
Chicago Freedom Struggle

"You always want to rationalize sin," King observed. "You ought to call sin, sin." The Chicago movement didn't just face a duplicitous mayor but also a president and Congress unwilling to address Northern segregation. In his State of the Union address back in January, Johnson had introduced his plans for this new Civil Rights Act. King had attended the March meeting with other civil rights leaders where Johnson had laid out his plans for the 1966 Civil Rights Act, which tackled housing discrimination, addressed discrimination in jury selection, allowed the Justice Department to bring suits around school segregation, and criminalized crossing state lines to incite a riot.[75] In the spring, King had felt Johnson was moving in the right direction around housing, though "antidiscrimination legislation was not enough."[76]

But Johnson was not even fully committed to this legislation and, according to political historian Ronald Shaw, over the spring and summer did not do the "behind the scenes pushing . . . that marked earlier civil rights legislation."[77] In the Montgomery bus boycott, the Freedom Rides, and the Birmingham and Selma campaigns, what led to real change was not local agreements but federal pressure, and legislation that enforced local change. Three years earlier, Rev. Shuttlesworth had worried in Birmingham around the enforcement of the Birmingham Agreement; what gave it actual teeth was Kennedy speaking out, the national media watching, and then the passage of the Civil Rights Act the next year. That was what was required in Chicago. The Chicago Summit Agreement was stronger than what King and SCLC had achieved in other single-city campaigns, but it was what the federal government did not do that made the difference.[78] King knew that federal pressure was needed here.[79]

The mainstream press gave relatively little coverage to the 1966 Civil Rights Act, though both the *New York Times* and *Washington Post* praised Johnson's efforts around the legislation. By the summer and fall of 1966, the mainstream media were consumed with "Black Power," publishing article after article that summer and into the fall of 1966. Historian Say Burgin has argued that the print media in 1966 became obsessed with Black Power and perpetually "got the story wrong."[80] In response to this media frenzy, dozens of Black ministers took out an ad in the *New York Times* decrying the "historic distortions" in the media's coverage of Black Power.[81] If not for media hysteria, Black Power might have been "little more than a healthy internal difference of opinion," King observed, but this gave cover for white Northerners to maintain their resistance to desegregation while waxing hysterical around Black Power.[82] Speaking to the National Newspaper Publishers Association, King criticized "the white-owned press" for covering the movement "as an ongoing popularity contest between the tribunes of black power and the apostles of nonviolence."[83]

Obsessed with Black Power, the national press largely ignored the persistent, systemic segregation in schools and housing, particularly outside the South, that remained mostly untouched by the 1964 Civil Rights Act, and what that meant for the lives of Black people across the country. The problematic and insufficient coverage of the Chicago movement that year also played a key role in the demise of the Civil Rights Act of 1966. For the 1964 Civil Rights Act, media coverage was much more substantive: the segregation and injustices it sought to correct were given significant attention, Southern officials were routinely questioned, and a righteous Black movement challenging Southern racism was covered seriously.[84] But with the 1966 Civil Rights Act, there were few substantive national news stories detailing the depth and breadth of housing segregation and the searing conditions Black people faced in segregated Northern ghettos. News outlets largely didn't question Northern officials like Daley who denied the city's segregation (while working hard to preserve it), unlike how they had approached Southern politicians. And they hadn't treated the CFM as a righteous movement facing a racist and wily city machine, as they had in Birmingham or St. Augustine. The press helped convey an expectation that Johnson needed to get the civil rights bill through Congress in 1964 to demonstrate his effectiveness as president, but not in 1966. In August at the SCLC's convention, King noted how "the shouts of desperation now fall on deaf ears."[85] According to historian Beryl Satter, only six references to the Chicago Freedom Movement were made during the congressional debates around the bill, and all of them were negative.[86]

Where the press was silent, ordinary white citizens filled in the gap. Whites across the country were determined to retain their right to keep Black people out of their neighborhoods. Johnson aide Joseph Califano described congressional offices besieged by calls from middle-class white constituents who did not want housing desegregation. Illinois senator Paul Douglas, who had supported open housing, was deluged with anger.[87] And there was little national leadership to call out this racism. The House passed the bill on August 9 by a 259–157 majority, only after introducing an exemption for homes, owner-occupied buildings, and buildings of fewer than five units and restricting the kinds of suits the US attorney general could bring around school segregation to exclude Northern "de facto" segregation. King blasted the exemption and the "surrender" of Johnson and the House to real estate interests and Northern parents and homeowners.[88]

Then it went to the Senate. One of the bill's chief opponents was Illinois senator Everett Dirksen, the Senate minority leader. The Republican Dirksen had helped break the Southern filibuster to get the 1964 Civil Rights Act passed, but here he helped lead the resistance to the 1966 act. Any attempts to address housing discrimination (even though much of Chicago's housing market would have been exempt) were anathema. Dirksen referred to the act as "a package of mischief for the country," while North Carolina senator Sam Ervin slammed Dirksen's hypocrisy and other previous civil rights–supporting senators once their own states were being targeted.[89] Two attempts to get a cloture motion in the Senate failed, and the bill went down to a filibuster on September 19 with Dirksen key to the opposition.[90]

Decrying Dirksen's "blatant hypocrisy," King lambasted Northern politicians for the defeat of the Civil Rights Act. "It is unfortunate for anyone to excuse the Congress for what they did by blaming the riots. The question is that the nation hasn't come to terms with housing integration."[91] White Northerners proved a powerful political force opposing any housing or school desegregation that touched them. In January 1967, historian C. Vann Woodward proclaimed 1966 marked the end of the Second Reconstruction. "As soon as this came north, the great withdrawal set in. . . . Amid the clamor (North and South together), the Civil Rights Act of 1966 . . . went down in crashing defeat."[92]

Congress had the chance to put some teeth behind the Chicago Agreement. Johnson could have used the relentless segregation the Chicago Freedom Movement had exposed and the violence directed at the marchers to mark the urgency—putting further pressure on Dirksen's hypocrisy. He might have been able to play Southern anger at the double standard of the 1964 Civil Rights Act and how it skirted addressing Northern segregation to grab a couple of votes. He most certainly could have used the bully pulpit of the presidency and given a

246

national address, as he'd done the year before after the Selma violence. But he didn't. Dejected, King saw that the act's failure "surely heralded darker days for this social era of discontent."[93]

The defeat of the 1966 Civil Rights Act garners little historical notice—in part because a number of its provisions would pass in the Civil Rights Act of 1968, more commonly known as the Fair Housing Act, signed a week after King's assassination. Biographers barely mention it.[94] In one of the greatest shell games of the civil rights era, well-oiled Northern white power, with the complicity of Congress, the president, and the media, protected its systemic racism while continuing to point to the South (as well as the movement) as the problem. It would take the blood of Martin Luther King to change that, in the process erasing their earlier sin. Had the 1966 Civil Rights Act passed and cities like Chicago, Los Angeles, Detroit, and Newark been required to address some of their own segregation, had the movement built on its victories in 1964 and 1965 with a third legislative victory in 1966, the tumultuous years of 1967 and 1968 would have been very different.

That failure sent a green light to Daley that it was still open season for housing segregation. In November 1966, just three months after making the agreement, Daley's machine discarded it.[95] Alderman Thomas E. Keane, Daley's second in command during the negotiations, declared at a City Council meeting, "There is no Summit Agreement," and that open housing was simply "a goal to be reached."[96] Shortly afterward, Daley claimed that the summit had just produced suggestions—a "gentlemen's agreement under a moral banner." Outraged, King called it at an "act of cruelty and a betrayal of trust."[97] At a press conference in March 1967, King highlighted "for all intents and purposes, the public agencies have [reneged] on the agreement and have, in fact, given credence to [those] who proclaim the housing agreement a sham and a batch of false promises." Daley knew he could renege, given the lack of national political response, and President Johnson would not cross him.

The national media could have held Daley to account for breaking the agreement, but they did not. Instead they blamed King and the movement "creat[ing] hate."[98] Refusing to illustrate the urgency of addressing the city's searing inequities, they used Daley's Black surrogates to cast King as out of step with the Black community. Unlike their coverage in the South, most news articles failed to document how wide, wily, and brutal Daley's power was. King would bemoan this coverage repeatedly, highlighting the many organizing accomplishments of the CFM and the problems of the white press.[99]

Daley was reelected in April 1967 by a landslide, his biggest victory. He campaigned by denouncing "outsiders" like King and appealing to "law and order." Even his Republican opponent accused him of stoking white backlash.[100] Daley won all fifty wards, vastly increasing his support among white voters but still keeping a majority of Black voters.[101] There was little place for Black voters to go, and Daley's precinct captains made sure people understood there would be punishment if they strayed.

Daley's true colors would start to garner more national attention when he told police to "shoot to kill" Black people who rose up following King's assassination in April 1968.[102] Then, in the summer of 1968, under Daley's orders, Chicago police brutally and indiscriminately attacked demonstrators outside the Democratic National Convention. Black Chicago police officer Howard Saffold flatly observed, "That was the first time White people in Chicago realized that the police were actually brutal." [103] Daley refused to help Humphrey's candidacy, and Illinois voted to send Richard Nixon to the White House in 1968. Then, on December 4, 1969, with assistance from the FBI, Chicago police raided the place where Black Panther leader Fred Hampton was staying and killed him and fellow Panther Mark Clark.

But even with all this evidence, Daley's segregationist politics, his violent police, his efforts to ghettoize Black Chicagoans, and Johnson's and Congress's complicity have been laundered by most writers. They largely cast King and the Chicago Freedom Movement as the failure rather than expose Daley's white segregationism and the failures of Congress and the Oval Office.

The Successes

In January 1967, the Kings moved out of their apartment in Chicago. Despite the betrayal by Congress and Daley, the CFM had garnered a number of less-heralded successes. Tenant organizing had produced a number of local wins. Then, in April, after a nine-month rent strike, the Lawndale Union to End Slums announced a historic agreement with the landlord agreeing to immediate repairs; in six months a nonprofit would buy the buildings, with each tenant's subsequent rent payments being allowed as payments to ultimately purchase their apartments.[104] Poor people would have the chance to own their own apartments.

Coretta Scott King highlighted two lasting victories of the Chicago campaign: the efforts of Operation Breadbasket to open economic opportunities and the organizing work with gang members. "Our challenge to decades of entrenched economic exploitation," she observed decades later, "produced a rich harvest that lingers to this day."[105] Historian James Ralph has also underscored the importance of the CFM's "creative approaches to economic injustice." The movement employed "new strategies to fight housing segregation," and "the sense of possibility" it engendered led to an expanded sense of Black political power and ultimately to the election of Harold Washington as mayor in 1983.[106]

In September 1966, the Chicago Freedom Movement joined pickets against Saks Fifth Avenue for refusing to recognize the certification of two unions of mostly Black, non-sales workers.[107] Operation Breadbasket continued to pressure companies to hire Black people in all positions, to increase commerce to Black businesses, to support Black products, and to ensure Black companies were getting the contracts in Black neighborhoods. Breadbasket's purpose, Jesse Jackson explained, was for Black people "to control the basic resources of their community . . . the banks, the trades, the building construction and the education of our children . . . to stop whites from controlling our community and removing the profits and income that belong to black people."[108] Between 1966 and 1971, its efforts led to 4,200 jobs for Black people and gains to Chicago's South Side Black community of $57.5 million annually.

Tired of negative media on the Chicago campaign, in April 1967 the ministers of Operation Breadbasket released a statement outlining their significant gains and "positive programs that Dr. King has initiated":

- over 1,000 jobs in dairy and soft drinks
- the ability to get "Negro products" on the shelves of major chain stores
- an alliance of Black garbage pickup men to service white companies in Black neighborhoods
- a Black construction company for the first time getting to build a chain store in a Black neighborhood, and
- Black banks actually getting significant business for white companies that do business in Black areas[109]

King and many others had been sickened by the profit so many people made off the city's slums. Breadbasket had worked to change that.

King returned to Chicago in October 1967 to call for a boycott of Certified Food Stores.[110] Coretta also came to Chicago to support Breadbasket's efforts, telling Martin it was one of the greatest spiritual experiences of her life.[111] In March 1968, Breadbasket announced a deal to begin selling Alabama Black farmers' products in Chicago's Black grocery stores. And the women of Breadbasket successfully exposed bad meat being sold in grocery stores serving Black people.[112] The local wins piled up.

The second ongoing success Coretta Scott King emphasized was in organizing gang members and their growing sense of leadership. Bernard Lafayette emphasized the "sense of pride, a sense of doing something to protect the community . . . and change these conditions."[113] These young men's visions of possibility expanded and both the Blackstone Rangers and Vice Lords got grants from the Ford Foundation and the US Office of Equal Opportunity to pursue community projects the next year. King had provided, according to the Blackstone Rangers' Jeff Fort, a model for their empowerment and community leadership as he linked violence between gangs to the larger oppressive conditions that impacted Black life in the city.[114] These young men started to push to change those conditions.

Daley and the CPD continued to be threatened. In March 1967, the CPD created a Gang Intelligence Unit; alarmed by the community organizing these gangs were now pursuing, the unit sought to infiltrate and undercut those community betterment efforts.[115] The Chicago Black Panther Party picked up the baton helping to grow this multiracial organizing, as it cultivated alliances with the Blackstone Rangers and Young Lords and the political and community organizing that grew out of that into a rainbow coalition.[116] In 1969, the Vice Lords, Blackstone Rangers, and Gonzato Disciples partnered to push to open up jobs in the construction industry.[117] The community work gang members pursued meant that during the summer of 1967, when uprisings and tensions exploded in Detroit and Newark, they did not do so in Chicago, and many directly credited gangs like the Rangers for that peace.[118]

But Chicago had provided a sobering lesson. The nation could not be counted on to care about Black immiseration, segregation, and white violence when it happened in the "liberal" North. Political leaders who had gone the distance to address Southern racism like President

Johnson, UAW leader Walter Reuther, or Senator Dirksen were unwilling to address Northern racism, indeed forming a barrier to change. An American public outraged by Selma had found Chicago a bridge too close to home. Again, the Kings experienced—as they had from graduate school onward—how allies disappeared around addressing Northern inequality.

Daley had developed colonial forms of disfranchisement, which stripped Black people of the collective power of their vote, punished people who stepped out of line, used policing to further disempowerment, and flaunted Black politicians willing to cover it up. City leaders successfully deployed fears of "crime" and "culture of poverty" theories that blamed Black family dysfunction and crime to shield the city's systematic segregation, deflect Black movements, and divide poor people. And the nation moved more toward expanded law enforcement.

But the CFM changed people and prepared them for further struggle. Black Chicagoans were transformed by the movement in ways that reverberated in the years to come. King was changed as well. He realized their strategies needed to evolve. He would not follow Rustin's and Randolph's path into Democratic Party politics, as the two men urged. Deepening their attack on false "sociological" explanations about Black "culture," they needed to go national. The task was to build Black political power, take on colonialism at home and abroad, and forge a multiracial movement that took on the interconnections of race, poverty, and war.

Many of SCLC's advisors couldn't see it—but Martin and Coretta Scott King could.

Act IV

1965–1968

King was repeatedly accosted by the press.

11

The Time Is Now

Building National Black Political Power, Anticolonial Solidarities, and Culture-of-Poverty Critique

When faced with opposition, Martin Luther King tended to double down. In the last two years of his life, he would do so again. They needed to go bigger. This was a both-and approach: antisegregation *and* antipoverty, Black *and* multiracial, drilling down with local organizing *and* developing national political power *and* taking on global peace work. Coretta had been pushing for years the need for an expanded global focus, and from the Chicago campaign their critique of colonialism at home and abroad had grown.

While King shied away from the refrain *Black Power*, he too had come to see they would have to build collective Black political power and bring their fight national to demand a national reprioritization of resources away from war and police to massive social spending. Part of what King liked about the thrust of Black Power was how it destroyed the shame of Blackness, built community strength, and foregrounded the need for collective Black political demands.[1] But with the slogan "Black Power," he felt "you have to spend too much time explaining what you're talking about" and field endless, annoying questions about violence and separatism. So King told Stokely Carmichael, "Let's not use the slogan, Let's get the power. . . . But somehow we managed to get just the slogan."[2]

Faced with the disappointing defeat of the 1966 Civil Rights Act, King began calling more stridently for a guaranteed minimum income and collective Black voting strength. While Rustin and Randolph urged political pragmatism and work with the Democratic Party, King understood that political deal making was not going to lead to the changes needed. They needed a broad-based confrontational movement to build national Black political power and economic transformation, concretizing the ways spending on war directly stole from people's needs at home. Only when faced with confrontational organized power were Congress and the president going to change course.

Meanwhile, as Coretta Scott King's peace activism and freedom concerts had grown, she saw the need to document her own history and tasked her sister Edythe, a professor, to write that book in 1966. Increasingly tired of the media and public seeing her as an appendage, Coretta had a family history of freedom fighting and her own political commitments. To facilitate it, the Kings paid for a sitter to watch Edythe's son to give her sister time to research and write. After "two years of reading, interviewing and combing through family documents," Edythe finished the book, which detailed the Scott family's history and Coretta's civil rights commitments through Montgomery at the beginning of April 1968. Days later, Martin was assassinated, and the book would be shelved to make way for Coretta's autobiography and then for another thirty-five years. In 2004 Coretta asked Edythe to resurrect and expand it; the book was finally published in 2012, six years after Coretta's death.[3] Coretta Scott King clearly understood her place in the struggle—and wanted to document her own roots and the ways she and Martin were a political partnership.

Like many activists, the Kings increasingly saw voting rights not simply as a matter of an individual vote but the ability of Black people to protect their community interests. Having the right to vote didn't mean much if Black people could only vote for candidates that the machine approved or were gerrymandered to dilute Black voting strength. On the heels of the passage of the Voting Rights Act in August 1965, King joined the movement for District of Columbia statehood and home rule. The majority-Black city of Washington, DC, did not have its own mayor or congressional representative, and Congress controlled its budget. It was only in 1961 that DC residents had even gained the right to vote for president. Black DC activists including SNCC's Marion Berry and Rev. Walter Fauntroy saw this for the colonial situation that it was and helped lead the fight for DC home rule. After leaving the signing of the Voting Rights Act, Fauntroy, King, Abernathy, and many others marched "straight down U Street to the White House, to rally for home rule," Fauntroy recalled.[4] King called for "massive nonviolent direct action" for DC statehood and compared DC with voter disfranchisement in the South.[5]

Speaking on CBS's *Face the Nation*, King called for a "massive march on Washington" for DC statehood, warning that the failure to grant home rule could lead to riots in DC.[6] District residents deserved to elect their own representative, instead of being governed by a Congress they had no role in electing. If the bill didn't make it out of committee in the House, King stressed, there would be the need for a much larger march. Five years after King's assassination, a limited District of Columbia Home Rule Act finally passed Congress, providing for an elected mayor of DC and a City Council. But to this day, Congress maintains authority over DC's budget, and residents still have no voting congressional representative.[7]

Building Collective Black Political Power

In both Los Angeles and Chicago, King had realized the need for collective Black political power given the colonial situation Black people lived in, where their vote was controlled and profit made from their ghettoization. In Cleveland, King hoped that could be changed and joined local efforts to give Black people real representation. Defeating the colonial situation in Northern cities was key to avoiding unrest, King understood.

Like many other Northern cities, school segregation and housing segregation had heightened in Cleveland. Jobs had been lost to automation—with Black people often the first fired. Black people could vote—but their votes were diluted by gerrymandering and elected officials felt little responsibility to Black issues. A robust school desegregation movement in Cleveland had grown. On April 7, 1964, Black parents and other community members including a twenty-seven-year-old white minister named Bruce Klunder aimed to block the construction of a new segregated school by lying down around a bulldozer. Klunder was run over and killed.

In 1967, Black state representative Carl Stokes was challenging incumbent mayor Ralph Locher in the primary to become the first Black mayor of Cleveland (or any large American city). Raising funds for voter registration alongside Black groups in Cleveland, SCLC would engage in months of organizing Black turnout.[8] King came to Cleveland numerous times in 1967 to further this effort, kicking off a coordinated voter registration drive in April because "things are worse for the mass of Negroes than they were twenty years ago."[9]

On April 26, 1967, King spoke at three Cleveland high schools and at the Cleveland Job Corps for Women. Underscoring the importance of Black voter turnout, he urged students to be "a committee of one to work with your parents if they have not registered and others in your community."[10] Since Montgomery, King had seen how young people often served as the vanguard in believing change was possible, pulling their parents along with them.

Fed up with Locher's leadership and the ignoring of Black concerns, a group of city pastors invited King to Cleveland in June to build Black political power. But Carl Stokes recoiled. Stokes didn't want King campaigning on his behalf, fearing whites would withdraw. King's bold push against Northern racism meant that many Northern Black politicians kept him at arm's length. In his autobiography, Stokes explained that he told King, "If you come in here with these marches and what not, you can just see what the reaction will be." While King acknowledged Stokes's concerns, he was undeterred, committed to helping build this voter mobilization in Cleveland.[11] Refusing to meet with King, Mayor Locher also viewed King's focus on Cleveland as a threat. King pressed for a change in Cleveland's police conduct as key to avoiding the uprisings that had occurred the previous summer.[12]

They were trying to build collective Black power, both politically and economically. In August, Operation Breadbasket had a win in its boycott of Cleveland-based Sealtest food when the company agreed to hire fifty Black workers.[13] According to Cleveland activist Ancusto Butler, Sealtest had refused to budge on hiring or negotiate at all, until King and the Breadbasket boycott pressured them: "You get no jobs . . . by trying to be nice."[14] But confrontational strategies had worked.

In 1967, journalist David Halberstam spent ten days with King for a lengthy 1967 *Harpers* feature, traveling with King to Cleveland, New York, and Berkeley, California.[15] Halberstam had spent his early career covering Nashville's emerging student sit-in movement as the urgent news story it was; John Lewis described Halberstam as "the only one covering us."[16] But here Halberstam's framing was different. With no mention of long-standing movements in these Northern cities, Halberstam called King "arrogant" and in danger of losing his way.[17] Halberstam longed for the "heady years" when King "was our beloved." In Northern ghettos, Halberstam claimed, "The schools are terrible, but there is no one man making them bad by his own ill will. . . . The jobs are bad, but the reasons Negroes aren't ready for decent jobs are complicated."[18] For Halberstam, Northern injustice might be bad, but its causes were amorphous, and Northern Blacks weren't necessarily "ready" for decent jobs anyway. This framing of Northern injustice was one that King—and Northern activists—had been challenging for years (though Halberstam refused to acknowledge it).[19] While the piece focused on King in Cleveland, Halberstam provided almost no attention to the segregation, police brutality, and disfranchisement that Black Clevelanders and King were challenging. He took note of King's anger at the hypocrisy of Northern mayors like Locher "calling me an extremist and three years ago, he gave me the key to the city and said I was the greatest man of the century. That was as long as I was safe from him down in the South." But Halberstam didn't care to probe this two-facedness of Northern liberal politicians nor King's criticism that the white press was distorting his Northern organizing (which Halberstam dismissed in a patronizing footnote).[20]

What they were doing in Cleveland, King explained, "was a Black Power move"—Black people organizing and voting as a bloc to achieve political power.[21] Black voter turnout was key for the Democratic primary with Black people making up 37 percent of Cleveland's population.[22] Stokes had run against Locher in the primary in 1965 and narrowly lost—with 87,716 votes to Locher's 87,858.[23] Many African Americans had stayed home, thinking he didn't have a chance. Alongside CORE, the NAACP, and numerous grassroots local efforts, King and the SCLC joined a massive voter registration and get-out-the-vote drive in Cleveland. A dozen SCLC members had been working in Cleveland since the summer.[24] King had been commuting to the city a couple of days a week for months to walk the streets, speaking to Black residents, going into barbershops, businesses, bars, and churches and attending registration drives.

On October 3, Stokes defeated Locher in the primary, garnering 53.6 percent of the vote, or 110,000 votes to Locher's 92,003.[25] In a conversation recorded by the FBI, Levison and King discussed the essential role Black turnout had played in Stokes's victory. "I am not sure Carl wants to recognize it as much as he should—but Carl is in office today because of SCLC and me, not in office because he won . . . the white vote, which was significant, but if the Negro vote had remained where it was the last time, which was 60%, he could not have won: we turned it to 75%, which was unheard of anywhere." Black voter turnout changed the game from Stokes's defeat two years earlier. "I know I walked 15 miles a day before the election, stopping in bars, pool rooms and everywhere I could find people," King told Levison.[26] Stokes also garnered two thousand Puerto Rican votes.

Black turnout in the general election was also the highest ever at

80 percent, with 90 percent voting for Stokes. But many commentators, like Stokes himself, focused on white support.[27] In fact, seventeen thousand more voters voted in the general election in 1967 than in 1965. The extent of community organizing supported by King and the SCLC might have been why, according to historian Stephen Oates, "Cleveland had no race riot" in 1967, unlike a hundred other cities.[28] The night Stokes won, King was back in Cleveland having spent the day turning out Black voters. King and Abernathy had talked to Stokes in his hotel suite earlier in the evening and the candidate had promised to call if he emerged victorious. But Stokes never called—again fearing being associated with King.[29] That disregard has continued in many accounts of Stokes's victory, which focus more on the white support that Stokes garnered and not the massive Black turnout that won it for him.

King saw the need for a "vigilant" people's movement to continue even after these victories, according to Belafonte, because he feared Black elected officials "would drift away from . . . meaningful Black interests."[30] This fear proved prescient with many newly elected Black politicians in the next decades. King returned to Cleveland numerous times in 1967 to build tenant unions, rent strikes, and economic protests, calling the city, like other Northern cities, "a teeming cauldron of hostility."[31]

King had grown increasingly frustrated by the ways the media kept wanting to write about divisions between him and Northern Black people. Unlike some Black leaders, Coretta observed, "Martin could walk alone anywhere. Even when there were reservations about his tactics, the respect people had for his personal bravery and honesty was a shield."[32] Yet most white journalists refused to see this, sticking to their belief that Northern Black people were different, angry, and alienated. King longed for a fresh story that documented this work and how everywhere he went, he "found nothing negative." Levison commiserated with King: "No use trying to get the *Times* or a magazine to do it because they don't have a conception of what a story there is here."[33]

This is not to say that all Northern Black activists joined arms with King. Like in the South, many disagreed sharply with his focus on nonviolence, favoring self-defense, more aggressive strategies, or more Black nationalist framings. Many from the Revolutionary Action Movement to the Nation of Islam to SNCC criticized King directly. And King at times disagreed publicly with them as well. But at key points, he refused to attack—even when Northern allies and other Black leaders called on King to disavow Black militancy. Like his unwillingness to repudiate Brooklyn CORE's stall-in in 1964, King refused to join a group of Black leaders who published a three-quarter-page ad in the *New York Times* on October 14, 1966, titled "Crisis and Commitment," in which they reaffirmed their faith in the importance of integration and repudiating violence—and implicitly condemned Black Power. King refused to sign because he didn't want to "excommunicate" anyone from the struggle and saw white criticism of Black Power as a smoke screen to cover up long-standing white resistance to Black demands that vastly predated the slogan.[34] Attacking Black Power was just the newest excuse to do nothing for many white officials and residents. "The Negro is not moving too fast, he is barely moving," he observed.[35]

The Kings tired of the ways the media tried endlessly to pit them against Black Power and, in particular, against SNCC's Stokely Carmichael. In Montreal in February 1967, Scott King told reporters Carmichael represented a "valid and important" part of the Black struggle. "[B]asically he wants what we want—justice." Carmichael, also in Montreal, similarly challenged this division, praising King's "great compassion" and bemoaning "the dilemma of white America . . . that it doesn't have the compassion of Martin Luther King."[36]

A decade earlier, in 1960, King and Randolph had marched on both parties' conventions, to try to make them take up Black issues. Increasingly, King saw the urgency to coalesce national Black political power to hold both parties accountable. A week before his assassination, he made three stops in Newark. Speaking to students and teachers at South Side High School, he told the students they were "black and beautiful" and deserved power. He marched through Newark's Central Ward with these young people and then paid a surprise visit to Black nationalist Amiri Baraka's house to discuss the importance of building a national Black political strategy. Hundreds of people trailed behind him, according to historian Komozi Woodard, and waited outside— and many of these students would become key Black Power organizers in the years ahead, recalling King's role in their politicization.[37]

Both Amiri and Amina Baraka were surprised and delighted with the visit, recognizing the inaccurate ways that King had been portrayed and the possibilities for collaboration. "If I had known he was coming, I would have baked a cake," Amina later said.[38] At the Barakas, King talked about how increasing divisions between Black leaders were dangerous and stressed the need for unified Black leadership to build Black political power. According to Woodard, "The meeting made an impression on Baraka and his organization and signaled the possibility for a broader black united front, one that would include such civil rights organizations as King's Southern Christian Leadership Conference." [39] It made an impression on King as well. The thirty-nine-year-old King confided in Harry Belafonte, "I have more in common with these young people than with anybody else in this movement." [40] Their meeting helped nurture the seeds for the convention movement that would flower in Newark and then nationally in 1972 with the National Black Political Convention in Gary, Indiana.

That night King spoke at Newark's Abyssinian Baptist Church, which bordered some of the densest housing projects of the Central Ward, and was greeted with huge cheers when he declared, "The hour has come for Newark, New Jersey, to have a Black mayor." [41] A couple of days later, he met with Representative John Conyers of Michigan and Gary, Indiana, mayor Richard Hatcher to strategize about developing a national political strategy to harness Black political power. The lessons of Chicago and defeat of the 1966 Civil Rights Act had demonstrated the need for a national Black political mobilization that would make Black interests undeniable to elected officials.

Baraka would announce plans for a Black political convention at a press conference in the wake of King's assassination. Coretta Scott King would also take up this focus that summer of 1968, as many Black people refused to endorse Democrat Hubert Humphrey for president. She played a key role at the planning meeting on September 24, 1971, to organize a National Black Convention, the only woman in the small confab of Black nationalists who gathered. The position paper she presented, "The Transformation of the Civil Rights Movement into a Political Movement," expounded on many of the same notes from Martin's meeting at Baraka's. Then, she was pivotal to the Gary Convention itself, held in March 1972.[42] The seeds of the modern Black Convention movement had been planted by the Kings before Martin was assassinated—a movement Coretta would continue to cultivate after his death.[43]

Global Solidarity and Justice

For many years, both Kings had linked the Black struggle at home to anticolonial movements around the globe.[44] In 1957, the Kings had

visited Ghana, and in 1959, India—deepening their analysis of colonialism and learning from anticolonial movements across the world. While
many commentators today cast King's antiwar work in terms of peace
and nonviolence, his anticolonial politics were there from the outset.

As was their critique of militarism and the mis-prioritization of national resources. The nuclear arms race alarmed them, and Coretta
Scott King embarked on a lifetime of global peace work, including
early opposition to US policy in Vietnam. In fall 1961, Martin had
visited London and spoken out on nuclear disarmament for a British
peace group. Eslanda Robeson was impressed, particularly that he
wasn't fazed by the hecklers who tried to interrupt him. Robeson had
gotten to meet him the day before at a smaller reception organized by
Black leftist Claudia Jones at Africa Unity House.[45]

While both Kings had a global vision and anticolonial understanding, Coretta influenced Martin's growing antiwar sentiment, yet many
historians have missed her impact on his thinking. Scott King remained steadfast in her public opposition from the early 1960s onward,
pressing him after the 1964 Nobel Prize about their global responsibilities to decry US conduct in Vietnam.[46] In March 1965, at North Carolina A&T, before joining Martin at the Selma-to-Montgomery march,
she emphasized the Black struggle was global. "It is in South Africa,"
she said. "It is in Selma, Alabama. We want to be free and we want to
be free now—everywhere."[47] In May 1965, bucking Cold War pressure,
she addressed the WILPF conference on the topic "Peace, Jobs, and
Freedom," and then in June she addressed a crowd of eighteen thousand at the "Emergency Rally on Vietnam" in Madison Square Garden, the only woman to speak. She and Martin decided together that it
was particularly important she go. After the Madison Square Garden
rally, she helped lead a march to the UN.

In March 1965, Martin spoke out against the war at Howard University, decrying the three "howling" evils of our time—war, racism, and
poverty—and condemning "the appalling silence of good people."[48]
That spring, condemning American use of force in the Dominican Republic and Vietnam, he drew controversy for contemplating going to
North Vietnam to sit down with its leader Ho Chi Minh.[49] NAACP's
Roy Wilkins chastised his hubris and qualifications.[50] In September,
after a meeting at the UN, Martin spoke out against US bombing of
North Vietnam and the refusal to seat the People's Republic of China
in the United Nations. President Johnson was furious. Congressmen

questioned his patriotism, and newspapers editorialized against him.[51] Again the SCLC board refused to support linking civil rights with the antiwar movement.[52]

Feeling the pressure, in November Martin backed out of an address to a DC peace rally, but Coretta Scott King kept her commitment to speak.[53] Addressing the 25,000 gathered, she underlined that "unless America learns to respect the right to freedom and justice for all, then the very things which we hold dear in this country will wither away in the hypocritical ritual of the preservation of national self interest."[54] Following her appearance, a reporter asked Martin if he had educated his wife on these issues. He replied: "She educated me."[55] They were a partnership, and while he led on some issues, she did on others. Two weeks later in Detroit, she questioned whether the US was doing all it could to negotiate peace in Vietnam, and if it was even interested in doing so. The *Detroit Free Press* called her "nearly as articulate as her husband." The FBI flagged the story and her potential danger.[56] But despite the fearsome red-baiting of antiwar activists, she wasn't going to back down.

In late 1965, Martin Luther King signed a statement with seven other Nobel Peace Prize winners including Linus Pauling and Albert Luthuli (but not Ralph Bunche) calling for "an immediate ceasefire and political settlement" in Vietnam.[57] An avalanche of criticism followed. Both Martin and Coretta condemned those who "confuse dissent with disloyalty."[58] He addressed WILPF's fiftieth-anniversary celebration in 1965. At the end of 1965, King wrote a column, after having been attacked by many friends for his antiwar stance: "How can I not be consistent and fail to say violence is as wrong in Hanoi as it is in Harlem?"[59]

Coretta Scott King pressed forward. In February 1966, she attended a WILPF conference in Chicago. Having kept tabs on her peace activism for years, the FBI designated her as a "subversive" to the Secret Service in March 1966.[60] Over and over, agents communicated to local FBI bureaus and state police of her travel plans and people she was meeting with—ominously making it clear "these agencies should be advised that we are merely passing on this information and not requesting protection for Mrs. King."[61] The movement and the Kings themselves faced two dangers from the FBI. Alongside the constant monitoring and harassment was the Bureau's unwillingness to protect them or seriously investigate as plans surfaced or violence took place. From Montgomery on, both Martin and Coretta were targets of white hatred and violence. Back in September 1963, Coretta was driven off the road by a white driver, but it was treated as an "auto accident." [62] The Bureau largely stood aside.

Coretta Scott King was not just leading her husband on this issue but leading the nation. In fall 1966, she became part of the steering committee of what became the National Mobilization Committee to End the War in Vietnam. She was one of the few Black people there; John Lewis, James Farmer, and Bayard Rustin were listed as endorsers but didn't show up. A small group of SNCC activists attended but got discouraged; "there's too many white folk here." [63] Yet commentators and journalists at the time and many writers subsequently missed her leadership around Vietnam. "Since the spotlight shone so brightly on Martin, the press overlooked my agenda and activities," she said. [64]

Thus both Kings had opposed the war in Vietnam long before his historic address at Riverside Church—and Coretta Scott King had forged the way despite "constant denunciation." [65] Martin grew tired of allies, SCLC associates, and even his father telling him he shouldn't criticize the war. "My sense is that the more his leadership was criticized," SCLC's Dorothy Cotton observed, "the stronger he seemed to hold his view that war was not the way." [66]

Many people made known their disapproval. At a fundraiser on Long Island, Martin was upbraided by the Urban League's executive director, Whitney Young, who found King's focus on urban poverty and Vietnam a sham. Both men raised their voices. "What you're saying may get you a foundation grant," King shot back, "but it won't get you into the kingdom of heaven." Young, observing Martin's weight gain and knowing he was sensitive about it and charges of hypocrisy, reproached, "You're eating well." Friends separated them before the argument got worse. Later King, embarrassed by his uncharacteristic tone, called Young to apologize. [67]

In February 1967, King gave a searing speech in Los Angeles casting US involvement in Vietnam as "perpetuat[ing] white colonialism" and rendering US global standing "pathetically frail." Highlighting the 1966 Civil Rights Act's failure, he called it arrogant that the same senators who "vote joyously to appropriate billions of dollars for War in Vietnam . . . vote loudly against a Fair Housing Bill to make it possible for a Negro veteran to purchase a decent home." [68] He stressed how Black people were "100% of a citizen in warfare" but "50% of a citizen on American soil . . . half of all Negroes live in substandard housing and Negroes have half the income of whites."[69]

In March, Scott King, identified as "a leader in several peace organizations," gave an extensive interview to the *Atlanta Constitution*. The US was spending billions on the war but "we ignore and even jeer at the plight of my people at home." She eloquently described how "we entered this war in support of colonialism . . . we equated our interests with a corrupt and dictatorial regime . . . we shunned efforts by the United Nations to stop the war . . . with the boastful but misguided notion that we have some mission to be the moral savior of the world. Yet most of the world disagrees with this policy."[70] Martin led his first peace march of five thousand in Chicago on March 25, 1967, calling the war "a blasphemy against all that America stands for."[71] He compared the $322,000 spent to kill each Vietnamese person with the $53 spent for each person in the "so-called" war on poverty and "much of the $53 goes to salaries for those who are not poor."[72]

And then, on April 4, 1967, he mounted the pulpit at New York's Riverside Church in front of a phalanx of reporters and gave a rousing condemnation of the war and its evils domestically and internationally. The public criticism from the NAACP to the *New York Times* (and even privately from Stanley Levison) was fast and furious.[73] The *Times* called his words "facile" and "slander"; the civil rights movement, the paper intoned, should concentrate on "the intractability of slum mores and habits."[74] Martin paid a "tremendous price," Coretta underscored, for his antiwar stance but was personally more at peace. His decision to go public gave courage to people who had been afraid to speak out and caused many clergy, including his own father, to reassess their positions.[75] Speaking to one of his "Big Six" detractors, he emphasized, "You know, for a long time I encouraged my wife to speak out, but I was the happiest man in the world when I came to a point where I could personally take a position against this evil war."[76]

Coretta was thrilled too, telling Martin, "Finally I will be able to march with you. All these years I've been marching for peace alone or as the only black and certainly the only woman" in leadership.[77] Standing out on this issue had been hard, so it was a joy to have him join her.

But unfortunately, a week later he was needed in New York City and she had to be on the West Coast. Martin Luther King spoke before a crowd of 200,000 in the city on April 15 while Coretta Scott King addressed a mass antiwar march of 40,000 in San Francisco, reminding the experts "that bombing only makes an oppressed people more determined to throw off the yoke of oppression."[78] Then, in May, she joined Dr. Benjamin Spock and others at a protest at the White House. The antiwar protests, rallies, and marches weren't having the effect they should, so Scott King began considering the power of appealing to Congress as women—as mothers, grandmothers, wives, and sisters— to break through the political morass. Organizers approached her in late 1967 to help lead a women's protest of Vietnam termed the Jean- nette Rankin Brigade (for former congresswoman Jeannette Rankin's long antiwar politics). She gave them her "100% support." This was ex- actly what she had already been thinking.[79]

Shortly after, Harry Belafonte convened a meeting at his house with various leaders from SNCC and SCLC, including Martin Luther King and Stokely Carmichael. According to Belafonte, tremendous energy came out of the meeting for plans going forward. Those gathered also agreed on a "moratorium" on public disagreement, given the urgency of the moment around US racial politics and the war and the ways the press was operating.[80]

King had been planning a historic trip to visit Israel in November to engage in interfaith fellowship, pray with other Christians in the Gal- ilee, and give a sermon on the Mount of Olives. But he canceled that trip after the June 1967 Six-Day War, where Israel displaced hundreds of thousands of Palestinians and seized control of Gaza and the West Bank. "I just think that if I go, the Arab world, and of course Africa and Asia for that matter, would interpret this as endorsing everything that Israel has done," he told Stanley Levison in a call recorded by the FBI, "and I do have questions of doubt."[81] In a television interview, he explained that it would "probably be necessary" for Israel to "give up this conquered territory" to the Palestinian people.[82]

A key problem of US militarism, the Kings believed, was that it di- verted attention and resources from addressing inequality at home. It also provided a cover for those uncommitted to addressing pov- erty to now claim it was unaffordable. King criticized groups like the NAACP, who condemned his antiwar message, for refusing to recog- nize how the war gave civil rights opponents the "opportunity" to say the country lacked the resources for education, housing, and health care.[83] King also had grown tired of trying to convince Black young people to reject violence when their own government was "running wild in the world."[84] He knew he had an urgent role to play, even if it was "unpopular," as the myriad costs of the war were increasingly clear in America's cities.[85]

The Uprisings of 1967

On the evening of July 23, 1967, a week after a four-day uprising had erupted in Newark, New Jersey, a group of Black Detroiters gathered at an illegal after-hours bar, known as a "blind pig," to celebrate the return of two men from Vietnam. Black people often socialized at these bars, because many Detroit bars didn't welcome Black customers and Black business owners struggled to get permits. Police would raid these establishments again and again—and Black Detroiters had been highlighting the pattern of police harassment and brutality for years, to no avail. That night, when police raided the bar at around 4 a.m., people refused to disperse. Cops swarmed the area and began arresting people. The crowd grew angrier as the morning came. More people arrived, as did more cops. Some people looted and burned buildings, and the police clamped down on the Black community. Congressman Conyers called it a "police riot." Police arrested 7,200 Black people, though most of the arrests would prove unfounded and dismissed for lack of evidence.[86] At the end of five days, forty-three people were dead—thirty of them Black, most at the hands of law enforcement.

King had been warning about this for years. Hearing what was taking place in Detroit, he fired off a telegram to President Johnson: "The chaos and destruction which now spread through our cities is a blind revolt against the revolting conditions which you courageously set out to remedy as you entered office in 1964. The conditions have not changed."[87] King was angry: "I'm no fireman." Four years earlier, he had marched with almost two hundred thousand Black Detroiters to stress that the city couldn't keep going as usual. Despite years of movements highlighting a pattern of police brutality, school segregation, the ravages of urban renewal, and job discrimination, the inequality remained. "My role is to keep fires from starting," King told the press, but that work had been roundly ignored.[88] Four months earlier, when King had cautioned that cities were "powderkegs" because "the nation has not done anything to improve conditions in these areas," Assistant Attorney General Roger Wilkins had called King "dangerous."[89]

Over and again, when King warned of the consequences of ignoring Black grievances on segregated schools, housing, and policing, news outlets and politicians accused him of "inciting" riots.[90] Here again, King reminded Johnson, these uprisings could have been prevented. He fingered Congress's cuts in housing, jobs, and urban development as kindling for rebellion. "They have declared a war on poverty, yet only financed a skirmish."[91] Then in August, at the Conference for New Politics, King put his disappointment even more plainly. For nearly twelve years "my promise of a better life for Negroes has simply not materialized and there is no evidence that Johnson's Great Society will ever get off the ground."[92]

Many Americans saw Detroit as a model city, with a liberal mayor, two Black congressmen, and a booming auto industry. King challenged that view. "Detroit has the same problems we find in other cities," he noted. "The [Black] unemployment rate is twice as high." Small progress, he underscored, "whets the appetite for greater progress, and if it isn't fast enough, then the despair sets in and this can lead to the kind of violence that we've seen."[93] Detroit's police were key to the problem. In 1960, the Detroit NAACP lambasted the "chronic" nature of the police brutality, presenting records of 244 cases of police brutality between 1955 and 1960, with 47 resulting in hospitalization.[94] In 1965, people marched to protest five police killings in two years— Cynthia Scott, Kenneth Evans, Clifton Allen, Nathaniel Williams, and Arthur Barrington—and the brutal beatings of six others.[95] Johnson's crime-focused approach magnified the problem. Federal spending for local policing skyrocketed from nothing in 1964 to $20 million in 1965 to $63 million in 1968.[96] Johnson's War on Crime poured military-style weapons into local police. In 1965, using new federal money made available after Watts, the Detroit Police Department created a Tactical Mobile Unit for "crowd control." Black Detroiters found it "Gestapo-like."[97]

On top of outright brutality, Detroit police regularly took money and other items of value from Black people they stopped. Any note of protest could lead to a beating and a trumped-up charge of drunkenness, disorderly conduct, or resisting arrest. Police expanded the practice of arresting Black people simply on "investigation"; indeed, about a third of their arrests were made for this reason. Detroit's Black newspapers, the *Michigan Chronicle* and Rev. Cleage's *Illustrated News*, recorded a steady litany of police abuse and harassment of Black Detroiters, but, according to Detroit NAACP leader Arthur Johnson, the city's major newspapers the *Detroit News* and *Detroit Free Press* "had a standing agreement not to cover issues of police brutality."[98]

Even though he remained steadfastly nonviolent, King highlighted the contexts that produce violence. Black people were increasingly determined to break down the walls of segregation, but "the white power structure is still seeking to keep the walls of segregation and inequality substantially intact."[99] Martin understood how violence often resulted from "legitimate grievances that deny people their human rights and economic opportunity," Coretta explained.[100] He was exhausted saying over and over "I condemn the violence . . . but I understand the conditions which caused them," and then time and again, the conditions were not corrected.[101]

Martin drilled down on popular discourses of rising "Black crime" that justified segregation and heightened policing. Upending the idea of the criminal, he highlighted the white illegality that produced Northern ghettos: "When we ask Negroes to abide by the law, let us also demand that the white man abide by law in the ghettos. Day-in and day-out . . . he flagrantly violates building codes and regulations; his police make a mockery of law; and he violates laws on equal employment and education and the provisions for civic services."[102] *His police.* King made clear that the police largely sought to control, not protect, the Black community. As Blackstone Ranger leader Jeff Fort elaborated, "Dr. King told us that it was wrong for the government to beat a man down for asking for equal treatment."[103]

Repeatedly, King faulted the "white majority . . . [for] producing chaos" and then blaming the chaos on Black people. "If the total slum violations of law by the white man over the years were calculated and were compared with the lawbreaking of a few days of riots, the hardened criminal would be the white man."[104] Insisting that white criminality and the criminality of the state were what bore investigating, he stopped using the phrase "law and order," instead calling for "law and justice."[105] King condemned the push for increased law enforcement in Black communities. "Many Americans would like to have a nation which is a democracy for white Americans but simultaneously a dictatorship over black Americans."[106] He also noted the increasing militarization of US society and "the bizarre spectacle of armed forces of the United States fighting in ghetto streets of America while they are fighting in the jungles in Asia."[107]

Reframing the press obsession with the "long hot summer," King focused on "long cold winters of delay" by Congress and local politicians that had preceded them. He continued to object to the term *white backlash*; it was "a new name for an old phenomenon" that flattered Northerners' self-conception when they had never favored change at home.[108] In a *Detroit Free Press* interview in 1967, King emphasized how the white power structures in many cities "plant the seeds for riots." Many white Northerners who supported the Southern movement against Bull

Connor "were not for genuine equality. . . . They're not for Negroes living next door. . . . The future of the Negro in this country will depend on the ability of white America to honestly face its racism and honestly respond to the demands that will not cease." [109] Over and again, he and Coretta attacked the focus on Black personal responsibility, which, as she put it, "let people off the hook who are oppressing you." [110]

Increasingly, King saw the need to offer a more accurate history of twentieth-century America, one that chronicled the far different opportunities that white people, including the surge of white immigrants in the early twentieth century, received—opportunities from which Black people were largely excluded:

> White immigrants in the 19th century were given free credit and land by the government. In the early 20th century a plethora of social agencies helped them to adjust to city life. The economy readily absorbed white workers into factories and trained them to skills. There were obstacles and privations for white immigrants but every step was upward; care and concern could be found. When the Negro migrated, he was substantially ignored or grossly exploited within a context of searing discrimination. He was left jobless and ignorant, despised and scorned as no other American minority has been.[111]

Numerous times, Martin Luther King outlined the history of benefits whites had received that Black people had not. This wasn't just a legacy of slavery, but also of federal policies in the late nineteenth and twentieth centuries. When people claimed white immigrants demonstrated the possibility to rise above discrimination by hard work in the United States, King pointed out the ways in which the government subsidized their land, home loans, and access to higher education. Speaking to the Teamsters union that same year, historian Michael Honey writes, King recounted "how the federal government had heavily subsidized white advancement at various stages—through land grants, the GI Bill and Federal Housing Administration loans, for example." [112] He retold the history of Black migration not as a journey from terror to the Promised Land but to a new Egypt that controlled and disfranchised them in new ways.

King used this history to challenge the ways that well-meaning white Northerners repeatedly cast their advantages as self-sufficiency, born of hard work and good values. No, King emphasized, the white middle class had also been given substantial state assistance after World War II through the GI Bill, access to home loans, higher education, and highway construction. These laws and policies had skewed the playing field in education, housing, and jobs toward white people, including white immigrants. The Kings condemned the false pride of many Americans: "Nobody does it on their own." [113]

Enduring white resistance had provided a sharp lesson for Black people of how "they must expect to remain permanently unequal and permanently poor. The so-called riots in a distorted and hysterical form were a Negro response that said inequality will now be resisted to the death," King stressed to the SCLC in August 1967.[114] Convinced violence wasn't the answer, King advocated mass disruption to "cripple the operations of an oppressive society and dislocate the functions of a city." [115] Again, the national media reacted hysterically. The *New York Times* lambasted King's call for disruption as "certain to aggravate the angry division of whites and Negroes into warring camps." [116] So did the *Washington Post*.[117]

Preaching His Heart Dry

The uprisings of that summer weighed heavily on Martin, according to Coretta. "People expect me to have answers and I don't have any answers," he agonized.[118] He was more depressed than she had ever seen him; his pain was "intense because he felt that our nation wasn't willing to live up to the basic causes of the riots. He knew there were solutions but despaired of the complacency and blame shifting and intransigence." [119] Little systemic change and constant white denial had brought many Black people, including King himself, to the breaking point. He talked about taking time off, but never could. "He just had to be involved," Coretta explained. "There was something about the isolation—he couldn't stand—only for very short periods of time." [120]

"More pained than weary," her sister Edythe noted, that summer Martin seemed changed.

He had deprived himself of much in life, traveling the country instead of spending time with his children. He had been beaten, stoned, and jailed; he had been reviled by his supposed friends and hounded by the federal government. And he had preached his heart dry to force the nation to face up to . . . the critical issues of this age. Yet when he looked back over his life, he saw a paltry, insignificant result for a lifetime of work and recognized the enormity of what remained to be done.[121]

Six months before his assassination, his efforts felt meager.

King had struggled with depression for years, having been ordered to bed for exhaustion and fever by doctors on at least five occasions.[122] Many of his advisors grew increasingly concerned, pushing him to get help. But he worried that it could get out and be used against him and the movement.

King liked to have fun. He loved good food and playing pool. He drank, smoked, and had impressed Coretta early on with his dancing. He was not a fundamentalist. He teased and joked a lot—and could keep Coretta, friends, and colleagues in stitches for hours. Sometimes he would joke when Coretta was in no mood. He would complain that she was too serious; annoyed, she would push back, "That's my nature. I can't be frivolous."[123]

When he was stressed, he smoked, drank, and ate even more. He gained weight and stopped sleeping—at times suffering from debilitating insomnia. He was painfully self-critical and perhaps self-sabotaging. As Belafonte and Levison eulogized after his death, "None of his detractors, and there were many, could be as ruthless in questioning his motives or his judgement as he was to himself."[124]

Like many men he knew, he also slept with other women, some of them long-term. It was one way he took after his father, though he had hoped not to. In 1964, the FBI had sent the Kings a tape of some of his indiscretions, hoping to ruin him. It took its toll but didn't stop them. For the most part, Coretta didn't acknowledge it, though she had known this dimension from their courtship.[125] Sometimes she directly denied it: "There are so many stories about Martin and me and our life that were fabricated, pure and simple."[126]

But in describing Martin's character, she said he always ultimately unburdened his conscience. "He would always tell me eventually . . . guilt would just eat him up."[127] And on one occasion, she explained, "If I ever had suspicions . . . I never would have even mentioned them to Martin. I just wouldn't have burdened him with anything so trivial."[128] She likely had more complicated feelings, and they may have had some sort of understanding. But seeing why she calls it "trivial" necessitates sitting with the myriad demands they dealt with, the fear they lived with, the level of pain King was struggling with, and the bond they shared. It may, indeed, have felt somewhat trivial.

"Little or No Role in Disclosing Truth": King Takes On Culture-of-Poverty Theories

King had long condemned the misuse of sociological arguments—in particular, "culture of poverty" theories that claimed the dislocations of slavery, Jim Crow, and Northern migration had produced "Black cultural adaptations" that now were what held Black people back.[129] Northerners favored such sociological framings about "Black culture" in part because they seemed reasoned, a far cry from Southern segregationism. But King saw the problematic cover they provided to oppose desegregation, normalize inequality, and increase policing. King criticized the problematic "turn to sociological arguments, the crime rate in the Negro community, the lagging cultural stands . . . [without realizing] that criminal responses are environmental, not racial."[130] Behavioral explanations for Black poverty and segregation "means having your legs cut off, and then being condemned for being a cripple."[131]

While King was concerned with Black family life and Black men's ability to support a family, the causality was being manipulated. The greatest problem facing the Black community was not the "tangle of pathology" of the Black family, he argued, but what had been and was continuing to be done to Black families. King had highlighted the Moynihan Report's menace: "The danger will be that problems will be attributed to innate Negro weaknesses and used to justify, neglect and rationalize oppression."[132] In May 1966, King received an award from Planned Parenthood. Coretta went to receive it in his stead, reading a speech that stressed that useful policies to address reproductive rights and civil rights were constantly thwarted. Politicians like Moynihan "overemphasiz[ed] the problem of the Negro male ego and almost entirely ignored the most serious element—Negro migration. In all respects Negroes were atomized, neglected and discriminated against."[133]

On September 1, 1967, King delivered a scathing address to the American Psychological Association on the ways US social science had fallen down on the job. "All too many white Americans are horrified not with conditions of Negro life," King observed, "but with the product of these conditions—the Negro himself." American social science had done little to expose those conditions, King argued, and because of that they had played "little or no role in disclosing truth." King challenged the ways social scientists focused on Black people's "cultural responses"—rather than those who created the conditions Black people were forced to live in. King continued,

> The policymakers of the white society have caused the darkness; they create discrimination; they structured slums; and they perpetuate unemployment, ignorance and poverty. It is incontestable and deplorable that Negroes have committed crimes; but they are derivative crimes. They are born of the greater crimes of the white society . . . The slums are the handiwork of a vicious system of the white society.[134]

Five months later, in a speech honoring W. E. B. Du Bois's centennial, King continued this critique: "White America drenched with lies about Negroes, has lived too long in a fog of ignorance."[135] King lambasted social scientists who had compromised their profession by not exposing the truth of structural racism and the history of white benefit and discriminatory action.

In a series of lectures in late 1967 for the Canadian Broadcasting Company, King further elaborated an alternate reading of the riots. The violence people committed during the uprisings, he noted, overwhelmingly focused on property. To King, property "is intended to serve life . . . it has no personal being." Harming property was a far, far cry from harming people. He contrasted that selectivity with "white hoodlumism in Northern streets." Then he explained:

> The focus on property in the 1967 riots is not accidental. . . . Because property represents the white power structure, which they were attacking and trying to destroy. A curious proof of the symbolic aspect of the looting for some who took part in it is the fact that after the riots the police received hundreds of calls from Negroes trying to return merchandise they had taken. These people wanted the experience of taking, of redressing the power imbalance that property represents.[136]

But King's observations about the nature and character of the riots have largely been missed. On multiple occasions, King stressed the ways these urban uprisings largely targeted property, not people. "Negroes in the ghetto goaded and angered by discrimination and neglect for the most part deliberatively avoided harming persons. They have destroyed property. But even in the grip of rage, the vast majority have

vented their anger on inanimate things, not people."[137] The selective
targets of the rioters contrasted with the conduct of law enforcement
who took dozens of people's lives in the rebellions in Detroit and Newark that summer.

King identified long-standing white resistance to Black demands for
equality as the first factor leading to riots. White shock at the uprisings
was a willful way to try to escape accountability, and King was not
having it, not when white politicians and local residents had "refus[ed]
to take the means which have been called for." These politicians and
residents preferred blaming ghetto dwellers for the run-down housing
and decrepit conditions that they lived with. "The slums are the hand-
iwork of a vicious system of the white society," King said. "Negroes
live in them but do not make them any more than the prisoner makes
a prison."[138]

Faced with the summer's uprisings, President Johnson convened
a commission headed by Illinois governor Otto Kerner. Kerner had
downplayed racism in Illinois for years, criticizing King back in 1963
for highlighting Chicago's relentless segregation.[139] The Kerner Commission report found—as many, including King, had long said—that
the uprisings were caused by rampant racial discrimination in housing, schools, jobs, and municipal services, and that Great Society
programs had not gone far enough. In February 1968, King read a summary and praised the report as "a physician's warning of approaching
death with a prescription for life. The duty of every American is to
administer the remedy without regard for the cost and without delay."
But a report would not change things. "Eloquence and analysis by
themselves do not bring change," he stressed. "Bitter experience has
shown that our government does not act until it is confronted directly
and militantly."[140] King's fears proved prescient. On March 25, King
again noted how Johnson "has not made any move toward implement-
ing any of the recommendations of that Commission."[141]

In March, King traveled to the elite white suburb of Grosse Pointe,
Michigan, for a speech. There, meeting with community activist Claud
Young beforehand, King put his head in his hands and, surprisingly,
began to cry. Undone by the possibility of further uprisings and the
level of poverty he had seen across the country, he told Young, "I saw
them cooking grass in an attempt to prevent starvation and I couldn't
help them."[142]

The Grosse Pointe speech would be the last time Rosa Parks saw
him.[143] There were so many threats to his life that the police chief

rode on King's lap as they drove up to the high school where King was scheduled to speak.[144] Massively heckled and repeatedly called a traitor that night, it was the most disruptive indoor audience he'd ever encountered. Parks described it as "a horrible mess. . . . It was an all-white city."[145] King persisted amid the heckling:

> And I must say tonight that a riot is the language of the unheard. And what is it America has failed to hear? It has failed to hear that the plight of the negro poor has worsened over the last twelve or fifteen years. It has failed to hear that the promises of freedom and justice have not been met. And it has failed to hear that large segments of white society are more concerned about tranquility and the status quo than about justice and humanity.

King's focus on the "unheard" takes on new meaning seeing him reminding white Detroiters about the years they'd ignored Black cries against the city's injustices. He also condemned the bootstrap philosophy that formed the backbone of many Northerners' solution to these inequalities. The solution was *not* more policing or more personal responsibility but "acting forthrightly on the recommendations of the Kerner Commission."[146]

In late March, King joined with a broad spectrum of Black leaders condemning the charges against SNCC leader H. Rap Brown for allegedly inciting a riot in Cambridge, Maryland. The fiery Brown had been shot by police after he'd spoken at a rally in Cambridge but now faced charges of incitement. Brown's arrest was a threat to everyone's liberty, King underscored: "[T]hose who sit silent while another's rights are violated inevitably come to one of two ends. . . . Either they ultimately compromise their principles to survive in a police state, or they are eventually crushed themselves when it is too late to resist."[147]

12

To Make the Nation Say Yes When They Are Inclined to Say No

The Poor People's Campaign

Martin "had left Chicago," Coretta explained, "but Chicago wouldn't leave him." Children without adequate clothes for the weather, the rats, the lack of health care, all haunted him: "Martin replayed the searing images in his mind."[1] The seeds for building a national campaign against racism and poverty had grown in Chicago. In the aftermath of the Chicago Agreement, he'd explained to his Ebenezer congregation, "I choose to identify with the poor. . . . If it means suffering a little bit, I'm going that way. . . . If it means dying for them, I'm going that way, because I heard a voice saying, 'Do something for others.' "[2]

That voice pushed him forward. In Chicago, they had started to develop a multiracial, multipronged attack on race-class oppression from housing to jobs to lead paint. But national change had eluded them. Only mass disruption of the country's business would be sufficient to call attention to the breadth of the issues facing the nation. This thinking coalesced in the Poor People's Campaign.

The urgency had escalated in June 1966 when King visited a Head Start center in Marks, Mississippi. He saw four kids eagerly awaiting lunch—which then consisted of the teacher giving each child a quarter of an apple. He unexpectedly broke into tears, telling Ralph Abernathy later, "I can't get those children out of my mind. . . . I don't think people really know that little school children are slowly starving in the United States of America."[3] King was adamant that a race-class approach was needed; he was *not* moving from race to class. Addressing the Senate in December 1966, he stressed that "[e]conomic improvement despite its importance without full citizenship rights can be a bribe to the excluded rather than a gateway to the free society."[4]

Instead of one city, they would "go for broke" and take on the federal government "to make the invisible visible."[5] King saw how the country rested on the comfort of not looking steadfastly at the devastations of segregation and poverty and blaming poor people for their poverty. King had witnessed the ways lobbying and closed-door meetings didn't do the trick. They had all the "studies, all the recommendations . . . and yet nothing was done."[6] On top of that, he and Coretta had long seen that massive Cold War funding for war meant that people's needs were ignored. Only through mass action of poor people and civil disobedience would Congress and Johnson be moved to act and provide tools for real economic and political self-sufficiency.[7]

King was quick to remind people that the kinds of assistance they were asking for had been given to others.

> At the very same time that America refused to give the Negro any land, through an act of Congress, our government was giving away millions of acres of land in the West and the Midwest which meant that it was willing to undergird its white peasants from Europe with an economic floor. . . . Not only that, today many of these people are receiving millions of dollars of federal subsidies not to farm and they're the very people telling the Black man to lift himself by his bootstraps. . . . When we come to Washington in this campaign, we're coming to get our check.[8]

From his work with Local 1199 onward, King had seen the power of interracial militancy. King telegrammed his support to Milwaukee's Father James Groppi, a white Catholic priest, who had attended the Selma march and returned to Milwaukee to lead a militant open-housing movement with the Young Commandos, a group of young Black militants. For two hundred nights in 1967, they marched to challenge the city's fierce housing segregation and faced bottle-throwing white Milwaukeeans and tear gas from the police. Inspired by their relentless interracial direct action, King praised their efforts in finding a "middle ground between riots and sentimental and timid supplications for justice."[9]

Welfare Rights

From Chicago on, King saw public assistance as a right. Where some labor leaders like Randolph saw public assistance undermining the pride and dignity of the Black man, King came to see it as an essential right. Initially believing it contributed to men leaving, he had come to see the racial disparities in how welfare was administered—and the importance of access. Welfare had a sordid racial history. The 1935 Social Security Act, besides creating unemployment benefits and Social Security, established Aid to Dependent Children (or welfare) to provide cash assistance to women and children. Because they feared losing African American and Latina women's agricultural and domestic labor, legislators added "suitable home" provisions to determine which children and their mothers qualified for aid, which gave caseworkers great discretion. These provisions were often enforced on a racial basis, and women of color gained little access to ADC in its first decades in the South or North.[10] A growing welfare rights movement in the 1960s pressed for access for all women eligible. They also strove to expand the assistance to meet a family's basic living need, while demanding an end to punitive invasive treatment.

King began to see the racial double standard for poor Black mothers. "Now we are going to get the right for our wives and our mothers not to have to get up early in the morning and run over to the white ladies' kitchen . . . but to be able to stay at home and raise their children."[11] It had become a key demand in the Chicago campaign. "We are tired of a welfare system which dehumanizes us," King proclaimed at a multiracial rally in Chicago in 1966, "and dispenses payments under procedures that are often ugly and paternalistic."[12]

King's change around welfare stemmed partly from Coretta as well as through interactions with welfare rights activists. Welfare rights leader Johnnie Tillmon had confronted King for not understanding the extent to which welfare policies dehumanized poor women and reproduced gender-based racial oppression. She criticized him for overly focusing on the need for jobs for men. "You know Dr. King, if you don't know, you should say you don't know." King said he had come to learn.[13] King's interactions with Tillmon and the welfare rights movement deepened his analysis of structural racism. He had come to see public assistance as an important component of social citizenship and Black self-determination.

King had long understood Black poverty through the lens of race *and* class. Racism provided an important tool of capitalist power, both by paying Black and Latino people less and by the wages of whiteness that fractured interracial solidarity and movement building among poor people. King's gender analysis was the least developed, but it was changing. King came to see the double standard around welfare—it was " 'welfare' for the poor but 'subsidies' for everyone else."[14] He gave his support for a nationwide Mother's Day march of welfare recipients in 1968. He also battled with many of his SCLC advisors to include expanded welfare and no work requirements (that Congress seemed poised to ask for) in their demands. Septima Clark saw how King was changing: "He really felt that black women had a place in the movement and in the whole world," unlike the other SCLC ministers.[15]

From his 1964 *Why We Can't Wait* on, King had also advocated for a living wage and guaranteed annual income.[16] King diverged from Randolph and some other male leaders, according to historian Sylvie Laurent, in his endorsement of "the guaranteed job or income . . . as nothing less than a right."[17] (Coretta Scott King too was a key advocate of guaranteed annual income and would deepen this campaign in the 1970s.)[18] But he saw a "formidable wall" against its passage because many people were "profiting from the low wages of Negroes."[19] To him the simplest approach to poverty made the most sense: "abolish it directly by a now widely discussed measure: the guaranteed income."[20] Martin believed in a guaranteed annual income, Coretta explained, because "America had helped immigrants to become adjusted. We helped businessmen—in the airlines, for example to get started by giving them subsidies. . . . We were asking only to be given our fair share."[21]

Since Coretta met him, Martin had possessed a strong critique of capitalism, which grew over time. According to Black Marxist C.L.R. James, King was "a man whose ideas were as advanced as any of us on the Left." King had confided in James some of his thinking but that he "couldn't say such things from the pulpit."[22] King was also a diehard unionist. When the American Federation of Television and Radio Artists went on strike in April 1967, King refused to cross the picket line to be on ABC's *Issues and Answers* program and was replaced by Barry Goldwater.[23]

By 1967, King and the SCLC had grown increasingly critical of Johnson's War on Poverty, which claimed to prioritize "maximum feasible participation" of the poor to determine the direction of programs but did little to facilitate and, at times, harmed the political organization of poor people. Mayors like Yorty and Daley used War on Poverty money as another lever of influence to be disbursed to those who played ball. On top of that, the escalation in Vietnam had caused cuts in funding to education, job training programs, and social services. Many in the Johnson administration subscribed to a cultural-deficit model for understanding poverty, simultaneously pursuing a war on crime and amplifying police power.

As much as they had tried to build Black people's voting power in Chicago and Cleveland, this required a national approach. The idea for the Poor People's Campaign (PPC) was to bring multiracial poor people from across the nation to the Capitol and stay until their needs were addressed by Congress and the president. A mass mobilization of poor people "as dramatic, as dislocative, as disruptive, as attention getting as the riots without destroying life or property" would force the issue into public consciousness, bring the city to a standstill, and hopefully move Congress to action.[24]

The idea had partly come from Marian Wright, a young lawyer working with the NAACP-LDF who was determined to expose the depths of Mississippi poverty. In April 1967 Wright brought a group of senators, including New York's Robert F. Kennedy, down to Mississippi to see hunger and poverty firsthand. The trip moved Kennedy tremendously. She then went to Atlanta to tell King what she had witnessed about the receptiveness and power of the Mississippi trip and how the next step was to bring poor people to DC and demand to be heard. King was elated by the idea—treating Wright like "an angel delivering a message."[25] His mind spinning with ideas and plans, he started reaching out to friends and trusted colleagues. He had his old enthusiasm back, Coretta saw.[26] The government is "not going to act unless it's forced to," and his spirits lifted at this concrete idea of how to do so.[27] The PPC was "the culmination of everything that King had been talking to us about in our private meetings," former Chicago field staff worker Lynn Adler saw.[28]

In September a Poor People's Action Committee was created within SCLC. Bernard Lafayette was put in charge. Lafayette recruited Tom Houck, a poor white high school dropout who had become the King family's driver, to go to Appalachia to bring poor whites into the PPC.[29] But many in SCLC were critical of the idea and thought it was destined to fail. Assistant secretary of the board Marian Logan found it inopportune, writing an uncharacteristic six-page litany of concerns.[30] She thought the PPC would be too wide and uncontrollable, that SCLC didn't have the capacity, and that Washington would hate it.[31] Some like Hosea Williams didn't trust the interracialism.

Many of King's longtime allies had grown more opposed to his political direction in his last years. As with Chicago and Vietnam, Rustin opposed the campaign. "Personally I cannot think of a situation more flammable," he carped.[32] James Bevel and Jesse Jackson wanted to prioritize the war; Andrew Young favored concentrating on Southern field operations. They saw Johnson and Congress as impossible to shift on these issues.[33] King was "devastated by betrayals from friends and movement comrades . . . [who] were loud and adamant, telling him he was failing," Andrew Young later recalled.[34]

James Orange, however, saw the PPC differently—as a way to tackle poverty and the war together: "to give all the poor peoples in this country an adequate income, they would have to take some of the money back home."[35] Coretta understood as well. The urgency of tackling the triple evils of poverty, racism, and war was not new for them. Nor was the pushback from advisors, but here it was much more intense. But King persisted, stressing that if the PPC failed, it would be the nation that failed, not the movement.[36] In many ways, Chicago had taught him that lesson.

King's foundation for the PPC was also deeply religious. Just as moving to Chicago had brought him to live among the poor, the idea for the PPC embodied God's justice on earth. "By the thousands we will move . . . to turn this nation upside down and right side up."[37] They would overturn the moneychangers' tables and take on Congress to get their rightful due. "You gotta have both the vision and the expectation," Marian Wright understood.

King's thinking further solidified when he was forced to go back to jail in early October 1967 on an old charge from the 1963 Birmingham campaign. Not an easy time, he was sick and couldn't sleep. His health was so poor that he had to see a prison doctor. After four days the judge released him, seemingly worried about King's health.[38] But King emerged further convinced of the need for mass disruptive action in DC to dramatize the plight of the poor and force action. These bigger, bolder steps with Chicago, with Vietnam, and now with the PPC, Coretta and Martin felt, brought him closer to his own death. "You have to pay the ultimate sacrifice if you stand up for what you really believe in . . . you don't try to save your life because, I think, history was moved forward as a result of the position that he took."[39]

In what would be the last winter of his life, he was "terribly distressed," Coretta Scott King explained.[40] He felt people wanted answers he didn't have. Whereas before she would hold him and her words could help lift him, "now my words took root only for a moment."[41] Coretta's centeredness had helped sustain them. From childhood on, "I was being prepared for this role. . . . Because if I had been less strong, physically, mentally and emotionally, it would have been just, almost impossible, I think. And it's interesting that Martin saw these things in me when we were, when he first met me." Looking back, she observed the immensity of what they were trying to do.

> I personally didn't feel . . . like I was straining to do what I did. It was like, I have a lot to do, but I'm gonna do it and I can do it. And every day, I mean, it was exciting. It's amazing, when I think back on it. I didn't realize how hard it was. If I had known how hard it was really, maybe, you know, things would have been different. But I didn't realize it was that hard.[42]

She continued to wish for more time together with the kids and more movement co-leading. "Best friends," Coretta would later say, they could "feel each other's wounds" and so his pain weighed heavy on them.[43] Still, he pushed forward with the Poor People's Campaign amid this despair and the skepticism of many advisors. His pace was frantic. At the same time, according to Harry Belafonte, the breathing tic King suffered seemed to be gone. When Belafonte asked about it, King said he had "come to terms with death"—not just his own death but the potential of Coretta, his kids, or other supporters being killed. He had come to embrace his responsibility to make decisions apart from considerations that somebody might die.[44] Dorothy Cotton noted how when someone would run up to them at the airport, she would get scared, while King would already have his hand out. The fear "didn't control his behavior."[45]

While they talked a lot about the possibility of his death and even joked about it, Coretta said he could never talk about what would happen to the children if he died—"this was too much to cope with."[46] For years, that had left Coretta to talk with the kids about the dangers their father's work entailed. She did not want to scare them or make them fearful, but she wanted them to understand the dangers and violence out there. She was someone who always faced things and didn't want to deceive them. She was proud that they too did not seem fearful.

On December 4, King announced the Poor People's Campaign at a press conference. He lambasted the "spectacle of cities burning while the national government speaks of repression instead of rehabilitation."[47] He zeroed in on the federal government's "primary responsibility for low minimum wages, for a degrading system of inadequate welfare, for subsidies to the rich and unemployment and underemployment of the poor." The nation had developed ways to ignore, hide, and criminalize the impacts of poverty—and part of the campaign's aim would be to force the country to "see the poor."[48] They would stay in DC until there was action, specifically:

- $30 billion annual appropriation for a real war on poverty
- congressional passage of full employment and guaranteed income legislation [a guaranteed annual wage]; and
- construction of 500,000 low-cost housing units per year[49]

This was the "absolute minimum," King made clear to the press.[50] For King, a guaranteed annual income wasn't enough; it required spending on and desegregation of housing and education as well. Poverty and racism needed to be addressed together.[51]

The press, as usual, was skeptical. The *Washington Post* called it "an appeal to anarchy."[52] Over and over, King was asked: "What if you fail?" But he made clear, "It won't be Martin Luther King, Jr. that fails. It will be America that fails."[53] The media were out of step with what people wanted, he stressed. When a Harris poll revealed "64 percent feel that the slums should be torn down and the communities rebuilt by the people who live in them, I believe we are moving around the right issue."[54] When questioned how he would train poor people to be nonviolent, King explained that militant direct action would keep people disciplined and nonviolent, citing the example of the Blackstone Rangers during the Chicago campaign as evidence.[55]

Back in June, amid much controversy about whether King should even have been invited, he addressed the annual Capitol Press Club Awards. King spoke directly to the disapproval swirling about him. "Booker T. Washington used pressureless persuasion and he was widely praised and called a responsible leader by white folks. Whenever I am called a responsible leader, it worries me because it often means you are not telling the truth."[56]

Having worked with groups across the country, the PPC hoped to coalesce its power to have "the ability, the assertiveness and the aggressiveness to make the power structure of this nation say yes when they may be desirous to say no."[57] This kind of policy change required substantial spending. "It didn't cost the nation one penny to integrate lunch counters," King observed during a February 1968 trip to Mississippi, "but now we are dealing with issues that cannot be solved without the nation spending billions of dollars and undergoing a radical redistribution of economic power."[58]

The Jeannette Rankin Brigade planned its antiwar march on DC for January 15 with the eighty-seven-year-old Rankin and Coretta Scott King as two of the leaders. On its eve, she and other SCLC women published a letter decrying the problems of hunger, hopelessness, and hatred prevalent in Southeast Asia and at home: "History shows us that no political ideology has ever been destroyed by military might, nor any political problem solved by the killing of young men."[59] On January 15, Coretta missed Martin's thirty-ninth birthday to help lead more than five thousand women in the protest.[60] Coretta was proud that many Black women participated. A delegation, including Scott King, took their petition calling for an end to the war and diverting funding to social spending to meet with Congress.

SCLC held a mandatory three-day retreat in mid-January 1968, at Ebenezer, for its staff to plan for the PPC. This internal work was essential, King said, before they went out to organize communities. "We made some strides toward the ending of racism but did not stride into freedom." He worried about the ways that the US Census deeply undercounted Black people—and particularly Black unemployment, joking, "I used to tell them when they told me they had a million Negroes in Chicago . . . 'I know it's more than a million Negroes in Chicago because I personally know a million folk in Chicago.' " Then he turned serious: "And whether we realize it or not, the poorest people in our country today . . . are working every day." King underlined the bitterness that develops from Black demands long disregarded. "I would rather be dead than ignored," a man had told King. The campaign would have to be confrontational and harness the energy that had spilled out in the riots in a powerful, creative way. It would require civil disobedience.[61] He bemoaned how former allies "were hollering . . . [because] some sacrifices will have to be made." But they were determined to go to Washington "to demand what is ours."[62]

In his last year, King had grown increasingly pointed at white liberal hypocrisy. He revealed the pretense of equality that most whites, even many allies, favored:

Negroes have proceeded from a premise that equality means what it says. . . . But most whites in America, including many of goodwill, proceed from a premise that equality is a loose expression for improvement. White America is not even psychologically organized to close the gap—essentially, it seeks only to make it less painful and less obvious but in most respects retain it. Most of the abrasions between Negroes and white liberals arise from this fact.[63]

The majority of white Americans, King stressed, "consider themselves sincerely committed to justice for the Negro. They believe that American society is essentially hospitable to fair play. . . . But unfortunately this is a fantasy of self-deception and comfortable vanity."[64] Indeed, a Gallup poll in 1967 found only 1 percent of white Americans believed that Black people were badly treated.[65]

King criticized the white liberal preference to focus on love and not justice: "It is not enough to say, 'We love Negroes, we have many Negro friends.' They must demand justice for Negroes. Love that does not satisfy justice is no love at all. It is merely a sentimental affection, little more than what one would love for a pet."[66] *A pet.* Professing affection for Black people without being willing to transform the political and economic fabric of the country was condescending and self-serving. This would take sacrifice and cost—and King pushed white allies to understand that.

On January 16, King announced the concrete plans for SCLC's work on the PPC. Sixty-six staff members would recruit and train three thousand demonstrators from fifteen poverty-stricken cities and rural areas. Three caravans of poor people coming from different parts of the country would converge on the Capitol.[67] "If necessary, we are willing to fill up the jails of Washington and surrounding communities," he declared.[68]

In late January, Coretta's sister Edythe came to stay with them because Coretta had fibroid surgery. Martin was home much of the time, but "he was not the same person I had known earlier," Edythe noted. "His conversations and demeanor reflected deep and unresolved pain."[69] Still Coretta would later say how glad she was that Martin was alive when she had to have this surgery.

On February 4, King's sermon at Ebenezer meditated on the lasting legacy of Jesus: "He was only thirty-three when the tide of public opinion turned against him. They called him a rabble-rouser. They called him a troublemaker. They said he was an agitator. He practiced civil disobedience; he broke injunctions. . . . Nineteen centuries have come and gone and today he stands as the most influential figure that ever entered human history." King then went on to talk about his own death:

If any of you are around when I have to meet my day, I don't want a long funeral. And if you get somebody to deliver the eulogy, tell them not to talk too long. . . . I'd like somebody to mention that day that Martin Luther King, Jr., tried to give his life serving others. . . . I won't have the fine and luxurious things of life to leave behind. But I just want to leave a committed life behind.[70]

At the end of January, Stokely Carmichael came on board with the PPC; in March, King told the press that Carmichael would provide housing and food support for the encampment but not participate.[71] Carmichael described how "the press started its stupidity, trying to pose King and some of us in the city in direct opposition to each other."[72] He wasn't having it.

King emphasized that the "huge promissory note" he'd referenced at the 1963 March on Washington was long overdue.[73] The lack of any action around the Kerner Commission's report demonstrated to King the absolute necessity of the PPC to demand Congress "bring the recommendations to life."[74] If Congress didn't take action, he worried about the possibility of even worse uprisings that summer and said he would favor demonstrations at the Democratic National Convention in August.[75]

With help from Highlander Folk School, the PPC's first gathering took place at Paschal's Motor Hotel in Atlanta on March 14, 1968. It brought together over fifty organizations representing poor Blacks, whites, Latinos, and Native Americans to engage, as King wrote, "in joint thinking."[76] Still recovering from the fibroid surgery, Coretta went, not wanting to miss this historic coming together. The meeting prompted a lot of cross-learning; people spoke about their particular needs and their common problem—poverty.[77] The meeting went long into the evening, past the 5 p.m. stated end time, with people singing Spanish songs, Appalachian folk tunes, and Native American "tongue talk."[78] Late that night, King spoke about the power that a united front of poor people possessed. "His comment was when you impede the rich man's ability to make money, anything is negotiable," farmworker organizer Baldemar Velasquez recalled decades later.[79]

Again, King put Gilberto Gerena Valentin in charge of organizing the Puerto Rican contingent to the PPC; they would print one hundred thousand PPC leaflets in Spanish and pledged several busloads from New York's Puerto Rican community to go to Washington.[80] Young people from Chicago and Milwaukee, including many Chicago gang members recruited to be marshals, and Peggy Terry from JOIN, formed the heart of the Midwestern Caravan.[81] King asked Father Groppi and the Young Commandos to help lead the PPC's Midwestern contingent.[82] Local 1199 would help organize the Northeastern delegation; six hundred 1199 members would journey to Washington in June for the PPC. The National Welfare Rights Organization would play a key role, along with the National Mobilization Committee to End the War in Vietnam, which Coretta had helped get on its feet.

King reunited with his friend Rabbi Heschel on March 25 when he spoke before the Rabbinical Assembly, Heschel echoing the importance of the PPC: "Martin Luther King is a sign that God has not forsaken the United States of America. . . . The situation of the poor in America is our plight, our sickness. To be deaf to their cry is to condemn ourselves."[83] The PPC pulled together so many people King had worked with over the years.

Exhausted, King was suffering intense insomnia, telling a reporter in March he had been "getting two hours of sleep a night for the past ten days."[84] He felt his own death more imminently. For the first time, in mid-March, he saw some synthetic red carnations in a window, wrote Coretta a note, and sent them to her. They were beautiful, but she was surprised since he'd always sent her real flowers. When she commented on it, he explained, "I wanted you to be able to keep them."[85]

The PPC was a "mammoth job"—the logistics, the transportation, food, mobilization, and the expenses of bringing caravans from all over the country. King was also committed to having Freedom Schools so people could learn Black history at the encampment.[86] Some of his closest advisors—Andrew Young, Jesse Jackson, and James Bevel— grew increasingly skeptical. In what would be the last week of his life, more stressed than ever, he exploded against them and their lack of support. King rarely used personal attacks, but their constant questioning had pushed him to the breaking point. He called the US a "burning house" and found their reluctance "selfish." Finally, a compromise was reached where some would go immediately to Memphis and others would devote their time to the PPC.[87] As SNCC's Zoharah Simmons came to recognize, King was "far ahead of even his closest colleagues . . . [understanding] the interlocking problems of the world's poor."[88]

The mainstream media was a drumbeat of criticism. The *Washington Post* published a cascade of increasingly negative coverage about the campaign in the winter-spring of 1968 fearing the "mayhem" it would cause and the ways it would "snarl traffic." The *Post* published a long article detailing Roy Wilkins's criticisms, like other newspapers using Wilkins to ventriloquize their fear and opposition.[89] The *New York Times* didn't print anything on the historic March meeting but instead published a fairly skeptical article on March 31 titled "Dr. King Hints He'd Cancel the March if Aid Is Offered."[90] King was not canceling, despite pressure to do so. He had received a dream offer to take a one-year sabbatical to lead New York's historic Riverside Church. But he turned it down. He was committed to going to DC.[91]

In what would be the last months of his life, according to Coretta, Martin worked at a "frantic pace," feeling a tremendous urgency to get things done. The idea of the PPC moved him at a spiritual level, giving him a different kind of energy. She, Abernathy, and others around him saw "a kind of a lion quality about him . . . they were in awe, as to how he could get that strength, when he obviously could be very low, and very much like any other human being. And then he could transcend and somehow be able to be above it."[92] He tried to ready his staff to continue in his absence. "If anything happens to me, you must be prepared to continue," he had said repeatedly.[93] It wasn't unusual for Coretta to awake before daybreak and see him at his desk working. "It was as if he were racing against a clock. . . . The faster he ran, the faster the clock."[94]

To build the PPC they were conducting "people-to-people tours" to recruit poor people from around the country. Martin loved these. From DC to Virginia, South Carolina, North Carolina, New Jersey, Maryland, Ohio, Michigan, and Illinois, he "would come back so inspired because he said the people came out in large numbers and they were so eager and interested in the whole idea."[95] He liked walking from house to house during the visits, requesting people not be told he was coming so he could see their real living conditions. Sometimes he would stay to eat with them.[96] Two weeks before his assassination, he took his two sons (Martin was ten and Dexter seven) on a "people-to-people" trip to rural Georgia along with Ralph Abernathy and his son.[97] Coretta had suggested it, Martin really liked the idea, and the boys were thrilled. They got home in the middle of the night excited but exhausted. Marty told her how tired he was but how hard Daddy worked and "was not even tired; he went off to the office and he's wide awake and talking."[98]

For King, what the nation needed to do was clear. In the last piece he wrote, published three days after his assassination, he again lamented "not a single basic cause of the riots has been corrected." He decried how "police, national guard, and other armed bodies are feverishly preparing for repression." And then he laid out the choice: "The American people are infected with racism—that is the peril. Paradoxically, they are also infected with democracy—that is the hope. . . . We have the opportunity through massive nonviolent action to avoid a national disaster. . . . All of us are on trial in this troubled hour." [99]

The FBI and the PPC

Johnson and the FBI viewed the PPC as a threat. In mid-March, the government announced that ten thousand members of law enforcement and the armed forces would be on standby to police the encampment. [100]

As Black Power had captured media attention over the previous few years, the FBI saw an opportunity to stoke more division. The Domestic Intelligence Division recommended that an article "indicting King for his failure to take a stand on the [Black Power] issue and at the same time exposing the degree of communist influence on him" be given to a newspaper contact "friendly" to the Bureau. [101] In March 1967, Director Hoover approved a recommendation by the Domestic Intelligence Division to furnish "friendly" reporters with questions to ask King. [102] That summer, after an editorial criticizing King as a "traitor to his race" had appeared in a Black newspaper, the FBI sent it around to major news outlets. [103]

In its multipronged campaign against King, the FBI had long tried to cultivate—and amplify—tensions between him and other civil rights leaders. The Bureau planted false rumors, magnified or even created rivalries, and then benefited from factionalism. [104] Using the press had long been key to the FBI's strategies against King. In a nine-hour meeting back in December 1963, the Bureau discussed twenty-one proposals to try to discredit King, looking at possibilities of using his housekeeper, disgruntled acquaintances, Black agents, and "aggressive" reporters. [105] Given the amount of coverage Black division garnered in the *Washington Post*, *New York Times*, and *Los Angeles Times* over the next five years, it is unclear what role the FBI might have had in stoking this narrative.

In 1964 the FBI had cultivated a relationship with *Atlanta Constitution* publisher Ralph McGill to assist in discrediting King. The FBI took note of "a rift possibly developing" between King and NAACP head Roy Wilkins. They instructed the New York and Atlanta offices to "remain particularly alert" to a possible feud for "utilization," hoping to feed information to McGill.[106] Other news outlets, including the *Chicago Tribune, Los Angeles Times,* and *New York Times,* also gave significant coverage over the next four years to Wilkins's criticisms of King.[107]

In 1964, the FBI tried to block a magazine article King was publishing (written by Clarence Jones) in the *Saturday Evening Post.* When it was were unable to do so, the Bureau got the magazine to "resist" efforts by King to soften criticism of other civil rights leaders that Jones had put in.[108] The FBI wanted to widen disagreement between King and other Black leaders. While it had less success cultivating journalists to cover King's sexual affairs, disagreements between Black leaders proved a fruitful avenue with journalists already enamored with stories about Black discord. The FBI stoked controversy around King's reluctance to join other leaders to critique Black Power—trying to plant stories and widen that disagreement into a feud.

Additionally, as historian Lerone Martin documents, the Bureau used Black clergy to launder their message.[109] Having scaled back its electronic surveillance, the FBI also cultivated a variety of paid informants, including James A. Harrison, a member of the SCLC's Atlanta staff, and Memphis Black photographer Ernest Withers. Beginning in October 1965, the FBI began paying Harrison $450–$600 a month for his services, increasing this amount over time.[110]

The FBI's campaign against him weighed on King. They "talked about it constantly," according to Harry Belafonte.[111] Sometimes the Kings talked in code on the phone.[112] It eroded their spirits, exacerbated tensions with other Black leaders, and corroded public opinion about him and the movement.

Hoover continued to report nearly weekly to Johnson directly. Regarding the Poor People's Campaign as "a grave threat to peace and order in this city," the FBI requested permission to wiretap the SCLC offices; when Attorney General Ramsey Clark said no, agents stepped up their informants.[113] The FBI managed to place informants into various PPC chapters, including Chicago, Detroit, and Washington, DC— who then attempted to cause internal dissension.[114] In Detroit, a special agent claiming to be a businessman offered to fund and provide buses; then when there were no buses, people would hopefully turn against the organizers.[115] The Miami FBI office paid the producer for a local

NBC television special on young Black leaders to make them look angry and incoherent on-screen. In Savannah, Georgia, the Bureau planted news stories that claimed King and the SCLC would strand activists sick and destitute in DC.[116] The FBI worked to place unfavorable articles on the PPC right up to (and beyond) King's assassination. Toward the end of March, it circulated a story that King was being irresponsible with money.[117] Knowing King faced dissension within the SCLC and was desperate for funds, the intention was to exacerbate the fighting and hobble their fundraising.

The Johnson administration's concerns about King continued to escalate. The White House counsel wrote the president worrying that "we have permitted the Stokely Carmichaels, the Rap Browns, and the Martin Luther Kings to cloak themselves in an aura of respectability to which they are not entitled." Calling King's work "criminal disobedience," he hoped "the President will publicly unmask this type of conduct for what it really is." [118]

And so on March 4, 1968, one month before King's assassination, Hoover sent a memo to forty-one field offices outlining the threat of a Black "messiah" developing and the efforts the FBI must take to stop that from happening. He named three men explicitly: Stokely Carmichael, Elijah Muhammad, and Martin Luther King.[119] Agents were instructed to figure out ways to discredit these three men, including amplifying and exploiting conflict between them.

Then, as King prepared to go to Memphis in early April, the FBI helped plant news stories that King had abandoned Black businesses by staying at the white-owned Holiday Inn the last time he'd been in town. So, when he returned to Memphis on April 3, he stayed at the Black-owned Lorraine Motel, as he often did, in room 306. His room number was printed in the newspaper.[120]

The Assassination

King had long highlighted how Black workers needed the protection of a union. On February 12, 1968, Black sanitation workers in Memphis had decided to strike after two more men had been killed on the job. Their wages were so low that many needed food stamps so their families had enough to eat. They demanded recognition of their union, better safety conditions, and a living wage. On February 26, daily marches began, with strikers bearing "I Am A Man" posters. The City Council voted to recognize the union, but the mayor refused, saying that only he had the power to do so. King's friend Rev. James Lawson, now living in Memphis, was dismayed at the mayor's intransigence and pleaded with King to come.

King agreed to join their struggle. Arriving in Memphis on March 18, he addressed a crowd of twenty-five thousand and urged a Black general strike if the sanitation workers' demands weren't met.[121] He was very moved, according to Coretta, by the unity and spirit of the people in Memphis.[122] Ten days later, on March 28, King returned to lead a march. It turned chaotic when people started throwing things and looting; King was rushed to a nearby hotel. Police responded violently, killing one teenager, using tear gas, and clubbing many people. Condemnation rained down on King for losing control; the *Chicago Tribune* editorialized against this "carnival of lawbreaking" by King "and his posse of pulpitless parsons." [123]

Martin was deeply discouraged. He had never left a march like this. Coretta bowed out of a church engagement that night to be home when he got there, knowing how demoralized he was. "After the tragedy occurred, I thought back on this and I thought, 'I'm so glad I was there that night to give him what consolation that I could.' " [124]

SCLC was divided on what to do. Many in the organization felt Memphis wasn't their fight. But after a contentious meeting, King decided to return to Memphis on April 3, believing he needed to continue the work he had begun there. As had become commonplace, a bomb threat forced them off the plane; the airplane was searched and then deemed safe. "Well, it looks like they won't kill me on this flight," King said to Abernathy as they reboarded.[125]

That night, people filled Memphis's Mason Temple to the rafters. It was storming and there were tornado warnings. Sick, King initially begged off, saying he was too worn-out, and sent Abernathy in his stead. He called Ebenezer to give them the title of his Sunday sermon—"Why America May Go to Hell." But Abernathy called him at the motel, saying the auditorium was packed and asking for King. In his pajamas, King agreed and shortly headed out into the rain.

An exhausted but smiling King began his speech around 9:30. "The nation is sick," he lamented. "Somewhere I read about freedom of speech. . . . Somewhere I read that the greatness of America is the right to protest for right." King had grown increasingly disillusioned at the country's refusal to address its own sins. "The illusion of the damned," King called it that night.[126] The speech continued to build: "I've seen the Promised Land. I may not get there with you. But I want you to know tonight, that we, as a people, will get to the Promised Land!" When Abernathy reached out to hug him after the speech, King was crying.[127]

Martin's brother A. D. showed up that night and they stayed up eating, laughing, and cavorting. On April 4, after a day of meetings and waiting for the judge to rule on the march, Martin and A. D. called their mom, trying to prank her since she didn't know they were together. Then, after an impromptu pillow fight to blow off steam, Martin stepped out of his room onto the Lorraine Motel balcony and was shot in the head at 6:05 p.m. It was a single shot.

As they rushed him to St. Joseph's Hospital, Jesse Jackson called Coretta and told her to get on the next plane. She started to gather her things. A breaking news story came on TV saying Martin Luther King had been shot. She tried to turn it down but Yoki heard and began crying, "Don't tell me, don't tell me." She then started to help her mom pack.

Coretta had just gotten to the airport when Dora McDonald, Martin's longtime jack-of-all-trades assistant (she "could be president," he had said), beckoned her into the bathroom.[128] King's sister Christine followed. Mayor Ivan Allen knocked on the door to tell her Martin had died. "That's how I found out my brother had died—in a bathroom in the Atlanta airport," Christine recalled.[129] The physician who did the autopsy said that thirty-nine-year-old King's heart looked like the heart of a man twice his age.

Coretta decided to turn around and come home, wanting to be with her children when they learned about their father's death. But the kids had already heard the news on TV by the time she got there. Yolanda had "sat them down and tried to comfort them," Coretta learned.

When Belafonte heard King had been shot, he called Coretta to see where she and the kids were and what they might need. To give Martin peace of mind, one of the things they'd put in place, according to Belafonte, was assurances "his family would never be left without care and attention."[130] Belafonte bought him a life insurance policy and would put money away for the children's college.

Now Belafonte also stressed the importance of Coretta's political role—to go to Memphis to lead the march that Martin was supposed to. "You're the only force in the universe who can do it as it needs to be done. . . . The leadership needs your strength and your resolve." Coretta said yes; she needed to make arrangements for the children but she would come.[131] She reflected on how Martin had felt his death would be redemptive to help bring about the change they believed in.[132] Edythe too thought she should go. It would have been what Martin wanted, they both agreed. They slept in the same bed that night, as they often had as kids. When they woke up, Coretta said, "I was crying when I woke up." "So was I," Edythe said.[133]

But Coretta Scott King rose to the occasion. "God was using us—and now he's using me, too," she thought. In a statement from Ebenezer two days after his death, she underscored how Martin knew America "was a sick society totally infested with racism and violence . . . that would ultimately lead to his death and he struggled with every ounce of his energy to save that society from itself."[134]

Four days after the assassination, she, along with the three oldest children, journeyed to Memphis to demonstrate through their own example that the struggle must continue. "I gave a speech from the heart and some people 'saw' me for the first time," she recalled.[135] "How many men must die before we can really have a free and true and peaceful society?" she demanded.[136] Carrying on the fight for racial and economic justice was the only appropriate way to honor Martin's death, she stressed: "The day that Negro people and others in bondage are truly free, on the day want is abolished, on the day wars are no more, on that day I know my husband will rest in a long-deserved peace."[137]

Media organizations and people across the country took note of her strength and political courage—many, like the *New York Times,* in a way they had not before.[138] Going to Memphis "made me feel better," she later recalled; seeing all the marchers, "his spirit lives on within all of those people."[139]

Colleagues and friends insisted that the responsibility for King's death lay not just at the feet of the shooter but with the nation as a whole. As his Morehouse mentor Benjamin Mays stressed, "The American people are in part responsible for Martin Luther King Jr.'s death. The assassin heard enough condemnation of King and of Negroes to feel that he had public support."[140] Mike Royko of the *Chicago Sun-Times* underlined the ways Northerners had sewn the climate of hate that had killed King: "It would be easy to point at the Southern redneck and say he did it. . . . What about the Northern mayor who steps all over every poverty program advancement, thinking only of political expediency. . . . Toss in the congressman with the stupid arguments against busing."[141]

The respect for Martin Luther King poured in from many corners. Head of Local 1199 Leon Davis stressed that statues or flowery tributes would not do justice to King: "[W]e would build no monuments in his memory, but would instead build our union in his image in the struggle to end poverty, racism, injustice and war. . . . King belonged to us, to our members, to the poor, to the ghetto dweller, to the black man and to the poor white man." [142]

A couple of days after the assassination, over a thousand Blackstone Rangers, ages twelve to twenty-one, met and pledged to react nonviolently to his death, making a temporary truce with the Gonzato Disciples.[143] Leader Jeff Fort said they had "loved" King and "will do all we can to promote peace in our communities." [144] Because of this, no uprisings happened on the South Side—though people rose up in other parts of Chicago.[145] Daley ordered the police to "shoot to kill" anyone carrying a Molotov cocktail. Similarly, in Newark, Baraka worked the streets after King's assassination, urging Black people, like King had wanted, to put their energies in building organized Black political power "so we can pick the candidates for every city office." [146]

Young activists across the country were angry and sickened. "When white America killed Dr. King last night," SNCC's Stokely Carmichael announced, "she declared war on us. It would have been better if she had killed Rap Brown . . . or Stokely Carmichael. But when she killed Dr. King, she lost it." In the week after King's assassination, hundreds of uprisings flared across the country. Young people poured into the streets and took over schools in anger over the assassination. Carmichael contextualized this "mass urban revolt" across the country: "If no reaction came for the death of King, then these racist pigs in the country will feel that they can kill anybody with impunity, so there must be some actions . . . to stay their hands against killing those who come to take a leadership position in fighting for the people." Carmichael drove from Washington, DC, to Atlanta for the funeral and the whole way he saw smoke—"a funeral pyre . . . giving him his proper burial." [147]

The day after King's assassination, President Johnson addressed the nation, saying he had asked Congress to receive him at the "earliest possible moment" to get the Fair Housing Act passed. No longer faced with an alive and eloquent King, Johnson and Congress acted with alacrity. A week after King's assassination, the act was signed into law, outlawing discrimination in the sale and rental of property including realtor-sold, single-family homes. Something "impossible" two years earlier was accomplished in a week. Unlike in 1966, the media played a significant role in laying out expectations that Johnson needed to get it done. The *New York Times* praised Johnson for saying it would happen "in our time." [148] This progress narrative erased what Johnson had not done—get fair-housing legislation passed in King's lifetime before more uprisings and suffering had occurred.

The Struggle Continues

Coretta Scott King was committed to a funeral that was as simple as possible "in keeping with the kind of life he lived, simple, dignified, beautiful." [149] Because Martin had loved the idea of the mule-train caravan for the PPC, part of his funeral included a march with his casket drawn by a mule and wagon.[150] Many of King's advisors walked alongside. President Lyndon Johnson did not attend the funeral.

Mays gave the only eulogy that day. He and Martin had made an agreement: he would preach Martin's funeral or Martin would preach his, depending on who died first.

> Martin Luther King Jr. was a prophet in the 20th century ... If Jesus was called to preach the Gospel to the poor, Martin Luther was called to give dignity to the common man. If a prophet is one who interprets in clear and intelligible language the will of God, Martin Luther King Jr. fits that designation. If a prophet is one who does not seek popular causes to espouse, but rather the causes he thinks are right, Martin Luther qualified on that score.[151]

In the days surrounding the funeral, so many people came by the house, called, and sent gifts of love. Coretta wished Martin "could see this, because he never—somehow I had the feeling that he never knew how much people thought of him. . . . I think he would have felt that his sacrifices were well worth it." [152]

King's assassination—and the uprisings that resulted—also led to a massive police escalation and militarized law enforcement. The next month, Scott King traveled to Harvard to give the Class Day address Martin was supposed to have given, highlighting this problem: "This is not time for business as usual and strengthening the police is business as usual, a tired and false answer." [153] She grew increasingly pointed about the targeting of Black activists: "If the FBI wants to find the wellsprings of radicalism . . . [t]ell them to look at the White House and in the marbled halls of Congress. The policies there radicalized more young people than a million books by revolutionaries." [154]

Coretta Scott King stepped forward after the assassination even more determined to continue their work. After leading the march in Memphis, three weeks later she delivered a powerful antiwar speech in New York's Central Park.[155] But she struggled with the ways she was being marginalized in SCLC: "Most thought that women should stay in the shadows; . . . for the longest time, way before I married Martin, I had believed that women should allow our essence and presence to shine, rather than letting ourselves be buried or shunted to the sidelines." [156]

"The men" in SCLC imagined she should be the widow and let them run things, but she refused. (That's how she referred to them, "the men," her longtime friend Mary Frances Berry laughingly recalled.)[157] Many believed she was lost without Martin and needed them to lead the way. Quite the contrary, her antiwar work and racial-economic advocacy work continued to grow. Scott King's steadfast efforts against the Vietnam War meant the FBI continued to spy on her for many more years, fearing she would "tie the anti-Vietnam movement to the civil rights movement." [158]

For some people, King's assassination broke open a dam of hopelessness.[159] But Coretta Scott King, Ralph Abernathy, and scores of activists around the country were determined that the Poor People's Campaign would continue. On April 29, one hundred community leaders presented their demands to government officials in DC. Then, on May 1, Coretta stepped out onto the balcony in Memphis where Martin had been shot and launched the Southern caravan of the PPC. She sang one of his favorite spirituals, "Sweet Little Jesus Boy, They Didn't Know Who You Was," and declared her own dream "where not some but all of God's children have food, where not some but all of God's children have decent housing, where not some but all of God's children have a guaranteed annual income in keeping with the principles of liberty and grace." [160]

Nine caravans of poor people of all races began making their way across the country. By bus, train, car, and mule train they traveled to DC. The most visible Black caravan—the Mule Train—with a hundred people and seventeen mule-drawn wagons, started out from Marks, Mississippi, the poorest county in the country, where King's idea for the PPC had begun two years earlier.[161] Two buses of poor white people came from Appalachia while caravans of Latinos and Native Americans journeyed thousands of miles to the nation's capital. A combination of local, state, and FBI officials kept the Mule Train under constant surveillance as it traveled the thousand miles to DC, and informants were planted in many of the delegations.[162]

Organizers broke ground on a tent city of plywood shanties on the National Mall named Resurrection City on May 12. Commandeering a bunch of teenage boys to build "a hundred and some houses," James Orange served as the "sheriff" of Resurrection City. About 2,500 people stayed there. Unprecedented heavy rain (seven and a half inches across the encampment) made the conditions of the tent city hazardous, the mud capturing media attention more than the issues.[163]

Members of the Blackstone Rangers and Egyptian Cobras made the trip to DC to take part in Resurrection City. An encampment of Chicanos led by Rodolfo Gonzales and Reies Tijerina set up at the Hawthorne School, and many Native Americans congregated at a nearby church. They held a Puerto Rican Day celebration on June 15, four thousand strong.[164] Johnnie Tillmon and the NWRO played a huge role. The PPC's vision promoted both interracial organizing and intraracial strength.

At the Mother's Day march with welfare recipients that Martin had endorsed before his death, Coretta Scott King criticized the hypocrisy of a society "where violence against poor people and minority groups is routine." She reminded the nation of its violence: "Neglecting school children is violence. Punishing a mother and her family is violence. . . . Ignoring medical needs is violence. Contempt for poverty is violence. Even the lack of will power to help humanity is a sick and sinister form of violence." [165] Marian Wright toggled between Resurrection City and Congress, trying to turn their demands into policies that various federal agencies the PPC visited would get behind. "I never understood then and I don't understand now why it was so hard to get hungry people fed in rich America and why the needs of poor children were always superseded by politics," she lamented.[166]

The high point of the PPC came on June 19, Solidarity Day. More than fifty thousand people gathered to hear Coretta Scott King, Ralph Abernathy, Rosa Parks, Gilberto Gerena Valentin, and others address the crowd. Scott King called for the transfer of funds from "the most cruel and evil war in history" to an effective war on poverty.[167] "The sickness of racism, the despair of poverty and the hopelessness of war have served to deepen the hatred, heighten the bitterness, increase the frustration and further alienate the poor in our society." She warned that the PPC might be "the last opportunity to save the nation and the world from destruction." [168]

Despite its well-defined demands for full employment, a guaranteed annual income, and construction of more affordable housing, the Poor People's Campaign was criticized by many congressmen and the media as needing "clarity." [169] The coverage of the PPC was skeptical and condescending. On July 7, 1968, the *New York Times* snidely observed that Resurrection City "had not looked much like a resurrection or a city." [170] As Jesse Jackson observed, "the press examined minutely the behavior of poor people and ignored the collective behavior of Congress." But serious coverage of the PPC, according to Mule Train photographer Roland Freeman, would have required acknowledging the role the media and public officials played in dismissing the urgent needs it highlighted. [171]

Resurrection City was torn down by police on June 24. While not succeeding in getting Congress to act, it made poverty visible and spurred more local organizing and a sense of possibility for the many Black, Latino, Native American, and white people who came. Many would go back to fight more strongly at home. "In Resurrection City," Jesse Jackson explained, "the poor whites began to see how they had been used as tools of the economic system to keep other minority groups in check . . . wallowing together in the mud of Resurrection City [allowed us] to hear, to feel and to see each other for the first time in our experience." [172]

The PPC altered local relations, as well. Bertha Johnson of Marks, Mississippi, explained that afterward, public officials were "very nice to me," afraid she might "call the SCLC." Programs addressing hunger—with free school lunch, nationwide nutrition for mothers, and food stamps—greatly expanded in the 1970s. Marian Wright Edelman explained that "the Poor People's Campaign now in retrospect played an enormously important role in making all of that happen." [173] Growing Native American militancy blossomed in the coming years—including a protest at the Bureau of Indian Affairs.

An expanded welfare rights movement continued to grow in the wake of the PPC, as did the movement for an annual basic income. Scott King stepped up to meet the challenge. She supported a bevy of other movements from various union strikes to the 1972 Gary Convention to a growing anti-apartheid movement to gay rights. She came to see, as Martin had, how important and cherished showing up for movements people were building across the country was. And show up she did. As she pressed forward over the next four decades, "the news media would tag me as 'Martin's widow.' . . . [S]ometimes I wondered how and when people would look beyond the name and see me as a woman of substance and commitment, working for the Cause each day of her life." [174]

For many who made the journey—Black, Latino, Native American, Asian American, and white—the PPC furthered a sense of political possibility and self-determination. From a powerful hospital workers' 112-day strike in Charleston, South Carolina, to the more militant welfare organizing of the 1970s to the transformation of Black political power in Mississippi, the sense of poor people's power took shape. In Mississippi a week before he was assassinated, outraged by the deep poverty people were forced to live in, Martin Luther King exhorted, "God does not want you to live like you are living." [175] They were entitled to demand their rights to sufficient food, decent housing, education, and health care.

A sense of their own power had developed as a result. As King had explained to convince SCLC staff of the PPC's importance, "In dangerous moments people begin holding hands that didn't know they could hold them." [176]

Epilogue

Be Careful What You Wish For: The Willful Ignoring of Dr. King's Challenge to Northern Racism

If our most dedicated ancestors
could look us alive in the eye right now
what kinds of apologies would we make
for invoking their names posthumously.

—Darius Simpson

King delighted in the spirit and determination of young people in Chicago and across the country.

Reckoning with King's lifelong critique of American structural racism—how he insisted that white liberal politicians, Northern residents, social scientists, and journalists be held to account—is sobering. With his eloquent preacher voice and nice suits, King decried

Northern racism and supported Northern movements for a dozen years. At times, Northern officials gave him awards, welcomed him to their podiums, and condemned the South. But they largely did not listen, let alone act, when he challenged their own segregation, demonizing him and the movements he supported locally. Recognizing King's lifelong critique of Northern liberalism contextualizes the bleakness and boldness of his tone in the last years of his life. Over and over, he had raised his voice on the structural racism endemic across the country, pursued disruptive nonviolent direct action alongside organized Northern Black communities across the country, and called on white liberals and the nation to walk the talk in their own cities. And over and over, most Northerners and the nation's leaders had sidestepped those calls or criticized him for it, smug in a sense of their own goodness.

It is easier to tell a history that King focused on the South. It is easier to think that injustice highlighted by a noble movement with an eloquent spokesman is injustice corrected in the United States. It is easier to frame Northern Black communities as angry and alienated rather than reckon with the myriad nonviolent movements and community institutions they built. It is easier to think that King was naïve or didn't have clear targets, that Northern young people refused organized nonviolent movements, or that Northern racism was more complicated—than it is to reckon with the extent many Americans went to protect and preserve American apartheid. It is easier to claim to love King than to listen to him.

The reality is far more complicated. As Harry Belafonte and Stanley Levison eulogized, "In the luminescent glare of the open streets he gave a lesson to the nation revealing who was the oppressed and who was the oppressor."[1] During his own lifetime, King was embraced and simultaneously rejected by many white politicians, journalists, and citizens who were proud to sit next to him, bring him to their cities or religious organizations, and at times decry Southern racism. But by and large, many had little interest in acting when he highlighted the similar systemic problems in their own cities—school segregation, housing segregation, police brutality, job discrimination—and rejected movements there. The mainstream media that covered his work more seriously and fulsomely in the South largely ignored, distorted, and demonized movements and King's work across the North.

But Martin Luther King and his political partner Coretta Scott King persisted, joining with movements challenging "the plank in their own eye," as the scripture called it, and calling out Northern hypocrisy. He listened, and that listening meant that his ideas deepened and that he loved and was cherished by a large swath of Black people, South and North, young and old, even many who didn't always agree with his nonviolence. Those Northern activists and Martin and Coretta themselves had immense freedom dreams and concrete plans to address America's slums and structures of racism, poverty, and militarism.

The problems we face today—segregated schools, police brutality, and rampant injustice in the criminal legal system, environmental racism, unequal city services, lack of decent, affordable housing, poverty wages—were issues for which many people, including Dr. King, had tangible solutions. What if the 1964 Civil Rights Act had actually been enforced against Northern school districts and their money had been taken until they desegregated their schools, addressed overcrowding and decrepit facilities, and changed teacher hiring? What if the media had covered Northern massive resistance—Proposition 14 proponents or white antibusing moms in Brooklyn—like massive resistance in the South? What if growing movements against police brutality in the early 1960s well before the uprisings had been taken seriously, leading to structural changes in policing and civilian oversight, instead of more policing, further weaponization, and new "tactical" units? What if a robust 1966 Civil Rights Act had passed in 1966, forcing Daley and white Chicagoans and New York City, Los Angeles, and other cities to implement policies that addressed unequal housing and the Black freedom struggle had scored another win with an alive King?

Well, then, we would be living in a very different United States today.

King insisted the United States needed to be honest about its history—that Black migrants to the North in the twentieth century found a new "Egypt." Long after the end of slavery, white people gained benefits of land, home loans, more resourced primary education, access to college, and neighborhoods with well-kept sanitation, parks, and municipal services. These created the floor for white success—but were benefits Black people largely couldn't access in the South *or* in the North. In other words, the inequality we live with today is modern, sanctioned, and reinforced, not simply a relic from a bygone time—and not so complicated that it is beyond state remedy.

During our own lifetime, this side of King has been hidden in plain sight. He is America's Black friend—held up and mythologized to punish activists who push too hard against the status quo—the "ultimate gaslight," students say, to today's activists. Our textbooks mark the success of Birmingham in 1963 and ignore the fierce school desegregation movements in Boston, Detroit, Chicago, and Los Angeles. They highlight the Watts uprising but not the myriad movements in LA before it. The March on Washington is pictured as a shining example of the power of American democracy and not also the inauguration of relentless FBI surveillance of Martin Luther King. Northern liberal politicians, journalists, and white citizens are seen as pivotal actors for racial transformation in the South—and not also crucial players preventing change in the North.

Reckoning with this side of King is urgent, particularly because this mis-history of the civil rights movement is regularly weaponized against contemporary movements. Be more like King, they tell young activists, when King was treated as "unreasonable," accused of "inciting violence," relentlessly policed, and harangued by the media and more moderate Black leaders. Be more like King, they tell young activists, when perhaps the greatest gift of his leadership was his embodied belief in the power of each person's action. Convinced that the systems of injustice before us did not have to stand, he insisted that we are enough to step forward and that what some cast as unimaginable could become possible.

Be careful what you wish for. Dr. King called out Northern hypocrisy in praising the movement in the South and decrying Black activism at home. He highlighted structural racism endemic across the country and denounced the pattern of police brutality and the ways it was countenanced by Northerners and the federal government, despite ongoing Black protests. He chastised allies more devoted to order than to justice, stressing that if "our direct action tactics alienate our friends, they never were really our friends." He rejected personal responsibility as a public philosophy, saw the leadership potential of criminalized gang members, and challenged Black faces in high places beholden to white power. He was committed to building real Black political power and the power of poor people to get the nation to respond.

Be careful what you wish for. He continued to speak truth to power to Northern mayors, public officials, and President Johnson himself, saying you can't consider yourself a friend of civil rights and not do what is necessary here. Resisting calls to be more pragmatic and less aggressive, he critiqued public officials, scholars, local citizens, and journalists who loved to focus on "Black crime" and "cultural pathology" rather than on state policies that produced segregation, slums, and police abuse. He saw that liberalism too often turned into a comfortable pose, rather than an on-the-ground commitment.

Like many activists today, he insisted that disruption and direct action were necessary to expose the urgency of injustice, that you don't blame the doctor for pointing out the cancer. He saw the power of young people's courage to pull adults into the struggle. He was resolute and steadfast, outraged and impatient, and deeply moved by people's suffering. He lambasted those who asked why Black people were so angry. Black people had the right and reasons to be angry. Why weren't they angry too?

Be careful what you wish for. When we tell young people to be more like King, this country needs to be honest about what being like Dr. King truly entails and the comprehensive measures he challenged the nation to undertake.

Acknowledgments

I come to this book from many places. I am the granddaughter of a family who fled the Armenian genocide, understanding the ways that history lives and is denied for powerful, political reasons. I am the daughter of a proudly determined Greek father who was a dogged historian of the FBI's abuses and an equally fierce Armenian mother who was a lifelong Christian left activist. I am the sister of a deeply thoughtful feminist educator George and an indefatigable Poor People's Campaign cochair Rev. Liz. I am the colleague and comrade of a community of scholars-activists who have worked to change the ways we understand the Black freedom struggle, insisted this history is essential for understanding the US we live in today, and pressed for racial justice and human rights from the policing to Palestine. I have brought all these sensibilities to this book: critical historian, activist, African American studies scholar, teacher, researcher, and Christian liberationist.

I was lucky in college to take a course on the civil rights movement with Julian Bond. Professor Bond proved to be a lifelong friend and mentor. But one of the first lessons he imparted to me was that there was *always* more to learn. Even as a crucial player in many of the movements we were studying, he kept reading and learning because there was context, vantage points, and perspectives he couldn't see or hadn't understood at the time. Julian died before I began this book, but I hope it honors that spirit. His teaching and activism infuse these pages.

So many Black freedom struggle activists have supported and encouraged me and my work: Doris Crenshaw, Judy Richardson, Zoharah Simmons, Barbara Smith, Komozi Woodard, Pam Horowitz, Ericka Huggins, Dorothy and Dan Aldridge, Mary Frances Berry, LeRoy Henderson, Gloria Richardson, John Bracey, and General Baker. I am blessed by their support and inspired by their example.

It is one of my life's greatest fortunes to teach Brooklyn College students. They are my first and last audience and continually renew my hope in a more just future where we learn together, tender with each other's dreams, and are fierce about history and social justice. When my confidence has waned, they have given me pep talks, underlining the transformative power of knowing this history. In particular, this book is immeasurably better because of my research assistants: Gabrielle White, David Rondeau, Tyra Smart, Matthew Mort, and Jessica Louis. They helped me investigate the ways the media covered Martin Luther King Jr. and Coretta Scott King—and this book is so much better for their insights, outrage, and careful readings.

This book would not be possible without all the people who have supported me over the past decade as I figured out new ways to bring Rosa Parks's history to the public and pushed back on the misuses of the civil rights movement in contemporary politics. Gayatri Patnaik, Say Burgin, Deborah Menkart, Jesse Hagopian, Johanna Hamilton, Yoruba Richen, Stephanie Melnick, Alex Marchevsky, Christalyn Hampton, Soledad O'Brien, Okhela Bazile-Charles, Marwa Amer, Bennett Ashley, Melissa Harris-Perry, LisaGay Hamilton, Robin Kelley, Bryan Stevenson, Jessica Rucker, Tiffany Patterson, Bill Bigelow, Ursula Wolfe-Rocca, Jessica Murray, William Barber, Joanna Green, Keisha Blain, and Amos Kennedy have helped me change and expand the ways this country now understands Rosa Parks and the movement.

Many people read portions of this book and offered helpful feedback, conversation, and insight. Most are scholars of the Black freedom struggle themselves, and I was blessed with this community of knowledge surrounding *King of the North*. I am so grateful to Erik Wallenberg, Jonathan Eig, Lerone Martin, Tenisha Hart Armstrong, Matt Delmont, Say Burgin, Robin Kelley, Arun Kundnani, Traci Parker, Aviva Stahl, Barbara Smith, Thomas Jackson, Noliwe Rooks, Ansley Erickson, Elizabeth Todd-Breland, LaShawn Harris, D'Weston Haywood, Aram Goudsouzian, Brian Purnell, Dolly Chugh, Todd Moye, Michael Ezra, Joseph Entin, Mary Frances Berry, Francis Gourrier, David Lucander, Nishani Frazier, Dominique Jean-Louis, Dayo Gore, Simon Balto, Alex Marchevsky, Arnold Franklin, Gaston Alonso, Tanya McKinnon, Karen Miller, Shailly Barnes, Evan Rothman, Dominick Braswell, Karin Stanford, Sammy Chomsky, Patrick Parr, Laura Rovner, and Sam Theoharis. Their ideas and work inspire me—and this book is markedly better for their thoughtful feedback, suggestions for sources, and tremendous enthusiasm. Komozi Woodard, Carl Hart, Mark Speltz, Patrick Duff, Jamon Jordan, Andrew Kahrl, Tom Sugrue, Margaret Burnham, Clarence Taylor, Peniel Joseph, Barbara Reynolds, David Garrow, David Stein, Tahir Butt, Colleen Wessel-McCoy,

Zebulon Miletsky, Dorothy Tillman, Lynn Adler, Hermene Hartman, Bob Artinian, and Ella Theoharis also provided assistance and encouragement.

More than twenty years ago, Komozi Woodard and I began a partnership to bring the history of the Northern Black freedom struggle out of the historical margins; it has been tremendous to watch this field grow. This book simply wouldn't exist without those two decades of collaboration, conversation, and friendship. Brian Purnell has been a friend and intellectual companion for more than fifteen years as we've plumbed the history of the Jim Crow North—these pages reflect countless discussions, laughter, and research. Jonathan Eig shared sources and insights, as we analyzed many aspects of Dr. King's life. Arun Kundnani, Lerone Martin, and Tenisha Hart Armstrong shared my joy and wonder at many junctures of this King research—providing key assistance, crucial sources, and tremendous encouragement that this history was urgent for our understandings of King and this country today. Matt Delmont shared his research on Coretta Scott King and has been one of my favorite thought partners for a decade on Northern history. Traci Parker helped me think through Coretta Scott King's story. Brandon Proia loved this book's many interventions and its importance for a new generation and helped me craft a better narrative. Say Burgin buoyed my spirits and puzzled through so many aspects of this history with me. Erik Wallenberg has been with me since well before the inception of this project, researching and imagining with me how to show the King of the North. That I have been able to tell this story is in good measure because of Erik's efforts and vision.

I am grateful to a number of editors—Olivia Waxman, Jen Parker, J. T. Roane, and Carly Goodman—who helped me develop early arguments of this book into op-eds. I am blessed to be part of a group of scholar-activists, who treat the work as collective, pursue justice, and see this history as urgent to understanding the way forward. My CUNY community has encouraged my work and inspired me with theirs: Gaston Alonso, Evan Rothman, Irene Sosa, Prudence Cumberbatch, Lawrence Johnson, Rhea Rahman, Dominick Braswell, Kris Burrell, Celina Su, Caroline Arnold, Jeffrey Severe, Daryl Barney, Mary Phillips, Karen Miller, Lucien Baskin, Naomi Braine, Naomi Schiller, Dominick Braswell, and Vikki Law. Joseph Entin and Alan Aja are tremendous colleagues, comrades, and co-conspirators.

My friends Karen Miller, Pardiss Kebriaei, Shane Kadidal, LaShawn Harris, Dayo Gore, Jennifer Bernstein, Aliyah Dunn-Salahuddin,

Robyn Spencer, Ansley Erickson, Brian Jones, Faisal Hashmi, Brenda Cardenas, Amy Jones, Melissa Madzel, Chitra Aiyar, and Deborah Menkart have shared my political and intellectual commitments, fought for justice alongside me, and supported me for years. Aviva Stahl and Say Burgin have held me up along this journey.

Marc Favreau loved this book from the very first moment—understanding the urgency of the King of the North for today and being creative and committed in ensuring my efforts to tell this history. Tanya McKinnon saw the necessity of having a feminist biographer of King and underlined for me the centrality of the media narrative. I am grateful to The New Press for their tremendous care, vision, and effort to bring this book to life. Special thanks to managing editor Maury Botton for shepherding the book through production, Sam Theoharis for designing the beautiful timeline, Vikki Law for her careful review of the proofs, Jibola Fagbamiye for the amazing cover design, and copyeditor Tom Pitoniak for his eagle eye and excellent queries.

I could not do what I do without my family: Luke, Sophia, Ella, Sam, Emilio, Gabriela, Gretchen, Chris, Julie, Ellen, Jason, Auntie Sue, Stephanie, Arnold, Alex, George, and Liz. Stephanie Melnick has been my friend all my life. Arnold Franklin has walked beside me for decades. Alex Marchevsky is a friend of my mind.

I began this book in earnest, without realizing it, in the early-morning hours of the first months of the pandemic. I had been collecting material for years and, annoyed at how there wasn't anything good to teach on King outside the South, decided to use this unforeseen time to write an article. I then realized how much bigger and more urgent this story was. We lost both of our parents in those first years. George and Liz have sustained me in so many ways—with ice cream and jokes, carrying on, political outrage, encouragement, and so much care. This book is dedicated to them.

List of Abbreviations Used

AJC: *Atlanta Journal-Constitution*
AN: *Amsterdam News*
BG: *Boston Globe*
BS: *Baltimore Sun*
BSB: *Bay State Banner*
CD: *Chicago Defender*
CE: *California Eagle*
CRDP: Interviews done for the Civil Rights Documentation
    Project, housed and digitalized by Moorland Spingarn
    Research Center, Howard University
CSK: Coretta Scott King (as author/speaker)
CST: *Chicago Sun-Times*
CT: *Chicago Tribune*
DFP: *Detroit Free Press*
Eyes I: Interviews done for *Eyes on the Prize*, Blackside
    Productions, housed and digitalized at Washington University
Eyes II: Interviews done for *Eyes on the Prize II*, Blackside
    Productions, housed and digitalized at Washington University
Hatch: Alden and Allene G. Hatch Papers, University of Florida
LAS: *Los Angeles Sentinel*
LAT: *Los Angeles Times*
MLK: Martin Luther King Jr. (as author/speaker)
MLKPP: Martin Luther King Papers Project, Stanford University
MLMLML: CSK, *My Life, My Love, My Legacy,* as told to Barbara
    Reynolds (New York: Henry Holt and Company, 2017)
NVLP: National Visionary Leadership Project, 2002, on file at
    American Folklife Center, Library of Congress
NYT: *New York Times*
PC: *Pittsburgh Courier*
PI: *Philadelphia Inquirer*
SOHP: Southern Oral History Program digitalized interviews
WP: *Washington Post*

Notes

Preface

1 "King Gives Progress Formula," *LAS*, June 21, 1962.

2 "Kingly Tribute," *LAS*, May 30, 1963.

3 MLK, "Beyond the Los Angeles Riots," *Saturday Review*, November 13, 1965.

4 This arc is evidenced in Taylor Branch's series: *Parting the Waters: America in the King Years, 1954–1963* (New York: Simon & Schuster, 1989), *Pillar of Fire: America in the King Years, 1963–1965* (New York: Simon & Schuster, 1999), and *At Canaan's Edge: America in the King Years, 1965–1968* (New York: Simon & Schuster, 2007); Stephen Oates, *Let the Trumpet Sound: A Life of Martin Luther King, Jr.* (New York: Harper, 1982); David Levering Lewis, *King: A Biography* (Urbana: University of Illinois Press, 1970); James Cone, *Martin and Malcolm and America* (New York: Orbis, 1991); Clayborne Carson, ed., *The Autobiography of Martin Luther King, Jr.* (New York: Warner Books, 2001); Thomas F. Jackson, *From Civil Rights to Human Rights: Martin Luther King Jr. and the Struggle for Economic Justice* (Philadelphia: University of Pennsylvania Press, 2007); Harvard Sitkoff, *King: Pilgrimage to the Mountaintop* (New York: Hill and Wang, 2009); Michael Eric Dyson, *I May Not Get There with You: The True Martin Luther King* (New York: Free Press, 2001); Cornel West, ed., *The Radical King* (Boston: Beacon Press, 2016); Peniel Joseph, *The Sword and the Shield: The Revolutionary Lives of Malcolm X and Martin Luther King* (New York: Basic Books, 2020); Tommie Shelby and Brandon Terry, *To Shape a New World: Essays on the Political Philosophy of Martin Luther King, Jr.* (Cambridge, MA: Harvard University Press, 2020); and Jonathan Eig, *King: A Life* (New York: Farrar, Straus and Giroux, 2023). Peniel Joseph argues that "Watts transformed King" and that King's experience in Chicago "gave proof of Malcolm X's characterization of racism as a national illness not quarantined in the South"—even though King himself had explicitly characterized it this way seven years earlier (246, 263). In *To Shape a New World*, Tommie Shelby and Brandon Terry list a range of issues animating King's political philosophy: "labor and welfare rights, economic inequality, poverty, love, just war theory, virtue ethics, political theology, violence, imperialism, nationalism, reparations, and social justice not to mention his more familiar writings on citizenship, racial equality, voting rights, civil disobedience and nonviolence." Northern racism and the limits of Northern liberalism didn't even make the list (187). Jonathan Eig notes that King "wasn't coming north because he'd suddenly discovered the issues of

urban poverty, police brutality, and slum housing," but the book's previous thirty-six chapters obscure that work. Eig claims that King's plan to attack the slums in Chicago was as "lacking in detail" as Daley's. Eig, *King*, 454–55, 478. Cornel West regularly castigates the Santa Clausification of King but includes nothing on King's long-standing critique of Northern racism and Northern liberalism in his introduction to *The Radical King*. Michael Dyson claims King's loss of faith in American liberalism begins "after defeat" in Chicago (84) while Sitkoff claims that King moved to Chicago in 1966 and *then* met with the CCCO, didn't anticipate white backlash to the white riots, and King's "rhetoric fell on deaf ears" in the Black community (177–186). Branch too dramatically undertells the Chicago movement in his 1,039-page study of 1965–1968 (*At Canaan's Edge*), then pronouncing "Chicago nationalized race, complementing the impact of Watts. Without it, King would be confined to posterity more as a regional figure" (523).

5 See Brandon M. Terry et al., eds., *Fifty Years Since MLK, Boston Review Forum* (2015); Michael Honey, *Going Down Jericho Road: The Memphis Strike, Martin Luther King's Last Campaign* (New York: Norton, 2008); Michael Honey, *To the Promised Land: Martin Luther King and the Fight for Economic Justice* (New York: Norton, 2019); Andrew Douglas and Jared Loggins, *Prophet of Discontent: Martin Luther King Jr. and the Critique of American Capitalism* (Athens: University of Georgia Press, 2021); James Ralph, Jr., *Northern Protest: Martin Luther King, Jr., Chicago and the Civil Rights Movement* (Cambridge: Harvard University Press, 1993); Sylvie Laurent, *King and the Other America: The Poor People's Campaign and the Quest for Economic Equality* (Berkeley: University of California Press, 2019); Robert Hamilton, *Dr. Martin Luther King Jr. and the Poor People's Campaign of 1968* (Athens: University of Georgia Press, 2020); Mary Finley et al., *The Chicago Freedom Movement: Martin Luther King Jr. and Civil Rights Activism in the North* (Lexington: University of Kentucky Press, 2016); and Thomas Sugrue, *Sweet Land of Liberty: The Forgotten Struggle for Civil Rights in the North* (New York: Random House, 2008).

6 MLK, Great Walk for Freedom speech, June 23, 1963.

7 "King Gives Progress Formula," *LAS*, June 21, 1962; "So They Say," *CST*, June 25, 1963.

8 See Brian Purnell and Jeanne Theoharis, "Introduction," *The Strange Careers of the Jim Crow North: Segregation and Struggle Outside of the South* (New York: New York University Press, 2019); Mary Dudziak, *Cold War Civil Rights: Race and the Image of American Democracy* (Princeton, NJ: Princeton University Press, 2000).

9 www.nobelprize.org/prizes/peace/1964/king/biographical/.

10 Vincent Harding, *Martin Luther King: The Inconvenient Hero* (New York: Orbis Books, 2008), 32.

11 Like Matthew Delmont's Black Quotidien project, which led to *Half American: The Epic Story of African Americans Fighting World War II at Home and Abroad* (New York: Penguin, 2022), looking at King through the eyes of

the Black press provides a markedly different window onto this period of American history and civil rights struggle.

12 *A More Beautiful and Terrible History: The Uses and Misuses of Civil Rights History* (Boston: Beacon Press, 2018); Eig, *King*; West, ed., *The Radical King*; Shelby and Terry, *To Shape a New World*; Joseph, *The Sword and the Shield*; Hajar Yazdiha, *The Struggle for the People's King: How Politics Transforms the Memory of the Civil Rights Movement* (Princeton, NJ: Princeton University Press, 2023).

13 "The New Coretta Scott King: Emerging from the Legacy," *WP*, January 15, 1978.

14 Henry Hampton, *Voices of Freedom: An Oral History of the Civil Rights Movement* (New York: Bantam, 1991), 470.

15 MLK, *Strength to Love* (New York: Harper & Brothers, 1963), 14.

16 See David Halberstam, "The Second Coming of Martin Luther King," *Harpers* 235 (August 1967); Anthony Lewis, "Since the Supreme Court Spoke," news analysis, *NYT*, May 10, 1964.

17 Les Payne and Tamara Payne, *The Dead Are Rising: The Life of Malcolm X* (New York: Liveright, 2020), 393.

18 Fred Carroll, *Race News: Black Journalists and the Fight for Racial Justice in the Twentieth Century* (Urbana: University of Illinois Press, 2017), 186.

19 See Zaheer Ali, Manning Marable, Les and Tamara Payne; Charles Payne, *I've Got the Light of Freedom: The Organizing Tradition and the Black Freedom Struggle* (Berkeley: University of California Press, 1995), 413.

20 MLK, *Where Do We Go from Here: Chaos or Community?* (Boston: Beacon Press, 1968), 3. King used the term *riot*, while many of his fellow radicals used *uprising* or *rebellion*. He occasionally employed the phrase "culture of poverty" while highlighting the structural racism in the North. This language might have made it easier to ignore what King was *actually* saying, that structural causes and policy were responsible.

21 CSK, *My Life with Martin*, 253.

22 Carroll, *Race News*, 168.

23 Important biographies by Eig, Joseph, Jackson, Garrow, Branch, Lewis, and Oates still overlook King's long-standing Northern attention and critique of Northern liberalism before 1965. Cone and Joseph detail the growing commonalties between King and Malcolm yet miss many of the campaigns both supported in Los Angeles and New York, their shared early critiques of Northern liberalism in the 1950s and early 1960s, and their anticolonial politics that began for both in the 1950s.

24 One of the most profound treatments of the Black freedom struggle, *Eyes on the Prize* furthered the misimpression that the movement from 1954 to 1965 was basically in the South. Because people criticized the first series' omissions, *Eyes on the Prize II* turned northward post-1965 to Malcolm X, Black Power, and King's last radical years. But it still largely missed the movements of the early 1960s in Chicago, Boston, Los Angeles, Detroit—making it seem like the uprisings came out of alienated Northern communities rather than cities with long-standing movements. Even so, Blackside

had much more trouble funding *Eyes on the Prize II*, particularly "The Promised Land" episode on King's last year.

25 This book takes as a model Thomas Jackson's *From Civil Rights to Human Rights*, which argues that King's economic analysis begins in the 1950s; King's attention to Northern inequality and challenge to Northern liberals begins there as well.

26 King's SCLC advisors did not consistently accompany him on these trips, so that has impacted many biographies.

27 Brandon Terry begins to challenge this in *To Shape a New World*.

28 "Martin as I Knew Him," *Michigan Chronicle*, January 17, 1987.

29 Harry Belafonte, *My Song* (New York: Knopf, 2011), 326–28.

30 MLK, interview by David Susskind, *Open End*, June 9, 1963.

31 Kenneth Clark, *King, Malcolm, Baldwin: Three Interviews by Kenneth Clark* (Middletown, CT: Wesleyan University Press, 1985), 39–40; MLK, *The Last Interview* (Brooklyn: Melville House, 2017), 50–51.

32 CSK interview, 2004, www.huffpost.com/entry/qa-with-the-late-cor etta_b_94899.

33 CSK, "Thoughts and Reflections," in *We Shall Overcome: Martin Luther King Jr., and the Black Freedom Struggle*, edited by Peter J. Albert and Ronald Hoffman (New York: Pantheon, 1990), 255. The conference included Clayborne Carson, John Hope Franklin, Cornel West, Aldon Morris, and David Garrow, among others.

34 Zoharah Simmons, "Martin Luther King Jr. Revisited," *Journal of Feminist Studies in Religion*, 2008.

35 This book follows the lead of Eric McDuffie and Komozi Woodard's revisionary treatment of Malcolm X and the women who shaped him: " 'If You're in a Country That's Progressive, the Woman Is Progressive': Black Women Radicals and the Making of the Politics and Legacy of Malcolm X," *Biography* 36:3.

36 Robin Kelley, *Freedom Dreams* (Boston: Beacon, 2002).

37 MLK, "A Time to Break the Silence," April 4, 1967.

38 MLK Papers, vol. 4, 2000, 222.

39 *Playboy* interview with MLK; *A Testament of Hope: The Essential Writings and Speeches of Martin Luther King, Jr.*, edited by James Washington (New York: Harper Collins, 1991), 348.

40 "Malcolm X Speaks Out on the NYC School Boycott," March 16, 1964, Peabody Awards Collection, Digital Library of Georgia.

41 Elizabeth Gillespie McRae, *Mothers of Massive Resistance* (New York: Oxford University Press, 2019).

42 See Frederick Harris, *The Price of the Ticket: Barack Obama and the Rise and Decline of Black Politics* (New York: Oxford University Press, 2012), for this useful formulation. Thomas Jackson argues Bayard Rustin was pivotal in shaping King's thinking on this.

43 Martin Luther King speaking at City Temple in London, December 7, 1964, at www.democracynow.org/2015/1/19/exclusive_newly _discovered_1964_mlk_speech.

44 MLK, "Why We Are in Chicago," *AN*, March 12, 1966.
45 MLK, Centennial of W. E. B. Du Bois, February 23, 1968, www.peoplesworld
     .org/article/dr-martin-luther-king-on-the-legacy-of-w-e-b-du-bois/.
46 Jenny Jarvie, "An Uneasy Standoff Between Police and Protesters as Black
     Lives Matter Returns to the Streets," *LAT*, July 9, 2016; Barbara Reynolds,
     "I Was a Civil Rights Activist," *WP*, August 24, 2015.
47 Gene Roberts and Hank Klibanoff's Pulitzer Prize–winning *The Race Beat:
     The Press, the Civil Rights Struggle, and the Awakening of a Nation* (New York:
     Knopf, 2006) furthered this hagiographic treatment of the media as he-
     roic accomplices in the civil rights movement. In the avalanche of praise
     for *The Race Beat*, few reviewers noticed the authors hadn't analyzed the
     ways the press covered Northern struggles. In a June 18, 2013, NPR inter-
     view, Klibanoff explained the Southern media's reluctance to cover Black
     protest: "Most news reporters at the time would not have had in their
     Rolodexes or address books the names of any African-Americans in town.
     They wouldn't know who to call, by and large. . . . There's no sense of 'let's
     live the lives of our readers.'" But this exact point could be made about
     the *New York Times* or the *Los Angeles Times* regarding Black life in their
     own cities. www.npr.org/sections/codeswitch/2013/06/18/193128475/how
     -the-civil-rights-movement-was-covered-in-birmingham.
48 Scholars of the Black press have thoughtfully examined the Southern
     movement but largely overlooked the Black press's coverage of King's
     work in the North. D'Weston Haywood, *Let Us Make Men: The Twenti-
     eth Century Black Press and a Manly Vision for Racial Advancement* (Chapel
     Hill: University of North Carolina Press, 2018); Kathy Roberts and Sid
     Bedingfeld, *Journalism and Jim Crow* (Urbana: University of Illinois Press,
     2021), 308; Carroll, *Race News*.
49 Barbara Reynolds, "The Biggest Problem with 'Selma' Has Nothing to
     Do with LBJ or the Oscars," *WP*, January 19, 2015.
50 "October 7, 1968 letter to Alden," Box 22, Folder 2, Hatch.
51 Mayerson described Coretta's "certain cold bloodedness in her attitude
     towards whites. . . . I questioned her about the death of Goodman and
     Schwerner . . . though she is sad that they died she felt that it was an im-
     portant event because it made the white community more aware of the
     problems than any number of Negro deaths would have done." Playing
     on race and gender stereotypes, Hatch told Mayerson that he "deliberately
     wrote it with very simple language that I believe would have a special ap-
     peal for the critics" and, when Coretta and Edythe objected to the book's
     tone, told Mayerson to call in the "big reserves" to intimidate Coretta to
     acquiesce. "March 2, 1969 Letter to Charlotte," Box 22, Folder 2, Hatch.
52 See, for instance, https://storymaps.arcgis.com/collections/2400b1aa1bb
     e44dea03539534d68dd2d?item=2.
53 For instance, three weeks before his assassination, King came to the elite
     suburb of Grosse Pointe, Michigan; forty years later, Grosse Pointers
     were invested in preserving that history. Similarly, his 1964 visit in San
     Diego, his 1967 APA address, and many more.

54 See the oral histories of Black LA at UCLA, the interviews done for the '63 *Boycott* documentary, Ruth Batson's papers at Radcliffe, and many others.

55 Such works on the North include Thomas Sugrue, *The Origins of the Urban Crisis: Race and Inequality in Postwar Detroit* (Princeton, NJ: Princeton University Press, 1996); Brian Purnell, *Fighting Jim Crow in the County of Kings: The Congress of Racial Equality in Brooklyn* (Lexington: University Press of Kentucky, 2013); Martha Biondi, *To Stand and Fight: The Struggle for Civil Rights in Postwar New York City* (Cambridge, MA: Harvard University Press, 2003); Matthew Delmont, *Why Busing Failed: Race, Media, and the National Resistance to School Desegregation* (Berkeley: University of California Press, 2016); Mark Speltz, *North of Dixie: Civil Rights Photography Beyond the South* (Los Angeles: J. Paul Getty Museum, 2016); Clarence Taylor, *Knocking at Our Own Door: Milton A. Galamison and the Fight for School Integration in New York City* (New York: Columbia University Press, 1997); Komozi Woodard, *A Nation Within a Nation: Amiri Baraka (LeRoi Jones) and Black Power Politics* (Chapel Hill: University of North Carolina Press, 1999); Jeanne Theoharis and Komozi Woodard, eds., *Freedom North: Black Freedom Struggles Outside the South, 1940–1980* (New York: Palgrave Macmillan, 2003); Patrick Jones, *The Selma of the North: The Civil Rights Insurgency in Milwaukee* (Cambridge, MA: Harvard University Press, 2009); Josh Sides, *LA City Limits: African American Los Angeles from the Great Depression to the Present* (Berkeley: University of California Press, 2003); Matthew Countryman, *Up South: Civil Rights and Black Power in Philadelphia* (Philadelphia: University of Pennsylvania Press, 2006); Angela Dillard, *Faith in the City: Preaching Radical Social Change in Detroit* (Ann Arbor: University of Michigan Press, 2007); Donna Murch, *Living for the City: Migration, Education, and the Rise of the Black Panther Party in Oakland, California* (Chapel Hill: University of North Carolina Press, 2010); Jacobi Williams, *From the Bullet to the Ballot: The Illinois Chapter of the Black Panther Party and Racial Coalition Politics in Chicago* (Chapel Hill: University of North Carolina Press, 2013); Rhonda Williams, *The Politics of Public Housing: Black Women's Struggle Against Urban Inequality* (New York: Oxford University Press, 2003); and Nishani Frazier, *Harambee City: The Congress of Racial Equality in Cleveland and the Rise of Black Power Populism* (Little Rock: University of Arkansas Press, 2017).

56 "The World of Coretta Scott King: A Word with Trina Grillo," *New Lady*, January 1966.

57 Harding, *Martin Luther King: An Inconvenient Hero*, 31.

58 Vincent Harding, "King for the 21st Century Calls Us to Walk with Jesus," speech, Goshen College, January 21, 2005.

59 In *The Rebellious Life of Mrs. Rosa Parks* (Boston: Beacon Press, 2013), I insisted on *Mrs.* in the title and used it throughout the book. Here I don't use *Mrs.* for a related reason. For Mrs. Parks, it was meant to defamiliarize us with her since she is typically called "Rosa Parks" in popular discourse and public honoring, while people who knew her well used the "Mrs." Coretta Scott King was obsessively called "Mrs. King" and "Mrs. Martin

Luther King" to the exclusion of her name so I use her first and full name to foreground her full personhood and activism. As she wrote in her autobiography, "Most people . . . know me as Mrs. King. . . . But I am more than a label. I am also Coretta."

1: Our First Protest: Martin Luther King and Coretta Scott Come of Age in the North

1 Anna Malaika Tubbs, *The Three Mothers: How the Mothers of Martin Luther King, Jr., Malcolm X and James Baldwin Shaped a Nation* (New York: Flatiron, 2021), 133. King was originally named Michael King Jr. after his father but his father changed both their names to Martin Luther when King was five.

2 Tubbs, *The Three Mothers*, 110.

3 Jackson, *Becoming King*, 41.

4 Jamon Jordan, "MLK Changed Detroit—but Only After Detroit Changed Him," *DFP*, January 16, 2022.

5 https://connecticuthistory.org/laboring-in-the-shade/.

6 Blake Harrison, "Mobility, Farmworkers and Connecticut's Tobacco Valley, 1900–1950," *Journal of Historical Geography*, April 2010.

7 Patrick Parr, *The Seminarian: Martin Luther King Comes of Age* (Chicago: Lawrence Hill Books, 2018), 7.

8 Parr, *The Seminarian*, 10.

9 Branch, *Parting the Waters*, 65.

10 Parr, *The Seminarian*, 11–12.

11 Parr, *The Seminarian*, 10, 13.

12 Clayborne Carson, "Martin Luther King, Jr.: The Crozer Seminary Years," *Journal of Blacks in Higher Education* (Summer 1997), 124.

13 Branch, *Parting the Waters*, 70.

14 Parr, *The Seminarian*.

15 Oates, *Let the Trumpet Sound*, 24.

16 See Parr, Eig, Branch, and Garrow.

17 See Purnell and Theoharis, *The Strange Careers of the Jim Crow North*, for further explication of this idea.

18 Parr, *The Seminarian*, 47.

19 Parr, *The Seminarian*, 62.

20 https://rabblerouser.blog/2022/04/16/mlk-historians-urge-nj-to-save-camden-home/.

21 Local historian Patrick Duff has done a great deal of legwork to ensure this incident has received its historical due. Taylor Branch, Harvard Sitkoff, Stephen Oates, and Clayborne Carson's *Autobiography* missed it altogether.

22 J. D. Mullane, "MLK's Rise to Civil Rights Icon Was Launched in Burlington County," *Burlington County Times*, April 4, 2018. See letter from Nichols's lawyer here: https://kinginstitute.stanford.edu/king-papers/documents/statement-behalf-ernest-nichols-state-new-jersey-vs-ernest-nichols-w-thomas.

23 Interview of Walter McCall by Herbert Holmes, Atlanta, GA, March 31, 1970, provided by Patrick Parr.

24 Parr, *The Seminarian*, 132; Biographical Investigation Final Report Presented to the New Jersey Department of Environmental Protection, Historic Preservation Office, December 12, 2017.

25 Carson, "Martin Luther King, Jr.: The Crozer Seminary Years," 124.

26 Parr, *The Seminarian*, 134, 137.

27 "Martin Luther King: He Never Liked to Fight!" *Afro-American*, June 15, 1957.

28 "Martin Luther King's Confrontation with a Bartender in Maple Shade," *PI*, January 21, 2015.

29 Parr, *The Seminarian*, 135.

30 Parr, *The Seminarian*, 137.

31 Interview of Walter McCall by Herbert Holmes, Atlanta, GA, March 31, 1970, provided by Patrick Parr.

32 As quoted in Biographical Investigation Final Report Presented to the New Jersey Department of Environmental Protection, Historic Preservation Office, December 12, 2017.

33 "Rev. King Lauds City on Strides to Integration," *Philadelphia Tribune*, October 28, 1961.

34 Sugrue, *Sweet Land of Liberty*, 149–50.

35 "They went there because they wanted to go there and they said it was freedom . . . because that was them," Lowery continued. This interview with Lowery was done sixty years after the event, as New Jersey considered putting her parents' former address on the historical registry. As quoted in Biographical Investigation Final Report Presented to the New Jersey Department of Environmental Protection, Historic Preservation Office, December 12, 2017.

36 Efforts by Patrick Duff sought to place the Hunts' house on the New Jersey Register of Historic Places. The state determined that King "neither lived or resided there" in Camden.

37 Parr argues that it also changed the sermons he gives that summer (139).

38 Phillip Hoose, *Claudette Colvin: Twice Toward Justice* (New York: FSG, 2009), 62.

39 Thanks to Patrick Duff for this information and flyer.

40 Parr, *The Seminarian*, 114–18.

41 Oral history with Marjorie Penney, Temple University, provided by Patrick Duff.

42 Parr, *The Seminarian*, 42.

43 Lewis, *King*, 33.

44 David Garrow, *Bearing the Cross*, 41.

45 Parr, *The Seminarian*, 39.

46 CSK interview, Box 22, Folder 4, Hatch.

47 Parr, *The Seminarian*, 218. Emphasis in original.

48 Carson, ed., *The Autobiography of Martin Luther King, Jr.*, 25.

49 Carson, "Martin Luther King, Jr.: The Crozer Seminary Years," 126.

50 Reinhold Niebuhr, "Walter Rauschenbusch in Historical Perspective," *Religion Today*, vol. 27, 1958.

51 CSK, *My Life with Martin*, 55.

52 MLK, "The Theology of Reinhold Niebuhr," April 1953–June 1954.

53 Mel King, *Chain of Change*, 25.

54 archives.bu.edu/videos/video?id=360433.

55 Adrian Walker, "When Martin Luther King Jr. Came to Boston," *BG*, January 16, 2012.

56 Lewis, *King*, 38.

57 Zebulon Miletsky, *Before Busing: A History of Boston's Long Black Freedom Struggle* (Chapel Hill: University of North Carolina Press, 2022).

58 "Martin Luther's King Jr.'s Boston Legacy," *BSB*, January 16, 2020; Oates, *Let the Trumpet Sound*, 42.

59 www.bu.edu/sth/memories-of-martin-luther-king-jr-as-a-bu-student/.

60 archives.bu.edu/videos/video?id=360433.

61 Adam Fairclough, "Was Martin Luther King a Marxist?" *History Workshop Journal* (Spring 1983): 118. While Fairclough claims "until 1965, King's radicalism was more intellectual than emotional" (120), paying attention to the North reveals King's early passion.

62 Ruth Batson, *A Chronology of the Educational Movement in Boston*, manuscript in Ruth Batson's papers, Box 1, Schlesinger Library, Radcliffe Institute.

63 Mel King, *Chain of Change*, 13.

64 Lewis Baldwin, *There Is a Balm in Gilead: The Cultural Roots of Martin Luther King Jr.* (Minneapolis: Fortress Press, 1991), 40.

65 CSK interview, Box 22, Folder 4, Hatch.

66 CSK interview, Box 22, Folder 4, Hatch.

67 Miletsky, *Before Busing*.

68 Baldwin, *There Is a Balm in Gilead*, 40.

69 Doug Most, "How Boston Shaped the Life of MLK, Jr.," *Bostonia Magazine*, January 22, 2019.

70 Joseph Rosenbloom, *Redemption: Martin Luther King Jr.'s Last 31 Hours* (Boston: Beacon Press, 2018), 127.

71 Edythe Scott Bagley, *Desert Rose* (Tuscaloosa: University of Alabama Press, 2012), 122.

72 CSK interview, NVLP.

73 Kristopher Burrell, "I Was Called Too: The Life and Work of Coretta Scott King," paper, CUNY.

74 Bagley, *Desert Rose*, 62.

75 "King's Wife Battles to Provide Calm Home Life," *Toronto Daily Star*, March 16, 1965.

76 Bagley, *Desert Rose*, 62.

77 CSK, Senior Paper, summary provided by Antioch College.

78 CSK, "Commencement Address to Antioch College," 1982.

79 CSK interview, Box 22, Folder 9, Hatch.

80 Bagley, *Desert Rose*, 84.
81 Burrell, "I Was Called Too."
82 "The World of Coretta Scott King," *New Lady*.
83 CSK interview, NVLP.
84 Bagley, *Desert Rose*, 84.
85 CSK interview, NVLP.
86 CSK interview, NVLP; CSK, "Address to Antioch Reunion," *Antiochian*, June 25, 2004. She had to do an additional year teaching at the Antioch campus private school to gain her credential.
87 www.washingtonpost.com/history/2022/01/17/coretta-scott-martin -luther-king-meeting/.
88 Shirley Graham, "Shirley Graham's Keynote Speech, 1948," Progressive Party, W. E. B. Du Bois Papers, University of Massachusetts Amherst Libraries.
89 David P. Stein, "'This Nation Has Never Honestly Dealt with the Question of a Peacetime Economy': Coretta Scott King and the Struggle for a Nonviolent Economy in the 1970s," *Souls*, 18:1, 83.
90 Bagley, *Desert Rose*, 81.
91 CSK, *MLMLML*, 28.
92 CSK interview, Eyes I.
93 Phillip Martin, "Coretta Scott King Quietly Blazed Trails of Her Own Before Meeting Her Future Husband in Boston," WGBH, www.wgbh.org /news/national-news/2023/01/13/coretta-scott-king-quietly-blazed-trails-of -her-own-before-meeting-her-future-husband-in-boston?fbclid=IwAR1w PdPWnuX9xurx61w1maz-nyVVv4UINOdtflHHX4AtDgS7eUskK5s631g.
94 CSK, *My Life with Martin*, 51.
95 CSK interview, Box 22, Folder 4, Hatch.
96 CSK Interview, Box 22, Folder 4, Hatch.
97 Eig, *King*, 69, 89.
98 Bagley, *Desert Rose*, 97; CSK interview, Box 22, Folder 4, Hatch.
99 Martin, "Coretta Scott King Quietly Blazed Trails."
100 Carson, ed., *The Autobiography of Martin Luther King Jr.*, 35.
101 CSK interview, NVLP.
102 CSK interview, Box 22, Folder 4, Hatch.
103 Jackson, *Becoming King*, 49.
104 https://learningenglish.voanews.com/a/what-it-takes-coretta-scott -king/4082415.html.
105 Christine King Farris, *Through It All: Reflections on My Life, My Family, and My Faith* (New York: Atria, 2009), 74; CSK interview, Tape 5, Hatch.
106 CSK interview, Box 22, Folder 4, Hatch.
107 CSK interview, Box 22, Folder 4, Hatch.
108 CSK interview, *MLMLML*, 38.
109 MLK, Letter to Coretta, July 18, 1952, MLKPP.
110 Eig, *King*, 106.
111 CSK interview, Box 22, Folder 4, Hatch.
112 James Baldwin, "The Dangerous Road Before Martin Luther King," in *Collected Essays* (New York: Library of America, 1998), 649–50.

113 CSK interview, Tape 5, Hatch.

114 CSK interview, NVLP.

115 Carson, ed., *The Autobiography of Martin Luther King Jr.*, 35.

116 "The New Coretta Scott King: Emerging from the Legacy," *WP*, January 15, 1978.

117 CSK interview on Tavis Smiley, January 2005 (aired February 2, 2006).

118 Bagley, *Desert Rose*, 123.

119 CSK interview, Box 22, Folder 4, Hatch.

120 Author interview with Mary Frances Berry, February 22, 2024.

121 Bagley, *Desert Rose*, 99.

122 Her second year, she was able to get money from the state of Alabama, which had no professional or graduate programs in music open to Black students. Alabama was willing to pay to maintain that segregation by supporting Black students' graduate education outside the state.

123 Eig, *King*, 89.

124 Bagley, *Desert Rose*, 100.

125 CSK interview, Box 22, Folder 4, Hatch.

126 *Daddy King*, 134.

127 CSK, *MLMLML*, 46.

128 CSK interview, Hatch.

129 CSK interview, Box 22, Folder 4, Hatch.

130 Dayo Gore, *Radicalism at the Crossroads: African American Women in the Cold War* (New York: New York University Press, 2011).

131 CSK, *We Shall Overcome*, 255.

132 Toni Morrison, *Beloved* (New York: Plume, 1988), 272–73.

133 I am grateful to Traci Parker for helping me crystallize this idea.

134 Author interview with Barbara Reynolds, November 8, 2023.

135 Clennon King, "Martin Luther King Jr. and Coretta Scott King in Boston: A Love Story," *Boston Magazine*, January 15, 2021.

136 CSK interview, Box 22, Folder 4, Hatch.

137 Martin didn't mind wearing an apron and thought it made him look manly. CSK, *MLMLML*, 52.

138 Patrick Parr, *Malcolm Before X* (Amherst: University of Massachusetts Press, 2024).

139 CSK interview, Box 22, Folder 4, Hatch.

140 CSK, *My Life with Martin*, 107.

141 MLK, *Stride Toward Freedom*.

142 Oates, *Let the Trumpet Sound*, 49.

143 Bagley, *Desert Rose*, 103.

144 "Meet Mrs. King," *PC*, March 30, 1957.

2: There Lived a Great People: King's Leadership Emerges, as Does His Critique of the North

1 CSK, *MLMLML*, 56.

2 CSK interview, NVLP.

3 Author interview with Mary Frances Berry, October 18, 2023.

4 Bagley, *Desert Rose*, 109.

5 Jordan, "MLK Changed Detroit."

6 Douglas Brinkley, *Rosa Parks: A Life* (New York: Penguin, 2000), 100. Aretha Watkins, "Mrs. Parks Recalls the First Time She Saw Dr. King," *LAS*, April 11, 1968.

7 Branch, *Parting the Waters*, 124.

8 Theoharis, *The Rebellious Life of Mrs. Rosa Parks*, 60–77.

9 Jo Ann Gibson Robinson, *The Montgomery Bus Boycott and the Women Who Started It* (Knoxville: University of Tennessee Press, 1987), 44–56.

10 Robinson, *The Montgomery Bus Boycott and the Women Who Started It*, 45.

11 Donnie Williams and Wayne Greenhaw, *The Thunder of Angels: The Montgomery Bus Boycott and the People Who Broke the Back of Jim Crow* (New York: Lawrence Hill, 2007), 60.

12 Earl and Miriam Selby, *Odyssey: Journey Through Black America* (New York: G.P. Putnam's Sons, 1971), 59.

13 MLK, *Stride Toward Freedom*, 21–22.

14 MLK, *Stride Toward Freedom*, 53–54.

15 Williams, *From the Bullet to the Ballot*, 66.

16 Edgar Daniel, Nixon interview, CRDP.

17 CSK interview, Eyes I.

18 Box 4, Folder 3, Preston and Bonita Valien Papers, Amistad Research Center, Tulane University.

19 Jackson, *From Civil Rights to Human Rights*, 66.

20 Oates, *Let the Trumpet Sound*, 87.

21 Hoose, *Claudette Colvin*, 80.

22 Lillie Patterson, *Coretta Scott King* (Champaign, IL: Garrard Publishing, 1977), 52.

23 Box 4, Folder 3, Valien Papers.

24 CSK interview, Eyes I.

25 Box III, A-273, Folder 3, NAACP Papers, Library of Congress.

26 CSK, *MLMLML*, 67.

27 Dan Berger, *Captive Nation: Black Prison Organizing in the Civil Rights Era* (Chapel Hill: University of North Carolina Press, 2014), 31–32.

28 CSK, *MLMLML*, 68.

29 Oates, *Let the Trumpet Sound*, 89.

30 Eig, *King*, 30–31.

31 Thanks to Lerone Martin for helping me see this.

32 CSK, *My Life with Martin*, 117.

33 Williams, *From the Bullet to the Ballot*, 133–34.

34 Garrow, *Bearing the Cross*, 61.

35 CSK interview, NVLP.

36 CSK interview, Eyes I.

37 "The World of Coretta Scott King," *New Lady*.

38 CSK interview, Academy of Achievement, 1997, www.youtube.com/watch?v=7DX5pyvAXz0.

39 Photo caption, *AN*, December 29, 1956.

40 Oates, *Let the Trumpet Sound*, 91.

41 Carson, ed., *The Autobiography of Martin Luther King Jr.*, 82.

42 Bagley, *Desert Rose*, 132.

43 CSK, *My Life with Martin*, 124.

44 CSK interview, Eyes I.

45 Haywood, *Let Us Make Men*, 143–44.

46 John D'Emilio, *Lost Prophet: The Life and Times of Bayard Rustin* (Chicago: University of Chicago Press, 2004), 236.

47 Haywood, *Let Us Make Men*, 145.

48 CSK interview, Box 21, Folder 10, Hatch.

49 Author interview with Dorothy Tillman, August 9, 2024.

50 CSK interview, Eyes I; Dorothy Cotton interview, SOHP.

51 CSK interview, Box 22, Folder 6, Hatch.

52 Oates, *Let the Trumpet Sound*, 93.

53 "Meet Mrs. King," *PC*, March 10, 1957.

54 Oates, *Let the Trumpet Sound*, 95.

55 Williams and Greenhaw, *Thunder of Angels*, 76; " 'Crime Wave' in Alabama," *NYT*, February 24, 1956.

56 Julian Bond, *Julian Bond's Time to Teach: A History of the Southern Civil Rights Movement* (Boston: Beacon Press, 2021).

57 Jackson, *Becoming King*, 130.

58 Jordan, "MLK Changed Detroit."

59 CSK interview, Box 22, Folder 4, Hatch.

60 "Her Involvement Not Planned Says Mrs. King," *Montreal Star*, February 24, 1967.

61 Belafonte, *My Song*, 296–97.

62 Marcia Walker-McWilliams, *Reverend Addie Wyatt: Faith and the Fight for Labor, and Gender Equality* (Urbana: University of Illinois Press, 2016), 95–96.

63 CSK interview, Eyes I.

64 Vicki Crawford, "Coretta Scott King and the Struggle for Civil and Human Rights," *Women in the Civil Rights Movement: Torchbearers and Trailblazers, 1941–1965* (Bloomington: University of Indiana Press, 1993).

65 "Meet Mrs. King," *PC*, March 10, 1957.

66 Oates, *Let the Trumpet Sound*, 107.

67 CSK, *My Life with Martin*, 255.

68 D'Emilio, *Lost Prophet*, 245.

69 Haywood, *Let Us Make Men*, 159.

70 MLK, *The Last Interview*, 3–5.

71 MLK, *The Last Interview*, 26–27.

72 Bond, *Julian Bond's Time to Teach*, 112–13.

73 D'Emilio, *Lost Prophet*, 266.

74 Barbara Ransby, *Ella Baker & the Black Freedom Movement: A Radical Democratic Vision* (Chapel Hill: University of North Carolina Press, 2003); Simmons, "Martin Luther King Jr. Revisited."

75 CSK interview, Ghana trip audio, Hatch.

76 https://baptistnews.com/article/martin-luther-king-preached-freedom -in-africa-too/.
77 Jackson, *Becoming King*, 153.
78 CSK, *My Life with Martin*, 144–46.
79 Oates, *Let the Trumpet Sound*, 118.
80 "Martin Luther King in London," *Guardian*, December 2, 2014.
81 Selma James, "Women's Key Role in Educating Martin Luther King," *Guardian*, December 4, 2014.
82 MLK, Temple of Isaiah address, February 1960.
83 "Chicagoans Preparing for Pilgrimage to Washington," *CD*, May 11, 1957.
84 MLK, "Give Us the Ballot," May 17, 1957, MLKPP.
85 MLK, *The Last Interview*, 32.
86 MLK, "A Look to the Future," September 2, 1957, MLKPP.
87 King, *Stride Toward Freedom*, 199–200.
88 Dudziak, *Cold War Civil Rights*.
89 Charles Mills, *The Racial Contract* (Ithaca, NY: Cornell University Press, 1998), 18–19.
90 MLK, *Stride Toward Freedom*.
91 CSK interview, Academy of Achievement, www.youtube.com/watch?v =7DX5pyvAXz0.
92 Arthur Johnson, *Race and Remembrance*, 68.
93 Carson, ed., *The Autobiography of Martin Luther King Jr.*, 105.
94 Cotton interview, SOHP.
95 Bagley, *Desert Rose*, 213.
96 Garrow, *Bearing the Cross*, 376.
97 Payne, *I've Got the Light of Freedom*, 76, 92–93.
98 Interview with Dorothy Aldridge, April 22, 2024.
99 Jordan, "MLK Changed Detroit but Only After Detroit Changed Him."
100 MLK, "Address at the Religious Leaders Conference," May 11, 1959, MLKPP.
101 Dudziak, *Cold War Civil Rights*.
102 "The World of CSK," *New Lady*; CSK, *My Life with Martin*, 150–51.
103 CSK, *My Life with Martin*, 168.
104 "What I Learned About Coretta Scott King," *AJC*, May 26, 1968.
105 *The Papers of Martin Luther King*, vol. 7, 145–47.
106 MLK's speech at Cornell College: https://news.cornellcollege.edu/dr -martin-luther-kings-visit-to-cornell-college/.
107 "Two events on June 3, 1964, featuring Dr. Martin Luther King Jr. in Arizona" transcript: https://repository.asu.edu/attachments/135805/con tent/mlk-at-asu-transcript-public.pdf.
108 MLK, "The Rising Tide of Racial Consciousness," September 6, 1960, MLKPP.

3: The Thin Veneer of the North's Racial Self-Righteousness: King and the Black Freedom Struggle in New York

1 Branch, *Parting the Waters*, 240.
2 Eig, *King*, 203.

3   Martin Sostre, "Martin Luther King Was a Lawbreaker," *Black News*, April 1970, https://offshootjournal.org/wp-content/uploads/2022/04/zine_4_11_final.pdf.

4   "King Packs Williams CME," *AN*, October 4, 1958.

5   "Students Set to March on the Capitol for Integration," *CD*, September 18, 1958.

6   Joseph, *The Sword and the Shield*, 49.

7   www.whsak.com/izola-story.html.

8   CSK, *My Life with Martin*, 155.

9   "Inside the Friendship between MLK Jr. and the Surgeon Who Saved Him," *New York Post*, September 19, 2018.

10   https://nyulangone.org/news/doctor-who-saved-preacher#:~:text=On%20September%2020%2C%201958%2C%20alumnus,was%20taken%20to%20Harlem%20Hospital.

11   Branch, *Parting the Waters*, 244.

12   Oates, *Let the Trumpet Sound*, 138.

13   "The New Coretta Scott King," *WP*, January 14, 1978.

14   "Rev. King Worries about His Crusade . . . not Death," *PC*, September 27, 1958. King was required to appear before a grand jury that indicted Curry. But she was found unable to understand the charges against her and was committed to the Matteawan State Hospital for the Criminally Insane.

15   Author interview with William Barber, June 28, 2017.

16   Claressa W. Chambliss, in *Reflections on Our Pastor Dr. Martin Luther King at Dexter Avenue Baptist Church*, edited by Wally Vaughn (Majority Press, 1999), 80.

17   Michael Eric Dyson, *April 4, 1968: Martin Luther King, Jr.'s Death and How It Changed America* (New York: Civitas Books, 2008). A 1978 NBC movie showed how King had "violent attacks of hiccups when he was frightened." "King Lays Bare an Ordinary Man of Inordinate Strength," *CT*, February 9, 1978.

18   Obery Hendricks, "The 'Macroethics' of Martin Luther King," *Salon*, January 16, 2016. Robert Vaughn describes King's hiccups when he saw him in Sweden in 1966. Robert Vaughn, *A Fortunate Life: Behind the Scenes Stories from a Hollywood Legend* (New York: Thomas Dunne, 2008).

19   CSK, *My Life with Martin*, 158.

20   CSK, *My Life with Martin*, 150–51.

21   CSK, *My Life with Martin*, 158.

22   Jackson, *Becoming King*, 169.

23   Daniel Perlstein, "Bayard Rustin and the Struggle for Racial Justice," *Civil Rights in New York City: From World War II to the Giuliani Era*, edited by Clarence Taylor (New York: Fordham University Press, 2011), 131.

24   MLK speech to 1199, 1968, https://www.seiu.org/blog/2015/7/when-martin-luther-king-jr-to-seiu-1199#.

25   Thanks to Evan Rothman for helping me think through this idea.

26   Fred Opie, *Upsetting the Apple Cart: Black-Latino Coalitions in New York City*

from Protest to Public Office (New York: Columbia University Press, 2015), 15.

27 Moe Foner, *Not for Bread Alone* (Ithaca, NY: Cornell University Press, 2002), 45.

28 www.seiu.org/blog/2015/7/when-martin-luther-king-jr-to-seiu-1199.

29 Alan Kraut, *Covenant of Care: Newark Beth Israel and the Jewish Hospital in America* (New Brunswick, NJ: Rutgers University Press, 2007), 149.

30 Foner, *Not for Bread Alone*, 49.

31 Leon Fink and Brian Greenberg, *Upheaval in the Quiet Zone: 1199/SEIU and the Politics of Healthcare Unionism* (Champaign: University of Illinois Press, 2009), 102–3, 127.

32 Opie, *Upsetting the Apple Cart*, 45.

33 youtube.com/watch?v=aZWPdibBbo8.

34 Fink and Greenberg, *Upheaval in the Quiet Zone*, 102–3.

35 Opie, *Upsetting the Apple Cart*, 45–47.

36 Cynthia Young, *Soul Power: Culture, Radicalism and the Making of the U.S. Left* (Durham: Duke University Press, 2006), 86.

37 "Randolph Calls Mass Labor Convention," *CD*, May 28, 1960.

38 "800 Attend Labor Council Bias Meet," *CD*, March 4, 1961; "King Urges Action on Bias," *CD*, February 15, 1961.

39 MLK's AFL-CIO address: umdlabor.weebly.com/uploads/2/9/3/9/29397087/speech_transcript.pdf.

40 "Challenge Labor to Realize Civil Rights Potential," *CD*, December 12, 1961.

41 Honey, *To the Promised Land*, 65.

42 Occasionally when Powell saw advantage, he would embrace King, but he largely opposed King's work.

43 MLK, "Statement Announcing the March on the Conventions Movement for Freedom Now," June 9, 1960, MLKPP.

44 Garrow, *Bearing the Cross*, 343.

45 Garrow, *Bearing the Cross*, 138.

46 D'Emilio, *Lost Prophet*, 296–99.

47 D'Emilio, *Lost Prophet*, 298.

48 D'Emilio, *Lost Prophet*.

49 E. Franklin Frazier, *The Negro Family in the United States* (Chicago: University of Chicago Press, 1939).

50 Tyrone Palmer, "Live Dog or Dead Lion: The Complex Masculinity of Martin Luther King, Jr.," unpublished paper in author's possession. Thanks to Tyrone Palmer for helping me see King's masculinity in new ways.

51 *Daddy King*, 155.

52 David Johnson, *The Lavender Scare: The Cold War Persecution of Gays and Lesbians in the Federal Government* (Chicago: University of Chicago Press, 2004).

53 MLK, "Face-to-Face," BBC, 1961.

54 CSK, *My Life with Martin*, 142.

55 Dyson, *I May Not Get There with You*, 212–13.
56 According to Eig, who cites Hosea Williams, sometimes King yelled at her to step back and leave (450).
57 Author interview with Mary Frances Berry, February 22, 2024.
58 CSK, *My Life with Martin*, 142.
59 Garrow, *Bearing the Cross*, 376; Fairclough, *To Redeem the Soul*, 50.
60 Cotton interview, SOHP.
61 Cotton, SOHP.
62 Cotton, SOHP; Fairclough, *To Redeem the Soul*, 4.
63 Cotton, SOHP.
64 CSK, *My Life with Martin*, 142.
65 Eig, *King*, 451.
66 Patterson, *Coretta Scott King*, 51.
67 See Jonathan Eig, Peniel Joseph, Brandon Terry, and Tommie Shelby.
68 Crawford, "Coretta Scott King," 111.
69 Tahir Butt, " 'You Are Running a De Facto Segregated University': Racial Segregation and the City University of New York, 1961–1968," *The Strange Careers of the Jim Crow North*.
70 "Rights Plea Made at City College," *NYT*, June 13, 1963.
71 "Negroes Here More Upset About Jobs than Segregation," *NYT*, June 18, 1963.
72 Jonna Perillo, *Uncivil Rights: Teachers, Unions, and Race in the Battle for School Equity* (Chicago: University of Chicago Press, 2012), 25.
73 Christina Collins, *"Ethnically Qualified": Race, Merit and the Selection of Urban Teachers* (New York: Teachers College Press, 2011), 224–25.
74 Hayes, *The Harlem Uprising*, 69.
75 Ella Baker interview, SOHP.
76 See Ransby, *Ella Baker.*
77 Testimony by Mallory (speaker #38) from the PS #10 PTA at the Board of Education Commission on Integration Public Hearing, January 17, 1957, as quoted in Back.
78 Adina Back, "Taking School Segregation to the Courts," unpublished chapter in author's possession. Back interviewed Mallory in 2000.
79 "Letters from Prison," Monroe Defense Committee, circa 1962, quoted in Jeanette Merrill and Rosemary Neidenberg, "Mae Mallory: Unforgettable Freedom Fighter Promoted Self-Defense," *Workers World*, February 26, 2009.
80 Back, "Taking School Segregation to the Courts."
81 Back, "Taking School Segregation to the Courts." These women organizers received little mainstream media coverage.
82 Adina Back, "Exposing the Whole Segregation Myth," *Freedom North*, 65.
83 Ashley Farmer, "Mae Mallory: Forgotten Black Power Intellectual," *Black Perspectives* (blog), June 3, 2016. FBI files in author's possession.
84 Taylor, *Knocking at Our Own Door.*
85 https://kinginstitute.stanford.edu/king-papers/documents/desegrega tion-and-future-address-delivered-annual-luncheon-national-committee.

86 MLK, "New Year Hopes," *AN*, January 5, 1963.

87 MLK, "Merits of Maladjustment," *AN*, January 19, 1963.

88 "Baldwin Clan Flops in a Meeting with RFK," *PC*, June 1963.

89 Belafonte, *My Song*, 269.

90 James Baldwin, "A Report from Occupied Territory," *The Nation*, July 11, 1966, www.thenation.com/article/culture/report-occupied-territory/.

91 Alex Haley, *The Autobiography of Malcolm X* (New York: Ballantine, 1965).

92 Clark, *Baldwin, Malcolm, King*, 33.

93 In the first years, SCLC executive director Wyatt Tee Walker assisted King with these columns; Andrew Young and Dorothy Cotton helped subsequently.

94 MLK, "Hall of Famer," *AN*, August 4, 1962.

95 Payne, *I've Got the Light of Freedom*, 393.

96 To document this pattern, I read hundreds of *NYT* articles, particularly from 1963 to 1966, but also across the decade.

97 "Negro Violence in the North Feared," *NYT*, May 27, 1963.

98 *The Papers of Martin Luther King*, vol. 7, 504–5.

99 Articles on the Southern struggles in 1963 were more substantive: "Negro Victory Fades in Georgia," *NYT*, March 14, 2024; "Dr. King Leaves Birmingham Jail," *NYT*, April 21, 1963; "Kennedy Studies New Legal Steps for Integration," *NYT*, May 23, 1963.

100 "Status of Integration: The Progress So Far Is Characterized as Mainly Tokenism," *NYT*, September 1, 1963.

101 "Dr. King Finds Setback in the North for Rights Drive," *NYT*, October 18, 1963.

102 "Dr. King Backing Holiday Boycott," *NYT*, September 27, 1963.

103 "Strike Against Santa Claus," editorial, *NYT*, September 28, 1963.

104 CSK interview, Box 22, Folder 9, Hatch.

105 MLK, "The School Boycott Concept," *AN*, April 11, 1964.

106 Sonia Lee and Ande Diaz, " 'I Was the One Percenter': Manny Diaz and the Beginnings of a Black–Puerto Rican Coalition," *Journal of Ethnic History* 26, no. 3 (Spring 2007): 52.

107 "The School Boycott," editorial, *NYT*, February 4, 1964.

108 Rustin FBI transcript from Jonathan Eig.

109 MLK, *The Last Interview*, 37. King's sustained support of Northern school boycotts has escaped the attention of nearly all of his biographers. Taylor Branch wrongly put King on the other side of the issue. Branch, *Pillar of Fire*, 243.

110 "Dr. King Urges Nonviolence in Rights Protest," *NYT*, March 15, 1964.

111 Thanks to Thomas Jackson for his research on Title III and the May 20, 1963, Oval Office transcript.

112 Delmont, *Why Busing Failed*, 50.

113 MLK, "May 17–11 Years Later," *AN*, May 22, 1965.

114 Purnell, *Fighting Jim Crow in the County of Kings*, 212–13.

115 "143 More Seized in Protests Here," *NYT*, July 24, 1963.

116 "Nab 40 More in 'Lie-Down' to Halt Work," *CT*, July 25, 1963.

117 See Purnell, *Fighting Jim Crow in the County of Kings*.

118 Purnell, *Fighting Jim Crow in the County of Kings*, 264.

119 Purnell, *Fighting Jim Crow in the County of Kings*, 264–66.

120 George Lipsitz, *A Life in the Struggle: Ivory Perry and the Culture of Opposition* (Philadelphia: Temple University Press, 1988), 82.

121 "Confidential Memorandum to Martin Luther King from Clarence Jones," April 15, 1964, from Jonathan Eig.

122 MLK, "The Stall-in in Review," *AN*, May 9, 1964.

123 Eig, *King*, 233.

124 Stephen and Paul Kendrick, *Nine Days* (New York: Farrar, Straus & Giroux, 2021), front matter.

125 "The New Coretta Scott King Emerging from the Shadows," *WP*, January 15, 1978.

126 *The Papers of Martin Luther King*, vol. 7, 444.

127 The eggs have been falsely blamed on Malcolm X supporters and on Communists. Sugrue claims definitively they were not followers of Malcolm but a "Harlem Christian minister" (303).

128 "Dr. King Is Target of Eggs in Harlem," *NYT*, July 1, 1963.

129 "Fruits of Old Distrust: Decades of Frustration Explode in Harlem Riots Aimed at Police," *LAT*, July 26, 1964.

130 Garance Franke-Ruta, "Martin Luther King Jr's. Amazing 1964 Interview with Robert Penn Warren," *Atlantic*, August 26, 2013.

131 MLK, "Hammer of Civil Rights," *The Nation*, March 9, 1964.

4: A New Form of Slavery Covered Up with Certain Niceties: Rethinking 1963 and King's Growing Frustration with Northern Intransigence

1 MLK, "Face to Face" interview, *BBC*.

2 Bond, *Julian Bond's Time to Teach*, 188–97.

3 "Martin Luther King: A Personal Portrait," interview, 1965, https://bmac.libs.uga.edu/index.php/Detail/objects/25153.

4 CSK interview, Box 21, Folder 8, Hatch.

5 CSK interview with the CBC, December 27, 1965, https://okra.stanford.edu/transcription/video/651227-005.mp4.

6 CSK interview, Box 22, Folder 6, Hatch.

7 CSK interview, Box 21, Folder 8, Hatch.

8 Carson, ed., *The Autobiography of Martin Luther King Jr.*

9 CSK interview, Eyes I.

10 "King's Wife Battles to Provide Calm for the Children," *Toronto Star*, March 16, 1965.

11 MLK, "Letter from a Birmingham Jail," April 16, 1963.

12 Jon Hale, *A New Kind of Youth: Historically Black High Schools and Southern Student Activism* (Chapel Hill: University of North Carolina Press, 2022), 144–45.

13 Bond, *Julian Bond's Time to Teach*, 224–25.

14 The *New York Times* ran many articles. See for instance: "Negro Victory

Fades in Georgia," *NYT*, March 14, 2024; "Dr. King Leaves Birmingham Jail," *NYT*, April 21, 1963; "Kennedy Studies New Legal Steps for Integration," *NYT*, May 23, 1963; "Not Token Freedom, Full Freedom," *NYT*, June 9, 1963.

15 "32 Negro Marchers Seized in Birmingham at Start of Prayer for Police Commissioner," *WP*, April 7, 1963.

16 CSK interview, WTTW, 1978, www.pbs.org/video/coretta-scott-king -process-social-change-pr0cgf/?continuousplayautoplay=true.

17 Full text: https://www.presidency.ucsb.edu/documents/radio-and-televi sion-report-the-american-people-civil-rights.

18 MLK interview with David Susskind.

19 Dillard, *Faith in the City*, 268.

20 "Detroiters Poised for Bias March," *DN*, June 23, 1963.

21 Cleage was dismayed by the others' willingness to compromise with white liberal leaders like Cavanagh and Reuther and months later split to form the Grassroots Leadership Conference; he mistakenly lumped King in with others, according to biographer Angela Dillard, missing that both he and King had similar critiques of white liberals. Angela Dillard, "Religion and Radicalism: The Reverend Albert B. Cleage, Jr., and the Rise of Black Christian Nationalism," *Freedom North*, 155–68.

22 Parks had lost her job during the boycott, as had her husband. They never found steady work again and continued receiving death threats, so eight months after the boycott's end, they were forced to leave Montgomery for Detroit, where her brother and cousins lived. She called it "the Northern promised land that wasn't."

23 Dillard, *Freedom North*, 268.

24 Sugrue, *Sweet Land of Liberty*, 299.

25 Author interview with General Baker, October 21, 2009.

26 "Martin Luther King Thrills Marchers," *Michigan Chronicle*, June 29, 1963.

27 https://kinginstitute.stanford.edu/king-papers/documents/address -freedom-rally-cobo-hall.

28 Brinkley, *Rosa Parks*, 184.

29 Suzanne Smith, *Dancing in the Street: Motown and the Cultural Politics of Detroit* (Cambridge, MA: Harvard University Press, 2001), 17.

30 Smith, 23–25.

31 "Whites to Aid Rally by Detroit Negroes," *NYT*, June 23, 1963.

32 "125,000 Rally to Protest Discrimination," *NYT*, June 24, 1963.

33 Jennifer Scanlon, *Until There Is Justice: The Life of Anna Arnold Hedgeman* (New York: Oxford University Press, 2016), 156–70.

34 Gilberto Gerena Valentin, *Gilberto Gerena Valentín: My Life as a Community Activist, Labor Organizer and Progressive Politician in New York City* (New York: City University of New York, 2013), 134–35.

35 Valentin was accused of working with Communists in his union work. "Man in the News; Puerto Rican Leader; Gilberto Gerena Valentin," *NYT*, March 2, 1964. In the 1950s the FBI stalked him and got him fired.

36 Johanna Fernandez documented this meeting in an independent oral history with Gilberto Gerena Valentin. See Johanna Fernandez, *The Young Lords: A Radical History* (Chapel Hill: University of North Carolina Press, 2020), 402 (n114).

37 Fernandez, *The Young Lords*.

38 Valentin, *Gilberto Gerena Valentín*, 105–8, 134.

39 "Rights Drive Set by Puerto Ricans," *NYT*, August 23, 1963.

40 Honey, *To the Promised Land*, 97.

41 https://transcripts.cnn.com/show/se/date/2003-08-28/segment/16.

42 Higginbotham foreword, *Freedom North*, ix.

43 Higginbotham, x–xi.

44 Scholars differ. Lee and Diaz, " 'I Was the One Percenter': Manny Diaz and the Beginnings of a Black-Puerto Rican Coalition," 65. Sonia Lee says just over two thousand Puerto Ricans go to the MOW but includes no citation to the figure, so it's unclear if it's referring to New York Puerto Ricans or Puerto Ricans from anywhere in the US. Sonia Lee, *Building a Latino Civil Rights Movement: Puerto Ricans, African Americans, and the Pursuit of Racial Justice in New York City* (Chapel Hill: University of North Carolina Press, 2014), 80. Thomas and Santiago say thousands. Lorin Thomas and Aldo Santiago, *Rethinking the Struggle for Puerto Rican Rights* (New York: Taylor & Francis, 2017).

45 Valentin, *Gilberto Gerena Valentín*.

46 https://centropr-archive.hunter.cuny.edu/centrovoices/chronicles/marching-martin-luther-king.

47 https://remezcla.com/lists/culture/mlk-latino-community/.

48 Eig suggests King was on board with limiting women's speaking at the MOW (325).

49 Farris, *Through It All*, 101–2.

50 CSK interview, Box 21, Folder 9, Hatch.

51 Scanlon, *Until There Is Justice*, 169.

52 Jackson, *From Civil Rights to Human Rights*, 182.

53 CSK interview, Box 21, Folder 9, Hatch.

54 Gary Younge, *The Speech: The Story Behind Martin Luther King's Dream* (New York: Haymarket, 2013); Speltz, *North of Dixie*, 117.

55 Kenneth O'Reilly, *Racial Matters: The FBI's Secret File on Black America, 1960–1972* (New York: Free Press, 1989), 130.

56 https://vault.fbi.gov/Coretta%20Scott%20King/Coretta%20Scott%20King%20Part%201%20of%205/view#document/p211.

57 Andrew Young, *An Easy Burden* (New York: Harper Collins, 1996), 467.

58 Stegall assumed custody of many of Johnson's personal, financial, and campaign files when Walter Jenkins left the White House in 1964.

59 Hoover to Johnson (digitized), Mildred Stegall papers, LBJ Presidential Library. Thanks to Jonathan Eig for many conversations to figure this out.

60 Sylvie Laurent, "MLK's Radical Alternative to Lyndon Johnson's War on Poverty," *Literary Hub*, January 2, 2019, https://lithub.com/mlks-radical-alternative-to-lyndon-johnsons-war-on-poverty/.

61 Cotton interview, SOHP.
62 Beverly Gage, *G-Man: J. Edgar Hoover and the Making of the American Century* (New York: Viking, 2022), 613–14.
63 "Rev. M.L. King," *Jet*, October 29, 1964.
64 Farris, *Through It All*, 108.
65 Athan Theoharis and John Cox, *The Boss: J. Edgar Hoover and the Great American Inquisition* (Philadelphia: Temple University Press, 1988), 357–59.
66 Gage, *G-Man*.
67 CSK, *We Shall Overcome*, 252.
68 Bagley, *Desert Rose*, 191.
69 "Johnson Hails Hoover's Service," *NYT*, May 9, 1964.
70 Gage, *G-Man*, 595.
71 "Screvane Links Reds to Rioting," *NYT*, July 22, 1964.
72 Jackson, *From Civil Rights to Human Rights*, 208; Taylor, *Fight the Power*, 114.
73 Taylor, *Fight the Power*, 112–13.
74 Lewis, *King*, 245.
75 Garrow, *Bearing the Cross*, 343.
76 MLK, "A Plan for New York," *AN*, July 18, 1964.
77 Hamilton, *Martin Luther King Jr. and the Poor People's Campaign*, 26.
78 See interview at www.democratandchronicle.com/story/news/2018/04/04/video-martin-luther-king-jr-1964-rochester-riots/485494002/.
79 "King Confers with Mayor and City Leaders on City and U.S. Rights Issues," *NYT*, July 28, 1964.
80 FBI transcript of call between King and Bayard Rustin, July 6, 1964, courtesy of Tenisha Armstrong.
81 D'Emilio, *Lost Prophet*, 383.
82 "The Real Story of Dr. King's New York Visit," *AN*, August 1, 1964. The article explicitly debunked the misinformation that King hadn't first come to Harlem.
83 "Dr. King Confers with Mayor on City," *NYT*, July 28, 1964.
84 MLK, "Press Conference Statement on New York," July 29, 1964, MLKPP.
85 Garrow, *Bearing the Cross*, 344; Hayes, *The Harlem Uprising*, 195.
86 Taylor, *Fight the Power*, 114; "Harlem Leaders Charge Dr. King," *NYT*, July 29, 1964; "King Confers with Mayor and City Leaders on City and U.S. Rights Issues," *NYT*, July 28, 1964; Hayes, *The Harlem Uprising*, 195; Joseph, *The Sword and the Shield*, 202.
87 MLK, "Press Conference Statement on New York," July 29, 1964, MLKPP.
88 "After the Riots," *NYT*, August 2, 1964.
89 Christopher Bonastia, *The Battle Nearer to Home: The Persistence of School Segregation in New York City* (Stanford, CA: Stanford University Press, 2022), 91–92. Branch called Powell's killing a small incident (417); Eig missed it altogether.
90 "Policeman Sues King, Others for 5 Million Dollars," *LAT*, May 27, 1965.
91 "Gilligan Sues King, Asks for 1.5 Million Dollars," *NYT*, March 4, 1966.
92 Nixon won the Midwestern states Illinois, Wisconsin, Indiana, and Ohio as well as California in 1968 (but not the Deep South, which went to

third-party candidate George Wallace). So Nixon's "Southern strategy" might be more aptly named a Midwestern or Northern strategy.

93 "Polls Show Whites in City Resent Civil Rights Protest," *NYT*, September 21, 1964.

94 Memo from Hoover to Moyers, October 20, 1964, in Stegall papers, from Jonathan Eig.

95 MLK, "Negroes-Whites Together," *AN*, August 15, 1964.

96 Sugrue, *Sweet Land of Liberty*, 361.

97 MLK, "Negroes Are Not Moving Too Fast," *Saturday Evening Post*, November 7, 1964.

98 MLK, "A Choice and a Promise," *AN*, December 5, 1964.

99 MLK, "Negroes Are Not Moving Too Fast."

100 MLK, *Playboy* interview; *A Testament of Hope*, 362.

101 Payne, *The Dead Are Rising*, 384–85.

102 Eig, *King*, 421–23. Transcript of *Playboy* interview provided by Eig.

103 Payne, *The Dead Are Rising*, 387–88. See also Manning Marable's research on Haley in *Malcolm X: A Life of Reinvention* (New York: Viking, 2011).

104 www.malcolm-x.org/docs/let_mart.htm.

105 "Pope and Dr. King Confer on Rights," *NYT*, September 19, 1964.

106 MLK, "The Un-Christian Christian," *Ebony*, August 1965.

107 "Mrs. Martin Luther King," *CD*, April 25, 1968.

108 CSK, *My Life with Martin*, 4.

109 CSK, *My Life with Martin*, 272–73.

110 MLK, "What the Nobel Prize Means to Me," *CD*, November 28, 1964.

111 King speech to British Christian Action, December 7, 1964, www.democracynow.org/2019/1/21/mlk_at_90_a_rediscovered_1965.

112 "Martin Luther King in London," *Guardian*, December 2, 2014.

113 "Dr. King Proposes a Rights Alliance," *NYT*, December 10, 1964.

114 CBC interview with CSK, December 27, 1965.

115 CSK interview, Box 31, Folder 1, Hatch.

116 "King's Wife Battles to Provide Calm for the Children," *Toronto Star*, March 16, 1965.

117 "New York Hails Martin Luther King," *AN*, December 26, 1964.

118 Garrow, *Bearing the Cross*, 367.

119 MLK, Armory speech: www.wnyc.org/story/community-salute-to-dr-martin-luther-king-jr/.

120 Ruth Batson, "Statement to the Boston School Committee," June 11, 1963, https://dsgsites.neu.edu/desegregation/wp-content/uploads/2015/04/neu_rx914286c.pdf.

121 "How a Collection of King's Personal Papers Ended Up in Boston," WGBH, April 4, 2018.

122 Michael Ross and William Berg, *"I Respectfully Disagree with the Judge's Order": The Boston School Desegregation Controversy* (Washington, DC: University Press of America, 1981), 49.

123 "Martin Luther King's Boston Legacy," *BSB*, January 16, 2020, archives.bu.edu/videos/video?id=360433.

124 https://openvault.wgbh.org/exhibits/boston_civil_rights/article#foot note-10.
125 Batson Chronology, 134.
126 Hampton, *Voices of Freedom*, 589.
127 Ross and Berg, *"I Respectfully Disagree with the Judge's Order,"* 70.
128 Andrea Jones Dunham, "Boston's Civil Rights Movement: A Look Back," found at openvault.wgbh.org/exhibits/boston_civil_rights/arti cle#footnote-165.
129 "Boston Schools Are Target for King, SCLC March," *CD*, April 20, 1965.
130 CSK, *We Shall Overcome*, 254.
131 "Interview with Ellen Jackson," in Ruth Hill, Black Women Oral History Project, 145–46.
132 "Martin Luther King's Address to the Mass. State Legislature," *BSB*, January 20, 2014.
133 Purnell, *Fighting Jim Crow*, 171.
134 Matthew Lassiter and Joseph Crespino, eds., *The Myth of Southern Exceptionalism* (New York: Oxford University Press, 2009), 27.
135 "Martin Luther King's Boston Legacy," *BSB*, January 16, 2020.
136 All-white schools, however, were not considered racially imbalanced in the Massachusetts law.
137 Batson Chronology, 201.
138 "King Will Lead Rights March Here and Speak at Boston Common," *Harvard Crimson*, April 14, 1965; "Dr. King Plans Boston March," *NYT*, April 14, 1965.
139 Adrian Walker, "When Martin Luther King Jr. Came to Boston," *BG*, January 16, 2012; Branch, *At Canaan's Edge*.
140 https://boston.cbslocal.com/2018/02/10/martin-luther-king-jr-s -special-connection-to-boston/.
141 "King Has Door Banged in His Face in Boston School," *CT*, April 23, 1965.
142 "Dr. King Leads 15,000 in Boston Rights March," *LAT*, April 24, 1965.
143 Batson Chronology, 201.
144 Ruth Batson, "Statement Made at King March on April 23, 1965," Ruth Batson Papers, Schlesinger Library, Radcliffe Institute.
145 "Dr. King in Boston," *CD*, April 29, 1965.

5: Voting for Ghettos: King and the Struggle in Los Angeles Before Watts

1 James Baldwin, "The White Problem," 1963.
2 "Dr. King Due Here May 26," *LAS*, May 16, 1963; "Dr. King to Get a Hero's Welcome," *LAS*, May 23, 1963.
3 "Kingly Tribute," *LAS*, May 30, 1963.
4 Marnesba Tackett, 1988, Oral History Program, UCLA: "Greatest Freedom Rally Here Nets Heroes Over $75,000," *LAS*, May 30, 1963.
5 Mike Davis and Jon Wiener, *Set the Night on Fire: L.A. in the Sixties* (New York: Verso, 2020), 79.

6 Tackett interview.

7 Karin Stanford, *The Enduring Spirit of Martin Luther King Jr. in Los Angeles*, January 2024, doi:10.13140/RG.2.2.14783.52646.

8 https://la.curbed.com/maps/martin-luther-king-los-angeles-locations -map.

9 "Huge Crowds Attend M.L. King Rallies," *Los Angeles Sentinel*, March 3, 1960.

10 https://la.curbed.com/maps/martin-luther-king-los-angeles-loca tions-map.

11 Monroe Jones interview, Black Power Archive, CSUN, https://www .csun.edu/bradley-center/black-power-archives-oral-history-project.

12 M. Keith Claybrook Jr., "Remembering Ronald X Stokes and the Politics of Solidarity," https://www.aaihs.org/remembering-ronald-x-stokes -and-the-politics-of-black-solidarity/.

13 Davis and Wiener, *Set the Night on Fire*, 66–71.

14 "King Gives Progress Formula," *LAS*, June 21, 1962.

15 Davis and Wiener, *Set the Night on Fire*, 73.

16 NAACP Branch Files, Reel 4, Schomburg Center.

17 Gerald Horne, *Fire This Time: The Watts Uprising and the 1960s* (New York: Da Capo Press, 1995), 57.

18 Sides, *LA City Limits*, 136.

19 *The Papers of Martin Luther King Jr.*, vol. 7, *To Save the Soul of America: January 1961–August 1962* (Berkeley: University of California Press, 2014), 482, 485.

20 *The Papers of Martin Luther King*, vol. 7, 480–83.

21 Honey, *To the Promised Land*, 114.

22 CSK, *MLMLML*, 97.

23 https://blackwomenssuffrage.dp.la/collections/claire-collins-harvey /hacc0315.

24 CSK interview, Box 22, Folder 8, Hatch.

25 CSK, *My Life with Martin*, 194–95; Amy Swerdlow, *Women Strike for Peace: Traditional Motherhood and Radical Politics in the 1960s* (Chicago: University of Chicago, 1993), 194–96.

26 CSK interview, NVLP.

27 www.armscontrol.org/act/2021-11/features/power-women-strike-peace.

28 "Women Strike for Peace Hear Mrs. Martin Luther King," *Afro-American*, November 16, 1963.

29 "Mrs. Martin Luther King Cited for Valor," *New Journal and Guide*, May 2, 1964.

30 digital.wustl.edu/e/eii/eiiweb/kin5427.0224.089corettascottking.html.

31 "Martin Luther King: A Personal Portrait," interview, https://bmac.libs .uga.edu/index.php/Detail/objects/25153.

32 MLK interview by David Susskind.

33 Sides, *LA City Limits*, 155.

34 "Letter to Claude Hudson from Roy Wilkins," September 12, 1962, Branch Files of the NAACP, microfilm Part 27, Series D, 1956–1965, Reel 4.

35 "Yorty Calls Racial Situation Tense," *LAT,* May 10, 1962.

36 "NAACP Head Blasts Report," *CE,* January 9, 1964.

37 Davis and Wiener, *Set the Night on Fire,* 205–6.

38 "30,000 at Rally Hear Plea for Civil Rights," *LAT,* May 27, 1963.

39 "Kingly Tribute," *LAS,* May 30, 1963.

40 "Large Support Reported for Negro Drive Here," *LAT,* June 1, 1963.

41 "Los Angeles Choice," *CE,* June 13, 1963.

42 "LA Integration Test Approaches," *LAT,* June 23, 1963.

43 " 'Happy Slave' View in Textbooks Scored," *CE,* November 15, 1962.

44 Branch Files of the NAACP microfilm, Part 27, Series D, 1956–1965, The West, Reel 3.

45 Judith Kafka, *The History of "Zero Tolerance" in American Public Schooling* (New York: Palgrave, 2011).

46 Marnesba Tackett interview by Michael Balter, 1988, Oral History Program, UCLA.

47 John Caughey, *To Kill a Child's Spirit* (Itasca, IL: Peacock Publishing, 1973), 15–16.

48 Tackett interview, 107, 143.

49 Davis and Wiener, *Set the Night on Fire,* 92.

50 "Report of the Ad Hoc Committee on Equal Education Opportunity, September 12, 1963," Box 164, John Caughey Papers, UCLA.

51 "Dymally Hits Unequal School Boundary Lines," *LAS,* September 6, 1962.

52 "Negro Students Dodge Eggs During Last Week at South Gate High," *LAS,* July 4, 1963.

53 Sides, *LA City Limits,* 163.

54 Barbara Dimmick, "CORE's Corner: Thurmond Quizzes the Secretary," *LAS,* August 8, 1963. The four were also in town for a massive benefit concert on August 8.

55 "Top Aides Deny Teacher Discrimination," *LAT,* August 6, 1963.

56 "Report of the Ad Hoc Committee on Equal Education Opportunity."

57 Jackson, *From Civil Rights to Human Rights,* 289; King, Address at St. Paul's Church, Cleveland Heights, Ohio, May 14, 1963.

58 Thanks to Thomas Jackson for helping me clarify this point.

59 Becky Nicolaides, *My Blue Heaven: Life and Politics in the Working-Class Suburbs of Los Angeles, 1920–1965* (Chicago: University of Chicago Press, 2002), 303.

60 Daniel HoSang, *Racial Propositions* (Berkeley: University of California Press, 2010).

61 "Housing Foes Picket King, CRB Banquet," *CE,* February 20, 1964.

62 "Hate Picket Thank God for Chief Parker," *CE,* May 7, 1964.

63 "Dr. King Blasts Move to Repeal Rumford Act," *LAT,* February 17, 1964.

64 "2000 Jam L.A. Church for Talk by King," *LAT,* February 17, 1964. Pastor at Friendship Baptist in Harlem from 1947 to 1963, Kilgore raised money for the Montgomery Bus Boycott and went back to school at Union Theological Seminary, writing his thesis on the Montgomery movement. In

1963 Kilgore moved to Los Angeles. He saw this new church, Second Baptist, as one that would appreciate his "aggressiveness" and he helped establish the SCLC's Los Angeles office, the only SCLC chapter on the west coast.

65 "Decision on Housing Initiative," editorial, *LAT*, February 2, 1964.

66 "S&Ls and Politics: There's a Natural Affinity," *LAT*, March 23, 1964; "Housing Laws Foes Winning," *LAT*, April 4, 1964.

67 "Housing Laws Foes Winning," *LAT*, April 4, 1964.

68 Davis and Wiener, *Set the Night on Fire*, 207.

69 "Brown Deplores Sit-in Effect on Rumford Act," *LAT*, March 11, 1964.

70 "California Points Up Impact of Militancy," *LAT*, April 27, 1964.

71 "Majority Still Favors Rumford Act Repeal," *LAT*, May 3, 1964.

72 "State Senators to Study Racial Bias in Housing," *LAT*, April 19, 1964.

73 Branch, *Pillar of Fire*, 242.

74 "Nightriders Fire on Dr. King's Aide," *NYT*, May 30, 1964; "Wagner Bolsters Police on Subway to Deter Attacks," *NYT*, June 3, 1964.

75 "Wine Group's Official Hits Boycott Plan," *LAT*, March 31, 1964.

76 "Dr. King Urges Speedy Passage of Rights Bill," *LAT*, June 1, 1964.

77 Seth Mallios and Breana Campbell, "On the Cusp of an American Civil Rights Revolution: Dr. King's Final Visit and Address to San Diego in 1964," San Diego History Center, https://sandiegohistory.org/journals/cusp-american-civil-rights-revolution/.

78 Mallios and Campbell, "On the Cusp."

79 Thanks to Brian Purnell for helping me clarify this idea.

80 Morrie Ryskind, "The Establishment vs. the Facts," *LAT*, April 15, 1964.

81 "Why Prop 14 Deserves a Yes Vote," editorial, *LAT*, October 18, 1964.

82 "King Urges NO on 14," *LAS*, October 29, 1964.

83 Proposition 14 would ultimately be overturned by the courts. The NAACP quickly filed suit; in 1966, in a 5–2 decision, California's Supreme Court declared it unconstitutional. In 1967, the US Supreme Court in a 5–4 decision upheld that decision.

84 MLK, "Beyond the Los Angeles Riots."

85 CSK interview, Eyes II.

86 www.mojo4music.com/articles/stories/harry-belafonte-interviewed/.

87 Belafonte interview, Eyes II.

88 digital.wustl.edu/e/eii/eiiweb/kin5427.0224.089corettascottking.html.

89 MLK, "The Nightmare of Violence," *AN*, March 13, 1965.

90 MLK, "The Nightmare of Violence."

91 digital.wustl.edu/e/eii/eiiweb/kin5427.0224.089corettascottking.html.

92 Grillo, *New Lady*, 37.

93 www.laobserved.com/archive/2015/01/when_martin_luther_king_s.php.

94 "Police Pull Out Stops for King," *LAS*, March 4, 1965.

95 Robert Bauman, *Race and the War on Poverty: From Watts to East L.A.* (Tulsa: University of Oklahoma Press, 2022).

96 www.npr.org/2015/02/26/388691152/in-hollywood-mlk-delivered-a-lesser-known-speech-that-resonates-today.

97   "The New Coretta Scott King," *WP*, January 14, 1978.

98   "Mrs. Martin King: Concert Tour Furthers Thrust for Freedom," *LAS*, September 10, 1964.

99   CSK interview, Box 23, Folder 3, Hatch.

100 Bagley, *Desert Rose*, 197.

101 "Mrs. King Set for Concert," *CD*, October 1, 1966.

102 "Fear and Doubt Aren't Unknown to King," *LAT*, March 4, 1965.

103 "Rights Fight Needs Women—Mrs. King," *LAS*, March 11, 1965.

104 Eig, *King*, 447.

105 Interview with Doris Crenshaw, March 23, 2024.

106 https://vault.fbi.gov/Coretta%20Scott%20King/Coretta%20Scott%20King%20Part%201%20of%205/view#document/p28.

107 Bagley, *Desert Rose*, 199–200.

108 MLK, "The Future of Integration," address delivered at UCLA, April 27, 1965, unpublished transcript, King Center, courtesy of Tenisha Armstrong.

109 www.youtube.com/watch?v=ny6qP0rb_Ag.

110 Roy Wilkins, "Despite Smokescreen North, South Differ," *LAT*, March, 29, 1965. King would criticize Wilkins for "becom[ing] so much of a part of the white establishment he is no longer an effective representative of black people."

111 Jackson, *From Civil Rights to Human Rights*, 238–39.

112 "Civil Rights Helps to Unite Churches, Presbyterians Told," *Cincinnati Enquirer*, May 19, 1965.

6: As Segregated as Birmingham: King in Chicago Before the Chicago Campaign

1   As Timuel Black recounts, Rev. Abraham P. Jackson was one of the people King first spent time with in Chicago; he visited Liberty Baptist Church every year. https://mediaburn.org/video/timuel-black/?t=09:13.

2   "King Group Unveils Novel Plan to Repair Slums," *CD*, February 24, 1966.

3   David Bernstein, "Martin Luther King Jr.'s Chicago Campaign," *Chicago Magazine*, August 2016, www.chicagomag.com/chicago-magazine/august-2016/martin-luther-king-chicago-freedom-movement/.

4   Sitkoff, *King*, 178.

5   Andrew Diamond, "From Fighting Gangs to Black Nations: Race, Power and the Other Civil Rights Movement in Chicago's West Side Ghetto," *Revue Francaise d'Etudes Americaines*, 2008, www.cairn.info/revue-francaise-d-etudes-americaines-2008-2-page-51.htm?contenu=article.

6   Elizabeth Todd-Breland, *A Political Education: Black Politics and Education Reform Since the 1960s* (Chapel Hill: University of North Carolina Press, 2018), 22, 25.

7   Simon Balto, *Occupied Territory: Policing Black Chicago from Red Summer to Black Power* (Chapel Hill: University of North Carolina Press, 2020), 189.

8   "Unholy Centennial of 1919 Race Riots Finds a City Fighting for Justice," *CST*, July 24, 2019.

9 Andrew J. Diamond, *Chicago on the Make: Power and Inequality in a Modern City* (Berkeley: University of California Press, 2020), 41–45.

10 Diamond, *Chicago on the Make,* 135–37.

11 "The Legacy of Boss Daley," *NYT,* June 7, 1995.

12 "Dr. King Talks in Lansing," *CD,* March 12, 1966; Scott King, *MLMLML,* 143.

13 Mike Royko, *Boss: Richard J. Daley of Chicago* (New York: Dutton, 1971), 120.

14 Adam Cohen and Elizabeth Taylor, *American Pharaoh: Mayor Richard J. Daley: His Battle for Chicago and the Nation* (New York: Little, Brown, 2001).

15 Royko, *Boss,* 129–30.

16 Sugrue, *Sweet Land of Liberty,* 417.

17 Royko, *Boss,* 129–32.

18 "Dr. King Launches Attack on Chicago School Set-up," *CD,* February 5, 1966.

19 Sugrue, *Sweet Land of Liberty,* 238.

20 "King Asks Righteous Pressure in Deerfield," *CD,* December 17, 1959.

21 "Fighters of Deerfield Bigotry Need Funds," *CD,* December 3, 1960.

22 "Martin L. King to Speak Here Oct 31," *CD,* October 16, 1962.

23 Jackson, *From Civil Rights to Human Rights,* 127.

24 "Self Portrait of a Symbol: Martin Luther King," *New York Post,* February 13, 1961.

25 "What Effect Will JFK Housing Ban Have?" *PC,* December 1, 1962.

26 "Way for Negroes Asked of Faiths," *NYT,* January 17, 1963.

27 Martin Luther King, "JFK's Executive Order," *AN,* December 22, 1962.

28 "Parley Can Help, Says Dr. King," *CT,* January 17, 1963.

29 Full text of Heschel's address: www.blackpast.org/african-american-history/1963-rabbi-abraham-joshua-heschel-religion-and-race/.

30 National Park Service, "African American Outdoor Recreation," study, 2022, 101–3.

31 "It Looks Like 'Open Season' on King," *CD,* June 6, 1963.

32 " 'Segregation' in Chicago Hit by Dr. King," *CT,* May 28, 1963.

33 "Negro Tired of Waiting," *CST,* May 28, 1963.

34 "Battle over Open *Occupancy* Law in City Council," *CD,* June 1, 1963.

35 " 'Segregation' in Chicago Hit by Dr. King."

36 "We Are Fed Up," *CT,* May 29, 1963.

37 "Portrait of a Christian," *CT,* September 23, 1958.

38 See Alan Anderson and George Pickering, *Confronting the Color Line: The Broken Promise of the Civil Rights Movement in Chicago* (Athens: University of Georgia Press, 1986), 208.

39 https://kinginstitute.stanford.edu/encyclopedia/raby-albert.

40 Finley, *The Chicago Freedom Movement,* 16–19.

41 Finley, "A Stone's Throw," *CD,* May 4, 1964.

42 https://mediaburn.org/video/timuel-black/.

43 Amy Sonnie and James Tracy, *Hillbilly Nationalists: Urban Race Rebels and Black Power* (New York: Melville House, 2011), 18–19.

44   Michelle Boyd, *Jim Crow Nostalgia: Reconstructing Race in Bronzeville* (Minneapolis: University of Minnesota Press, 2008), 43.

45   www.history.com/news/chicago-public-school-boycott-1963-freedom -movement-mlk.

46   "We Are Fed Up."

47   "Intimidation Is Intended," *CST*, July 1, 1963.

48   Delmont, *Why Busing Failed*, 59.

49   "Negroes Win Big Victory; Willis Quits!" *CD*, October 5, 1963.

50   Dominic Pacyga, *Chicago: A Biography* (Chicago: University of Chicago Press, 2009), 351.

51   www.encyclopedia.chicagohistory.org/pages/1357.html.

52   Delmont, *Why Busing Failed*, 59; https://news.wttw.com/2013/10/22/1963 -chicago-public-school-boycott.

53   Sonnie and Tracy, *Hillbilly Nationalists*, 18–19.

54   "B.C. Willis, 86, Led Chicago Schools for 13 Years," *NYT*, August 31, 1998.

55   www.history.com/news/chicago-public-school-boycott-1963-freedom -movement-mlk.

56   Edwin Berry interview, CRDP.

57   Franklin, *The Young Crusaders*, 120–26.

58   Diamond, *Chicago on the Make*, 177.

59   Diamond, *Chicago on the Make*, 178.

60   Ralph, *Northern Protest*, 19.

61   Ralph, *Northern Protest*, 15.

62   https://casetext.com/case/webb-v-board-of-education-of-city-of-chicago.

63   "Benjamin C. Willis, Ex-City Schools Chief," *CT*, August 30, 1988.

64   Sugrue, *Sweet Land of Liberty*, 453.

65   Ralph, *Northern Protest*, 19.

66   Finley, *The Chicago Freedom Movement*, 19.

67   Balto, *Occupied Territory*, 173.

68   Todd-Breland, *A Political Education*, 28.

69   "We Must March Says Rights Leader," *CST*, August 27, 1963.

70   Delmont, *Why Busing Failed*, 61.

71   Ralph, *Northern Protest*, 21.

72   Todd-Breland, *A Political Education*, 30.

73   "Kerner Raps Civil Rights Criticism of Illinois," *CST*, July 29, 1963.

74   Albert Raby interview, Eyes II.

75   "King in Visit to Cheer Gregory," *Afro American*, August 31, 1963.

76   "What Were Willis Wagons That Got Bernie Sanders Arrested in 1963?" *CT*, February 29, 2016, swww.chicagotribune.com/news/break ing/ct-willis-wagons-explainer-20160223-story.html.

77   Finley, *The Chicago Freedom Movement*, 17.

78   Erin Blakemore, "Why MLK Encouraged 225,000 Chicago Kids to Cut Class in 1963," History.com, March 14, 2018.

79   Sugrue, *Sweet Land of Liberty*, 454.

80   Lawrence Landry interview, CRDP.

81   Todd-Breland, *A Political Education*, 46.

82 https://chicago.suntimes.com/2021/5/20/22442511/chicago-school
-segregation-brown-vs-board-of-education.

83 Delmont, *Why Busing Failed*, 62.

84 history.com/news/chicago-public-school-boycott-1963-freedom-move
ment-mlk.

85 "Rev. King Raps Willis Segregation Policy," *CD*, October 28, 1963.

86 Todd-Breland, *A Political Education*, 29; Landry, CRDP.

87 Toussaint Losier, *War for the City* manuscript, in author's possession;
Franklin, *Young Crusaders*, 131.

88 King, "The School Boycott Concept."

89 Cohen and Taylor, *American Pharaoh*, 314.

90 "Tribune vs. Rights," *CD*, March 16, 1964.

91 Garrow, *Bearing the Cross*, 431–32.

92 "Black and White—They Cared! Dr. King Enchants Huge Throng at
Rights Rally," *CD*, June 22, 1964.

93 Reese Cleghorn, "Martin Luther King Jr. Apostle of Crisis," *Saturday Evening Post*, June 15, 1963.

94 Cleghorn, "Martin Luther King Jr. Apostle of Crisis."

95 Martin Luther King, "Civil Right No. 1: The Right to Vote," *NYT*,
March 14, 1965.

96 "Dr. King Carries the Fight to Northern Slums," *Ebony*, April 1966, 100,
102.

97 *King in Chicago*, documentary.

98 Raby interview, Eyes II.

99 David Bernstein, "Martin Luther King Jr.'s Chicago Campaign," *Chicago Magazine*, July 26, 2016; Jackson, *From Civil Rights to Human Rights*, 237.

100 Lewis, *King*, 295; Jackson, *From Civil Rights to Human Rights*, 237. Those
opposed included Jones, Williams, and Rustin.

101 Hamilton, *Dr. Martin Luther King Jr. and the Poor People's Campaign*, 29.

102 Oates, *Let the Trumpet Sound*, 379.

103 "Dr. King: Death Won't Stop Drive," *BG*, March 15, 1965.

104 Bagley, *Desert Rose*, 203.

105 CSK, *My Life with Martin*, 148.

106 "Foundation Buys King's Vine City Home," *AJC*, January 24, 2019.

107 Oates, *Let the Trumpet Sound*, 379.

108 Raby interview, Eyes II.

109 Ronald Shaw, "A Final Push for National Legislation: The Chicago Freedom Movement," *Journal of the Illinois State Historical Society*, Autumn
2001, 304–32.

110 CSK, *My Life with Martin*, 252.

111 See Fairclough, *To Redeem the Soul*.

112 "Chicago—Target of Movement," *CD*, April 17, 1965.

113 Sam Hitchmough, "Missions of Patriotism: Joseph H. Jackson and Martin Luther King," *European Journal of American Studies*, Spring 2011.

114 "King to Push Rights Drive into Chicago," *CT*, April 2, 1965. The *Los Angeles Times* took note of the decision as well.

115 "Offensive Threats," editorial, *CT*, April 7, 1965.

116 "The Violence of Nonviolence," guest editorial, *CT*, April 18, 1965.

117 "Judges of Their Own Cause," editorial, *CT*, April 24, 1965.

118 "Dr. King Carries the Fight to Northern Slums," *Ebony*, April 1966, 102.

119 "Urge Rent Strike to Fight Woodlawn Slum Housing," *CD*, May 24, 1965.

120 "The Men Behind Martin Luther King Subject: Hosea Williams," *CD*, May 26, 1965.

121 Dorothy Tillman interview, August 9, 2024.

122 Raby interview, Eyes II.

123 "The Day King Marched in Chicago," *Negro Digest*, March 1966.

124 "They're Going to Have to Clean House," *CD*, August 3, 1965.

125 Mary Barr, "Segregation without Segregationists," *The Strange Careers of the Jim Crow North*, 181.

126 Branch, *At Canaan's Edge*, 265.

127 Branch, *At Canaan's Edge*, 266.

7: Police Brutality in the North Is Rationalized, Tolerated, and Usually Denied: King Takes On White Shock After Watts

1 As quoted in https://kinginstitute.stanford.edu/encyclopedia/chicago-campaign.

2 "Dr. King to Fight Bias in the North," *NYT*, August 6, 1965.

3 Sides, *LA City Limits*, 169.

4 Quintard Taylor, *In Search of the Racial Frontier* (New York: Norton, 1998), 300.

5 Davis and Wiener, *Set the Night on Fire*, 213.

6 www2.census.gov/library/publications/1966/demographics/p23-017.pdf; Elizabeth Hinton, *From the War on Poverty to the War on Crime: The Making of Mass Incarceration in America* (Cambridge: Harvard University Press, 2016), 67.

7 Horne, *Fire This Time*, 99; Oates, *Let the Trumpet Sound*, 377.

8 Interview with Cynthia Hamilton, Watts Oral History Project of the Southern California Library.

9 Horne, *Fire This Time*, 3.

10 Tackett interview.

11 Celes King interview, 1988, Department of Special Collections, UCLA.

12 David Sears and T. M. Tomlinson, "Riot Ideology Among Los Angeles Negroes," *Social Science Quarterly*, vol. 49, no. 3 (December 1968).

13 Kirse Granat May, *Golden State, Golden Youth: The California Image in Popular Culture, 1955–1966* (Chapel Hill: University of North Carolina Press, 2002), 160.

14 MLK interview with David Susskind.

15 MLK, "In a Word—Now," *NYT*, September 29, 1963.

16 "King Maps Course with Much Broader Goals," *LAT*, August, 15, 1965.

17 Nicolaides, *My Blue Heaven*, 324–25.

18 "LA Disorders Prolonged by Terrorists," *CT*, August 17, 1965.

19 Theodore H. White, "Lessons of Los Angeles," *LAT*, August 22, 1965.

20 "A Summer Carnival of Riot," editorial, *LAT*, August 13, 1965.

21 "A Time for Prayer," editorial, *LAT*, August 15, 1965; "A City Demands the Answers," editorial, *LAT*, August 17, 1965.

22 "We Must Speak to Each Other," editorial, *LAT*, August 29, 1965.

23 "What King Said in Meeting with Daley," *CD*, March 28, 1966.

24 "Inquiry on Causes Urged by Wilkins," *NYT*, August 16, 1965.

25 Davis and Wiener, *Set the Night on Fire*, 224–25.

26 "LA Disorders Prolonged by Terrorists," *CT*, August 17, 1965.

27 CSK interview, Box 21, Folder 10, Hatch.

28 "King Spurns Brown to Fly Here Today," *LAT*, August 17, 1965.

29 https://storymaps.arcgis.com/stories/74bab7e62e30485cbcd89ea79a33817a.

30 CSK, *My Life with Martin*, 253.

31 https://la.curbed.com/maps/martin-luther-king-los-angeles-loca tions-map.

32 https://laist.com/2017/01/16/mlk_1965_speech.php.

33 "Dr. King Going to Los Angeles," *The Sun*, August 16, 1965.

34 www.youtube.com/watch?v=diLC4hbJVF4&t=57s.

35 Alfred Ligon interview by Ranford Hopkins, 1988, Oral History Program, UCLA.

36 "King Did Overcome Hostility to Reason with L.A. Youths," *Jet*, September 2, 1965.

37 "Dr. King Hears Watts Protest over Heckling," *LAT*, August 19, 1965.

38 Eig, *King*, 463; Garrow, *Bearing the Cross*, 439.

39 CSK, *We Shall Overcome*, 254.

40 "King Assailed by Yorty in Stormy Meeting," *LAT*, August 20, 1965.

41 Hinton, *From the War on Poverty*, 70.

42 "McCone Heads Panel of 8 to Study Riots on the Coast," *NYT*, August 20, 1965; "Coast Riot Area Gets $1.7 Million for Cleanup Job," *NYT*, August 19, 1965.

43 Jackson, *From Civil Rights to Human Rights*, 241.

44 Oates, *Let the Trumpet Sound*, 378.

45 Oates, *Let the Trumpet Sound*.

46 Branch, *At Canaan's Edge*, 298.

47 Mike Marqusee, *Redemption Song: Muhammad Ali and the Spirit of the 1960s* (New York: Verso, 2000), 183.

48 "L.A. Lacks Leadership on Rights," *LAT*, August 21, 1965.

49 "King Assailed by Yorty in Stormy Meeting," *LAT*, August 20, 1965.

50 "Parker Warns Disrespect for Law Imperils US," *LAT*, August 22, 1965.

51 "Commission Named to Probe Causes of Los Angeles Riot," *CT*, August 20, 1965.

52 "Police Shoot Up Mosque," *CT*, August 19, 1965.

53 Christopher Strain, *Pure Fire: Self Defense as Activism in the Civil Rights Era* (Athens: University of Georgia Press, 2005), 124.

54 Maya Angelou, *A Song Flung Up to Heaven* (New York: Virago, 2002), 82–83.

55 "Capitol Nervous About L.A. Riots," *LAT*, August 17, 1965.

56 "300 at LA City Hall Protest King Arrest," *LAT*, February 3, 1965; "Yorty Cites King During Local Visit," *LAS*, March 4, 1965.
57 "King Talks with L.A. People: Calls for Ouster of Police Chief," *AN*, August 28, 1965.
58 "McCone Heads Panel of 8 to Study Riots on the Coast."
59 "Police Shoot Up Mosque, Seize 60 Black Muslims," *CT*, August 19, 1965.
60 Jackson, *From Civil Rights to Human Rights*, 240.
61 "Preserving a Good Police Force," editorial, *LAT*, August 22, 1965.
62 "Martin Luther King Could Share Bertrand Russell's Pitiable Fate," *LAT*, August 20, 1965.
63 Honey, *To the Promised Land*, 105.
64 CSK, Christmas message—1968, Box 23, Folder 5, Hatch.
65 Eig, *King*, 464–65.
66 Branch, *At Canaan's Edge*, 305–8.
67 Hinton, *From the War on Poverty*, 76–77.
68 Nick Kotz, *Judgment Days: Lyndon Baines Johnson, Martin Luther King Jr., and the Laws That Changed America* (New York: Houghton Mifflin Harcourt, 2005), 341.
69 Jackson, *From Civil Rights to Human Rights*, 240.
70 Lewis, *King*, 306.
71 CSK, *My Life with Martin*, 253.
72 See Lisa McGirr, *Suburban Warriors*; Mike Davis, *City of Quartz*.
73 MLK, "Feeling Alone in the Struggle," *AN*, August 28, 1965.
74 Robert Fogelson, "White on Black: A Critique of the McCone Commission Report on the Los Angeles Riots," *Political Science Quarterly* 82, no. 3 (September 1967); "Commission Named to Probe Causes of Riot," *CT*, August 20, 1965.
75 Jill Lepore, "The History of the Riot Report," *New Yorker*, June 15, 2020.
76 Fogelson, "White on Black."
77 Caughey, *To Kill a Spirit*, 29.
78 Felker-Kantor, *Policing Los Angeles*.
79 Gerald Horne has argued that it was researchers who were the "ultimate beneficiary of those fires of summer." He quotes the *Los Angeles Free Press*, "The special investigations and reports, surveys, articles, books, lectures, conferences and programs virtually defy enumeration." Horne, *Fire This Time*, 39.
80 Thomas Pynchon, "A Journey into the Mind of Watts," *NYT*, June 12, 1966.
81 MLK, "Beyond the Los Angeles Riots."
82 Franke-Ruta, "Martin Luther King Jr.'s Amazing Interview with Robert Penn Warren."
83 Historian Tom Sugrue notes that "nothing compared to the extensive coverage, both in newspapers and on television, of the role of southern law enforcement officials in resisting civil rights." Sugrue, *Sweet Land of Liberty*, 328.

84 Johnson, *Race and Remembrance*, 57.

85 Elizabeth Hinton, "Why We Should Reconsider the War on Crime," *Time*, March 20, 2015.

86 www.presidency.ucsb.edu/documents/commencement-address -howard-university-fulfill-these-rights.

87 Anderson and Pickering, *Confronting the Color Line*, 171–72.

88 Hinton, *America on Fire*, 241.

89 Hinton, *America on Fire*, 11; Law, *Corridors of Contagion*, 47.

90 "Boundary Problems 1st in School Probe," *CT*, January 3, 1966.

91 Cohen and Taylor, *American Pharaoh*, 350.

92 Jackson, *From Civil Rights to Human Rights*, 289.

93 Raby interview, Eyes II; Anderson and Pickering, *Confronting the Color Line*, 180.

94 "A Man Among Midgets," editorial, *CT*, October 6, 1965.

95 "A Man Among Midgets"; "Humiliating and Outrageous," editorial, *CT*, October 5, 1965.

96 Cohen and Taylor, *American Pharaoh*, 352.

97 "Dr. King Focuses on Drive in Chicago," *NYT*, October 11, 1965.

98 "King's Chicago Shakeup Could Help Republicans," *CD*, January 15, 1966.

99 Anderson and Pickering, *Confronting the Color Line*, 181.

100 "Dr. King Focuses on Drive in Chicago," *NYT*, October 11, 1965.

101 "Federal Aid: The Head of the Class," *Time*, October 15, 1965.

102 Cohen and Taylor, *American Pharaoh*, 353. Keppel then took a job in the private sector in 1966.

103 "Chicago School Fund Released," *CT*, October 6, 1965.

104 Raby interview, Eyes II.

105 Delmont, *Why Busing Failed*, 65–68.

106 MLK, "The Last Steep Ascent," *AN*, April 23, 1966.

8: Warrior Without a Gun: The Kings Move to Chicago

1 MLK, "Let Justice Roll Down," *The Nation*, March 15, 1965.

2 "Rev. King's Wife Sees Job to Be Done," *Fresno Bee*, April 26, 1966.

3 "Dr. King to Open Drive in Chicago," *NYT*, July 8, 1965.

4 " 'Racism Is Genocide': King Shakes Up Chicago," *CD*, July 24, 1965.

5 MLK, "A Prayer for Chicago," republished in *AN*, April 9, 1966.

6 "Dr. King Starts Drive in Chicago," *NYT*, July 25, 1965.

7 "King Shakes Up Chicago," *CD*, July 24, 1965; "Dr. Martin Luther King Spotlights Movement Here," *CD*, July 26, 1965.

8 Sugrue, *Sweet Land of Liberty*, 416.

9 "Dr. King Starts Drive in Chicago"; "Chicago No Promised Land, Says King," *CD*, July 27, 1965.

10 "Chicago No Promised Land, Says King."

11 "Dr. King Starts Drive in Chicago."

12 "Enough Predictions of Rioting," editorial, *CT*, August 31, 1965.

13 "Two Societies," *Eyes on the Prize*.

14 Williams, *From the Bullet to the Ballot*, 43.
15 Kelley, *Freedom Dreams*.
16 Erik Wallenberg, "The Young Lords Fight for Environmental Justice in New York," *Edge Effects*, July 29, 2021.
17 Finley, *The Chicago Freedom Movement*, 275.
18 Hamilton, *Dr. Martin Luther King Jr. and the Poor People's Campaign*.
19 Finley, *The Chicago Freedom Movement*, 278–79.
20 It is now known that levels exceeding 10 micrograms impact children's health. Finley, *The Chicago Freedom Movement*, 279.
21 "Lead Poisoning Claims Child," *CD*, September 7, 1960.
22 Finley, *The Chicago Freedom Movement*, 275–76.
23 "Lead Poisons Slum Tots," *CD*, March 27, 1961.
24 Finley, *The Chicago Freedom Movement*, 276–77.
25 https://kinginstitute.stanford.edu/encyclopedia/lafayette-bernard.
26 "Rights Forces, After Wide Legal Gains, Grope for New Ways to Bring Negro Equality," *NYT*, August 15, 1965.
27 www.mtsu.edu/first-amendment/article/618/gregory-v-city-of-chicago.
28 Ralph, *Northern Protest*, 7.
29 "C.C.C.O. to Ask Daley for a Meeting," *CT*, August 13, 1965.
30 Oates, *Let the Trumpet Sound*, 380.
31 "King Movement Faced Kid Gangs," *CD*, April 5, 1966.
32 Lafayette interview, Eyes II.
33 Author interview with Dorothy Tillman, August 9, 2024.
34 Tillman interview.
35 James Orange interview, CRDP.
36 MLK, "Beyond the LA Riots," 34.
37 MLK, "My Dream: Myth of the Promised Land," *CD*, December 18, 1965.
38 "Dr. King Is Writing Column for Papers," *NYT*, November 21, 1965.
39 "September 7, 1965," memo, Stegall Papers.
40 Eig, *King*, 475.
41 MLK, *Where Do We Go from Here*, 49–50.
42 MLK, "My Dream," *CD*, February 12, 1966.
43 Copy of the Chicago plan at www.crmvet.org/docs/6601_sclc_mlk_chicagoplan.pdf.
44 "Statement by Martin Luther King Jr., Chicago, Illinois, January 7, 1966," from Eig.
45 www.crmvet.org/tim/tim66b.htm#1966chicago.
46 Finley, *The Chicago Freedom Movement*, 116.
47 Finley, *The Chicago Freedom Movement*, 245.
48 MLK, "Going to Chicago," *AN*, January 15, 1966.
49 MLK statement, Chicago, January 7, 1966; MLK, "Going to Chicago," *AN*, January 15, 1966.
50 Oates, *Let the Trumpet Sound*, 388; Jackson, *Becoming King*, 282.
51 Cohen and Taylor, *American Pharaoh*, 357–59.
52 Cohen and Taylor, *American Pharaoh*, 358.
53 MLK, "My Dream," *CD*, February 12, 1966.

54 Ethan Michaeli, *The Defender: How the Legendary Black Newspaper Changed America* (New York: Houghton Mifflin, 2016), 400–401.

55 Lewis, *King*, 315; "Rights Leader Launches Hard-Hitting Campaign Against Slum Colonialism in Chicago," *Ebony*, April 1966.

56 "Dr. King's Flat, Altho Painted, Is Very Dismal," *CT*, January 26, 1966. The building the Kings moved into was owned by one of the largest tax-buying predators in the city, Allan Blair. Tax buyers would swoop in when people got behind on their property taxes and profit while people were forced to either scrape together much more money to pay the back taxes plus interest or lose their property altogether. People like Blair controlled a lot of property in the city's ghettos and contributed to their disrepair. Andrew Kahrl, *The Black Tax* (Chicago: University of Chicago Press, 2024), 121–27.

57 "Dr. King Carries the Fight to Northern Slums," *Ebony*, April 1966, 94.

58 "Dr. King Shows How to 'Cure' a Slum," *CD*, January 24, 1966.

59 "Dr. King's New Address Just off 'Bloody 16th St.,' " *Chicago Daily News*, January 25, 1966.

60 "Dr. King Shows How to 'Cure' a Slum."

61 "King and Wife Move into Slum," *CD*, January 27, 1966.

62 Statement by MLK, Chicago, January 7, 1966.

63 CSK, *MLMLML*, 144.

64 Oates, *Let the Trumpet Sound*, 388.

65 CSK, *MLMLML*, 143.

66 https://africasacountry.com/2020/07/we-are-all-brothers.

67 Jackson, *From Civil Rights to Human Rights*, 281.

68 MLK, "Why We Are in Chicago," *AN*, February 5, 1966.

69 MLK, "My Dream," *CD*, January 8, 1966.

70 "Africans Host Negro Refused Georgia Seat," *LAT*, January 22, 1966.

71 Oates, *Let the Trumpet Sound*, 390; "Dr. King Carries Fight to Northern Slums," 96.

72 Oates, *Let the Trumpet Sound*, 389.

73 CSK interview, Box 21, Folder 10, Hatch.

74 Author interview with Lynn Adler, August 20, 2024.

75 digital.wustl.edu/e/eii/eiiweb/kin5427.0224.089corettascottking.html.

76 CSK interview, Eyes II.

77 Finley, *The CFM*, 30.

78 Tillman interview.

79 Finley, *The CFM*, 30–31.

80 CSK interview, Box 21, Folder 10, Hatch.

81 digital.wustl.edu/e/eii/eiiweb/kin5427.0224.089corettascottking.html.

82 Letter from Jeff Fort, April 18, 2024.

83 Letter from Jeff Fort, July 22, 2024.

84 "Gangs That Came to Rule in Seats of Power," *CT*, June 22, 2012.

85 Fernandez, *The Young Lords*.

86 Diamond, "From Fighting Gangs to Black Nations"; Balto, *Occupied Territory*.

87 David Dawley, *A Nation of Lords: The Autobiography of the Vice Lords* (New York: Waveland Press, 1992), 107.
88 "How Lords, Cobra Gangs Organize and Expand," *CD*, September 14, 1965.
89 "Dr. King Will Occupy Slum Flat in New Rights Campaign," *CD*, January 8, 1966; "The Roots of the Chicago Freedom Movement," *Chicago Reporter*, February 1, 2016.
90 Franklin, *The Young Crusaders*, 201.
91 "Dr. King Meets with Top Cops," *CD*, January 29, 1966.
92 Eric Gerard Pearman, "Martin Luther King Jr. and Chicago's Gangs," *The Sphinx*, Spring 1997.
93 Brandon M. Terry, "MLK Now," *Fifty Years Since MLK*.
94 Pearman, "Martin Luther King Jr. and Chicago's Gangs."
95 Letter from Jeff Fort, July 22, 2024.
96 Pearman, "Martin Luther King Jr. and Chicago's Gangs."
97 Letter from Jeff Fort, April 18, 2024.
98 CSK interview, Box 21, Folder 10, Hatch.
99 Natalie Y. Moore and Lance Williams, *The Almighty Black P Stone Nation: The Rise, Fall, and Resurgence of an American Gang* (Chicago: Lawrence Hill, 2011), 41.
100 Franklin, *The Young Crusaders*, 201.
101 CSK, *My Life with Martin*, 262.
102 Finley, *The Chicago Freedom Movement*, 30–31.
103 Letter from Jeff Fort, July 22, 2024.
104 Moore and Williams, *The Almighty Black P Stone Nation*, 40–42.
105 Letter from Jeff Fort, April 18, 2024.
106 Author interview with Doris Crenshaw, March 23, 2024.
107 Kwame Ture interview, Eyes II.
108 MLK, "A Time to Break the Silence."
109 Oates, *Let the Trumpet Sound*, 392.
110 Oates, *Let the Trumpet Sound*.
111 Dawley, *A Nation of Lords*, 107.
112 "The Big Freedom Festival? It was a Smash!" *CD*, March 14, 1966.
113 Finley, *The Chicago Freedom Movement*, 297.
114 www.cairn.info/revue-francaise-d-etudes-americaines-2008-2-page-51.htm.
115 Hamilton, *Dr. Martin Luther King Jr. and the Poor People's Campaign*.
116 Ralph, *Northern Protest*, 93.
117 Ralph, *Northern Protest*, 95.
118 Moore and Williams, *The Almighty Black P Stone Nation*, 71, 74.
119 See "King Picks 'Typical' Flat; 8 Men Repair It," *CT*, January 23, 1966; "Dr. King, Mate Live in Flat for One Day," *CT*, January 27, 1966; "People," *Time*, February 25, 1966.
120 Ralph, *Northern Protest*, 55. King typically spent Wednesday through Saturday in Chicago, flying back to preach at Ebenezer on Sundays.

121 Author interview with Judy Richardson, December 14, 2023.

122 "Social Change," editorial, *CD*, February 9, 1966.

123 "Dr. King Carries the Fight to Northern Slums," 102.

124 MLK, "My Dream," *CD*, February 12, 1966.

125 Branch, *At Canaaan's Edge*, 372, 428–29.

126 Lewis, *King*, 316.

127 www.chicagoreporter.com/the-chicago-freedom-movement-and-the-fight-for-fair-lending/.

128 "Charge Rats Killed Baby Disputed," *WP*, February 12, 1966.

129 "Slum Rats Chew Out Baby's Eye," *Jet*, February 24, 1966.

130 Sitkoff, *King*, 180.

131 The *Washington Post* devoted a whole piece to how Adams did not die of rat bites but malnutrition, which echoed Daley's disturbing claim.

132 digital.wustl.edu/e/eii/eiiweb/kin5427.0224.089corettascottking.html.

133 Finley, *The CFM*, 32.

134 "Rev. Abernathy to Move In Next Door to Dr. King's," *CD*, February 12, 1966.

135 Lewis, *King*, 317.

136 digital.wustl.edu/e/eii/eiiweb/kin5427.0224.089corettascottking.html.

137 "Dr. King Barred from Slum Flats," *NYT*, April 6, 1966.

138 "City Stays Clear of Slum Grab," *CT*, February 26, 1966; "Martin Luther the Lawgiver," editorial, *CT*, February 25, 1966; "Dr. King Seizes a Slum Building," *NYT*, February 24, 1966.

139 Lentz, *Symbols*, 198–99.

140 "Dr. King Seizes a Slum Building"; "Dr. King Assailed for Slum Tactic," *NYT*, February 25, 1966; "Landlord Sues Dr. King over Building Grab," *LAT*, March 5, 1966; "Chicago Slum Owner Given 4 Weeks to Fix Violations," *NYT*, March 10, 1966.

141 "King Ordered Out of Flats," *CT*, April 6, 1966.

142 "Dr. King and the Law," *CD*, April 13, 1966.

143 "What's It Like in a Westside Flat," *CD*, March 14, 1966.

144 Ralph, *Northern Protest*, 57.

145 Michaeli, *The Defender*, 405.

146 Oates, *Let the Trumpet Sound*, 391–92; "Dr. King and the Law."

147 "Officials Across the Nation Battle to Remove Slum," *CD*, February 26, 1966.

148 Author interview with Lynn Adler, August 20, 2024.

149 Bernardine Dohrn et al., "Session V: Lawyers for the Chicago Freedom Movement, 1965–1966," *Northwestern Journal of Law & Social Policy* 10, no. 3 (Fall 2016).

150 "Another Seizure of Private Property," editorial, *CT*, April 9, 1966.

151 "Despite Bombing Opposition Remains," *NYT*, September 22, 1963; "Accord in Birmingham Viewed as a Milestone," *WP*, May 12, 1963.

152 "331 Slum Flat Rent Cut-Offs," *CD*, February 12, 1966.

153 "Group Seizes Second Tenement on South Side," *CT*, April 21, 1966.

154   "The Tardy Campaign Against Slums," *CT*, April 14, 1966.

155   Laurent, *King and the Other America*, 91.

156   Ralph, *Northern Protest*, 214. According to Sitkoff, Levison grew increasingly concerned about King's tenant organizing, saying it made SCLC come off like a "gang of anarchists" (183).

157   WVON call-in show, 1966, https://w.soundcloud.com/player/?url=https%3A%2F%2Fapi.soundcloud.com%2Ftracks%2F244099630&.

158   "Dr. King's Campaign in Chicago," *CT*, January 13, 1966.

159   "Useful Work for the Rev. Martin Luther," editorial, *CT*, February 15, 1966.

160   "Martin Luther the Lawgiver"; "Useful Work for the Rev. Martin Luther."

161   "Reader Wants King to Aid Destitute in Ala.," *CD*, March 12, 1966.

162   "Words of the Week," *Jet*, August 15, 1968.

163   MLK, "Why We Are in Chicago," *AN*, March 12, 1966.

164   MLK, "My Dream," *CD*, February 19, 1966.

165   MLK, "Chicago and Civil Rights—Drive to End Slums," *Christian Science Monitor*, March 14, 1967.

166   "Board Tackles Jenner Row Today," *CD*, February 23, 1966.

167   Dionne Danns, "Chicago High School Students' Movement for Quality Public Education," *Journal of African American History* 88, no. 2 (Spring 2003): 140.

168   "King to Speak Out on Jenner Issue," *CD*, February 22, 1966.

169   "Jenner Boycott Delayed," *CD*, April 4, 1966.

170   "Boycott Holds in 4th Day," *CD*, April 21, 1966.

171   "The Jenner Boycott Proves Numerical Success," *CD*, April 23, 1966.

172   "Pupil Boycott Foes Line Up," *CT*, April 20, 1966.

173   Garrow, *Bearing the Cross*, 470.

174   "Biased Schools Not Only in the South," *AN*, May 28, 1966; "King Group's Novel Plan to Repair Slum," *CD*, February 24, 1966.

175   "He Wants to Unseat Dawson," *CD*, March 2, 1966; Sitkoff, *King*.

176   Finley, *The CFM*, 19. The six were William Campbell, Robert Miller, William Harvey, Benjamin Lewis, Ralph Metcalf, and Claude Holman.

177   Lafayette interview, Eyes II.

178   Ralph, *Northern Protest*, 44–45.

179   Tillman interview; Bernstein, "Martin Luther King Jr.'s Chicago Campaign."

180   Raby interview, Eyes II.

181   Lawrence Landry interview, CRDP.

182   Bernstein, "Martin Luther King Jr.'s Chicago Campaign."

183   Cohen and Taylor, *American Pharaoh*, 359.

184   John Tweedle, *A Lasting Impression: A Collection of Photographs of Martin Luther King, Jr.* (Columbia: University of South Carolina Press, 1983), edited by Hermene Hartman, xvii.

185   Hampton, *Voices of Freedom*, 300.

186   Cohen and Taylor, *American Pharaoh*, 359–60.

187 "Were Chicago Ministers Wrong to Go to Albany," *CD*, September 11, 1962; Finley, *The CFM*, 38–39.

188 Williams, *From the Bullet to the Ballot*, 43.

189 Sam Hitchmough, "Missions of Patriotism: Joseph H. Jackson and Martin Luther King," *European Journal of American Studies*, Spring 2011.

190 Cohen and Taylor, *American Pharaoh*, 359.

191 "Dr. King, Rev. Jackson Air Differences," *CD*, July 7, 1966.

192 "Dr. King Assailed by Committee of 100," *CT*, March 8, 1966. Some biographers too have often portrayed this as a bona fide civil rights organization, as opposed to a Daley front group.

193 Lewis, *King*, 313.

194 "Dr. Martin Luther King Urges Chicagoans to Register—and Vote," *CD*, May 14, 1966.

195 MLK, "Why We Are in Chicago."

196 Jackson, *From Civil Rights to Human Rights*, 282.

197 Nancy Jefferson interview, Eyes II.

198 Author interview with Lynn Adler, August 20, 2024.

199 "Dr. King to Meet Mayor," *CD*, March 24, 1966.

200 "What King Said in Meeting with Daley," *CD*, March 28, 1966.

201 "Daley, Clerics Again Discuss City Problems," *CT*, March 25, 1966.

202 Laurent, *King and the Other America*, 91.

203 Black interview, https://mediaburn.org/video/timuel-black/?t=87:28.

204 Belafonte, *My Song*, 308–9.

205 "King in Paris Tells Negro Gains in U.S.," *CT*, March 29, 1966.

206 Oates, *Let the Trumpet Sound*, 394.

207 "Daley, Aides Have Word for King: 'Go,' " *CD*, April 16, 1966; Cohen and Taylor, *American Pharaoh*, 373.

208 MLK, "My Dream: Never Negative Normalcy," *CD*, March 12, 1966.

209 Jackson, *From Civil Rights to Human Rights*, 276.

210 Deppe, *Operation Breadbasket*, 5.

211 https://kinginstitute.stanford.edu/encyclopedia/operation-breadbasket; "Breadbasket Launches Boycott," *CD*, April 11, 1966.

212 Finley, *The CFM*, 243.

213 "Martin Luther King Says Riots Can't Win," *DFP*, October 22, 1967.

214 Ralph, *Northern Protest*, 94.

215 "3000 Teens Will 'Close Chicago,' Bevel Says," *CD*, May 11, 1966.

216 "Launch Moves to Improve Housing for Negroes," *CD*, June 4, 1966.

217 Finley, *The CFM*, 330.

218 Lyrics provided by Tenisha Armstrong.

219 Andrew Diamond, *Mean Streets: Chicago Youths and the Everyday Struggle for Empowerment in the Multiracial City, 1908–1969* (Berkeley: University of California Press, 2009), 270–71.

220 Ralph, *Northern Protest*, 94.

221 https://interactive.wttw.com/dusable-to-obama/dr-kings-chicago-crusade.

222 "Barriers Restrict Whites, Says Mrs. King," *Toronto Star*, May 14, 1966.

223   "Civil Rights Round 3," *Time*, May 6, 1966.

224   Garrow, *Bearing the Cross*, 467.

225   MLK speech at Southern Methodist University, March 17, 1966, www .smu.edu/News/2014/mlk-at-smu-transcript-17march1966.

226   "Dr. King Talks in Lansing," *CD*, March 12, 1966.

227   Lewis, *King*, 321.

228   "Approve Tenants Union," *CT*, July 14, 1966.

229   "Skip School Tuesday, City's Negroes Urged," *CT*, May 15, 1966.

230   "Willis to Give Explanation of U.S. Aid Cut," *CT*, May 18, 1966.

231   Joseph, *The Sword and the Shield*, 248–49.

232   Lewis, *King*, 312.

9: One Day That Man Wants to Get Out of Prison:
The Organizing Deepens but So Does White Resistance

1   Beryl Satter, *Family Properties: Race, Real Estate, and the Exploitation of Urban America* (New York: Henry Holt, 2010).

2   "Inmates Beat Whites Charged with Negro's Death," *Jet*, June 16, 1966.

3   Three of the teenagers would be convicted of voluntary manslaughter (serving less than five years); the charges were dropped on the fourth for testifying against them. Many Black Chicagoans were outraged at the "extremely light sentence." "White Toughs Get 9–20 Years," *Jet*, June 1, 1967. His family attempted to bring a wrongful-death suit against the town of Cicero, but the court rejected it.

4   James Loewen, *Sundown Towns: A Hidden Dimension of American Racism* (New York: New Press, 2005).

5   Dawley, *A Nation of Lords*, 107.

6   "Black Chicago Teen's Death Fueled Cicero March During 1966 protests," *CT*, September 2, 2016.

7   ciceroindependiente.com/cicero-protest-series-2020/opinion-we-dont -have-to-repeat-ciceros-racist-history.

8   "Black Chicago Teen's Death."

9   Carroll, *Race News*, 187–88.

10   "Rocks Hit Dr. King as Whites Attack March in Chicago," *NYT*, August 6, 1966.

11   See, for instance, Lewis, *King*.

12   Robert Lucas interview, CRDP.

13   Belafonte interview, Eyes II.

14   Huey's death didn't merit a mention in Taylor Branch's 1,000+-page *At Canaan's Edge* or Eig's 650-page book *King: A Life*; Eig short-shrifts the Chicago organizing.

15   Hamilton, *Dr. Martin Luther King Jr. and the Poor People's Campaign*, 38.

16   Hamilton, *Dr. Martin Luther King Jr. and the Poor People's Campaign*, 4.

17   "King Calls for Puerto Rican Meet," *CD*, June 15, 1966.

18   Finley, *The Chicago Freedom Movement*, 302.

19   Diamond, *Chicago on the Make*, 190.

20 Finley, *The Chicago Freedom Movement*, 299–300. Various girl gangs included the Vice Ladies, the Rangerettes, and the Black Angels.
21 Simon Balto, "MLK's Forgotten Plan to End Gun Violence," *Portside*, July 8, 2013.
22 Author interview with Dorothy Tillman, August 9, 2024.
23 "SCLC Organizing Young Gangs on a City Basis," *CD*, June 13, 1966.
24 "SCLC Organizing Young Gangs on a City Basis."
25 Finley, *The Chicago Freedom Movement*, 300–301.
26 Finley, *The Chicago Freedom Movement*, 301.
27 "SCLC Organizing Young Gangs on a City Basis."
28 Balto, *Occupied Territory*, 144–53, 172–75.
29 Balto, *Occupied Territory*, 166.
30 Finley, *The Chicago Freedom Movement*, 300.
31 For more on the first Rainbow Coalition, see Williams, *From the Bullet to the Ballot*, and the documentary *The First Rainbow Coalition*.
32 Jon Rice, "The World of the Illinois Panthers," *Freedom North*, 54.
33 Royko, *The Boss*, 151–52.
34 https://centropr-archive.hunter.cuny.edu/digital-humanities/puerto -rican-labor/puerto-ricans-riots-chicago-1966.
35 "King Calls for Puerto Rican Meet." For more on the 1966 Division Street Riots, see Melvin Mendez, "Recollections: The Division Street Riots," *Dialogo* 2, no. 1 (1997); workers.org/2006/us/chicago-0706/.
36 Mendez, "Recollections."
37 Mendez, "Recollections."
38 Gordon Mantler, "Black, Brown, and Poor: Martin Luther King, Jr., the Poor People's Campaign, and Its Legacies," dissertation, Duke University (2008), 90.
39 "Rev. King Asks Latin Leaders to Join March," *CD*, June 16, 1966.
40 Mendez, "Recollections."
41 Cohen and Taylor, *American Pharaoh*, 379.
42 "Puerto Ricans Hold Protest in Chicago," *NYT*, June 29, 1966.
43 Mantler dissertation, 91.
44 "Youth Gangs to Join Big March," *CD*, June 13, 1966; Franklin, *The Young Crusaders*, 201–2.
45 Gerena Valentin, *Gilberto Gerena Valentín*, 196–97.
46 Joseph, *The Sword and the Shield*, 256.
47 "A Global Vision for Black Cats," *Globe and Mail*, April 15, 1967.
48 Rosenbloom, *Redemption*, 9. King released a six-page statement on Black Power in October 1966.
49 Author interview with Judy Richardson, December 13, 2023.
50 CSK interview, Box 21, Folder 10, Hatch.
51 Ture interview, Eyes II.
52 Eig, *King*, 493.
53 CSK, Box 22, Folder 9, Hatch.
54 CSK interview, tape 23, Hatch.

55   CSK, *MLMLML*, 145.
56   Carson, ed., *The Autobiography of Martin Luther King Jr.*, 302.
57   Hamilton, *Dr. Martin Luther King Jr. and the Poor People's Campaign*.
58   Jackson, *From Civil Rights to Human Rights*, 283.
59   "Thousands Go to Soldier Field Rights Rally," *CT*, July 11, 1966.
60   Cohen and Taylor, *American Pharaoh*.
61   "Thousands Go to Soldier Field Rights Rally."
62   Finley, *The CFM*, 302.
63   Franklin, *The Young Crusaders*, 202.
64   Finley, *The CFM*, 303.
65   Sugrue, *Sweet Land of Liberty*, 418.
66   "Here's What Dr. King Told Vast Thousands," *CD*, July 11, 1966.
67   "Here's What Dr. King Told Vast Thousands."
68   "King Discloses Plan for Rally, March on City Hall on June 26," *CT*, May 27, 1966.
69   "30,000 Hear Dr. King at Soldier Field Rally," *CD*, July 11, 1966.
70   Ralph, *Northern Protest*, 107.
71   "King Tells Goals, March on City Hall," *CT*, July 11, 1966.
72   CSK, *MLMLML*, 145–46.
73   digital.wustl.edu/e/eii/eiiweb/kin5427.0224.089corettascottking.html.
74   Ralph, *Northern Protest*, 107.
75   "King Tells Goals, March on City Hall."
76   "A Digest of What Dr. King's Demanding," *CD*, July 11, 1966.
77   "King to Seek City Income Tax, $2 Wage," *CT*, June 9, 1966.
78   "30,000 Hear Dr. King at Soldier Field Rally."
79   Honey, *To the Promised Land*, 107.
80   "50 Years Ago: MLK Jr's Speech at Soldiers Field, March to City Hall with Demands for Daley," *CT*, July 10, 2016; "Common Sense Prevailed," editorial, *CT*, July 12, 1966.
81   "35,000 hear King at Chicago Rally," *CT*, July 23, 1966.
82   Ralph, *Northern Protest*, 108.
83   Raby interview, Eyes II.
84   "Daley, King, Aides, Meet on Rights," *CT*, July 12, 1966.
85   "Daley Critical of Some Civil Rights Moves," *CT*, July 13, 1966.
86   Anderson and Pickering, *Confronting the Color Line*, 208.
87   Michaeli, *The Defender*, 413.
88   Anderson and Pickering, *Confronting the Color Line*, 212.
89   National Park Service, "African American Outdoor Recreation: Study," 115–16.
90   Anderson and Pickering, *Confronting the Color Line*, 210.
91   Branch, *At Canaan's Edge*, 562; Finley, *The Chicago Freedom Movement*, 303.
92   Anderson and Pickering, *Confronting the Color Line*, 211.
93   CSK, *My Life with Martin*, 266–67.
94   Franklin, *The Young Crusaders*, 202.
95   Raby interview, Eyes II.
96   "Churches Fail Humanity by Silence," *CT*, July 18, 1966. He sent a taped

speech instead, his frustration evident: "Millions of American Negroes, starving for the want of the bread of freedom, have knocked again and again on the door of the so-called white churches. But they have usually been greeted by cold indifference or blatant hypocrisy."

97   "Chicago Officials Voice Concern Over Apparent Gang Alliance with Rights Leaders," *NYT*, July 20, 1966.
98   https://johnpwalshblog.com/tag/albert-raby/.
99   Ralph, *Northern Protest*, 111.
100 "Battleground Chicago," *CBS News*, July 15, 1966.
101 Diamond, *Chicago on the Make*, 192–93.
102 "Dr. Jackson Joins Archbishop in Peace Plea," *CT*, July 16, 1966.
103 Ralph, *Northern Protest*, 111.
104 "Dr. Jackson Joins Archbishop in Peace Plea."
105 Garrow, *Bearing the Cross*, 492; "Daley Names 23-Man Review Board," *CD*, July 26, 1966.
106 Ralph, *Northern Protest*, 143.
107 "Martin Luther King Says Riots Can't Win."
108 Branch, *At Canaan's Edge*, 504–5.
109 Deppe, *Operation Breadbasket*, 12.
110 Ralph, *Northern Protest*, 111.
111 Robin Kelley, "Birmingham's Untouchables," in *Race Rebels: Culture, Politics, and the Black Working Class* (New York: Free Press, 1994), 77–101; Diane McWhorter, *Carry Me Home: Birmingham, Alabama* (New York: Simon & Schuster, 2001).
112 Jackson, *From Civil Rights to Human Rights*, 289.
113 Ralph, *Northern Protest*, 182.
114 Ralph, *Northern Protest*.
115 Transcript of the Daley-Johnson call: https://prde.upress.virginia.edu /conversations/4006262.
116 Garrow, *Bearing the Cross*, 468.
117 https://prde.upress.virginia.edu/conversations/4006262.

10: Never Seen Mobs as Hostile . . . but the Nation Turns Its Back

1   "Approve Tenants Union," *CT*, July 14, 1966.
2   Jackson, *From Civil Rights to Human Rights*, 289–90.
3   Dohrn, "Session V."
4   Raby interview, Eyes II.
5   Ralph, *Northern Protest*, 116.
6   Author interview with Doris Crenshaw, March 23, 2024.
7   Lewis, *King*, 339.
8   *The Janes*, documentary, HBO.
9   Sonnie, *Hillbilly Nationalists*, 43.
10 Anderson and Pickering, *Confronting the Color Line*, 224.
11 "Rights Hecklers Burn Cars," *CT*, August 1, 1966.
12 John Dittmer, *The Good Doctors: The Medical Committee for Human Rights* (New York: Bloomsbury, 2009), 112.

13 Raby interview, Eyes II.
14 "Plan March into Belmont Cragin Today," *CT*, August 2, 1966.
15 "Demonstrators Cancel Their 3rd Gage Park March," *CD*, August 2, 1966.
16 "Chicago Vice Wears 'Black Face,' " *CD*, January 6, 1968.
17 https://interactive.wbez.org/curiouscity/chicagonazineighborhood/.
18 "Rights Hecklers Burn Cars"; "Urges Public: Keep Cool in Race March," *CT*, August 7, 1966; Anderson and Pickering, *Confronting the Color Line*, 225.
19 Jefferson interview, Eyes II.
20 Lafayette interview, Eyes II.
21 Diamond, *Chicago on the Make*, 193.
22 Franklin, *The Young Crusaders*, 202.
23 "Peace Among Teenage Gangs Still in Doubt," *CT*, August 1, 1966.
24 "King in Chicago: Has White Power Killed Love Power?" *Village Voice*, August 11, 1966.
25 Ralph, *Northern Protest*, 123.
26 Jeffrey Haas, *The Assassination of Fred Hampton: How the FBI and the Chicago Police Murdered a Black Panther* (Chicago: Chicago Review Press, 2011), 30.
27 Ralph, *Northern Protest*, 123; "King in Chicago"; https://johnpwalshblog.com/tag/albert-raby/.
28 https://johnpwalshblog.com/tag/albert-raby/.
29 Jones, *Selma of the North*, 125.
30 "Dozens Hurt During March in Chicago," *LAT*, August 6, 1966.
31 Raby interview, Eyes II.
32 Franklin, *The Young Crusaders*, 202.
33 Lafayette interview, Eyes II.
34 Moore and Williams, *The Almighty Black P Stone Nation*, 41–42.
35 Moore and Williams, *The Almighty Black P Stone Nation*, 42.
36 "50 Years Ago, MLK's March in Marquette Park Turned Violent, Exposed Hate," *Chicago Tribune*, July 28, 2016.
37 Belafonte interview, Eyes II.
38 "Perspective: The Nation," *LAT*, August 14, 1966.
39 Haas, *The Assassination of Fred Hampton*, 29–30.
40 Haas, *The Assassination of Fred Hampton*, 31.
41 "5 Cops Hurt in Race Disorders," *CT*, August 15, 1966.
42 chicagoreporter.com/the-chicago-freedom-movement-and-the-fight-for-fair-lending/.
43 MLK, "Meet the Press Interview," *A Testament of Hope*, 385.
44 MLK, "Meet the Press Interview," 388.
45 "Wife Reassures Leader Husband," *Calgary Herald*, August 22, 1966.
46 "Wife Reassures Leader Husband."
47 Balto, *Occupied Territory*, 186.
48 "Archbishop Embroiled in Civil Rights Storm," *LAT*, August 12, 1966.

49 Garrow, *The FBI and Martin Luther King*, 176.

50 "Demonstrations Should End, Cody Says," *CT*, August 11, 1966.

51 ncronline.org/news/justice/54-miles-freedom-catholics-were-promi
nent-1965-selma-march.

52 Ronald Shaw, "A Final Push for National Legislation: The Chicago Freedom Movement," *Journal of the Illinois State Historical Society*, Autumn
2001.

53 Roy Wilkins, "Stoning of King Raises Question of the 'Best Means,' "
LAT, August 15, 1966.

54 Ralph, *Northern Protest*, 183.

55 Kotz, *Judgment Days*, 368.

56 Cohen and Taylor, *American Pharaoh*, 398–99.

57 Garrow, *Bearing the Cross*, 505.

58 Garrow, *Bearing the Cross*, 513.

59 "King Plans Rights Test," *CT*, August 19, 1966.

60 "The Orderly Way," editorial, *CT*, August 20, 1966.

61 "King Assails Ruling; He May Ignore It," *CT*, August 20, 1966.

62 Hamilton, *Dr. Martin Luther King Jr. and the Poor People's Campaign*.

63 Lucas interview, CRDP.

64 Cohen and Taylor, *American Pharaoh*, 397.

65 "They Came to Lead," editorial, *CT*, August 22, 1966.

66 Bernstein, "Martin Luther King Jr.'s Chicago Campaign."

67 MLK, "Address at the Palmer House," August 26, 1966, MLKPP.

68 "The Settlement," *CD*, August 30, 1966.

69 Raby interview, Eyes II.

70 Lucas interview, CRDP.

71 https://reverendcrawford91.wixsite.com/faithinc/history-of-wso.

72 www.crmvet.org/tim/tim66b.htm#1966b-16.

73 Jabari Asim, *We Can't Breathe: On Black Lives, White Lies and the Art of Survival* (New York: Picador, 2018).

74 crmvet.org/tim/tim66b.htm#1966b-16.

75 "Status of Major Bills Now Before Congress," *LAT*, July 4, 1966.

76 March 21, 1966, FBI memo, Stegall Papers.

77 Shaw, "A Final Push for National Legislation."

78 Branch, *At Canaan's Edge*, 558.

79 Bagley, *Desert Rose*, 209.

80 Say Burgin, " 'The Trickbag of the Press': SNCC, Print Media, and the
Myth of the Anti-Whiteness of Black Power," *Journal of Civil and Human
Rights* 8, no. 1 (Spring/Summer 2022).

81 Burgin, " 'The Trickbag of the Press,' " 3.

82 Carroll, *Race News*, 168.

83 Michaeli, *The Defender*, 432–33.

84 For the kind of serious coverage the *New York Times* could have brought
to Chicago, see its approach covering Birmingham: "Negroes Uniting
in Birmingham," *NYT*, April 11, 1963; "Negroes Defying Birmingham

Writ," *NYT*, April 12, 1963; "Contempt Trial of Dr. King Opens," *NYT*, April 23, 1963.

85 Kotz, *Judgment Days*, 370.

86 Satter, *Race, Real Estate, and Family Property*.

87 Rick Perlstein, "1966—When Everything Changed," History News Network, https://historynewsnetwork.org/article/51156.

88 "Rights Groups Accuses Johnson of Surrender," *LAT*, August 12, 1966.

89 Branch, *At Canaan's Edge*, 530.

90 https://library.cqpress.com/cqalmanac/document.php?id=cqal66-1301767.

91 "Dr. King Laws Rights Defeat to Prejudice," *CT*, October 25, 1966.

92 C. Vann Woodward, "What Happened to the Civil Rights Movement," *Harpers*, January 1967.

93 Jones, *Selma of the North*, 172.

94 Nick Kotz, in his five-hundred-page study of King and Johnson, *Judgment Days*, devotes only a few pages, naturalizes its failure, and doesn't question Johnson's inaction.

95 Marqusee, *Redemption Song*, 185.

96 Royko, *Boss*, 154.

97 Cohen and Taylor, *American Pharaoh*, 427.

98 "Negro Pastors in Chicago Bid Dr. King End the Marches," *NYT*, April 20, 1967.

99 Halberstam, "The Second Coming," 43.

100 "Daley Courts White Backlash," *CT*, March 27, 1967.

101 Anderson and Pickering, *Confronting the Color Line*, 323–24.

102 " 'Kill Rioters,' Daley Ordered," *CD*, April 15, 1968.

103 Howard Saffold interview, Eyes II.

104 "Plan to Convert 11 Tenements to 'Condominiums for the Poor,' " *CT*, April 27, 1967.

105 CSK, *MLMLML*, 147–48.

106 See Ralph, "Interpreting the Chicago Freedom Movement," in Finley, *The CFM*, 92–93.

107 "The Nation," *LAT*, September 18, 1966.

108 Deppe, *Operation Breadbasket*, 27.

109 "Breadbasket Clerics Come to King's Aid," *CD*, April 25, 1967.

110 Deppe, *Operation Breadbasket*, xxxv.

111 "Mrs. King Praises Operation Breadbasket," *CD*, November 25, 1968.

112 "Breadbasket Aids Black Farmers' Co-op," *CD*, March 16, 1968; "Breadbasket Women Rap Bad Meat," *CD*, February 3, 1968.

113 Lafayette interview, Eyes II.

114 Fort letter, April 18, 2024.

115 Balto, *Occupied Territory*, 201.

116 Williams, *From the Bullet to the Ballot*.

117 Finley, 306.

118 James McPherson, "Chicago's Blackstone Rangers," *Harpers*, May 1969.

11: The Time Is Now: Building National Black Political Power, Anticolonial Solidarities, and Culture-of-Poverty Critique

1 MLK, *The Last Interview*, 96–97.
2 MLK, *The Last Interview*, 95.
3 Bagley, *Desert Rose*, ix–x.
4 https://wamu.org/story/15/01/09/how_a_civil_rights_struggle_in_the _south_helped_dc_elect_its_own_leaders/.
5 https://dcstatehoodyeswecan.org/j/index.php?option=com_content &view=article&id=407:dr-martin-luther-king-jr-and-the-district-of-co lumbia&catid=100:mlk-dc&Itemid=80.
6 Jackson, *From Civil Rights to Human Rights*, 238.
7 "King Warns of Big D.C. March," *CT*, August 30, 1965.
8 Frazier, *Harambee City*.
9 Garrow, *Bearing the Cross*, 559.
10 "Martin Luther King Speech: April 26, 1967," annotated, *Cleveland Plain Dealer*, January 14, 2012, cleveland.com/pdextra/2012/01/martin_luther _king_jr_april_26.html.
11 Carl Stokes, *Promises of Power: A Political Autobiography* (New York: Simon & Schuster, 1973).
12 Garrow, *Bearing the Cross*, 566.
13 Joseph, *The Sword and the Shield*, 283.
14 Ancusto Butler interview, CRDP.
15 Halberstam, "The Second Coming."
16 John Lewis with Michael D'Orso, *Walking with the Wind: A Memoir of the Movement* (New York: Simon & Schuster, 1998), 112.
17 Halberstam continued his critique of King: "He has finally come to believe his myth just as the people in the Pentagon believe theirs."
18 Halberstam, "The Second Coming."
19 "King admits he is becoming a more radical critic of the society," Halberstam writes, "and that the idea of 'domestic colonialism' represents his view of the North. I suggest that he sounds like a nonviolent Malcolm."
20 Halberstam bizarrely employed a footnote in a magazine to contradict King: "But many white reporters sympathetic to King, who thought the most important thing that could happen in America last year was for King to succeed in Chicago, consider his Chicago program a failure and a great tragedy."
21 MLK, *The Last Interview*, 97.
22 "Carl Stokes Dies," *CT*, April 3, 1996; teachingcleveland.org/money -and-mobilization-volunteers-in-the-stokes-mayoral-campaign-by-elis -ribeiro/.
23 https://www.ourcampaigns.com/RaceDetail.html?RaceID=548262.
24 Branch, *At Canaan's Edge*, 650.
25 https://www.ourcampaigns.com/RaceDetail.html?RaceID=548323.
26 MLK-Levison transcript from FBI surveillance, provided by Jonathan Eig.

27 teachingcleveland.org/money-and-mobilization-volunteers-in-the
    -stokes-mayoral-campaign-by-elis-ribeiro/.
28 Oates, *Let the Trumpet Sound*, 445.
29 Branch, *At Canaan's Edge*, 650–51.
30 Belafonte interview, Eyes II.
31 https://storymaps.arcgis.com/collections/2400b1aa1bbe44dea035
    39534d68dd2d?item=2.
32 CSK, *My Life with Martin*, 254.
33 MLK-Levison transcript from FBI surveillance.
34 Sugrue, *Sweet Land of Liberty*, 339. But the *New York Times* was so en-
    amored to frame King as antagonistic, the newspaper claimed he had
    signed it. King was frustrated with the *Times* article and how reporters
    had distorted what he said. Not wanting to get lumped in with the Urban
    League and NAACP on Black Power, he thought these press tactics were
    meant to weaken the movement. According to FBI surveillance, King
    and Levison believed the administration was trying to divide "us"—
    Levison convinced that Rustin had done this. They decided they would
    need to write the *Times* to correct the story. "Crisis and Commitment,"
    unsigned editorial, *NYT*, October 16, 1966; October 17, 1966, memo, Ste-
    gall Papers.
35 Garrow, *Bearing the Cross*, 533.
36 "King's Wife Accepts Carmichael," *Montreal Gazette*, February 24, 1967.
37 Author interview with Komozi Woodard.
38 Woodard interview.
39 Woodard, *A Nation Within a Nation*, 94.
40 Douglas and Loggins, *Prophet of Discontent*, 1–2.
41 Woodard, *A Nation Within a Nation*, 94.
42 Woodard, *A Nation Within a Nation*, 194.
43 Woodard interview.
44 MLK speech at Cathedral of St. John the Divine, New York, May 19, 1956.
45 Barbara Ransby, *Eslanda: The Large and Unconventional Life of Mrs. Paul
    Robeson* (New Haven: Yale University Press, 2013), 261–62.
46 CSK, *My Life with Martin*, 272–73.
47 "Negro Role in Society Defined," *Winston-Salem Journal*, March 22, 1965.
48 "Dr. King Asks Settlement in Vietnam," *BS*, March 3, 1965.
49 "Farmer Blocks Vietnam Issue," *Call and Post*, July 10, 1965.
50 "Wilkins Queries King's Tactics," *BS*, July 5, 1965.
51 "Capital Spotlight," *Afro-American*, October 2, 1965; "Dr. King and Viet-
    nam," *Christian Science Monitor*, July 8, 1965.
52 Jackson, *From Civil Rights to Human Rights*, 312.
53 Branch, *At Canaan's Edge*.
54 "25,000 Viet Protesters Throng US Capitol," *AJC*, November 28, 1965.
55 Jackson, *From Civil Rights to Human Rights*, 313.
56 "Mrs. King: Peace Warrior," *DFP*, November 29, 1965, https://vault.fbi
    .gov/Coretta%20Scott%20King/Coretta%20Scott%20King%20Part%20
    5%20of%205/view#document/p16.

57 "Dr. King, Other Nobel Winners Sign War Appeal," *Afro-American*, August 28, 1965.
58 "King Urges Peace Moves in Vietnam," *Afro-American*, December 4, 1965.
59 MLK, "Peace, God's Business and Man's," *Cleveland Call and Post*, December 25, 1965.
60 https://vault.fbi.gov/Coretta%20Scott%20King/Coretta%20Scott%20 King%20Part%201%20of%205/view#document/p234.
61 https://vault.fbi.gov/Coretta%20Scott%20King/Coretta%20Scott%20 King%20Part%201%20of%205/view#document/p245.
62 "Wife of Martin Luther King in Auto Accident," *Black Dispatch*, September 20, 1963.
63 "Typical Marcher: Middle Class Adult," *NYT*, November 28, 1965.
64 CSK interview, Box 22, Folder 8, Hatch.
65 "Many Have a Strong Feeling Against War," *AJC*, March 13, 1967.
66 Dorothy Cotton, *If Your Back's Not Bent: The Role of the Citizenship Education Program in the Civil Rights Movement* (New York: Atria, 2012), 250.
67 Sitkoff, *King*, 213–14.
68 aavw.org/special_features/speeches_speech_king02.html.
69 https://investigatinghistory.ashp.cuny.edu/module11D.php.
70 "Many Have a Strong Feeling Against War."
71 "Dr. King Leads Chicago Peace Rally," *NYT*, March 25, 1967.
72 "Speaks Before Peace Rally Here," *CT*, March 26, 1967.
73 "Rights Leader Hits Dr. King's Viet Tactics," *CT*, April 15, 1967.
74 "Dr. King's Error," editorial, *NYT*, April 7, 1967.
75 CSK interview, Box 22, Folder 8, Hatch.
76 CSK interview, NVLP.
77 CSK, *MLMLML*, 150.
78 Honey, *To the Promised Land*, 115; "Antiwar Rally Called 'Just Beginning,' " *Palo Alto Times*, April 17, 1967.
79 CSK interview, Box 22, Folder 8, Hatch.
80 Belafonte interview, Eyes II.
81 Levison FBI recordings.
82 Garrison Hayes, "We Don't Have to Guess What Martin Luther King Thought about the Israel-Palestine Conflict," *Mother Jones*, November 9, 2023.
83 "King Raps NAACP 'Myth' on Views," *CD*, April 13, 1967.
84 Jackson, *From Civil Rights to Human Rights*, 337.
85 "How Would America Be Different if King Had Lived," *WP*, April 3, 1988.
86 Say Burgin, " 'The Shame of Our Whole Judicial System': George Crockett, Jr., the New Bethel Shoot-In, and the Nation's Jim Crow Judiciary," *The Strange Careers of the Jim Crow North*.
87 Oates, *Let the Trumpet Sound*, 445.
88 "Four Negro Chiefs Assail Riots," *CT*, July 27, 1967.
89 "Dr. King Criticized for 'Violence' Talk," *NYT*, April 21, 1967.

90 "95 Theses of Martin Luther King," editorial, *CT*, April 19, 1967.
91 Michaeli, *The Defender*, 436.
92 Michaeli, *The Defender*, 439–40.
93 "Face to Face Interview," in *A Testament of Hope*, 401–2.
94 "Summary Statement," December 14–15, 1960, Box III: C65; 5, NAACP Papers, Library of Congress.
95 May 15, 1963, flyer, projects.lib.wayne.edu/12thstreetdetroit/exhibits/show/beforeunrest/panel6.
96 Elizabeth Hinton, "Police Violence," in *Myth America* (New York: Basic Books, 2022), 240.
97 Nancy Milio, *9226 Kercheval: The Store that Did Not Burn* (Ann Arbor: University of Michigan Press, 1971), 105.
98 Johnson, *Race and Remembrance*, 56–57.
99 MLK, "A New Sense of Direction."
100 CSK interview, 2004, huffpost.com/entry/qa-with-the-late-coretta_b_94899.
101 CSK interview, Box 23, Folder 2, Hatch.
102 MLK, "The Role of the Behavioral Scientist in the Civil Rights Movement," American Psychological Association, September 1967, apa.org/monitor/features/king-challenge.
103 Fort letter, April 18, 2024.
104 www.aavw.org/special_features/speeches_speech_king03.html.
105 Jackson, *From Civil Rights to Human Rights*, 337.
106 Honey, *To the Promised Land*, 115.
107 aavw.org/special_features/speeches_speech_king03.html.
108 Joseph, *The Sword and the Shield*, 280, 277.
109 "Martin Luther King Says Riots Can't Win."
110 CSK interview with WTTW's John Callaway, 1978, pbs.org/video/coretta-scott-king-structural-roots-social-problems-ojqubm/?continuousplayautoplay=true.
111 MLK, "The Crisis in American Cities," SCLC address, August 15, 1967.
112 Honey, *To The Promised Land*, 115.
113 CSK interview, WTTW.
114 MLK, "The Crisis in American Cities."
115 Jackson, *From Civil Rights to Human Rights*, 335.
116 "Formula for Discord," *NYT*, August 17, 1967.
117 Joseph, *The Sword and the Shield*, 285.
118 Eig, *King*, 530.
119 CSK, *My Life with Martin*, 276.
120 Box 22, Folder 6, Hatch.
121 Bagley, *Desert Rose*, 211.
122 Rosenbloom, *Redemption*, 5. These included October 1964, February 1965, August 1966, April 1967, and February 1968.
123 "Widow's Might," *AJC*, February 1, 1976.
124 CSK, *My Life with Martin*, 311.

125 As Coretta explained in an interview about Juanita Sellers, "He really could have hurt me then, at one point in my life I thought whatever he did didn't really matter but he really could have hurt me then." CSK interview, Tape 5, Hatch.

126 CSK, *My Life with Martin*, 128–30.

127 Eig, *King*, 104.

128 Garrow, *Bearing the Cross*, 374.

129 These included Frazier's *The Negro Family in the United States*; St. Clair Drake and Horace Cayton, *Black Metropolis* (New York: Harcourt Brace, 1945); Gunnar Myrdal, *An American Dilemma: The Negro Problem and American Democracy* (New York: Harper & Row, 1944). King's critique was prescient, as this tendency would grow in the late 1960s with works like Lee Rainwater's *Behind Ghetto Walls*, Ulf Hannerz's *Soulside*, and Eliot Lebow's *Tally's Corner*. For more on this turn, see Alice O'Connor's *Poverty Knowledge*.

130 MLK, *Where Do We Go from Here*, 126.

131 MLK, *Where Do We Go from Here*, 127.

132 Lewis, *King*, 309.

133 MLK acceptance speech, Planned Parenthood.

134 MLK, "The Role of the Behavioral Scientist."

135 MLK, "Honoring Dr. DuBois," *Freedomways*, February 23, 1968.

136 West, ed., *The Radical King*.

137 aavw.org/special_features/speeches_speech_king03.html.

138 MLK, "The Crisis in American Cities," address to SCLC, August 15, 1967; Jackson, *From Civil Rights to Human Rights*, 336.

139 "Kerner Raps Civil Rights Criticism of Illinois," *CST*, July 29, 1963.

140 Oates, *Let the Trumpet Sound*, 466–67. The interim Kerner Report's staff summary of 1,500 pages of data and testimony was ruled too controversial; when the White House got its hands on the draft, the budget was cut and most of the staff terminated. Mark Krasovic, *The Newark Frontier: Community Action in the Great Society* (Chicago: University of Chicago Press, 2016), 140–43.

141 Conversation with Martin Luther King at Rabbinical Assembly, March 25, 1968. https://www.rabbinicalassembly.org/sites/default/files/assets/public/resources-ideas/cj/classics/1-4-12-civil-rights/conversation-with-martin-luther-king.pdf.

142 "Martin as I Knew Him."

143 MLK, "The Other America," March 14, 1968, www.gphistorical.org/mlk/index.htm.

144 freep.com/story/opinion/contributors/2018/01/14/martin-luther-king-grosse-pointe/1030581001/.

145 Parks, Millner interview in Garrow, *The Walking City*, 566.

146 gphistorical.org/mlk/mlkspeech/index.htm.

147 Peter Levy, "The Media and H. Rap Brown: Friend or Foe of Jim Crow?," *The Strange Careers of the Jim Crow North*, 294–95.

12: To Make the Nation Say Yes When They Are Inclined to Say No: The Poor People's Campaign

1 CSK, *MLMLML*, 152.
2 Garrow, *Bearing the Cross*, 524.
3 Wright, "The 1968 Poor People's Campaign," 110.
4 Laurent, *King and the Other America*, 90.
5 "MLK Dispatches Recruiting Corps Goal," *CD*, January 17, 1968; MLK, *The Last Interview*, 107.
6 MLK and Rabbinical Assembly.
7 "MLK Dispatches Recruiting Corps Goal," *CD*, January 17, 1968.
8 Laurent, *King and the Other America*, 120–21.
9 Jones, *Selma of the North*, 254.
10 Dorothy Roberts, *Killing the Black Body: Race, Reproduction, and the Meaning of Liberty* (New York: Vintage, 1988), 207; Mary Poole, *The Segregated Origins of Social Security* (Chapel Hill: University of North Carolina Press, 2006).
11 Jackson, *From Civil Rights to Human Rights*, 346.
12 Laurent, *King and the Other America*, 128–29.
13 Premilla Nadasen, *Welfare Warriors* (New York: Routledge, 2005), 72.
14 Laurent, *King and the Other America*, 171.
15 Jackson, *From Civil Rights to Human Rights*, 346.
16 civilrightsmuseum.org/50-voices-for-50-years/posts/dr-kings-dream-deferred.
17 Laurent, *King and the Other America*, 128.
18 Stein, " 'This Nation Has Never Dealt Honestly with the Question of a Peacetime Economy.' "
19 Jackson, *From Civil Rights to Human Rights*, 251.
20 MLK, *Where Do We Go from Here*, 163, 173.
21 CSK, *My Life with Martin*, 278.
22 Dyson, *I May Not Get There with You*, 88.
23 "Terms Talks to End TV Feud as 'Critical,' " *CT*, April 9, 1967.
24 Douglas and Loggins, *Prophet of Discontent*, 45.
25 Marian Wright Edelman interview, Eyes II.
26 CSK, *My Life with Martin*, 277.
27 CSK interview, Box 23, Folder 2, Hatch.
28 Author interview with Lynn Adler.
29 Hamilton, *Dr. Martin Luther King Jr. and the Poor People's Campaign*, 89.
30 Marian Logan Memorandum to Martin Luther King, March 8, 1968. Martin Luther King, Jr., Papers, Martin Luther King Center, Atlanta, GA.
31 Three nights before he was killed, King went over to Logan's; she, her husband, and King stayed up all night, as King endeavored unsuccessfully to change her mind. Marian Logan interview, Eyes II.
32 Eig, *King*, 537.
33 Dyson, *I May Not Get There with You*, 89.
34 Cornel West, "Hope and Despair: Past and Present," in *To Shape a World*, 327.

35 Orange interview, CRDP.

36 Amy Nathan Wright, "The 1968 Poor People's Campaign, Marks, Mississippi and the Mule Train," in *Civil Rights History from the Ground Up*, edited by Emilye Crosby (Athens: University of Georgia Press, 2011), 110.

37 Colleen Wessel-McCoy, *Freedom Church of the Poor* (New York: Lexington, 2021), 95.

38 Oates, *Let the Trumpet Sound*, 649.

39 digital.wustl.edu/e/eii/eiiweb/kin5427.0224.089corettascottking.html.

40 Eig, *King*, 538.

41 CSK, *MLMLML*, 151–52.

42 CSK interview, NVLP.

43 CSK, *MLMLML*.

44 Belafonte interview, Eyes II.

45 Cotton interview, SOHP.

46 CSK interview, Box 22, Folder 6, 9, Hatch.

47 MLK, "Statement Announcing the Poor People's Campaign," December 4, 1967.

48 Wright, "The 1968 Poor People's Campaign," 110–11.

49 Jackson, *From Civil Rights to Human Rights*, 343.

50 "King Keys His Tactics," *WP*, February 8, 1968.

51 Rosenbloom, *Redemption*, 86.

52 "How Would America Be Different if King Had Lived."

53 digital.wustl.edu/e/eii/eiiweb/kin5427.0224.089corettascottking.html.

54 Wessel-McCoy, *Freedom Church of the Poor*, 20.

55 Hamilton, *Dr. Martin Luther King Jr. and the Poor People's Campaign*, 59.

56 "King Still Holds Sway as US 'Conscience,' " *CD*, June 14, 1967.

57 Wessel-McCoy, *Freedom Church of the Poor*, 10.

58 Honey, *Going Down Jericho Road*, 186.

59 "Women Cry Out Against War," *AJC*, January 10, 1968.

60 CSK interview, Box 22, Folder 8, Hatch.

61 MLK, "Why We Are Going to Washington DC," January 15, 1968.

62 MLK, "Why We Are Going to Washington DC."

63 MLK, *Where Do We Go from Here*.

64 MLK, *Where Do We Go from Here*.

65 Carroll, *Race News*, 186.

66 MLK, *Where Do We Go from Here*.

67 Honey, *To the Promised Land*, 125.

68 "King Recruits for DC March," *WP*, January 17, 1968.

69 Bagley, *Desert Rose*, 233.

70 MLK, Drum Major Sermon, February 4, 1968, https://bethlehemfarm.net/wp-content/uploads/2013/02/DrumMajorInstinct.pdf.

71 "King, Stokely Join Capital Camp-in," *CD*, January 30, 1968; "King's DC Drives Begins April 22," *CD*, March 5, 1968.

72 Ture interview, Eyes II.

73 "King Keys His Tactics."

74 "King's DC Drive Begins April 22," *CD*, March 5, 1968.

75 "King's DC Drives Begins April 22"; "King Issues Warning on Dems Parley," *CT*, February 1968.

76 Valentin, *Gilberto Gerena Valentín*, 199; Sonnie, *Hillbilly Nationalists*, 58.

77 CSK interview, Box 23, Folder 2, Hatch.

78 Hamilton, *Dr. Martin Luther King Jr. and the Poor People's Campaign*, 100–104.

79 Honey, *To the Promised Land*, 131.

80 Mantler dissertation, 298, 149.

81 Mantler dissertation, 203.

82 Jones, *Selma of the North*, 239.

83 Branch, *At Canaan's Edge*, 724–25.

84 Rosenbloom, *Redemption*, 82.

85 CSK interview, Box 22, Folder 6, Hatch.

86 Hamilton, *Dr. Martin Luther King Jr. and the Poor People's Campaign*, 108–9.

87 Belafonte, *My Song*, 328–29; Eig, *King*, 546.

88 Simmons, "Martin Luther King Jr. Revisited," 208–9.

89 "LBJ Views King's Camp-In as Mistake," *WP*, February 3, 1968; "King Keys His Tactics"; "Wilkins Fears Riots Could Mar March," *WP*, April 3, 1968.

90 "Dr. King Hints He'd Cancel the March if Aid Is Offered," *NYT*, March 31, 1968.

91 Rosenbloom, *Redemption*, 158.

92 CSK interview, Eyes II.

93 CSK, *My Life with Martin*, 280.

94 CSK, *MLMLML*, 153.

95 CSK interview, Box 23, Folder 2, Hatch.

96 Hamilton, *Dr. Martin Luther King Jr. and the Poor People's Campaign*, 108.

97 CSK, *MLMLML*, 154, 156.

98 Box 22, Folder 6, Hatch.

99 MLK, "US Plays 'Roulette with Riots,' " *WP*, April 7, 1968.

100 "10,000 to Keep 'Poor People's' DC 'Sit-in' Under Control," *CD*, March 11, 1968.

101 Memorandum from Frederick Baumgardner to William Sullivan, October 28, 1966, https://sites.google.com/site/cointelprodocs/dr-martin-luther-king-jr-case-study#n412.

102 Memorandum from Charles Brennan to William Sullivan, March 8, 1967, https://sites.google.com/site/cointelprodocs/dr-martin-luther-king-jr-case-study#n420.

103 Garrow, *The FBI and Martin Luther King*.

104 Betty Medsger, *The Burglary: The Discovery of J. Edgar Hoover's Secret FBI* (New York: Knopf, 2014), 346–48.

105 FBI work paper, "Questions to Be Explored at Conference 12/23/63 re: Communist influence in Racial Matters," https://miscdocs.neocities.org/dr-martin-luther-king-jr-case-study.html.

106 SAC, Atlanta memorandum, April 14, 1964.

107 "N.A.A.C.P. Decries Stand of Dr. King on Vietnam," *NYT*, April 11, 1967.

108 FBI memorandum, November 3, 1964, "Church Committee Final Report—Book III: Supplementary Detailed Staff Reports on Intelligence Activities and the Rights of Americans," 21, https://sites.google .com/site/cointelprodocs/dr-martin-luther-king-jr-case-study#n280.

109 Lerone Martin, *The Gospel According to J. Edgar Hoover, How the FBI Aided and Abetted White Christian Nationalism* (Princeton, NJ: Princeton University Press, 2023), 233–34.

110 Martin, "Bureau Clergyman," 28. King had worried about Harrison's spending and Clarence Jones apparently had suspected Harrison, warning King, but Harrison remained on staff. Garrow, *Bearing the Cross*, 584.

111 Belafonte interview, Eyes II.

112 Rosenbloom, *Redemption*, 142.

113 Branch, *At Canaan's Edge*, 708.

114 Garrow, *Bearing the Cross*, 607.

115 Rosenbloom, *Redemption*, 146.

116 Branch, *At Canaan's Edge*, 709.

117 Memorandum from George Moore to William Sullivan, March 26, 1968, https://sites.google.com/site/cointelprodocs/dr-martin-luther-king -jr-case-study#n443.

118 Garrow, *The FBI and Martin Luther King*, 185.

119 Gage, *G-Man*, 658.

120 Eig, *King*, 546–47.

121 "King Urges Work Stoppage by Negroes to Back Strike," *Commercial Appeal*, March 19, 1968.

122 CSK interview, Box 23, Folder 2, Hatch.

123 "More Nonviolence," editorial, *CT*, March 30, 1968.

124 CSK interview, Box 22, Folder 6, Hatch.

125 Eig, *King*, 546.

126 Eig, *King*, 533.

127 Eig, *King*, 540.

128 Cotton interview, SOHP.

129 Harris, *The Price of the Ticket*, 30.

130 Belafonte interview, Eyes II.

131 Belafonte, *My Song*, 331.

132 CSK interview, Box 22, Folder 6, Hatch.

133 Bagley, *Desert Rose*, 238.

134 "Mrs. King Pleads for All to Fulfill Husband's Dream," *WP*, April 7, 1968.

135 Crawford, "Coretta Scott King and the Struggle for Civil and Human Rights," 113.

136 Bagley, *Desert Rose*, 241.

137 Honey, *To the Promised Land*, 454.

138 "Right's Leader's Undaunted Widow," *NYT*, April 9, 1968.

139 CSK interview, NVLP.

140 Jason Sokol, *The Heavens Might Crack: The Death and Legacy of Martin Luther King, Jr.* (New York: Basic Books, 2018), 89.

141 Mike Royko, "Millions in His Firing Squad," *Chicago Daily News*, April 5, 1968.

142 Young, *Soul Power*, 86–87.

143 McPherson, "Chicago's Blackstone Rangers."

144 Moore and Williams, *The Almighty Black P Stone Nation*, 82.

145 "1000 Rangers Make Plans for Peace in Area," *CD*, April 8, 1968.

146 Woodard, *A Nation Within a Nation*, 96–97.

147 Ture interview, Eyes II.

148 "President Signs Civil Rights Bill; Pleads for Calm," *NYT*, April 12, 1968.

149 CSK interview, Box 22, Folder 6, Hatch.

150 CSK, *MLMLML*, 167–68.

151 https://time.com/5224875/martin-luther-king-jr-eulogy/.

152 CSK interview, Box 22, Folder 6, Hatch.

153 CSK, "We May Yet Not Only Survive, We May Triumph," Class Day speech, *Harvard Alumni Bulletin*, July 1, 1968.

154 "King Widow Speaks," *BS*, May 29, 1072.

155 Martha Burk, "Black Women Make History Too: An Interview on Coretta Scott King," *Huffington Post*, February 12, 2012.

156 CSK, *MLMLML*, 189.

157 Author interview, with Mary Frances Berry, February 22, 2024.

158 "FBI Spied on Coretta Scott King," *LAT*, August 31, 2007.

159 Sonnie, *Hillbilly Nationalists*, 90.

160 "Rally Hears Mrs. King's March Plea," *BS*, May 2, 1968; Roland Freeman, *The Mule Train* (Nashville: Rutledge Hill Press, 1998), 23.

161 Wright, "The 1968 Poor People's Campaign," 110.

162 Wright, "The 1968 Poor People's Campaign," 128.

163 sites.si.edu/s/topic/0TO1Q000000U4xHWAS/city-of-hope-resurrection-city-and-the-1968-poor-peoples-campaign-poster-exhibition?t=1593615883430.

164 Mantler dissertation, 300.

165 Jackson, *From Civil Rights to Human Rights*, 358.

166 Edelman interview, Eyes II.

167 "Protest Asks End of War," *WP*, June 20, 1968.

168 "50,000 at Poor Rally Get Warning of Last Chance for America," *BS*, June 20, 1968.

169 John Kelley, "Before Occupy There Was Resurrection City," *WP*, December 2, 2011.

170 "The anger and problems and sickness of the poor of the whole nation were in this one shantytown," *NYT*, July 7, 1968. Forty-nine years later, the *Times* ran a long feature with numerous unpublished photos from the PPC, noting the negativity of its original coverage. "In 1968, a 'Resurrection City' of Tents, Erected to Fight Poverty," *NYT*, February 18, 2017.

171 Wright, "The 1968 Poor People's Campaign," 137.

172 Wessel-McCoy, *Freedom Church of the Poor*, 83.
173 Wright, "The 1968 Poor People's Campaign," 131–34; Edelman interview.
174 CSK, *MLMLML*, 184.
175 Wessel-McCoy, *Freedom Church of the Poor*, 30.
176 Wessel-McCoy, *Freedom Church of the Poor*, 83.

Epilogue
1 CSK, *My Life with Martin*, 310.

Index

About the Author

Jeanne Theoharis is Distinguished Professor of Political Science at Brooklyn College of City University of New York. She is the author of the *New York Times* bestselling *The Rebellious Life of Mrs. Rosa Parks* and winner of the 2014 NAACP Image Award for Outstanding Literary Work Biography/Autobiography and the Letitia Woods Brown Award from the Association of Black Women Historians. Her book has been adapted into a documentary of the same name, executive produced by Soledad O'Brien for NBC-Peacock where Theoharis served as a consulting producer. Her young adult adaptation with Brandy Colbert, *The Rebellious Life of Mrs. Rosa Parks for Young People,* was included in the Best Books of 2021 by the Chicago Public Library and *Kirkus Reviews.* Her book *A More Beautiful and Terrible History: The Uses and Misuses of Civil Rights History* won the 2018 Brooklyn Public Library Literary Prize in Nonfiction and was named one of the best Black history books of 2018 by *Black Perspectives.* Theoharis's writing has appeared in the *New York Times*, the *Washington Post*, MSNBC, *The Nation, Slate,* and *The Atlantic.* She lives in Brooklyn.

Publishing in the Public Interest

Thank you for reading this book published by The New Press; we hope you enjoyed it. New Press books and authors play a crucial role in sparking conversations about the key political and social issues of our day.

We hope that you will stay in touch with us. Here are a few ways to keep up to date with our books, events, and the issues we cover:

- Sign up at www.thenewpress.com/subscribe to receive updates on New Press authors and issues and to be notified about local events
- www.facebook.com/newpressbooks
- www.x.com/thenewpress
- www.instagram.com/thenewpress

Please consider buying New Press books not only for yourself, but also for friends and family and to donate to schools, libraries, community centers, prison libraries, and other organizations involved with the issues our authors write about.

The New Press is a 501(c)(3) nonprofit organization; if you wish to support our work with a tax-deductible gift please visit www .thenewpress.com/donate or use the QR code below.